THE
APPROPRIATE
WORD

THE APPROPRIATE WORD

*Finding the Best Way to Say
What You Mean*

J. N. HOOK

ADDISON-WESLEY PUBLISHING COMPANY, INC.

Reading, Massachusetts   Menlo Park, California
New York   Don Mills, Ontario   Wokingham, England
· Amsterdam   Bonn   Sydney   Singapore   Tokyo
Madrid   San Juan   Paris   Seoul
Milan   Mexico City   Taipei

Library of Congress Cataloging-in-Publication Data

Hook, J. N. (Julius Nicholas)
  The appropriate word : finding the best way to say what you mean /
Julius N. Hook.
    p. cm.
  ISBN 0-201-52323-X
  ISBN 0-201-57703-8 (pbk.)
  1. English language – Synonyms and antonyms.   I. Title.
PE1591.H66 1990   89-18616
428 – dc20

Cover design by Marianne Perlak
Set in 10-point Bembo by DEKR Corporation, Woburn MA

1 2 3 4 5 6 7 8 9–MW–9594939291
First printing, May 1990
First paperback printing, April 1991

to RGH

INTRODUCTION

"Is this the appropriate word?" is a question not often fully articulated, but writers may need to answer it one or more times in almost any sentence. The question is not new, although the answers change somewhat with each generation. Joseph Conrad and Gustave Flaubert spent hours searching for the exact word, Elizabeth Barrett Browning put pyramids of possible alternatives in her margins, and many literate people remember Mark Twain's often-quoted statement that the difference between the right word and the almost-right word is as great as that between lightning and the lightning bug.

As professional authors, these nineteenth-century writers had effective ways to find the words that were appropriate for their times, their topics, and their readers. *The Appropriate Word* is intended to help today's people who write, especially nonprofessionals, in making many of their choices. A reference tool alongside a dictionary and a thesaurus, it should be of help to office workers, students, beginning or would-be authors, and anyone else who hopes to write clear, effective, and concise modern English that fits the circumstances.

FF and SWE

Books on English usage typically tell their readers, "This is right, but that is wrong. Say this, but don't say that."

The Appropriate Word is different. It says:

- There are no absolutes in language. What is standard in this century may have been taboo in the past or may become nonstandard in the future.
- A word may be "right" in some circumstances but not necessarily in others. Some of the words that are quite satisfactory at home or at a party or a bar may be less suitable in other places and with other people.

I use repeatedly in this book the letters FF (for "family and friends") to represent the casual, unplanned, carefree, and frequently slangy expressions that most Americans employ most of the time in conversing with or writing to people they know well or other people with backgrounds similar to their own.

I use SWE to refer to "standard written English." Some people call SWE "edited writing" instead, because its usages are similar to those found in such well-edited newspapers as the *New York Times* and the *Christian Science Monitor* or such magazines as the *Atlantic* and the *New Yorker*.

FF must not be equated with "wrong." The idea that every word or phrase is right or wrong was long ago repudiated by linguists. "Levels of usage" superseded "rightness" and "wrongness," but even that concept suggests superior levels and inferior levels. The contention in this book is that *most* words are appropriate in both formal and informal contexts but that at this time, late in the twentieth century, *some* words and expressions are appropriate in informal family-friends contexts but are regarded as less appropriate or inappropriate in relatively formal writing (as well as speaking). A word used in an inappropriate context is a weed.

A weed is defined by some botanists as "a plant out of place." A weed is not right or wrong, but is inappropriately located, perhaps in the middle of your manicured bluegrass lawn. A word, similarly, sometimes appears in an inappropriate place. As a word, it is not right or wrong, but in its location it may be suitable or unsuitable, appropriate or inappropriate.

For example, one of my college undergraduates, praising Emily Dickinson, said that she was "an exceptionable woman." *Exceptionable* doesn't belong in that context, because it means "objectionable," and my student was in no way objecting to or taking exception to that great American poet. He meant, of course, that she was *exceptional*, defined as "unusual, extraordinary, possessing unexpected or uncommon attributes." The student's *exceptionable* is a perfectly good word, definitely not wrong, but it was a weed in his sentence. This book will assist in the continuing and many-fronted fight against such weeds.

Appropriateness, then, involves adapting language to circumstances and to the intended receivers of the message. Almost everyone does some adapting, usually without thinking about it. When Daddy tells a story to Karen and Jason, he uses different words and even somewhat different grammatical structures and sentence lengths from those he uses in talking with adult friends or in writing a report to be used in his business or profession. Mama talks differently to the children, her own mother, her husband, her close friends, her business associates, and the pediatrician, and she writes differently to an old college friend, now living in Europe, from the way she writes to the seafood company that doesn't work hard enough to avoid killing dolphins, or to the congressional representative who perhaps can do something about it.

FF draws from the same vocabulary that SWE does, and countless FF sentences, addressed to family and friends, are identical to those employed in more formal contexts. Both FF and SWE are "good English" if they convey whatever information and emotion the writer or speaker intends. But FF is contrastable to SWE in these ways and perhaps in others:

- FF is ordinarily spontaneous, off-the-cuff, unplanned. We seldom think much about choice of words when we are conversing with a spouse, our children, or a good friend. We know that the words will come when we start chatting, and that if something is not clear, we'll be asked, "Whaddaya mean?"
- To the user of FF, language is just a tool, employed as unthinkingly as a spoon or a toothbrush. The FF speaker or writer seldom asks himself, "Is this word exact, completely clear, and in conformity with what Miss Snyder taught us in junior high school?" FF tends to be relaxed – linguistically and stylistically unconcerned.
- Because it is unplanned, FF is less meticulous than SWE. SWE generally differentiates, for instance, between *less* and *fewer, enemy* and *adversary*, or *disapprove* and *reject*, but most users of FF pay little attention to such distinctions.
- FF often exaggerates and exclaims. It may praise a small achievement as "Great!" or describe a merely unpleasant experience as "Horrible!"
- Some, but not all, users of FF either do not recall or do not obey teachers' admonitions not to use *ain't*, double negatives, *my mother she*, and other nonstandard forms such as those in "He done his work real good."
- FF usages are less consistent, less predictable, than those of SWE. Some FF users may say "I saw it" in one sentence but "I seen it" a little later.
- FF adopts innovative language, especially slang, more quickly than SWE does. As a synonym of *excellent*, FF in one decade may use *swell*; in another, *boss*; in another, *real cool*; and in still another, *ba-ad* or *wicked good*. But SWE may stay unswervingly with *excellent*. (It is true, though, that SWE eventually does accept a small percentage of originally slang words, especially if they are shorter, clearer, or more expressive than their synonyms. See the entry on MOB as an example.)
- FF more frequently than SWE uses words commonly regarded as profane or obscene. Some servicemen in two world wars were said – although certainly not accurately – to have vocabularies of only seven words, all of them at that time unprintable.

- FF tends to be more repetitive than SWE. It contains many redundancies, wasted words. It is sometimes succinct, but more often not. It may say "in the neighborhood of a hundred dollars" instead of "about a hundred dollars," or "a huge, big, immense building" instead of settling for a single adjective.
- The vocabulary of FF tends to be more limited than that of SWE. A person whose usual FF vocabulary may be only a few thousand words may use several times as many in business or professional work. Because of the greater meticulousness of SWE, its users take time to find the word that comes closest to conveying their precise meaning.
- FF is more varied than SWE. Its users range from near-inarticulateness to the edge of SWE. Some FF users are more slangy, profane, exclamatory, or hyperbolic than others. Some are less repetitive, more succinct, more versatile in word choice, more colorful, or more often observant of Miss Snyder's linguistic precepts than others.

A few people never need SWE at all. These are persons who have almost no contact with people other than those in their own limited environment and rarely need to communicate in writing. In fact, unless the job demands SWE, a whole week, a whole year, may be spent largely in FF contexts.

At least occasionally, however, most people do need to write letters to strangers, an explanation to the IRS, a memorandum or even a report to the boss. In an age when communication is increasingly called "the lifeblood of business and industry" and when the livelihoods of millions of Americans require considerable amounts of communication, a high degree of precision and consistency of word choice is desirable and often essential. This means SWE, not the FF that is appropriate mainly in contexts that are unlikely to penalize rather imprecise and inconsistent language.

Although SWE means "standard *written* English," its characteristics are present also in much *spoken* English, typically outside one's own intimate circles. SWE is especially likely in discussions of relatively serious subjects. If we are ever called on to address a convention of meteorologists, we will probably use SWE, but in talking about the weather with a chance acquaintance on the golf course, we use FF.

To describe SWE in part, we need only to turn upside down what has already been said about FF. SWE is usually:

- somewhat planned, seldom just spontaneous; it is thoughtful in regard to language, considering it an instrument that can be finely tuned to help a writer attain whatever his or her purpose may be.
- fairly careful in word choice.
- seldom exclamatory or hyperbolic.

- in general accord with conventional modern standards (although today less constrained than before by rules that now seem artificial, such as most of those about split infinitives and *shall* vs. *will*).
- consistent in choice of verb forms, pronoun cases, and the like.
- not more than moderately slangy, or in some contexts not at all.
- unlikely to be profane or obscene (except possibly in direct quotations).
- not wasteful of words, not repetitious except when repetition serves a purpose.
- furnished with a sizable vocabulary from which may be selected the words that most accurately convey intended information, ideas, or emotion from writer to reader.
- less extreme in its variations than FF, although its users are certainly not like peas in a pod. They differ especially in degree of formality, with some almost always preferring a light touch, and others most often serious without being stiff. They also shift gears as necessitated by context and purpose; for instance, a lawyer may be constrained to use legalese in official documents but may try to talk in layman's terms to his clients.

It can be argued that a no-man's-land exists between FF and SWE, a shaded area that cannot be categorized. I accept this argument and so occasionally use such terms as "informal SWE" or "marginally SWE" or "moving toward SWE."

An occasional entry in this book uses the acronym SANE, perhaps as in this short example:

appear on the scene, arrive on the scene   SANE says, "Delete three words in each."

SANE is an imaginary organization, the Society for the Avoidance of Needless Effort. It especially dislikes writing, typing, or speaking more words than are needed and forcing readers or listeners to read or listen to more words than they must. SWE generally follows SANE's precepts, but sometimes I have felt the need to suggest a change that I consider mere common sense. Then I say, in effect, "SANE recommends . . ."

Toward More Natural Expression

English language usages change slowly but constantly, as any reader of Chaucer, Shakespeare, or even a nineteenth-century author can easily see. Perhaps the greatest change in this century has been a move away from stiffness, long sentences, and greater-than-necessary formality. On average, today's SWE is less formal than that of 1940 or even 1960 or 1970, although a few circumstances demanding considerable formality still exist.

Modern American usage reflects lifestyles that in this century have steadily become less structured, more relaxed. A writer in the nineteenth century at least figuratively donned his Prince Albert coat before dipping his pen into the inkwell. Today's writer is likely to sit in shirtsleeves in front of the word processor.

Modern good writing, such as that in the best-edited magazines and newspapers, is characterized by relatively short sentences and paragraphs, lively verbs, an occasionally surprising noun or adjective, and especially a lack of starchiness. It reflects the influence of journalism but not journalistic excesses; it combines the lively styles of good reporters with the care and verbal precision of literary craftsmen.

By no means, then, have all the usage bars been let down. "Anything goes" has not become the rule governing SWE. The lowest common denominator, the language of the high school dropout, has not taken over. Today's even moderately careful users of SWE do not write, for instance, "had took" or "Me and her wasn't to blame nohow," nor do most of them confuse *apex* and *nadir* or *bisect* and *dissect*. They still adhere to a degree of orthodoxy, as is suggested by the fact that each year they spend millions of dollars on word processors or typewriters that alert them to spelling misdemeanors or provide lists of synonyms to remind them of choices that may be available. But in their writing, despite this leaning toward orthodoxy, they try to avoid stodginess, stiffness, and any hint of being old-fashioned.

Not only journalists and authors and editors of magazine articles have become less rigid. So have many of the people who write or dictate the correspondence coming from the nation's multitudinous places of business. Writers of business letters, for example, long ago stopped saying things like "Yours of the tenth inst. rec'd and contents noted. . . . Yr. obedient servant." Symptomatic of the trend are most of the articles in the *Wall Street Journal, Nation's Business, Forbes,* or probably any other widely read business publication.

Even scholarly writing has become less stiff. Paul Halmos is one of the world's leading researchers in mathematics and the editor of the prestigious *American Mathematical Monthly*. He tells of an early article of his that while in draft stage was criticized by a colleague for its occasional use of contractions, such as *isn't* rather than *is not*. At that time the use of contractions, as well as almost any other hint of informality, was taboo in scholarly writing. Halmos ignored the criticism, his article was published, and two years later it was awarded the coveted Chauvenet Prize for mathematical exposition.

In his autobiographical *I Want to Be a Mathematician*, published in 1985 by the Mathematical Association of America, Halmos expressed this belief about writing, a point of view increasingly accepted by scholars in many disciplines:

Expository writing must not be sloppy in either content or form and, of course, it must not be misleading; it must be dignified, correct, and clear. Within these guidelines, however, expository writing should be written in a clear, colloquial style, it should be evocative in the same sense in which poetry is, and it should not be stuffy, but friendly and informal. The purpose of writing is to communicate, and style is a tool for communication. It should be chosen so as to put the reader at his ease and make the subject seem as easy to him as it already is to the author.

Halmos was not the first to make such a plea. During most of the first half of this century, *Publications of the Modern Language Association of America* (PMLA), which prints articles by literary scholars, was almost invariably dull and stodgy, sometimes described as "a thin trickle of text and a river of footnotes." Its authors tended to display polysyllables and Latinate prose, and even though many of them were no doubt likable and good-natured, seldom did a trace of their amiability show up in their weighty PMLA articles.

Then in the 1940s along came an eminent Milton scholar, William Riley Parker. He was MLA secretary and PMLA editor. Like Halmos, Parker realized that scholarly accuracy and dignified writing were not incompatible with readability, a moderate degree of informality, and at least a touch of friendliness. He described in detail the expository qualities that he would insist on, and because of his prestige and that of the journal, he was able to get them – although some struggles did occur. Scholarly writing as a whole has become much more readable because of the work of such people as Halmos and Parker, and its contributions to human knowledge have not decreased in amount or significance.

Much more widely read than scholarly journals are many of the hundreds of popular magazines that fill today's newsstands. I once made a quick comparison of articles in a modern *Harper's* and an issue of a century earlier. Modern sentences average about half the length of the older ones, each word is much more likely to have six or eight letters rather than ten or twelve, even fairly technical subjects are treated so that almost any interested layman can understand them, and the words *flow*. Most published authors, such as those who write for today's best magazines, are not afraid to show that they are human beings, even making use of occasional wit and humor.

The Entries

The number of entries in *The Appropriate Word* is over 2,300, not counting cross-references. The total number of words treated (since many of the entries deal with two or more words) is close to 4,000.

How were the terms chosen? Admittedly, I had to be both selective and subjective. The book could have been much fatter; some readers may moan about what they consider unforgivable omissions. From varied sources I chose terms that reflected wordiness or misinformation or provoked uncertainty. These sources were many thousands of pages of college student writing, freshman themes through doctoral dissertations; local newspapers bought during my frequent travels, papers ranging from the weekly *Corn Belt Sentinel* to most of the nation's metropolitan dailies and their bloated Sunday editions; TV commentators and sports announcers, whose attempts at liveliness and cleverness vary in success. My wife and I for years have read regularly the *New York Times* and a semirural Illini or Hoosier daily. Large numbers of books from the past couple of decades make our bookshelves sag. We subscribe to some forty magazines (not always the same ones), including the *New Yorker*, the quite different *New York*, and the *Atlantic*, through *Newsweek*, *Good Housekeeping*, hobby magazines, *Arizona Highways*, an occasional West Coast periodical, and *Harrowsmith* (a delightful New England journal of rural life). To see what many other people read, we now and then buy tabloids and other periodicals, some of which we find it judicious to hide in the shopping cart under a box of cornflakes.

And in our travels in fifty states, my wife and I like to listen to people talk. Some might call us shameless eavesdroppers. We enjoy the many dialects, and we tuck away in our minds and sometimes on paper countless instances of words and constructions that occur in speaking but only rarely, if ever, in *House Beautiful*, for instance.

In writing about each term that I selected, how did I decide whether it was FF or SWE, or both (as is not unusual)? How did I decide that a word or expression was formal, informal, slangy, stiff, old-fashioned, wordy, or something else? I recalled, with my wife's help, its customary environment(s), noting whether it thrives in a lively breeze or in calm air, what its neighbors are like, how high-class its surroundings are (the languages of corner bars and of ritzy hotel bars differ considerably), whether it sometimes seems discordant in a given context. My wife and I try to be constantly alert to what is happening in the language, noting words or usages new to us, and other words or usages that seem to be getting established or dropping out of sight.

My wife, more conservative than I, often tempers my premature enthusiasm for some of the more eccentric coinages and innovative, or at least uncommon, usages. She also begs me not to call *imply* and *infer* interchangeable in SWE, even though a few respected publications treat them as though they are. And she implores me never to get what she calls "too permissive" about *unique*. Precision, she says, is important, even though the *New York Times* and other reputable publications are sometimes imprecise. The language is weakened, she believes, when it loses a needed word for which there is no exact synonym. This is what happens, for instance, when *unique*, which means "pertaining to the only one of its kind," is used to mean merely "unusual," because the language then has no remaining short, clear way to say "the only one of its kind." My wife's reasoning is sometimes very convincing. It shows up in a few entries in which I say, in effect, "SWE does so and so, but it would make more sense to do it this other way. SANE recommends . . ."

Abbreviations Used
in Entries

FF: family and friends
SANE: Society for the Avoidance of Needless Effort (a fictitious organization)
SWE: standard written English

References Mentioned
in Entries

AHD: *American Heritage Dictionary*. Boston, Houghton Mifflin, 1981 edition.

Bernstein: Theodore Bernstein, *The Careful Writer*. New York, Atheneum, 1977.

Bryant: Margaret Bryant, *Current American Usage*. New York, Funk & Wagnalls, 1967.

Copperud: Roy H. Copperud, *American Usage: The Consensus*. New York, Van Nostrand Reinhold, 1970.

————, *Webster's Dictionary of Usage and Style*. New York, Avenel Books, 1982 edition.

Crisp: Raymond D. Crisp, *Changes in Attitudes Toward English Usage*. Unpublished doctoral dissertation, U. of Illinois, 1971.

Evans: Bergen and Cornelia Evans, *Dictionary of Contemporary American Usage*. New York, Random House, 1957.

Flesch: Rudolf Flesch, *Lite English*. New York, Crown Publishers, 1983.

Flexner: Stuart B. Flexner, *Listening to America*. New York, Simon & Schuster, 1982.

Follett: Wilson Follett, *Modern American Usage*. New York, Hill & Wang, 1966.

Fowler: H. W. Fowler, *Dictionary of Modern American Usage*. Oxford and New York, Oxford U. Press, 1950 edition.

Howard: Philip Howard, *The State of the Language*. New York, Oxford U. Press, 1985.

Lamberts: J. J. Lamberts, *Short Introduction to English Usage*. New York, McGraw-Hill, 1972.

Morris: William and Mary Morris, *Harper Dictionary of Contemporary Usage*. New York, Harper & Row, 1975.

Nicholson: Margaret Nicholson, *Dictionary of American-English Usage*. New York, Oxford U. Press, 1957. (American edition of Fowler)

OED: *Oxford English Dictionary*. London, Oxford U. Press, 1971. (micrographic edition)

Oxford: *Oxford American Dictionary*. New York and Oxford, Oxford U. Press, 1980.

Partridge: Eric Partridge, *Usage and Abusage*. London, Hamish Hamilton, 1959 edition.

RHD: *Random House Dictionary of the English Language*. New York, 1987. Second edition.

Strunk and White: William Strunk and E. B. White, *The Elements of Style*. New York, Macmillan, 1979. Third edition.

Webster III: *Webster's Third New International Dictionary*. Springfield, Mass., Merriam, 1961.

THE
APPROPRIATE
WORD

A

a, an/per Purists of the sort who have asserted that *television* is a bad coinage because it combines Greek and Latin roots and thus is horribly miscegenetic have also said that *per*, from Latin, should not be used as a companion for words from Anglo-Saxon. SWE discards such reasoning as nonsense. Countless comparable mixtures exist in English and other languages. In the sense of "for each" or "by each," *per* and *a* (or *an*) are usually interchangeable: "a dollar per (or *a*) gallon." *Per* is especially likely in scientific contexts. Sometimes *a* may cause some odd-sounding sentences that *per* does not. "Output a man" is harder to understand than "output per man." Bernstein found this delightful example: "Belgium is rated third, with a yield a cow a year of 3,760 kilograms of milk." SWE would prefer ". . . an annual yield of 3,760 kilograms of milk per cow."

a/some "Some man told us how to get to Staunton" is FF. SWE: "A man . . ."

abandoned/depraved/vicious Each suggests immorality, but of different sorts. The *abandoned* person indulges frequently in "sin" and is not repentant. The *depraved* person actively searches for unusual sexual experiences and goes to extremes in use of alcohol or other drugs. The *vicious* person tries to hurt others, but the most likely victim of the abandoned or depraved person is himself.

abdicate/abrogate To *abdicate* is to relinquish formally, to give up: "Edward VIII abdicated the throne." To *abrogate* is to nullify or cancel: "Spain abrogated the treaty."

ability (verb with) SWE uses *ability* plus an infinitive rather than *ability* plus *of* plus an *-ing* form: "ability *to speak*" rather than "ability *of speaking.*"

ability/capacity 1. *Ability* and *capacity* both refer to qualities enabling a person to accomplish something, and sometimes may be used interchangeably. With reference to performing a specific act, however, *ability* is more likely: "ability to solve problems," ". . . to jump high." *Capacity* is a little more general and is more likely to be inborn rather than developed: "mental capacity," "capacity for painstaking research." One definition of the word is "ability to contain." 2. SWE tries to avoid the pompousness of sentences such as "In what capacity does he work?" It prefers "What kind of work does he do?" or "Precisely what is his job?"

abjure/adjure To *abjure* is to swear off, to renounce, to recant sol-

---

For meanings of abbreviations and full names of references, see page xvi.

A slash mark separating headwords indicates that they are contrasted. A comma between them indicates treatment as a unit. Capital letters signify a short general article rather than one on specific words.

emnly: "Her husband abjured drinking and gambling." To *adjure* is to command solemnly or to beg earnestly: "My father adjured me to stay out of bars."

able For the most part, only animate beings have ability; inanimate things in general are not "able" in the usual sense of the word: "We were able to hear the ocean waves from our cottage," or "From our cottage the ocean waves could be heard," but not "From our cottage the ocean waves were able to be heard." The restriction to animate beings is usually not applied to complex or "intelligent" machines, electronic gear, and so on: "My car is able to smooth out many of the bumps." "My computer is able to produce elaborate graphics."

aborning Used in SWE, though uncommon, for "getting started" or "while barely under way": "The strategy was yet aborning."

about (redundant) SWE omits *about* when the context makes it unnecessary, as in "She estimated that the task would take (about) ten or fifteen hours" (*estimated* implies "about").

about/around/round (adverb or preposition) *Around* or *round* emphasizes circularity more than *about* does. Thus "walked around (or *round)* the house" suggests a tour of the outer edges, but "walked about the house" suggests moving from one place to another but perhaps not following a circular path.

above (adjective, noun) With the meaning "mentioned above," *above* is SWE as an adjective but may seem stiff or awkward, as in "The above accusation was impossible to prove." SWE often rephrases, possibly as "The accusation referred to earlier . . ." *Above* as a noun is also SWE, although it suggests legalistic writing: "Two witnesses confirmed the above." In most SWE, "confirmed that statement" or something similar is likely.

above/more than SWE prefers *more than* in indicating time or measure: "more than five weeks," "more than a meter." *Above* more often suggests a physical location: "above the treetops."

abridged/unabridged An *abridged* dictionary, such as the various editions of *Webster's Collegiate*, is shortened from a full-length, *unabridged* one, such as Webster III. To abridge is to shorten or condense.

abrogate See ABDICATE/ABROGATE.

ABSOLUTE COMPARISONS See **COMPARISON OF ABSOLUTES**; PERFECT.

abstruse/obscure Something *abstruse* is difficult for most people to understand because it is complex or specialized. Most of us still consider Einstein's theory of relativity abstruse, but many scientists do understand it. Something *obscure* is perhaps not clearly understood by anyone at all. Alternatively, it may be expressed in an unclear way: "The causes of some diseases are still obscure." "Many explanations are obscure because badly written."

ABSTRACT AND GENERAL WORDS Although abstract and general words are often needed to avoid endless lists of concrete and specific terms, many inexperienced writers use too many of them. To write effectively, one must make readers see, feel, hear, smell, and taste. *Oppression* brings forth no image, no pain, really no sensation except vague dislike and pity. But *sting of the lash* or *three years in a dank dungeon* makes readers see, feel, perhaps even hear. *Plant* draws little response, nor does *pretty flower* draw very much, but *purple petunia* evokes a colored picture and possibly the recollection of a pleasant odor. *Said* conveys only the idea that someone spoke, but *whispered* or *screamed* makes the speaker live.

The good poet and the experienced novelist and almost every other excellent writer think in concrete, specific terms. They have learned to observe, and they do not lack the power to abstract or to generalize. But because they want not merely to inform but also to portray and often to move, they generally express themselves concretely, specifically. They often use examples or metaphors to make an abstraction seem real. They frequently provide only what is needed for readers to draw their own conclusions. In doing so, they are likely to use specific language. Thus Shakespeare's King Lear, who has given his kingdom to his children and whose daughter Goneril has deprived him of most of his attendants, does not prate about "selfishness," or "unkindness," or "ingratitude." Instead Lear says, "How sharper than a serpent's tooth it is to have a thankless child!" *Sharper, serpent's tooth, child* – all relatively concrete and specific, but Shakespeare made them shape for him the abstract thought he wished to convey.

academic As in "The question is only academic." The implication of such usage may be resented by university scholars who each year considerably increase human knowledge and some of whom are responsible, intentionally or not, for inventions and discoveries that increase human comfort, add to the food supply, and prolong human life. To equate *academic* with *trivial* is insulting. To equate it with *truth-seeking* is accurate. All truths are worth knowing: that is the center of academic belief. Most SWE writing, but not all, reflects this practice: if something is unimportant or trivial, say so, but don't call it academic.

accent/accentuate In the sense of "emphasize," often interchangeable, although one or the other may sound better in context. *Accentuate* is more common with abstractions: "'Accentuate the positive' is a line from an old song," but "Accent the first syllable."

accept/except *Accept*, a verb, means "receive as satisfactory or at least passable": "She accepted her prize with a gracious little speech." *Except* is usually a preposition meaning "with the exception of": "None of the girls except Sue won a medal." *Except* may also be a verb for "to make an exception of": "Because of John's illness, the teacher excepted him from the requirement."

acceptive/receptive Someone willing to accept something may be called *acceptive*: "Today she was in an acceptive mood, believing everything he told her – in sharp contrast to yesterday's stubborn incredulity." Much more commonly used, however, is *receptive*, with about the same meaning. Some writers prefer to use *acceptive* for a general tendency to accept, *receptive* with reference to a particular thing: "receptive to the latest offer."

accessorize A dubious modern coinage, most often used by advertisers and by salespeople suffering from inflammation of the vocabulary. Possible substitutes: *trim, add gadgets* (or *ornaments*) *to*. See also –IZE.

accident/mishap Although an *accident* certainly may result from bad luck, *mishap* emphasizes the mischance. *Mishap* is likely to refer only to small incidents, involving perhaps the loss of a glove or stumbling over a rock but not loss of life or even a large sum of money.

accounted for by Awkward as a synonym for *consists of:* "Most of his income consists of (or *comes from* or *is derived from*, but not *is accounted for by*) dividends from common stock."

accrue Because of the financial and legal connotations, SWE usually avoids *accrue* in highly personal contexts. "Much happiness accrued from their marriage" suggests cold, automatic increase, like that of compound interest.

accumulative/cumulative SWE prefers the shorter.

accustomed/inured We become *inured* to unpleasant or perhaps painful things that keep happening to us, such as television commercials: "Prison inures convicts to boredom." We become *accustomed* to pleasures, luxuries, or even everyday events that are neither pleasant nor especially objectionable.

acme/apex/epitome *Apex* and *acme* both refer to the highest point of something, but the former is generally used literally, the latter figuratively: "the apex of the cone," "the acme of pianistic attainment." *Epitome* has nothing to do with highest points. It may (rarely) mean a summary, as in "the epitome of this philosopher's beliefs." More often it means "an excellent representative of its type," as in "Sister Teresa is the epitome of selflessness."

acoustics (verb with) With reference to the science, takes a singular verb: "Acoustics is the science of sound." With regard to the qualities of carrying, reflecting, or absorbing sound, takes a plural verb: "The accoustics in Avery Fisher Hall were not good at first."

acquaintanceship SWE generally settles for *acquaintance*, and SANE applauds: "her acquaintance with Henri." The longer word still appears occasionally.

acquiesce Usually followed by *in:* "acquiesced in the decision." Note that a person may acquiesce in a proposal even though not wholeheartedly agreeing with it. One may acquiesce merely by not opposing.

ACRONYMS Acronyms are not mere initials but are pronounceable as words: AWOL (absent without leave), CARE (Cooperative Agency for the Relief of Europe), or SANE (which I use for Society for the

Avoidance of Needless Effort). In using an acronym that is not very well known, SWE normally identifies it when it first appears, perhaps like this: Mutual of New York (MONY).

ACTIVE VOICE See **PASSIVE VOICE**.

activity Overused, especially by some weather forecasters. One of them in four minutes used the word eleven times – usually preceded by *shower* or *thunderstorm*. He even predicted that "shower activity" would be "active" again the following day, when "fresh thunderstorm activity" might move into the valley. At least one viewer pushed a button to *deactivate* him.

actual, actually SWE omits these words if no change of meaning results, as is true in these sentences: "He did not know the (actual) truth." "He (actually) sprayed paint on her."

actual fact Because there are no "unactual" facts, SWE deletes *actual*.

acute/chronic An *acute* illness is severe, one that may have serious consequences. A *chronic* illness is one that lasts a long time; it may or may not be severe.

A.D./B.C. Customarily, A.D. precedes a year. *A.D. 962* means "in the year of our Lord 962" – more logical than "962 in the year of our Lord." With reference to a century, however, as in "the third century A.D.," the abbreviation follows *century*. (No one pays attention to the illogicality of "the third century in the year of our Lord.") B.C. customarily and logically follows a number: *47 B.C.* means "47 years before Christ."

ad Short for *advertisement*. Frequently used in SWE, but most often in fairly informal contexts.

adage An adage is an old saying, so SWE avoids the repetitiousness of *old adage*. *Old cliché* is similarly repetitious.

added fillip Most SWE omits *added* unless a first fillip has already been named. (Few people seem to know that a fillip is a snap of the fingers, or a sharp tap, or anything that goads, stimulates, or excites.) "The ice dancers' costumes were startlingly ragged, and an added fillip came from their choice of ragtime music."

addicted to/dependent on Addiction is generally harmful: "addicted to gin" but probably not "addicted to health foods." Dependency may be undesirable but is usually less difficult to overcome than addiction is: "He became dependent on prune juice as a laxative."

additional(ly), in addition SWE omits any such word if the sentence already has *more, another, add*, or the equivalent: "(In addition), one more point must be made." "Add (an additional) window on this side."

address/lecture Unlike a speech, an *address* is likely to be formal and most likely is delivered by a prominent person; it ordinarily concerns a topic of wide significance, such as an international treaty. A *lecture*, too, is likely to be somewhat formal or at least carefully prepared for, but it is more likely to concern a narrow or specialized topic:

"Today the topic of the professor's lecture was the mating habits of earthworms."

adequate   This word is often used to damn with faint praise. Although the literal meaning is "sufficient to meet the need," it has come to suggest "barely enough," especially with reference to quality: "Her word-processing skills are adequate." (Use of this word might result in a decision not to hire the candidate for the job.)

adjacent/adjoining   In a hotel or motel, *adjacent* rooms are usually next to each other. So are *adjoining* rooms, but they have a door connecting them. The distinction has been important in divorce suits in which infidelity has been the issue: did the defendants have unobservable access to each other? In other contexts, *adjacent* may mean either "next to" or "very near." *Adjoining* means "touching." Thus two plots of land touching at any point are adjoining.

adjure   See ABJURE/ADJURE.

adjust/readjust   Sometimes *readjust* is used when *adjust* would be more accurate. Unless there has been a previous adjustment, there cannot be a readjustment. In writing about adjustments or readjustments in pay or prices, SWE notes that such changes can be either upward or downward; too often only upward changes are considered, as in "Recent bad weather may result in price adjustments."

administer/minister   A person given help or care is *ministered* to. The help (medicine, for example) is *administered* to him. Last rites are either administered or ministered.

admission/admittance   Both are widely used in the sense of "permission to enter." Thus the signs "No Admission" and "No Admittance" are likely to be interpreted in the same way. However, the former *may* be interpreted as "No admission fee is charged." When any such ambiguity is possible, "No Admittance" is preferable.

admit to/confess to   *To* is often redundant. A criminal may either *admit* or *confess* a misdeed. He or she may, of course, *admit* (something) *to* a police officer or *confess to* a priest.

adopted/adoptive   Parents who get legal permission to rear a child are adoptive parents, and the child is an *adopted* child. (Some dictionaries now say that *adoptive* is possible for both senses but that a distinction is customary.)

adore   FF often applies *adore* to a color of lipstick, a hairdo, a quiche, or any other relatively unimportant thing. SWE customarily restricts *adore* or *adoration* to worship or extremely high affection and respect.

advance/advanced   *Advance* (adjective) indicates a time earlier than normal: "advance notice," "advance payment"; or a forward position: "the advance platoon." *Advanced* usually refers to figurative rather than actual time or position: "an advanced thinker," "socially advanced legislation," "advanced mathematics."

advance reservations, future plans   Because reservations and plans necessarily involve the future, SWE omits *advance* and *future* with such terms.

advent/arrival *Advent* is normally reserved for something of great or at least considerable importance: "the advent of better relations with Russia." *Arrival* is suitable for less significant things: "the arrival of the new spring fashions," ". . . of the mail."

adversary/antagonist/enemy/opponent An *enemy* ordinarily shows deep and steady hostility and is regarded with strong dislike. The role of an *adversary, antagonist*, or *opponent*, however, is often of short duration: "the opponent in tonight's game," "The attorneys had been courtroom adversaries once before." An *antagonist* is especially likely to show overt hostility that may be or become physical: "The antagonists glared at each other and clenched their fists." One may like, respect, or even admire an adversary or an opponent and sometimes even an antagonist: "an antagonist (or *foe*) worthy of his steel," as the cliché has it. But one is unlikely to feel affection or admiration for an enemy, although respect may be present.

adverse/averse A person is *averse* to something: "Mr. Willis is averse to taking separate vacations." *Adverse* is used to characterize opposing circumstances or anything else working against someone: "Adverse weather caused delays in harvesting corn." "Her adverse remarks surprised him." "He was averse to her making adverse remarks."

advice/advise *Advice* is a noun: "to give advice." *Advise* is a verb: "The professor advised me." "The judge advised counsel that such a motion was improper." Old-fashioned business letter jargon: "Please be advised . . . ," "This is to advise you that . . ."

advisedly/intentionally An act is performed *advisedly* if it follows careful investigation and thought. It is performed *intentionally* if it does not occur by chance. Partridge makes the point with this quotation from a professor: "Many intentional acts are not carried out advisedly."

affect/effect To *affect* is to have an influence on or bring about a modification in: "Her illness affected her disposition." To *effect* is to cause or to bring about: "The new law effected a reduction in bankruptcy declarations." As a noun, *effect* means "result or outcome": "an unexpected *effect* of the medicine," "Whatever affects a wife has an effect on her husand." As a noun (a rare use), *affect* is largely a psychological term for "emotion."

affirmative/negative SWE avoids these words if *yes* or *no* will suffice. It prefers "She said no" to "She answered in the negative."

affluent/opulent/rich/wealthy *Rich* is the all-embracing and therefore least specific of these words. An *affluent* person is rich enough to buy almost anything possessable that he or she wants. The word often connotes comfortable but unostentatious luxury. An *opulent* person wants, buys, and especially likes to display possessions and perhaps achieve social prestige. *Opulent* may also be used to describe things: "opulent furnishings." *Wealthy* implies a stability that may be less characteristic of the other words. A wealthy family, for instance, often has possessed wealth for two or more generations. SWE tends toward but does not uniformly observe these distinctions.

aforementioned   Useful legalese. Too stiff in most other contexts.

after my own heart   "A man after my own heart" means "a man I am fond of because we are alike in some important ways." The expression is a cliché, but it does have the advantage of brevity.

after the end of   "After the end of the war" is longer but no better than the SANE-approved "after the war."

afterward, afterwards   Interchangeable.

again   See RE- + AGAIN OR BACK.

age, aged, ages   These words can often be omitted: "a boy of twelve" rather than "a boy of age twelve" or "a boy aged twelve." Similarly, "children four to six" rather than "children of the ages of four to six." "At sixteen" is much better than the redundant "at the age of sixteen years old."

agenda (verb with)   A Latin plural meaning "things to be done." But in English the meaning has shifted to "a list of things to be done," so *agenda* is now almost always treated as a singular. The plural *agendas* ("lists of things to be done") is also not uncommon in today's SWE, despite the anguish of people who know Latin and consider a double plural as bad as bigamy or a double negative. The singular *agendum* is rare. It refers to one item to be done.

aggravate/annoy, irritate   Conservatives still insist that *aggravate* can mean only "to make worse," as in "The damp weather aggravated my cold." In SWE, however, the meanings "annoy, irritate, vex" are no longer rare, even though the usage aggravates (vexes) many people. The shift is one example of a formerly FF usage that has become frequent in SWE.

agnostic/atheist   An *agnostic* does not know whether God exists. An *atheist* believes that God definitely does not exist.

agonize, agony   Used in SWE only for acute pain and suffering, usually prolonged. Dubious: "When I first glanced at the examination questions, I was in agony."

ah/aw   Although the distinction is not always made, *ah* goes with something pleasant, *aw* with the unpleasant: "Ah, what an aroma!" "Aw, this place stinks!" Both are FF, of course.

ahold   FF says, "They took ahold of both ends." SWE says, "They took hold . . ." In sentences where *a hold* is needed, it is written as two words: "The swimmers secured a hold on the edge of the raft."

aid/aide   Today the spelling *aide* is usual with reference to a person: "a military aide," "aide-de-camp," "an aide to the president." Sometimes the spelling *aid* is used for a person, but SWE customarily uses that form for something inanimate. There is an obvious difference between "a nurse's aide" and "a nurse's aid (*help* or *tool*)"; the choice of spelling makes the distinction clear. A disposable thermometer is an example of a nurse's aid. Another sense is illustrated in "An intern came to the nurse's aid."

aim to   As in "They aim to arrive before dawn," the expression was once regarded as nonstandard American dialect, but it is now SWE in both the United States and England. However, it still has a more folksy air than *intend to* or *strive to*.

ain't   Although used at least occasionally in the speech of many – perhaps most – Americans, *ain't* in most writing and in semiformal or formal speaking is still regarded as slovenly. It is sometimes defended because the contraction is brief and was used by some of the Founding Fathers, and because *amn't* is awkward and never has caught on. *See also* AREN'T I.

air (verb)   Sometimes used in SWE as a synonym for *broadcast*: "The network will air the program tomorrow." Journalists, however, tend to overuse the word in other senses, as equivalent to *discuss, explain, justify, explore, make clear*, or what have you: "Congressman Adams will air his views today."

a.k.a. (also AKA, aka)   An abbreviation for "also known as": "We added a spoiler, a.k.a. an air dam." Its use has grown in recent years, but it may still puzzle many people. SWE geneally reserves it and other abbreviations for space-saving purposes, but sometimes uses it where the more familiar *alias* would fit as well.

akin   See KIN.

à la   French for "in the," elaborated to "in the manner of." SWE in a few expressions such as *à la carte, à la king* (although *la* is feminine and *king* masculine), and *à la mode* ("in fashion" but now more frequently "with ice cream"). The *à* is now often printed without the accent mark. *À la* in recent years has been used tiresomely and not always clearly with people's names: "dresses à la Oleg Cassini," "poetry à la Edgar A. Guest," "smiling à la Ronald Reagan," "bats à la Hank Aaron."

albeit   This synonym of *although* once seemed to be dropping out of the language, then came part of the way back, but still is not frequent in SWE and is almost nonexistent in FF. *Although, though*, and *even if* do the job well enough, but *albeit* can impart an old-time touch reminiscent of a Dickensian lawyer's office.

alias   See A.K.A.

alibi (noun, verb)   Technically, an *alibi* is evidence that a person was elsewhere when a misdeed was committed. SWE says, "His alibi was that he was working on his novel when the bank was robbed." In FF and much less often in SWE the word is substituted for *excuse*, as in "His alibi was that his hand slipped." A rarer FF use, as a verb, is derived from that sense: "'My hand slipped,' he alibied."

all during   *All* may be redundant. Instead of "all during the year," SWE may prefer "during the year," "during the whole year," "throughout the year," "all year," or "all year long."

all ready (adjective)/already (adverb) *All ready* means "completely prepared, completely available": "We are all ready to eat." (Note that *all* can be omitted without affecting the meaning.) *Already* means "previously" or "at this early time": "She has already spent the money." "She has already arrived."

all right/alright (adverb) *Alright* often appears in FF letters and the like, but most SWE users consider it no better than *alwrong* would be.

all that (adverb) FF in such expressions as "the news wasn't all that bad." SWE: "The news was less bad than they expected" or "Not all the news was bad."

all the farther *As far as* appears more logical and is much more common in SWE: "This is as far as I can go." *All the farther* appears often in FF. Similar comments apply to "This is all the higher I can reach," "all the taller it will grow," and countless others. See also AS FAR AS; FARTHER/FURTHER.

all together/altogether *All together* means "as a group": "Sheep often move all together, cows usually in a crooked line." *Altogether* means "in all" or "entirely": "Altogether there are three bushels in the two piles." "That is altogether too many potatoes for us."

all told Equivalent to *in all* or *altogether*, as in "Her mother counted twenty-seven of Mary's excuses, all told." *All told*, however, is less widely used than its synonyms and has suffered from feeble jokes, such as "That night she kissed sixteen boys. All told." The origin of the phrase lies in an old meaning of *tell*, "to count," as in "A nun was telling her beads." *All told* thus is literally "counting all, counting everyone or everything."

all-around/all-round SWE uses either one to mean "versatile," as in "an all-around athlete" and "an all-round athlete." See also ROUND.

allege This verb suggests something bad: "He is alleged to have been a spy," but not "He is alleged to have been a good Samaritan." The journalistic "alleged murderer" is intended to protect the media against a possible libel suit, and perhaps does so to a degree, but by itself may not fulfill that purpose, especially if no grand jury or other authority has actually alleged the crime. In other words, SWE avoids writing that something has been alleged if it is impossible to prove an official allegation.

allergenic/allergic People may be *allergic* to dust, chocolate, and so on, but the dust or chocolate itself is *allergenic* ("allergy-creating"). Some products are correctly advertised as *nonallergenic*.

allergic/antipathetic A person may be *allergic* to pollen or many other substances. In FF (informally or humorously) many of us are also allergic to work, a person, a theory, or almost anything else. In SWE a more accurate word or expression is preferred: *antipathetic* (rather stiff), *against, averse to, not friendly toward*, and so on, unless an allergy is actually involved.

allision/collision Although *collision* is used for the forceful meeting either of two moving objects or of a moving and a stationary object, a valuable but seldom-used word for the latter is *allision*. Reporters and lawyers in particular should find *allision* useful in making distinctions. It refers, for instance, to an auto hitting a telephone pole or a parked vehicle: "Allisions in parking lots are frequent." The verb form of *allision* is *allide*: "The car swerved and allided with a stone wall."

ALLITERATION SWE avoids alliteration in most prose. Some readers of poetry applaud the humming *m*'s in Tennyson's "The *m*oan of doves in i*mm*emorial el*m*s,/ and *m*urmuring of innu*m*erable bees," but in prose the repeated sounds call too much attention to themselves. Even in poetry, alliteration is less frequent than it once was.

allude/refer These words are often used interchangeably, but many careful writers of SWE use *allude* in the sense of "hint" or "mention indirectly": "She did not say so, but may have been alluding to a burglary." *Refer*, in contrast, names directly: "She referred to a burglary at the Ellisons'."

allusion/illusion An *allusion* (see also ALLUDE/REFER) is an indirect or brief reference: "Dr. Brady made only one allusion to previous research." An *illusion* is a mistaken impression or belief, or something imagined rather than real: "Millions of people still share the illusion that the world is flat."

ALLUSIONS Most good writers are allusive. They make many of their points by alluding or referring to people, events, ideas, or things that their readers are likely to know about and that help to clarify or brighten parts of their writing. Here are a few suggestions for selecting allusions:

- Keep in mind the prospective readers. If you mention Joe DiMaggio, can they identify him? Will they understand that "Milton's mighty line" has to do with blank verse, not with part of the football team of a small Wisconsin college?
- In writing for a large readership, avoid inside jokes, local references, or news events that may soon be forgotten.
- The Bible and Shakespeare's works are better known to the English-speaking world than any other books. For this reason they are still among the richest sources of allusions and quotations. Don't misquote or give even a slightly incorrect source. Verify, no matter what the source is or how sure you are of the wording.
- Choose no allusion that does not serve a useful purpose. Don't show off. Allusions should be relevant and enlightening.
- The best allusion is one that comes unbidden to your mind as a natural outgrowth of your thinking about the subject.
- In spite of the limitations just suggested, the whole world *is* your oyster. Everything you know is related to or at least parallel to

countless other things. Each time you use an allusion, you may help your readers to see one or more of those relationships and parallels.

almighty dollar Cliché. Now that the U.S. dollar is much less powerful than it was when Washington Irving coined the phrase in 1836, we may as well give up the adjective.

almost/most (adverb) In FF such expressions as *most all* and *most anybody* are customary, but in SWE *almost all, almost anybody*, and the like are usual. *Most*, however, has been crossing the line recently and has brevity to commend it.

almost, much, sometimes, somewhat (no hyphen after) In SWE no hyphen is placed after such adverbs when they modify a following adjective: "an almost uncontrollable temper," "a much debated question," "a sometimes unnecessary declaration," "a somewhat misleading statement."

alms The word has an *s*; not "an alm." Generally, the verb in SWE is plural: "His alms were generous," although the singular is occasionally seen.

along with, as well as, in addition to, together with None of these phrases determines whether the verb is singular or plural: "Horace, along with (*as well as, in addition to, together with*) other Roman poets, was (not *were*) popular in the eighteenth century" (the subject of the sentence is *Horace*). Contrast with "Several other Roman poets, as well as Horace, were (not *was*) popular . . . ," in which the subject is *poets*.

alongside (of) *Of* is not needed. Seldom SWE: "The car was abandoned alongside of a row of poplars."

aloud See OUT LOUD.

already See ALL READY/ALREADY.

already existing SWE usually deletes *already*, which generally is redundant.

alright See ALL RIGHT/ALRIGHT.

also *Also* is seldom used in SWE for *and* in a series. In: "Bolivian mines yield tin, silver, copper, zinc, lead, also a little gold," SWE usually would substitute *and* for *also*, or possibly insert it before *also*. *Also* is occasionally used, however, in a sentence such as "She is tall, also slender."

altar/alter An *altar* is likely to be in a church. To *alter* is to change or to castrate.

altercation An *altercation* is a quarrel or an argument but does not ordinarily involve physical force: "The altercation did not degenerate into a fistfight."

alternate/alternative Usually the adjective *alternate* refers to taking turns, changing back and forth: "Baseball teams have alternate turns at bat." *Alternative* refers to choices: "You may select from three alternative chemical processes." With reference to substitution, however, either word may be used: an alternative plan is the same as an alternate plan. See also ALTERNATIVE.

alternative Because *alternative* is derived from Latin for "another," some purists have argued that it must refer to one of only two choices. In real life, however, three or more choices (alternatives) are often possible. So SWE does not follow the purist line here, but writes, "She suggested four alternative plans," ". . . several alternatives." See also ALTERNATE/ALTERNATIVE.

although/though *Although* is a little more formal than *though* and is more likely to be the choice for the beginning of a sentence: "Although (or *Though*) Congress rejected a similar bill, the President expects this one to pass." *Though* more commonly introduces a later clause, especially if it is short and in a relatively informal context: "It may rain, though I doubt it." After *even, though* (not *although*) is required.

although/while *While* can be used to mean either "during the time that" or "although," with the former more common, as in "While the debate was going on, people outside the hall began to shout and mill around." The meaning "although" is illustrated in "While the debate was intended to present opposing views, the debaters seemed to be largely in agreement." A problem arises if readers cannot be sure which meaning is intended or at best are momentarily confused: "While the cloth is woven in Alabama, the sewing is done in Mexico." In such a sentence, SWE chooses *although*.

although See also ALBEIT.

alumna (and so on) *alumna:* female former student; *alumnus:* male former student; *alumnae:* female former students; *alumni:* male former students, or male and female former students as a group: "alumni of the University of Maine." Note that graduation is not a requirement for being an alumnus or an alumna. If completion of a degree program is to be shown, SWE uses *graduate:* "Graduates are fewer than alumni."

A.M./P.M. May be written with lowercase or capital letters. Printers often use what they call "small caps." SWE does not use these terms with *in the morning* or *at night* because of redundancy.

amateur/novice A *novice* is one just starting, usually in a kind of work or a game. He or she may be either an amateur or a recently turned professional: "a novice in (or *at*) tennis," "a novice printer." A religious novice is taking preliminary or probationary training. An *amateur* is a "lover" in the sense that he or she engages in something not for money but because of liking it. In sports an amateur is one who is not paid for participating, although possibly very proficient.

amazing/astounding These are strong words that in SWE are not cheapened to mean only "unusual." If the thing being described does not truly amaze or astound, a more workaday substitute can certainly be found. Prices of eggs or soap powders, for instance, are not likely to be amazingly or astoundingly low (or even high). Rents for apartments in large cities – well, maybe.

ambiance/environment   *Ambiance* (also spelled *ambience*) ordinarily refers to atmosphere, tone, taste, and attractiveness as well as to strictly physical things. It is likely to be associated with wealth and man-made comforts, not with hovels or glades. *Environment* is a much broader term, applicable to any kind of surroundings.

AMBIGUITY   Although William Empson's classic in literary criticism, *Seven Types of Ambiguity*, demonstrated that ambiguity in poetry is often important or even essential, in most prose a twofold meaning is undesirable and usually confusing.

Lexical ambiguity involves two meanings for the same word. Is a *fine* comb one that is expensive and perhaps bejeweled, or is it one with thin, closely set teeth? Does a sign that says "Fine for Fishing" tell the angler that he is likely to catch fish there or that he may be fined if he tries? Structural ambiguity, more common, appears in various forms, and sometimes a sentence that is clear when spoken is unclear when written. Thus "It was another moving day for the Allen family" may mean that the family was again transporting its belongings or that the day was a highly emotional one. The intonations of speech may show which meaning is intended. Professor Norman Stageberg, in articles in the *English Journal*, once classified structural ambiguities. Some of the following examples have been borrowed from him. He says that modifiers of nouns cause much of the trouble. Is "a wonderful cold morning breakfast" a cold breakfast or one for a cold morning? Is "modern English teaching" the teaching of modern English or the modern teaching of English? Is "a French teacher" French or a teacher of French? Is "a black man's hat" a hat of a black man or a hat that is black? Would you stay at the Little Charm Motel?

When several nouns follow an adjective, how far does the adjective reach? In "fat hogs, sheep, and cattle," are only the hogs fat or all three kinds of animals? "Antique lamps and pottery" probably means that both are antiques, but we cannot be sure. What is the Temporary Spouse Membership Card offered by a chain of motels?

Two or more words with the last followed by a phrase or a clause may cause the reader to wonder whether the modifier applies to one or to all. A catalog description says that shirts are available in "gray, blue, or tan with white stripes." Do the gray and blue shirts have white stripes? Stageberg quotes from students' papers: "Zola was able to describe the characters, the places they went, and the things they did very well." "He used an arm stroke and a kick which propelled him rapidly through the water." Phrases and clauses also cause trouble when they may conceivably refer to either one of two terms or to both. In "She sat looking at the children in the house," was she in the house, were the children, or were both? In "We went to a restaurant on Palm Street which was gaily decorated for the Christmas season," what was decorated? (The use of *which* in this example points up the fact that much ambiguity is caused by faulty reference of pronouns. Many a *he, she, it,* or *they,* and not only *which,* is impossible for readers to pin down.) Adverbial modifiers create their own share of ambiguity. Stageberg quotes "the bottle on the table there." Is the bottle or the table "there"? In "I hit the man with the bottle," who had the bottle?

Common sense and trying to put oneself in the readers' place can eliminate most ambiguities. See also **ANTECEDENT**; **WHICH**.

ambiguous/equivocal Both words describe statements that can be interpreted in two or more ways: "She enjoys interesting men." *Ambiguity* is usually unintentional, except sometimes in poetry or in humor. But an *equivocal* statement is an intentionally deceptive one. The advertising claim "All prices slashed up to 50 percent" is equivocal because it suggests large, storewide reductions, but it may mean that most items are reduced, say, 1 percent, and that perhaps no more than one or two items have a 50 percent reduction. See also **WEASEL WORDS**.

ambivalent Ordinarily, *ambivalent* in SWE means "having conflicting feelings and thoughts," such as simultaneous liking and disliking. But even in SWE the word has lost clarity, often being diluted to "different," as in "There will be ambivalent effects of the new tax." Such weakening can lead to the death of a valuable word.

ambivalent/vacillating (adjective) A person who cannot decide whether to favor one thing or another is *ambivalent*; he or she may see strong arguments on each side. The person is *vacillating* when changing his or her mind, especially when moving from one opinion or solution to a second, a third, or even more. The vacillating person is likely to seem wishy-washy and indecisive; the ambivalent person, thoughtful but not yet decided.

amend/emend *Emend* is a specialized term, used to refer to editing (making changes, corrections, improvements) in written or printed copy: "She emended the text by making the punctuation consistent and by correcting several factual errors." *Amend,* the more common word, may be used in various contexts, such as "amending ('adding to') the Constitution," "amending (or *mending*) one's ways," "amending earlier practices."

America, American *America* and *American* should cover North, Central, and South America. Generally, though, other nations resignedly accept the usurpation of the term by the United States. In important documents, however, *the United States* or *residents of the United States* should be used for absolute clarity, sometimes with *of America* added. Various replacements for *American* have been suggested, but none has caught on. One possibility: USan (pronounced you-*ess*-un).

amiable/amicable Usually interchangeable, although *amicable* emphasizes friendliness and peacefulness, and *amiable* suggests good nature and a smiling demeanor.

amid, amidst Interchangeable. Sometimes regarded in SWE as too literary for normal use, but either is a good, short substitute for *in the middle of* or *surrounded by*.

among/between In general, *between* is used in SWE with two persons, *among* with three or more: "the differences between you and me," "the differences among the five of us." However, when each of several participants acts individually, *between* is preferable: "A formal agreement between the six nations will be signed this week" (each nation agrees and signs, in effect, with each one of the other nations). "Between traveling, practicing, and performing, a musician may have little time for composing." FF often uses *between* where SWE prefers *among*: "Just between the four of us, I believe . . ."

amongst Often used in Great Britain for *among* but infrequently in the United States.

amoral/immoral An animal or a person with extremely low intelligence may be *amoral*, "without morals," "having no comprehension of moral standards." An *immoral* person comprehends the accepted standards but chooses to disregard them.

amount/number *Amount* is often used in FF when SWE chooses *number*. In brief, if something is countable, SWE prefers *number*: "the number of pages (*cans, apples*)," "the amount of paper (*soup, applesauce*)." Exceptions occur when actual counting is unlikely: "The amount of guns and gun parts was huge." "The amount of beans was about ten pounds." Sometimes even apples: "The amount of apples to be shipped is at least eight truckloads."

& (ampersand) See + (PLUS SIGN) AND/& (AMPERSAND).

ample Not "ample enough." *Ample* is enough. Both *ample* and *enough* mean "sufficient," but *ample* hints at more than sufficient. A man of "ample girth" probably should consider dieting.

amplify on SWE generally omits *on*.

amused See BEMUSED.

ANACHRONISM Anachronisms usually involve putting a thing or a person in the wrong historical period, but sometimes in the wrong place. An imaginary conversation between Washington and Lincoln would be anachronistic because Washington was dead before Lincoln was born. Shakespeare was anachronistic in referring to striking clocks in ancient Greece and to tigers in the New World. Language, too, can be anachronistic – for example, in the use of twentieth-century slang in a novel set in the eighteenth century.

ancestor/descendant Your *ancestors* are your parents, grandparents, and so on. Your *descendants* are your children, grandchildren, and so on. This newspaper sentence did not conform to SWE: "Ancestors of Civil War veterans can barely imagine the bitterness that once existed between North and South."

ancestress *Ancestors* covers both males and females. If a special need exists to limit a statement to females, however, *ancestress* is available: "Many of our ancestresses gave birth to more children than most modern women do."

ancient *Ancient* fashions in dress are those described by Homer or worn by the Assyrians, for instance. Ancient history is mainly that of the pre-Christian era. SWE avoids using *ancient* for something that happened last year or even five hundred years ago.

and (as sentence opener) It's no crime or even a stylistic fault in SWE to begin an occasional sentence with *and*. Doing so is likely to suggest greater emphasis on what follows. But the use should be infrequent, because each repetition of a stylistic device reduces its force. Similar comments apply to *but, nor, or, so,* and *yet* as sentence openers.

and (for *to*) FF says, "She came and saw him in June." Usual SWE says, "She came to see him in June."

and moreover Ordinarily, SWE omits *and*.

and/or If *and* or *or* alone will make the intended meaning clear, SWE avoids *and/or*: "There were no corrections or (not *and/or*) additions to the minutes." "Park visitors can enjoy fishing and (not *and/or*) boating." The expression is sometimes useful in business or law to indicate three possibilities involving two persons or things: *A* alone, *B* alone, or both *A* and *B*: "The CEO and/or the president must be notified at once." In ordinary prose a more graceful substitute is usually possible.

and which, and who, and whom In SWE, used only after an earlier *which, who,* or *whom*; not "He was a brave leader, and whom his followers trusted implicitly" (SWE deletes *and,* or rewords). For another example, SWE may say, "Marian is a woman who works hard and who is completely honest," or, more concisely, "Marian is a hard-working, honest woman." As the examples show, a construction with *and who* and the like can often be avoided.

angle Now SWE for "position, point of view, approach," as in "What is his angle?" "What angle shall we take in writing this news story?" "From my angle it seems that . . ."

angry with/angry at Books on usage generally prescribe *angry at* for references to things: "angry at the table leg that broke his toe"; but *angry with* for persons: "Lois was angry with her mother." More and more, however, *angry at* seems to be taking over both functions, perhaps by analogy with the colloquial *mad at*, but perhaps also because *with* suggests reciprocity – that both persons shared the anger. Maybe Lois was the only angry person, and her mother did not reciprocate. SANE recommends *angry at*, although SWE usage is divided. You may, of course, be *angry about* SANE's recommendation.

angry/mad A teacher once said, "I teach my students to say 'get angry' instead of 'get mad,' but I have to admit that I get mad when they disregard my advice." Older teachers insisted that *mad* necessarily means only "insane," ignoring the fact that many words have multiple meanings. Ultraconservatives still gnash their teeth when they hear or see *mad* where they prefer *angry*, but fortunately the gnashing is only figurative or their dentists' bills would be higher.

animals (*that* vs. *who*) See DOG WHO.

annihilate, destroy, flay, manhandle, massacre, slaughter, slay, smash, thrash Sports pages are filled with verbs of mayhem even in accounts of games in which no one suffered as much as a broken fingernail. Writers who tire of *beat, defeat, overcome, shut out*, and other accurate verbs often resort to bloody hyperbole. People who are not sportswriters can ordinarily use less violent language.

annoy (see AGGRAVATE/ANNOY/IRRITATE.

annual See BI-/SEMI-.

answer, reply, response; rejoinder/repartee/retort *Answer, reply*, and *response* are used interchangeably, although *response* may suggest slightly more formal circumstances. The other three words differ somewhat. A *rejoinder* is moderately sharp and contradictory. *Retort* conveys not only sharpness but also some hostility: "His retort was, 'That's an outright lie!'" *Repartee* is quick, good-natured, and often witty.

antagonist See ADVERSARY/ANTAGONIST/ENEMY . . .

ANTECEDENT In grammar an antecedent is a word or group of words to which a pronoun refers. Some sentences are not clear because readers cannot be sure about the antecedents of *he, she, it, they, this, that, which, who*, or other pronouns. In "When you get the old chair out of the crate, throw it on the junk pile," is *it* the chair or the crate? In "He ordered me to build a fire under the mule, *which* I was reluctant to obey," the antecedent of *which* is unclear for a moment. The SWE principle: When you use a pronoun (especially those listed), you should ask yourself, "Will readers instantly know what this pronoun refers to?" Debate goes on about whether *which* may ever refer to the whole idea of a phrase or a clause. The modern SWE answer is "Yes, but not if any confusion is possible." This sentence is clear: "That the undertaking might be dangerous, *which* had not previously occurred to him, now became apparent." When a noun comes just before the *which*, however, the construction may be temporarily misleading. That is true of the sentence about the mule and also of this: "He disregarded the offer, *which* surprised his friends." Here, *offer* seems to be the antecedent, and readers are consequently confused for a moment.

anticipate/expect Although *anticipate* and *expect* may often be used as synonyms, the former may seem a little pretentious, as in "We anticipate only a five-cent profit." *Anticipate* is needed, however, in the sense of doing something about whatever is likely to happen. In baseball, for example, a batter not only expects or awaits the next pitch but also may anticipate it by deciding ahead of time what the pitcher is likely to throw.

antipathetic See ALLERGIC/ANTIPATHETIC.

anxiety/apprehension/care/concern/worry *Anxiety* is normally longer lasting and perhaps deeper than *apprehension*. For example, one may suffer for years from anxiety about the possibility of cancer but is likely to feel apprehension about catching a cold. *Care*, often *cares*, is usually associated with responsibilities: "family cares." A *concern* most frequently is of short duration and usually has a specific cause: "Her concern was that the rain would start before two o'clock." *Worry* is likely to be long, persistent: "a farmer's worry that the coming summer will be as dry as the present one."

anxious/eager *Anxious* is related to *anxiety*, *eager* to *eagerness*. We are anxious ("worried") about harmful things that may happen, eager about things we want to happen. In FF we may be *anxious* to see a movie, get home early, and so on, but in SWE the customary word for pleasant activities is *eager*.

any (redundant) FF: "The apology didn't help him any." SWE generally avoids the unnecessary word: "The apology didn't help him."

any and all SANE advises and SWE concurs: in sentences such as "Any and all offers will be considered," choose *any* or *all*, but not both.

any is/any are *Any* may be either singular or plural, depending on context and intended meaning. In "Any of those cakes is eligible for first prize," the meaning is that any single one may win. In "If any of the pears are badly bruised, they must be discarded," the meaning is that all the damaged pears are not to be sold.

any more/anymore In "There are not any more bills left to consider" and similar sentences in which *more* is an adjective, *any more* is written as two words. In adverbial uses, as in "Annie doesn't live here anymore," the meaning is "at present" or "henceforth, from this or that time." Both spellings are used, with *anymore* gaining. In SWE, adverbial *anymore* or *any more* appears only in negative contexts, as in the example, or possibly interrogative: "They never invite him anymore." "Will they invite him anymore?" In FF, however, especially in some dialects, it appears in positive contexts: "Young folks used to get drunk, but anymore they get high on dope."

anybody, anyone (one word or two) As a pronoun, each is written as a single word: "Anybody (or *Anyone*) may bring a friend." In the rather rare nonpronominal use, each is two words: "The posse could not find any body ('corpse')." "If any one (single) theory seems most likely . . ." *Anybody* and *anyone* are interchangeable, although some people feel that *anyone* is slightly more formal.

anybody, anyone (verb or pronoun with) As shown by "anybody (or *anyone*) is . . . ," each word is singular. "If anybody in these tenements is most endangered, it is the infants." Technically, and most often but not uniformly when a following pronoun refers to *anybody* or *anyone*, that pronoun also should be singular: "If anyone wants to object, *he* (or *she*, or *he or she*) should feel free to do so." In FF, however, *they* is far more widely used: "If anyone wants to object, *they* should . . ." (The reason for this widespread use of *they* is that it makes unnecessary a choice between *he* and *she*.) SWE users who are conservative or are addressing conservative readers generally choose a singular pronoun rather than *they*.

anybody, anyone (with *else*) Just as *other* is used in SWE in a sentence such as "Jack is younger than any other boy on his team," so *else* is needed in "Jack is younger than anyone (or *anybody*) else on his team." Clearly, Jack could not be younger than anyone on his own team.

anyone See ANYBODY/ANYONE.

anyplace (adverb) Divided usage is found in SWE, as in "She could not find such statistics (anyplace or anywhere)." About half of the writers on usage insist on *anywhere* in formal contexts, but the rest say, in effect, "Take your choice." So – take your choice. Similar comments apply to *everyplace, noplace, someplace*, which may be used interchangeably with *everywhere, nowhere, somewhere*.

any time/anytime *Anytime* is used adverbially: "Little Suzie answers the phone anytime someone calls." As a noun, two words are required in SWE: "Any time you select will be satisfactory."

any way/anyway/anyways *Anyways* is FF (dialectal) for *anyway*. *Anyway* (one word) is SWE for the meanings "nevertheless" and "at any rate": "They went ahead anyway." "Anyway, they did not get lost." For the meaning "in any manner," both *any way* and *anyway* are SWE: "Spell it any way (or, less often, *anyway*) you like." Obviously, two words are required in a context such as "We could not find any way through the dense thicket," in which *way* is clearly a noun.

anywhere See ANYPLACE.

anywheres This is FF; SWE drops the *s*.

apex See ACME/APEX/EPITOME.

apiary/aviary No, you'll not find apes in an *apiary*, but you will find bees. (The Latin for "bee" is *apis*.) Because the Latin for "bird" is *avis*, a place where birds are confined is an *aviary*. *Aviator* and *aviation* are from the same source.

APOSTROPHE (punctuation) Examples of SWE usage: In contractions: *I'm, he'll, she'd, doesn't, it's* (only when the meaning is "it is" or [more rarely] "it has"); the apostrophe occupies the place where one or more letters have been removed. In possessives of nouns: the Queen's English, this *doctor's* husband, these *doctors'* husbands. In decades: the *1990's* or the *1990s* or the *nineties*. In plurals of symbols, and of letters or words referred to as letters or words: +'s, two *c*'s and one *s* in *occasion*, too many *and*'s. Not in plurals of nouns: *Tomatoes* for Sale (not *Tomato's* or *Tomatoes'*); the *Browns* (not the

Brown's or the *Browns'* unless possession is shown, as in "the *Browns'* dog").

apparent   SWE checks for ambiguity. An apparent mistake, for example, can be either what appears to be a mistake (but may not be) or a mistake that is easily seen.

apparent/evident/obvious   These three words are virtually interchangeable, meaning "easily perceived or recognized." But *evident* and *apparent* do differ somewhat. Something is *evident* if clear, easily obtainable evidence (facts) can be obtained. It is *apparent* or *obvious* if it can be seen at a glance. *Apparent* and *apparently*, however, sometimes cast a little doubt on the accuracy of an observation. Thus "Apparently he is telling the truth" shows less certainty than does *evidently* or *obviously*. On a believability scale, *obviously*, *evidently*, and *apparently* rank 1, 2, and 3.

appealing   Headline: "Singer Tina Turner is Appealing." Many male readers no doubt agreed. But the story said that she was appealing a legal decision. SWE is wary of ambiguous words.

appear   Some danger of ambiguity when an infinitive follows: "She appeared to testify against the defendant." Does this mean that she seemed to testify against him, or that she made a court appearance in order to do so?

appear on the scene, arrive on the scene   SANE says, "Delete three words in each."

appendices/appendixes   Both these plurals are standard. Surgeons, however, remove *appendixes*, and books are likely to have *appendices* rather than appendixes.

appendix (verb with)   According to FF, "Her appendix *have* been bothering her again. *They* gave her trouble last year, too." Because the appendix is a single organ, SWE chooses *has* and *It*.

apply downward pressure   Hoity-toity. Why not *press down*?

APPOSITIVE   An appositive uses different words to rename something that comes just before it in a sentence: "My brother, *the captain of the team*, led the scoring." Most often an appositive is set off by commas, as in the example. When necessary for identification and not just for further information, however, it is not set off. In "Ward's son, *John*, accompanied him," the implication is that Ward has only one son, and we are told what his name is. But in "Ward's son *John* accompanied him, but his son *Frank* remained at home," *John* and *Frank* are both necessary for identification and are not set off. Other examples: "the painter *Rubens*," "Mark Twain's novel *Tom Sawyer*," "We *boys* won," "for us *boys*." If the appositive is a pronoun, it is in the same case as the word with which it is in apposition. Thus in "The two men, *Graham and he*, fled," the form *he* is in the same case as the subject, *men*. But in "A posse pursued the two men, *Graham and him*," the objective *him* is chosen because it is in apposition with the direct object, *men*. Bernstein has commented on the superiority of the "post-appositive" over the "pre-appositive." He objects rightly to the ungainliness of "Ohio Supreme Court Judge and former trial lawyer James Garfield." Much more gainly is "James Garfield, Ohio Supreme Court Judge and former trial lawyer." Even more ridiculous, Bernstein suggests, is such journalese as "West 135th Street scrubwoman and subway rider Anna Johnson" (for this, perhaps, even a normally placed appositive would not be very graceful).

apprehension See ANXIETY/APPREHENSION/CARE . . .

approach SWE uses *to* after the noun *approach*, but not after the verb: "The approach to the mansion was a long, narrow lane." "We approached the mansion slowly."

apt/liable/likely Followed by *to* and referring to probability, *apt* and *likely* are interchangeable: "They are apt (or *likely*) to turn here." *Apt* may also refer to an inborn tendency, ability, aptitude: "an apt student of mathematics." Especially but not exclusively in FF, *liable* is often used as *apt* and *likely* are, to indicate probability: "They are liable to turn here." But in SWE *liable* refers most often to unpleasant or otherwise undesirable possibilities: "We are liable to encounter a blizzard," ". . . liable to lose money." In legal use, *liable* can mean "responsible": "She is liable for her husband's debts."

arbitrate/mediate In labor negotiations a person who *arbitrates* is empowered not only to gather facts and discuss them with all disputants but also to make a decision that all are bound to accept (although some preconditions may apply). One who *mediates* has less power. He or she may serve as go-between, gather and share information, give advice, and make recommendations, but not impose a settlement.

ARCHAIC LANGUAGE Language of a bygone period is generally avoided in SWE except when the writer is trying to reconstruct that period. A historical novelist, in writing about a medieval battle, may use old words for parts of armor (e.g., "a *greave* and a *cuisse* protected the calf and the thigh"), and the characters' speeches in the novel may be laced with archaisms typical of the era (*quoth*, *eftsoons*).

archetype/prototype Often used interchangeably, but one distinction is frequent in SWE: An *archetype* is an early model (e.g., of a machine) that is followed with little or no change in later models. (Jungian psychology has a special definition, related to survivals of inherited characteristics.) A *prototype*, also an early model, may later be considerably modified. Thus early Fords were prototypes of the Fords driven today. The word is also used to refer to something or someone that is a typical representative of a class or group: "He was the prototype of the New Deal legislator."

area Often can be omitted: "In the area of statistics, it is easy to mislead people." SWE here is likely to delete *the area of*, or to increase readability by writing, "Through misuse of statistics . . ." or "It is easy to mislead people by misusing statistics."

aren't I This expression is illogical, for probably no one says "I are not?" or "Are I not?" But because the contraction *ain't* is widely condemned, *amn't* seems awkward, and *am I not* may sound forced and unnatural, *aren't I* is widely used in FF though rarely in SWE. Despite misgivings, SWE writers usually settle for *am I not*. See also AIN'T.

arguably   Overused. Dubious in "Charles is arguably a handsome young man" or "Cherry is arguably the best kind of pie." Something is arguable if it is worth arguing about or at least can be argued about intelligently. A court decision or a congressional bill is usually arguable, but such things as handsomeness and taste are likely to be considered more emotionally than thoughtfully. As the saying goes, "There can be no disputing individual tastes." *Inarguably* (or *unarguably*) means, in effect, "This is one question that has only one side."

arithmetic progression/geometric progression   1, 5, 9, 13 . . . represents an *arithmetic progression* or *arithmetic series*, in which the same number is added at each step. (The accent in the adjective is on *met*.) 3, 9, 27, 81 . . . represents a *geometric progression*, using the same multiplier each time. It is also called a *geometric series* and is related to a *geometric mean*. See also AVERAGE.

armed to the teeth.   Cliché. Few people today carry daggers or other weapons between their teeth – not even figuratively.

armed with   This expression is used in SWE mainly when referring to actual arms or something else usable in offense or defense. Satisfactory: "armed with a shotgun," "armed with convincing evidence of the defendant's guilt." Dubious: "armed with kindly words," "armed with a birthday cake."

arm-twisting   Used figuratively to mean "vigorously trying to influence; putting pressure on." Although still slightly informal in tone the expression is widely used in SWE: "The president may have to do still more arm-twisting to get his bill through the Senate."

around   See ABOUT; ALL-AROUND; ROUND.

arrest   Although *arrest* may mean merely "stop," as in "to arrest the flow of water," it more often means "to take into custody." A person who is stopped for speeding, jaywalking, or any other relatively minor infraction and who is merely given a ticket or a reprimand is not arrested in the legal sense.

arresting/impressive/striking   An *arresting* sight is one that catches attention and holds it for more than a moment. An *impressive* sight impresses the viewer by its size, majesty, or some other quality. A *striking* sight is unusual, surprising.

arrogance/conceit/haughtiness/pride/vanity   *Pride* has a good face and a bad. The good one reflects self-respect and justifiable satisfaction and pleasure; "pride in a job well done," "pride in one's children." The bad face of pride is an excessively high opinion of oneself or of one's accomplishments or possessions. This face may reveal *arrogance* ("insolent claim or show of superiority"): "the arrogance of kings." Pride may also be *haughtiness*, not much different from arrogance but showing itself in supercilious looks, holier-than-thou words or insinuations, high-handedness: "the haughtiness of some wealthy dowagers." *Conceit* is false pride, the sort which "goeth before destruction," exaggerating one's own little abilities or triumphs. *Vanity* is similar to conceit but is more commonly associated with personal appearance. Arrogance, haughtiness, conceit, and vanity are snapshots of the bad face of pride, taken from different angles.

artifact An *artifact* is something made by human beings, often with the aid of tools. One does not speak, then, of dinosaur bones or similar archeological findings as artifacts, although shards (fragments of pottery) are. "Man-made artifact" is obviously a redundancy.

artificial/ersatz/fake/imitation/spurious/synthetic All suggest a replacement of a "real" or an "original" thing, and all include a hint of inferiority, although some replacements may actually be improvements. *Artificial*, as in "artificial diamonds," means "man-made, not natural." *Ersatz*, borrowed from German in World War II, means "substitute." Ersatz meat, for example, has been made from seaweed. *Spurious* and *fake* are used to refer to imitations passed off as genuine: "fake pearls," "a spurious property deed"; because of the deceptiveness, these adjectives are the most critical or pejorative. *Synthetic* means "developed in a chemical laboratory in imitation of something else": "synthetic sweeteners." *Imitation* is a broad term meaning "copied from or based on an original."

artisan/artist/artiste In today's usage an *artisan* is a skilled craftsman, such as a glassblower. An *artist* is usually engaged in the visual arts, such as painting, but anyone who does or makes attractive things can be so designated, for example, a cook, hairdresser, or dancer. *Artiste* is most likely to be applied to a performer, such as a singer, dancer, or possibly an actor. Webster III adds "often a woman," but other dictionaries make no mention of gender here. The word has a French flavor that some people like, but the *e* ending may carry a connotation of effeminacy.

as a whole/on the whole Not quite interchangeable. *As a whole* suggests that the statement is true of the whole group but not necessarily of each individual: "As a whole the police department gets more money now, but officers' salaries are down." *On the whole* is equivalent to *generally* or *for the most part*: "On the whole our national economy suffered little."

as . . . as/so . . . as Some purists prefer to use *so . . . as* in negative comparisons: "not so big as Indianapolis." SWE occasionally but not constantly draws such a distinction; more often it uses *as . . . as* in both positive and negative contexts.

as/because/since *As* or *since* may refer to either time or reason. Careful writers make clear which meaning is intended. Time: "As Roy was strolling past the edge of the crowd, he saw a female pickpocket at work." Reason: "As Roy was law abiding, he looked around for a police officer." Ambiguous: "As (*When* or *Because?*) Roy moved cautiously toward the suspect, she was unaware of her danger." Ambiguous: "Since (*After* or *Because?*) her first lift turned out successfully, she felt more sure of herself." In the ambiguous sentences, *because* or a time word is more likely than *as* or *since* to be chosen by SWE.

as concerns, as regards A sentence such as "As regards Judge Milligan, he is competent, thorough, and fair" may well be trimmed to "Judge Milligan is . . ."

as far as A weather forecaster might say, "Here's the picture as far as the clouds in the Midwest." SWE advises, "Add *are concerned* at the end to complete the clause." See also ALL THE FARTHER.

as good or better than Conservatives advise completion of the comparison more clearly by adding *as* before *or:* "Joyce's reasoning seemed as good as or better than his," or, less awkward, ". . . as good as his or better." Quality magazines, including a journal for professors of English, do often omit the second *as*, but sometimes include it. The SWE verdict: play it either way.

as/as if/like A noted author, Laura Hobson, once changed brands of cigarettes because she objected to the slogan "Winston tastes good like a cigarette should." Such strong feeling is shared by other conservatives, many of whom insist that *as* but not *like* may be used as a conjunction, as in "Do (*like* or *as?*) I do." Most teachers and editors condemn conjunctive *like*, but the public uses it unhesitatingly. Shakespeare was not consistent in his choice, and sometimes preferred *like as*. So did the men responsible for the King James Bible. Fear of conservative opinion has driven some people to use *as* where it definitely does not belong: "She can run as a deer." Conjunctive *like* for *as if* or *as though* has been condemned similarly, as in "France acted like another war was imminent."

Perhaps Mrs. Hobson looks down from Heaven and thinks she might as well have stuck with Winstons or that the distinction isn't worth the fuss. She and SANE might advise other writers, "Unless you are especially eager to gain the approval of conservatives, use whichever of the words you prefer. Other folks won't notice at all." SWE wavers but still more often than not disapproves of the Winston slogan.

as if, as though Equally good. SWE uses the one that sounds better in a given sentence. In a sentence such as "It looked as if (or *as though*) it (*was* or *were?*) going to snow," SWE chooses *was* if it really did snow, *were* if it did not. The noncommittal *might snow* is also possible. See also AS/AS IF/LIKE; WISH I WAS.

as is Items that are damaged and not guaranteed are sometimes sold *as is:* at the buyer's risk. *As are* is not SWE even though several items may be involved.

as long as As an equivalent of *because*, *as long as* is most likely to appear in FF. Sometimes it is ambiguous, as in "As long as it's snowing so hard, you'd better stay in the house." (Does *as long as* here mean "because" or "while"?) In SWE *as long as* most often means "while" and less often "since" or "provided that."

as of (with a time word) In "as of now," SWE usually deletes *as of* but may substitute "at this time." For "as of Tuesday," SWE often substitutes "on Tuesday."

as per Largely outdated business jargon. Instead of "As per your order of June 6, we are shipping . . . ," a modern business person is likely to fax, "As you requested . . ."

as such This expression usually can be omitted without affecting meaning: "Athletes (as such) constitute a sizable part of the entertainment industry." Possible: "Her letters as such were not masterpieces, but as portrayals of an unstable mind they were fascinating."

as the crow flies This is a cliché. The ornithology is faulty. Crows and most other birds only occasionally fly very far in a straight line, unless perhaps on long migratory flights.

as to **I.** SWE uses the term for "concerning" in sentences such as "As to the jewels, they have not yet been appraised." **2.** In both "as to whether" and "as to why," *as to* is usually cut in SWE: "They were uncertain (as to) whether the owner permitted hunting." "The president gave no explanation (as to) why he vetoed the bill." (More compact: "The president did not explain why . . .")

as was true of, as with Often SWE substitutes *like* for brevity: "Male deer, as is true of some other antlered animals, shed their antlers annually." (Changing to *like* saves three words.)

as well as See ALONG WITH, AS WELL AS, IN ADDITION TO . . .

as with See AS WAS TRUE OF/AS WITH.

ascend up *Up* is unnecessary. Neither does anyone *descend down*. See also UP.

Asians/Asiatics Many people from Asia prefer being called *Asians*, not *Asiatics*. Similarly, Chinese people prefer *Chinese* to *Chinamen*.

ask/demand/inquire *Inquire* is a slightly more formal word for *ask*, but the two are in effect interchangeable. To *demand* is to ask more vigorously, perhaps from a position of authority: "'Where were you?' the sergeant demanded." Unlike *ask* and *inquire*, it may also mean "order": "Her employer demanded an apology." See also DEMAND/ORDER.

assassin/murderer An assassin is a murderer, but most murderers are not assassins. An assassin (1) kills a well-known person, and (2) does so for political reasons.

assay/essay (verbs) To *assay* is to examine chemically or test or assess in some other way: "To assay gold is to determine its purity and value." To *essay* is to try or try out: "He essayed reopening the lawsuit." This verb is less often used than in the past.

assemblage/assembly *Assembly* refers to a meeting of an organized group of people, such as a school assembly or the General Assembly of the United Nations. An *assemblage* is often less formally organized and need not consist of people: an assemblage of starlings, of wheels and bolts, of transoceanic passengers.

assert   See CLAIM.

assignation/assignment   Referring to a secret meeting between lovers, SWE uses *assignation*. *Tryst* and *rendezvous* are other possibilities. In legal use, the transfer of property, rights, or interest may be called either an *assignation* or an *assignment*. Although dictionaries give *assignment* or *the act of assignment* as synonyms of *assignation*, teachers and students always use *assignment* in referring to a prescribed academic task.

assume/presume   SWE often uses these words interchangeably, but some writers attempt a rather subtle differentiation. With the meaning "suppose," *assume* includes the idea of taking something for granted, but with little supporting evidence: "She assumed that her husband, as usual, would call from the airport when he returned." *Presume* is more like *guess*; we presume something that we consider reasonable, even though there may be no evidence at all: "I've never met her young friend, but I presume that he is at least old enough to tie his own shoes, if not his own necktie."

assumed name/pen name/pseudonym   *Assumed name* has connotations of criminality because newspapers often refer to the *assumed name* or *alias* of a criminal. *Pseudonym* (false name) is less likely to have such connotations. *Pen name* (French *nom de plume*) should be reserved for writers. See also A.K.A.

assure   SWE insists on an object: "Congressman Myers assured (us, his hearers, his constituents, and so on) that he would not vote for new taxes."

astounding   See AMAZING.

astronaut/cosmonaut   These Greek ancestral words are translated respectively as "star sailor" and "space sailor," but the work of each person is approximately the same. Americans prefer the former term, Russians the latter (*kosmonavt*).

astronomical   SWE does not use the word with relatively small numbers. Dubious: "She paid an astronomical price for those slippers."

at (unnecessary)   1. SWE omits *at*, but FF sometimes keeps it, in sentences such as "Where is it at?" 2. SWE checks to see whether *at* is needed in such expressions as "at about" or "at around." *At* is not needed in "The plane will arrive at about (or *at around*) three o'clock," but is needed in "The land was bought at about (or *at around*) a thousand dollars an acre."

at the corner (intersection).   Wordy. Why not "at First and Maple" instead of "at the corner of . . . "?

at the present time/at this time   Both often occur in SWE, but SANE says they waste words. The first is a rather stately way to say "now" or "today" or "this year." Good writers first note whether an expression of time is needed at all. If it is, they see whether a shorter substitute will do as well. *At this time* is not stately and usually is not superior to *now*. See also POINT IN TIME.

at the rear of Will *behind* suffice?

at this juncture SWE usually downshifts to *now* or *then*.

atheist See AGNOSTIC/ATHEIST.

athletic/athletics An *athletic* coach is one who himself or herself engages in sports. An *athletics* coach might be confined to a wheel-chair; he or she coaches athletes who engage in athletic contests.

atrocious A strong word, related to *atrocity*: "an act of unspeakable cruelty." SWE uses it only when something deserves such strong condemnation. It ordinarily does not apply the word, except humorously, to jokes, stories, or somebody's looks.

attached hereto/attached together *Attached hereto* is a phrase from an old-fashioned business letter. In *attached together*, SWE deletes *together*.

attack/assault/rape The newspaper practice of using *attacked* or *assaulted* because they're "nicer" words than *raped* has almost disappeared, partly because frankness has increased, and partly because *attack* and *assault* have other, more common meanings.

attire This is a general word for *clothing*, but SWE often searches for a more specific word: perhaps *coat*, *dress*, *a ragged shirt*.

attorney/attorney at law/lawyer Technically, an attorney is any person, not necessarily a lawyer, legally authorized to represent someone else. But in the United States, *attorney* and *lawyer* are generally considered synonymous. Not all attorneys are attorneys at law. An attorney at law is one who is authorized to make court appearances on behalf of clients (not all attorneys have such authorization).

attorney general (plural of) Formally, *attorneys general* is the usual plural, but because this is out of step with, for example, *major generals* or *lieutenant colonels*, the usage is gradually shifting to *attorney generals*.

au naturel (1) Note the spelling. (2) Why not say *nude* or *naked* instead of resorting to a cutesy French phrase?

audience/congregation/spectators Basically, an *audience* hears (e.g., a concert or a lecture), *spectators* watch (e.g., an athletic event), and a *congregation* worships together. Obviously, hearing and seeing – and even worshiping – often occur simultaneously.

aught/naught These old-fashioned words are on rare occasions still seen in SWE in expressions such as "for aught he knew," "all for naught." See also NAUGHT/NOUGHT.

augment/supplement To *augment* means "to increase," "get more of the same thing": "The candy company augmented its supply of sugar by purchasing huge quantities of it from other Caribbean countries." To *supplement* means "to add something," usually of a different sort: "The candy company supplemented its supply of sugar by purchasing artificial sweeteners."

aural/oral *Aural* refers to hearing, *oral* to speaking.

authentic/genuine Almost but not quite, interchangeable in SWE. *Authentic* suggests that experts can attest that the object is really what it is claimed to be: "an authentic signature, according to handwriting analysts." *Genuine* lacks the connotation of examination by experts but does not preclude such examination: "These look like genuine rubies."

author (verb) Increasingly, a usage such as "She has authored seven books" is seen in SWE. Although some people object to this conversion of noun to verb, it is defensible on the ground that "authoring" involves not only writing but also gathering material, planning, revising, typing and perhaps retyping, and sometimes helping to sell.

29

automatic/pistol/revolver A *pistol* is any handgun. One variety of pistol is a *revolver*, in which a cylinder holds the cartridges and revolves slightly after each shot, ejecting the spent shell and moving in a replacement. An *automatic*, another variety, has no cylinder; it uses recoil to eject a shell, insert a new one, and recock the weapon, which will fire again if the trigger is still being pulled.

automation/mechanization When a job formerly done by one or more persons is done by a machine, we refer to *mechanization*. But if a machine or machines are controlled by a thermostat or by any sort of electronic device, the result is *automation*. A fully automated factory would have all its machines under the "supervision" of one or more electronic "brains," although sometimes human beings might have to repair both the brains and the machines.

avenge/revenge The distinction is not clear-cut, but some writers believe that *avenge* usually has as its subject a person other than the one who was harmed: "He avenged his sister." "He avenged her death." The subject of *revenge* is most often the person wronged, and its object is likely to be *himself* or a similar word: "He revenged himself (or *gained revenge*) for Dora's being unfaithful to him."

aver An increasingly rare substitute for *say, state, declare*. *Aver* suggests more force or confidence than does *say*. It is unlikely in informal contexts.

average SWE omits *each* or *apiece* with *average*. An average is based on two or more items. Illogical: "These chickens each average three pounds" or ". . . average three pounds apiece." Logical: "The average weight of these chickens is three pounds" or "These chickens average three pounds." If the chickens consistently weighed three pounds *each* or *apiece*, *average* could be superseded by one of those words.

average/common, ordinary *Average* is not a synonym of *common* and *ordinary* in SWE. The latter words mean "familiar, usual." But a description of an average man (if one existed) would result from arithmetical calculations based on size, age, intelligence, and all other characteristics of all the men in the world.

average/mean/median All three words refer to averages, but of different kinds. To find the *average*, as the *arithmetic mean* is commonly called, of the five numbers 3, 4, 6, 13, and 14, add them and divide by five. (Answer: 8.) There is also a *geometric mean*, which is the *n*th root of a product of *n* factors. To find this for two numbers, multiply the two and take the square root. For instance, $4 \times 36 = 144$. The square root of 144 is 12, the geometric mean of 4 and 36. (The *average* would be 20.) For three numbers, the cube root of the product of the three is taken; for four numbers, the 4th root. Statisticians say that when highly disparate numbers are involved, the geometric mean is less deceiving than the arithmetic mean. For example, if populations of three places are 500, 14,000, and 7,000,000, the arithmetic mean is c. 2,338,167, but the geometric mean is 36,593. To find the *median*, arrange the numbers in order and see which is the middle one. For 2, 4, 7, 10, and 15, the median is 7. When the sequence consists of an even number of items, the median is the average of the two middle items. For 3, 4, 7, 11, 13, and 14, the median is 9.

averse See ADVERSE/AVERSE.

avert/avoid/prevent *Avert* may mean "turn away": "Marjorie averted her eyes from the horrible sight." It may also be a synonym of *prevent* or *ward off*: "Clyde averted a crash by making a sharp right turn." *Avoid* means "stay clear of, shun": "The best way to avoid being disbelieved is to tell the truth."

aviary See APIARY/AVIARY.

avocation/vocation An *avocation* is a hobby. A *vocation* is one's life work, or a "call," for example, to the ministry.

avoid like the plague This is a cliché. SWE follows the advice.

avoid See AVERT/AVOID/PREVENT.

aw See AH/AW.

awake SWE has a rich variety of choices for the past tense of a verb meaning "stop sleeping": *awoke, awakened, awaked, wakened, waked, woke,* or *woke up*.

award/reward In general an *award* is given for "long and distinguished service," as the cliché has it. A *reward* usually is for a particular act, such as the familiar "$5,000 reward for information leading to the arrest and conviction of . . ."

awesome This fad word is often used in FF to mean "big," "surprising," or "very (almost anything)." A young California boy used it in accordance with SWE after his family survived a moderately strong earthquake: "It was *awesome*." One dictionary definition is "filling with respect tinged with fear."

awful The historic meaning of *awful*, "awe-inspiring," is now so little known that "God is awful" sounds blasphemous. The meaning has switched to "bad, extremely unpleasant," or in some dialects to "good, praiseworthy." In SWE those meanings are not objectionable, but in precise writing a less chameleonic term is desirable – perhaps *terrifying, horrifying, dreadful,* or *awe-inspiring* – to fit different contexts.

awfully The comments on *awful* apply here. *Awfully* in FF as a rule modifies an adjective and means "very": "awfully stupid." In SWE *awfully* may be omitted or replaced by *extraordinarily, unbelievably,* and so on.

awhile (adverb)/a while (noun) "Stay awhile" illustrates the adverbial use, comparable to "Stay here." "Stay for a while" is a noun use, comparable to "Stay for an hour." "Stay a while" is being used increasingly in SWE.

B

babe/baby In SWE *baby* is almost always used, although *babe* survives in hymns, the cliché *babe in the woods,* and elsewhere. *Babe* suggests even more innocence and lack of experience than *baby* does: "a mere *babe.*" (Probable exception: the grown "babe" who is addressed as "Babe.") In talking to an infant affectionately, some adults may say, "Don't cry, babe."

baby boom/baby boomer After World War II (c. 1947–1955) an unusually high birthrate prevailed in the United States and many other countries. As a result the period was called "the baby boom." The term now appears unlabeled in dictionaries. So does *baby boomer,* for a person born during the boom. Both are SWE.

baby boy (girl) In expressions such as "gave birth to a baby girl," *baby* is redundant. All boys and girls are babies when they are born.

baby/child/infant In legal terms an *infant* is any minor, and a *child* is a son or daughter of any age whatsoever; *baby* is not a category in the eyes of the law. In customary SWE, with some exceptions, *baby* and *infant* are interchangeable, with *baby* being more frequent; each usually signifies a boy or girl from birth to the out-of-diapers or weaned age. *Infant* is often, but not consistently, used for a very young baby. *Child* is used for those between infancy and puberty.

bachelor Any unmarried man, even if previously married, is a *bachelor.* Some women dislike the fact that there is no feminine equivalent, although *single woman* may be used. *Bachelorette,* although listed in dictionaries, has never caught on because of the diminutive, condescending, "cute" sound, and *bachelor girl* doesn't sound appropriate for a woman of fifty. Perhaps we should start using *bachelor* for both sexes, as we do *officer, bartender,* and many other words.

back See RE-.

BACK-FORMATIONS See ENTHUSE.

back of/in back of *In back of* is mainly FF. *Behind* and (less often) *back of* are SWE.

bad These uses are FF: *Bad* (or *badly*) *off:* "His health is poor. He's really bad off." "Financially, he's not bad off." *In bad:* "She's in bad with the law" (SWE: *in trouble*). *Not half bad*: "This pie is not half bad" (understatement for "very good").

bad/badly See FEEL (GOOD/WELL).

badmouth FF (slang) for "speak unfavorably of." Sometimes hyphenated.

bag and baggage Earlier, *bag* referred to items belonging to an entire military unit, and *baggage* to personal belongings. At that time it made sense to say that the unit moved out *bag and baggage*. Now the expression is a cliché, as dead as those old-time soldiers.

bag/poke/sack The words may be used interchangeably, although *bag* seems a little more common than *sack* and much more so than *poke*. Some speakers use *sack* only for a cloth container also known as *gunnysack* or *burlap bag*. *Poke* is a vanishing dialectal term, formerly often heard in the South, Midland, and West. Perhaps most familiar is the advice "Don't buy a pig in a poke."

baggage/luggage The words are usually interchangeable, although in airports the sign *Baggage* is more likely to be seen. Stores sell *luggage*, not *baggage*. The implication is that *luggage* means especially the suitcases and trunks themselves, but *baggage* includes their contents as well. (Dictionaries, however, do not make this distinction.) See also BAG AND BAGGAGE.

bagpipe(s) The word is *bagpipe* in the United States, *bagpipes* in Scotland, its native home. SWE uses both.

bail/bale These words have several meanings: *bale* of hay or cotton; to *bale* hay; to *bail* water from a boat; to *bail* out from a plane; to raise *bail* for a prisoner; the *bail* of a kettle or pail.

balance In a checking account, *balance* is the standard word for what remains after checks have cleared. But *balance* to mean the remainder of something nonfiscal is a debated usage, appearing increasingly in SWE.

balance/remainder/rest (verb with) Usually *balance* or a similar word requires a singular verb, but when countable things or persons are referred to, a plural verb is needed: "Some of the apples were delivered to children's homes, and the *balance* (*remainder, rest, others*) *were* distributed among elderly people."

balding Although some writers on usage dislike *balding* for "becoming bald," it is concise and comprehensible, and besides, no one objects to the comparable *graying*. Both *balding* and *becoming bald* are found in SWE.

bale See BAIL/BALE.

balmy Weather may be balmy, but *balmy* as an FF (slang) term meaning "eccentric" or "slightly insane" is based on a confusion with British *barmy*, referring to the foam of ale or beer and to people too well acquainted with it.

band/orchestra The traditional distinction is that an orchestra includes stringed instruments but a band does not. The distinction has blurred in this century, however. Jazz bands often have a string bass or two, and rock bands have a string bass and one or more guitars.

bank on   This substitute for "rely on," originally a gambling term, hovers between informal and formal, and occurs fairly often in SWE.

bank/shore   *Bank* is customary for the edge of a creek or small river; *shore*, for that of an ocean or a sea, lake, pond, or large river: "the banks of the Wabash far away," "Lakeshore Drive."

barbaric/barbarous   Often used interchangeably. *Barbaric* means "crude, typical of barbarians": "the barbaric custom of eating with the fingers." *Barbarous*, although it, too, suggests crude and uncivilized behavior, adds to it the idea of cruelty: "barbarous treatment of captured enemy soldiers." Note the spelling – no *i*.

barely . . . when   See HARDLY . . . THAN.

based on   In SWE, should have something to modify. What is based on what? Dangling: "Based on a few months at the United Nations, he has concluded that peace in the Middle East is unlikely in this century." "He" is clearly not based on anything. SWE prefers "Based on his few months at the United Nations, his conclusion is that . . ."or "After spending a few months at the United Nations, he has concluded that . . ."

bash   **1.** *Bash* is FF for "lively or wild party." **2.** It is SWE, although informal in tone, for "strike a heavy blow": "A falling tree limb bashed his head." If the blow was crushing, ". . . *bashed in* his head." **3.** Related to 2, but apparently a rather recent borrowing from England or Canada, *bash* is SWE for "criticize severely, condemn," usually in the form *bashing*: "In the 1930s Roosevelt-bashing was the favorite occupation of Republicans."

basis of (or *that*)   Often *the basis of* (or *the basis that*) is wordy and can be omitted: "The students' writing was judged on (the basis of) its content, organization, and clarity."

bath   See MATUTINAL ABLUTIONS.

BATHOS   **1.** Bathos is a sudden and unintentional descent from elevated language to the petty, mundane, or at least relatively unimportant: "For God, for Country, and for Yale!" (Yale graduates may substitute Princeton or Harvard.) **2.** A second meaning is "general dullness and commonplaceness in content or style." For instance, a political speech full of clichés about the glories of the nation, the dignity of labor, and the sacredness of motherhood could be described as *bathetic*. **3.** A third meaning is "false pathos," like that of the sob sister who tries to make readers cry over the sad lot of the millionaire actress who has just been divorced by her fourth husband.

batty   Once an eccentric, somewhat demented, or even violently insane person was said in slang to have "bats in his belfry." The no-less-slangy FF *batty* is probably derived from that expression.

bazaar/bizarre   A *bazaar* (also *bazar*) is a market of a specialized kind:

"a church bazaar," "the bazaars of India." *Bizarre*, an adjective, means "odd, fantastic in a generally unpleasant way": "bizarre acts of crime," "bizarre ice formations."

B.C. See A.D./B.C.

be being Sometimes logical but always awkward. "He must be being operated on by now," said a relative in the waiting room of a hospital. In those circumstances no one should be a critic of language, but usually in SWE *be being* is avoided: "The operation has probably begun by now." *Is being, were being*, and the like are not objectionable. See also BEING.

beat/beaten SWE prefers *beaten* as the past participle: "was beaten" "has been beaten," "will be beaten." The informal expression "can't be beat," however, is so well established that "can't be beaten" sounds strange. (Modern dictionaries list both *beat* and *beaten* as the past participle.)

beat (up) Although most likely to be seen on the sports page, *beat* ("defeat") is SWE. *Beat up* and *beat up on* ("thrash, harm physically") are informal but not rare in SWE.

beauteous Beauty shouldn't hiss as the last sound in *beauteous* does. *Beauteous* is an unpleasant and rarely used synonym of *beautiful*.

because/for Often interchangeable. *Because* clearly indicates cause or reason: "They stayed at home because it was snowing." *For* (after a comma) normally joins two independent statements and may suggest cause, reason, or evidence. Cause or reason: "They stayed at home, for it was snowing." Evidence: "They may have decided to drive into town, for faint tire tracks remain in their driveway."

because See AS/BECAUSE/SINCE.

become/get *Become* is a little more sedate than *get*, and is sometimes pretentious. Most folks get tired, get angry, get red in the face. *Become* is fine for people who aren't folks.

befall Has an archaic flavor.

before/no later than In SWE "before Friday" means "no later than Thursday midnight." "No later than Friday" means "no later than Friday midnight."

beget The past tense is *begot*; the past participle, *begotten*. The word is archaic or biblical, especially the alternative past tense *begat*, which today is often used humorously.

behest Old-fashioned for "command" (noun): "Sir Bedivere rode away at King Arthur's behest."

behold Somewhat archaic, but still used in SWE, mainly by preachers. *Lo and behold* is also rather old-fashioned.

beholden This word is old-fashioned for "indebted" or "obligated," but is still used now and then in SWE.

behoove "It behooves me" is Shakespearean English for "I ought."

being This word is overused by inexperienced writers: "Alicia, (being) the shorter of the two girls, could not remove the shelf, (it being) just an inch above her fingertips." See also BE BEING.

being as how/being that/bein's as how   FF for *because*: "Being as how she was only seventeen, she could not order a drink."

bells/o'clock   "Four bells" is not the same as "four o'clock." A day on a ship has customarily been divided into six four-hour watches, starting at twelve, four, and eight o'clock, with a bell sounding at half-hour intervals. So four bells would signify the midpoint of a watch – two, six, or ten o'clock.

belly   SWE or FF. For no good reason some people consider *belly* somewhat vulgar, although it has served the English language well since the Middle Ages. Modern writers sometimes choose a substitute out of deference to those people, but the substitutes offer problems of their own. *Stomach* refers to only one part of the alimentary canal. *Abdomen* and *intestines* bring up pictures of clinics or hospitals and white-clad people poking and kneading. The boundaries of *midsection* are uncertain, and *tummy* is baby talk. See also TUMMY.

belly-up   FF for "dead," "bankrupt," or possibly "defeated": "He started a publishing business, but it went belly-up." *Belly up to* (e.g., a bar) is sometimes used in FF for "stand close to."

below   Objecting to the redundancy of "fell to the ground below," the late *New York Times* editor Theodore Bernstein remarked wryly, "*Below* is where the ground usually is."

bemused (adjective)   Not at all like *amused* in meaning. A person lost in thought is *bemused*: "She sat bemused by the window for an hour." (An old sense of *bemuse* ["to stupefy or confuse"] has almost disappeared from the language.)

benedict   This is a vanishing word for "a confirmed bachelor who recently married." Some purists might spell it *benedick* because it may be based on Benedick in Shakespeare's *Much Ado About Nothing*. See also BACHELOR.

benefactor/beneficiary   Kindly Mr. Lavine paid George's way through college. Lavine was George's *benefactor*. George was the *beneficiary* of Lavine's generosity. The distinction is between the giver and the receiver.

beneficent/benevolent   A *benevolent* person is literally a "good-wisher": a kindly, considerate person. He or she can also become *beneficent*, "a good-doer," by being helpful and generous to those who need assistance. Note the last four letters of *beneficent*. It is sometimes misspelled and mispronounced as *beneficient*.

beside/besides   *Beside* means "alongside, at the side of": "Walk beside him." *Besides* means "in addition (to)": "Besides, they attended a Puccini opera." "Besides the opera, they heard a concert in Symphony Hall."

best of all/. . . of any/. . . of every   SWE most often chooses *best of all*, as in Voltaire's "best of all possible worlds."

best/better   According to one version of an old story, at a pep rally before a Yale-Harvard football game the Yale coach ended his remarks with "May the *best* team win!" The Harvard coach began by asking condescendingly, "Don't you mean the *better* team?" "No," said Yale, "I brought sixty-six players – six teams. May the *best* team win!" SWE ordinarily follows the conservative use of *better* when referring to two, *best* for three or more, but an occasional "best of the two" slips in.

better than/more than In expressions such as "better (or *more*) than a hundred yards" or "better (more) than ten pounds," SWE usage is split, with *more than* somewhat ahead. The AHD usage panel split 69–31 for *more than*, with one panelist calling *better than* "rustic and illogical. Is anything *better*, or *worse*, than a mile?"

between/among See AMONG/BETWEEN.

between . . . and/between . . . to A • B Note that the dot is *between* A *and* B. SWE reasons that it is illogical to substitute *to* there, or to say, as at least one weather forecaster does, "Temperatures will range between the mid-sixties *to* seventy."

between every (or *each*) SWE users consider it nonsense to say, "Ray paused between every word" or ". . . between each word." They prefer ". . . paused between every two words" or ". . . after each word." SANE agrees.

between you and (I, me) In SWE, always *me*, as with other objects of prepositions: "from me, to you and me, for her and me, at you and him, toward them and us." When two objects are involved, each should be the same as it would be if the other weren't there.

beyond (or *outside*) the Pale *Pale* is used here as "palings, a fence." In medieval times *Pale* referred to English or Irish holdings in Ireland, and anyone "beyond the Pale" (an imaginary border fence) was likely to be regarded as hostile. History suggests, then, that a serious context – not a trivial one – is most appropriate for the phrase. Even then, only rather well-schooled readers are likely to understand it.

bi-/semi- To avoid confusion in references to time, SWE uses *bi-* to mean "two" and *semi-* to mean "half." A biweekly paper is published every two weeks, a semiweekly every half week. Dictionaries define *biannual* as "every half year" and *biennial* as "every two years" or "lasting two years." Life would be simpler if *semiannual* were always used for the first of those definitions. SWE usually but inconsistently follows that practice.

bias/partiality/prejudice *Bias* represents an inclination rather than a judgment. It is a leaning toward or away from one side of an opinion, a controversial issue, or a person or a group. *Partiality* is based on a favorable opinion and is normally revealed in some sort of action: "Tom Smothers complained about the partiality toward Dick shown by their mother." *Prejudice* is literally "prejudging," making up one's mind without considering all evidence. One is usually prejudiced *against* something, although it is possible to be prejudiced *for*.

bid (principal parts) For "to make an offer or a proposal" and in phrases such as *bid defiance, bid fair*, and *bid in*, the principal parts are *bid, bid, bid*. For "to command" or "to utter" (a greeting or farewell), the principal parts are *bid, bade, bidden*.

biennial See BI-/SEMI-.

BIG WORDS See MATUTINAL ABLUTIONS; **PRETENTIOUSNESS**.

billet-doux Apparently the telephone call has largely supplanted the love letter, the love note, and the French word for either of those, *billet-doux*. For people who still do such writing, the plural is *billets-doux*.

billiards Takes a singular verb: "Billiards is great fun."

billion In the United States, France, and Germany, a *billion* is 1,000,000,000 – a thousand million. The British call the same number a *milliard*. The British billion is a thousand times as much: 1,000,000,000,000.

bisect/dissect To *dissect* (pronounced dis-*sect*) is to cut into parts, usually for purposes of examination. The number of parts may vary – not necessarily just two – and the parts need not be equal. To indicate cutting into two equal or almost equal parts, *bisect* is standard. Redundant: "bisect in two."

bison/buffalo The true buffalo are Asian or African animals such as the water buffalo, but the name is widely applied to the American bison, not closely related. The misnomer has long been used and perhaps causes no serious harm. "Bison Bill" would pack less wallop than "Buffalo Bill." There is also a European bison, larger but with a shorter mane and beard than the American version.

bit (with an adjective) *A little bit* for "a small amount" is slightly informal but does occur in SWE, usually with *of:* "a little bit of attention." *A little bit tired* or the like is informal. *The whole bit*, like *the whole schmeer*, is FF (informal or slang). *Bit part* (as in a play), *a bit much, bit by bit*, and *do one's bit* are SWE.

bite the bullet Cliché, but occasionally used in SWE for "meet the situation bravely," "accept the consequences." The phrase originated in wars of long ago, when a patient undergoing surgery would bite a soft lead bullet to keep from screaming.

bitter/bitterly (cold) SWE uses both. John Keats's line "St. Agnes' Eve – Ah, bitter chill it was!" contributed to making *bitter cold* acceptable.

bizarre See BAZAAR/BIZARRE.

black/Black Although for a while some Americans of African descent insisted on a capital letter (Blacks), most later agreed that, as in *whites*, the lowercase should suffice.

black humor/sick humor Both kinds treat in a comic way serious subjects such as alcoholism, death, AIDS, criminality, or the assumed pointlessness of life. Sick humor, however, may be more macabre, grotesque, and perverted, and more concerned with depicting small incidents than with a sustained treatment. A sick joke might concern, for example, two homosexuals on a desert island – a man and a woman.

blame for, blame on Some writers on usage, including the British Fowler, have called *blame on* wrong in sentences such as "The farmer blamed his crop failure on the heavy rains." Fowler would prefer ". . . blamed the heavy rains for his crop failure." Nevertheless, *blame on* has become SWE, which uses both the *for* and *on* alternatives.

blasé/sophisticated *Sophisticated* no longer means only "urbane, worldly." With reference to tools, robots, weapons, and other technically advanced instruments – even electronically controlled houses – SWE often uses *sophisticated* in the sense of "complex," "state-of-the-art." A truly sophisticated *person* is worldly-wise, has "been around," is aware of the conditions of people in various economic and social circumstances, knows that all human beings have strengths and weaknesses, and is willing to forgive most transgressors. A false sophistication exists also – that of the jet set or others who equate it with wealth, travel, the superficial trappings of what they consider the good life. A *blasé* person may well be one of the false sophisticates. He or she is "tired of it all," has experienced too much too soon, and is likely to pretend that a new experience is really not new, or if it is, it isn't worth getting excited about.

blatant/flagrant *Flagrant* carries a suggestion of wrongdoing that *blatant* may not. In basketball, for instance, a foul that seems avoidable and malicious is flagrant, not blatant. "He seduced his guest's wife – a flagrant breach of hospitality." *Blatant* often suggests something glaring and unpleasant to the ears or, less often, the eyes: "the blatant, drunken laughter," "blatant colors."

blaze/blazon One may *blaze* a trial but not *blazon* one. To blazon is to decorate, display, or loudly make known. In olden days knights wore their coats of arms blazoned (or *emblazoned*) on their shields.

BLENDS (E.G., BRUNCH) See SMOG.

blitz A standard word, shortened from *Blitzkrieg* ("lightning war") as practiced by the Nazis in World War II. Now SWE uses the word (both noun and verb) to refer to any intensive campaign: "With their well-filled coffers, the Republicans can afford a television blitz in the final week before the election."

blizzard Technically, a blizzard involves much snow, persistently high wind, and sustained temperature of $-10°$ F or below. Snow alone does not make a blizzard. Figuratively, *blizzard* means an extraordinarily large number or amount of something almost at one time: "a blizzard of applications for financial help."

bloc/block *Bloc*, not *block*, is SWE for "group united in a common cause," such as a business or legislative bloc.

blond/blonde Usage is inconsistent in SWE. *Blond* may refer to either a male or a female, but usually a male. *Blonde* is ordinarily SWE for female. SANE recommends *blond* for both sexes. See also BRUNET/BRUNETTE.

blood, sweat, and tears What Winston Churchill really told the

38

British was that winning the war required "blood, toil, tears, and sweat." The shorter version is a misquotation.

bloom/blossom Essentially interchangeable, these words refer to a flower, and phrases such as *in bloom* and *in blossom* are often used without distinction. However, *blossom* is more common with regard to fruit trees: "apple-blossom time" rather than "apple-bloom time," "the scent of orange blossoms" rather than ". . . orange blooms."

boast 1. In the sense of "be proud to possess," *boast* has been frowned on by many good writers but seems to be gaining ground in SWE. It may be misinterpreted to mean "brag about," however, in a sentence such as "This church boasts a membership of over a thousand." **2.** SWE accepts both *boast* and *brag*, but regards *brag* as slightly more informal. *Brag about* is more common than *brag on*, which may be classed as dialectal.

boat/ship People in navies as well as most landsmen insist that a *boat* is a small vessel, a *ship* a large one: "You can carry a boat on a ship, but you can't carry a ship on a boat." Some dictionaries, however, treat the words as synonymous. SANE advises: join the navy.

bogus Now SWE. An Americanism for "counterfeit, fake, sham:" "a bogus twenty-dollar bill." *Phony* is an equivalent.

boo-boo FF (childish) for a silly or careless mistake.

bookie/bookmaker Although most dictionaries label *bookie* as slang or informal for *bookmaker* ("one who takes bets"), SWE uses it frequently. Many readers think of a bookmaker as someone who assembles parts of books, and thus may be momentarily confused when *bookmaker* refers to gambling. *Bookie* is therefore preferable in its limited context.

boondocks Now SWE as a disparaging term for "backcountry." Used with *the* and a plural verb. FF (slang): *boonies*. (*Boondocks* is one of the few English words from the Filipino Tagalog language.)

born/borne These examples represent SWE usage: "Melba was *born* in Missouri. Her mother had *borne* two other children; one of them, a boy, was *born* deaf and crippled. Melba's mother has *borne* that burden with patience."

borrow See LEND/LOAN.

boss, bossy *Boss* for "employer, foreman, supervisor" or "leading politician" is SWE. So is the comparable verb, as well as the adjective *bossy*. The adjective *boss* in the sense of "first-rate," however, is FF (slang): "He's a boss guitarist."

both/each FF says, "Both fighters claimed that the other had fouled him." What other? SWE says, "Each fighter claimed . . ." and "Both fighters complained about the referee." So, of course, did each fighter. Unclear: "Both boys earned a thousand dollars." Clear: "Each boy earned five hundred (or *a thousand*) dollars."

both (redundant) Omitted in SWE when another word in the same sentence carries a similar meaning, as in these FF redundancies: "both went together," "both are equal," "both are similar." So SWE avoids sentences such as "Ralph and Walter both agree." FF says, "the both of you"; SWE deletes *the*.

bottom line This business term, relating to the profit-or-loss line in an official report, has been taken over in figurative use to mean any final result. The term is SWE but in recent years has been greatly overused.

bought/boughten SWE uses *bought* as both verb and adjective: "Antonia had bought a dress." "Antonia had a bought dress." Many Northerners and North Midlanders, however, dislike the sound of "a bought dress" and are likely to say (possibly write) "a boughten dress" or to evade the issue: "a manufactured (or *store-bought, tailormade*) dress," "baker's bread" (instead of "bought [or *boughten*] bread").

bovine (and similar words) Conservatives prefer to restrict words such as *bovine, canine,* or *equine* to adjectival use: "an equine face." But most dictionaries now recognize a noun usage as also standard: "a bovine was . . . ," "two canines." SWE is still undecided but leans toward the conservative position.

boyish/puerile *Boyish* is more favorable than *puerile*: "a boyish grin," "boyish daring," but "puerile boastfulness and bravado," "puerile silliness." See also JUVENILE.

brag See BOAST.

brand/kind/variety Although *brand* seems to be moving toward general acceptance in SWE in such phrases as "her brand of humor," many writers still prefer to restrict it to commercial use: "a good brand of tapioca," and to say "her kind (or *variety*) of humor."

breach/breech/bridge *Breach* is historically related to *break*. So we refer to a breach of a law, in a dike, of promise, in good relations. As a verb, to *breach* is to make a hole in: "breach the enemy's line." "A whale breaches when it breaks through the surface of the water." *Breach the gap* is an amusing slip. There's not much sense in making a hole in a gap. It makes more sense to *bridge* a gap. A *breech* may be the back part of a firearm, the lower part of a pulley, or the buttocks. A *breechcloth* covers the loins. Other uses appear in *breech delivery, breeches* (slang *britches*), *breeches buoy, breechloader*.

break up In "His jokes break me up," the term means "to cause to laugh almost uncontrollably." It's FF, but sometimes appears in SWE because it packs more punch than "I find his jokes extremely amusing."

breakdown This word is used too often when *analysis, profit-and-loss sheet,* or something else may be preferable. Sometimes *breakdown* is momentarily ambiguous. Does "He gave me a breakdown" mean that he showed me a chart, caused my car to stop running, or disturbed me so much that I needed a psychiatrist?

breech See BREACH/BREECH/BRIDGE.

British Isles/England/Great Britain/United Kingdom *England* is one part of *Great Britain*, which also includes Scotland and Wales. The *United Kingdom* is Great Britain and Northern Ireland (before 1922, all of Ireland was included). The *British Isles* include the United Kingdom and the islands near it. Ireland (Eire) is included in the British Isles but is not part of the United Kingdom or Great Britain.

Britisher/Briton Residents of Great Britain prefer to be called *Britons* but may call themselves *Britishers* informally. In the United States, *Britisher* in the late eighteenth or early nineteenth century was a somewhat derogatory term, but that usually is no longer true.

broke (adjective) Although some dictionaries call *broke*, meaning "without money," informal, Bryant's well-researched study says, "In America the use of *broke* [in this sense] is standard English, as in '. . . any United States citizen, be he wealthy or broke' (The *New York Times*)."

broken down When using this term to mean "classified," SWE is careful not to get a result like this: "Mrs. Leigh presented a report on the pitiable condition of many of the town's elderly people, broken down by sex."

browse/graze 1. If your cow is eating grass, she is *grazing*. *Browsing* is a more inclusive term, most often referring to eating leaves and soft twigs of trees or bushes, but also to eating grass or other low-lying vegetation. 2. In FF, a person who chooses among various possible snacks and eats one or more may be said to be *grazing*. 3. *Browsing* is SWE for looking leisurely at items in a shop or for glancing at or through printed material.

brunch See SMOG.

brunet/brunette *Brunette* applies to females, *brunet* usually to males but occasionally to females. If *blond* (rather than *blonde*) gains ascendancy, SANE recommends the comparable *brunet*.

buff SWE for "enthusiast": "rock music buffs," "computer buffs." A buff may be less knowledgeable about his subject than an aficionado is, but the difference is not great.

buffalo See BISON/BUFFALO.

bug 1. (eavesdropping device) "Spies placed a bug inside a lamp." "They bugged the lamp." Originally considered slang, but now SWE as both noun and verb because no other short, convenient term exists. 2. The verb *bug* for "annoy," as in "Don't bug me," is FF. 3. *Bug off* (or *out*) and *Butt out* are FF (slang) for "Don't bother me" or "Go away." 4. *Bug* is used loosely for *insect* in SWE and especially in FF. Entomologists generally restrict the term to hemipterous insects such as bedbugs or squash bugs.

building/edifice SWE uses *edifice* for an unusually large, expensive building. Although such structures are now numerous, the word appears less and less, perhaps because it suggests unnecessary extravagance. Builder Donald Trump has been said to have an "edifice complex."

bulk of SWE doesn't write "the bulk of the senators" unless the reference is to their physical size. It chooses *most* or *the majority of*. With noncountable nouns (rice, sand, water, and so on), either *bulk of* or *most of* is used, but *bulk* may cause some readers to think mainly of the amount of space occupied. *Most* will not be so misinterpreted.

bullet/cartridge/round/shell/shot Hunters usually refer to shotgun *shells*, not *cartridges*. A rifle or handgun fires *cartridges*, but (confusingly) these are sometimes called *shells*. A *bullet* is the (usually) lead part of a cartridge, the part that leaves the gun when fired. The small, round projectiles in a shotgun shell are called *shot*. In counting the number of shells or cartridges available or used, military people and some hunters say *rounds*, as in "fifty rounds of ammunition."

bum idea (or *rap, steer*) *Bum*, in the sense of "poorly chosen," "worthless," or "undeserved," is FF.

bump *Bump* is FF but moving toward SWE for "displace someone from a job or position": "The airlines bumped several passengers because the plane was too heavily loaded." "Today two drivers were bumped from the qualifiers for the Indy 500 because two others posted faster times."

bunch In SWE *bunch* refers to things that grow together, such as grapes, or that can be fastened together, such as roses. In FF it may refer to a small group of chairs, people, jobs, even love: "I love you a whole bunch."

bunk/bunkum *Bunk* for "foolish talk" is classified by dictionaries as slang or informal, and *bunkum* (alternatively *buncombe*) as standard. Yet *bunkum* or *buncombe* is almost never seen in print, while *bunk* is not infrequent. Consider *bunk* SWE.

bureaucracy, bureaucrats In most people's minds these words have unfavorable connotations. SWE writers use them sparingly, and not when they believe that their readers should like or be neutral toward these people. Middle-of-the-road designations are *government workers, federal employees*, and the like.

burglarize, burgle Both words are based on *burglar* and are now SWE, with *burglarize* more common and less informal.

burglary/holdup/robbery/theft *Theft* ("taking something belonging to someone else") is a general word encompassing the other three. *Burglary* is stealing from inside a building entered unlawfully. In legal use, forcible entrance, even without stealing, may be considered burglary. *Robbery* involves use of threats or force. (*Mugging*, somewhat informal, is a form of robbery.) A *holdup* involves a gun or other weapon.

burst/bust Pipes *burst*, they *burst* (not *bursted*) last night, they *have burst*. *Bust* in the sense of *burst* or *break* is FF and is often considered a mark of illiteracy. The term *drug bust*, however, is widely used informally and in magazine articles and books, since there is no other conveniently short term. Consider it SWE.

bus (verb) Although a few people still object to "They *bused* (or *bussed*) the children" and similar uses of a noun as a verb, the usage is SWE. It is comparable to "*shipped* the crates" or "*trucked* the melons."

bush, bush league   *Bush* as an adjective meaning "inferior, second-rate" is FF. So are *bush league* and *bush leaguer* for "minor league," "minor league player." They do appear on sports pages, especially in columns written by supercilious big-city residents.

bust   See BURST/BUST.

but (for *except*)   When *but* means "except," it is a preposition and takes an object: "all but (or *except*) me (*us, him, her, them*)," "All the guests but you and me were formally dressed." Some grammarians have said that in a sentence such as "No one saw it but I (or *me*)" *I* is "proper" because the last part is a shortened version of "but I did." That argument is weak, because for that meaning *else* would be added: "No one else saw it, but I did." SWE almost invariably chooses the objective case; "No one . . . but me."

but/however, nevertheless   *But* is a lighter connective than the rather ponderous *however* or *nevertheless*. Between clauses of a compound sentence, the punctuation reflects this difference: "Laboratory explosions are rather frequent, but usually no one is hurt" (note the comma). "Laboratory explosions are rather frequent; however, usually no one is hurt" (semicolon). Obviously redundant are *but however* and *but nevertheless*.

but that/but what   Both forms occur sometimes in SWE: "Most congressmen do not doubt but what (or *but that*) the president will sign the bill." The construction, though, is a variety of double negative; it is also ungraceful. In the example, *that* alone will suffice. "I don't know but what (or *that*) you are right" may be simplified to "I believe you may be right" or "Perhaps you are right."

but which, but who, but whom   See AND WHICH, AND WHO, AND WHOM.

but (with a negative)   When *but* means "only," it is not SWE to use it with a negative. Instead of "There aren't but six," SWE prefers "There are but six" or, more likely today, "There are only six." Instead of "I couldn't see but one," SWE chooses "I could see only one" or "I couldn't see more than one."

butt out   See BUG.

buy   **1.** FF for "believe" or "accept": "When a president becomes a lame duck, Congress is less likely to buy his recommendations." **2.** (As a noun) Once criticized by people who dislike using one part of speech as another, *buy* is now SWE in expressions such as "a good buy."

by means of   Often *by* or some other preposition is enough, so why wear out the word processor? "Pioneers harvested their grain with (not *by means of*) crude tools."

by nature   This expression adds nothing to the meaning in sentences such as "By nature he is taciturn but not unpleasant," or a weather forecaster's "Precipitation, snow in nature, will fall over the Great Lakes."

C

cacao/coca/cocoa/coconut   The small, tropical *cacao* tree produces seeds from which *cocoa* (source of chocolate) is made. *Coca*, however, is a South American shrub or small tree whose leaves are the source of cocaine. Still different is *coconut* (*cocoanut*), a tree that provides the large, hard-shelled nut with white flesh used, for example, in coconut cream pies.

cactus (plural)   The late J. J. Lamberts of Arizona State wrote, "A member of a garden club in Indiana or Ohio will probably use the plural *cacti*, but a rancher in New Mexico who lives with them all the time may say *cactuses*." When in Rome . . . SANE sides with the rancher, and in general favors the anglicizing of foreign plurals.

cadge   SWE for "get by begging or by imposing on others": "Although not poor, he cadges every meal he can."

calculate/reckon/suppose   SWE generally reserves *calculate* and *reckon* for mathematical statements: "He calculates (*reckons*) his assets to be ten million dollars." *Reckon* is slightly old-fashioned. In the sense of *suppose*, both are FF (dialectal or informal).

caliber (or *calibre*)   Note the decimal point in reference to guns: "a .22-caliber rifle." The bore of such a rifle or handgun or the size of its cartridge is .22 inches.

Calvary/cavalry   *Cavalry* refers to military units employing horses or, more recently, motorized vehicles. *Calvary* is a place near ancient Jerusalem where Christ was crucified. A calvary (small *c*) is an artistic portrayal of the crucifixion.

can/may   In SWE, *may* is customary in regard to permission: "Only the Supreme Court may legally make that decision." *Can* in SWE normally refers to ability or possibility: "No human being can run a three-minute mile." In FF *can* is often used where SWE prefers *may*. A discourteous reply to "Can I park here?" is "You can, but you may not." See also CAN'T/MAYN'T.

canine   See BOVINE.

cannon/canon/cañon/canyon   The most common meanings are these: *cannon*: a mounted gun; *canon*: principle or law, group of books or other writings recognized as standard, type of musical composition, church official; *canyon*: deep valley (Americanized spelling of Spanish *cañon*).

cannot   **1.** *Cannot* is the usual spelling. *Can not* provides more emphasis. The contraction is *can't*. **2.** *Cannot but*, as in "They cannot but be proud," has literary standing but is awkward and may be misunderstood. SWE prefers *can only* or *must*. *Cannot help but* (*agree*, and so on), although sometimes criticized, is SWE, equivalent to *cannot help*. **3.** *Cannot seem to* (*think straight*, and so on) appears in SWE, although *seem to* is generally omitted. *Seems unable to* may be substituted. Similar comments apply to *could not help but* and *could not seem to*.

can't hardly   SWE is *can hardly*. *Can't hardly*, a double negative, is widely regarded as an indicator of inadequate education, in that way similar to *doesn't have none*.

can't seem to   See CANNOT.

can't/mayn't   FF almost never, and SWE seldom, uses *mayn't*, even when permission is involved, although for permission the uncontracted form may be usual. In both FF and SWE, "Why can't towns make such decisions for themselves?" is customary. In "They can't (vs. *mayn't*) have more time," both FF and SWE often choose *can't*. *Mayn't*, like *may* and *may not*, is sometimes ambiguous, referring to either permission or possibility.

canyon   See CANNON/CANON/CAÑON/CANYON.

capable   The usual idiom is *capable of doing*, not *capable to do*. With a word such as *sufficiently* or *enough*, however, the *to*-construction is SWE. "Mrs. Larson is sufficiently capable (or *capable enough*) to manage the whole office."

capacity   See ABILITY/CAPACITY.

capital/capitol   The state *capital* is the city in which the *capitol* (building) stands. Some people remember the *o* in *capitol* by thinking of the *o* in *dome*.

carat/caret/carrot/karat   *Carat* or *karat*: a jeweler's term for 200 milligrams; *caret*: a mark (ˆ) showing a place to insert written or printed material; *carrot*: a kind of vegetable.

cardinal/ordinal   *Cardinal* numbers are 1, 2, 3, and so on. *Ordinal* numbers are *first, second, third*, and so on. The endings *st, nd, rd*, and *th* are used less frequently than formerly with ordinals: "June 1" or "1 June" rather than "*June 1st.*" In SWE, it's "the seventh son" rather than "the 7th son." With long ordinals, *127th* is customary rather than *one hundred twenty-seventh*. In tables, *1st, 2nd*, and so on are less likely than *1, 2*, and so on.

care of   For the abbreviation, as in an address, SWE uses *c/o*, not %.

care   See ANXIETY/APPREHENSION/CARE . . .

careen/career   In earlier usage, *careen* was applied only to boats leaning to one side, and *career* referred to fast, erratic movement of wagons or cars. Now, however, perhaps because of other, quite different meanings of *career*, *careen* is used for wheeled vehicles and sleds as well as boats: "Two cars careened crazily toward each other."

career   Pretentious or humorous when used to refer to a job held only briefly. In SWE *career* signifies the major professional activity of a lifetime. References to "my high school career" or "my three-week career as a hosiery salesman" appear either highfalutin or funny.

careful (*close*) scrutiny   *Scrutiny* by definition is careful and close. SWE most often omits the modifier.

caret, carrot   See CARAT/CARET/CARROT . . .

cartridge   See BULLET/CARTRIDGE/ROUND . . .

case   This word is overused in the sense of "situation" or "circumstances." Partridge quotes this amusing example: "There was a greater scarcity of crabs than in the case of herrings."

cast/caste   A playbill lists a *cast* of characters. In India and sometimes elsewhere a class of society is called a *caste*: "The four major Hindu castes are Brahman, Kshatriya, Vaisya, and Sudra."

casual/causal   Frequently confused by typists. *Casual* means "occasional, incidental, haphazard, indifferent, or informal": "a casual visitor," "casual clothing." *Causal* is derived from *cause*: "the causal relationship between friction and wear."

casualty   In military and accident reports a casualty may be a person either killed or severely injured. A military casualty list may also include names of seriously ill, captured, deserted, or missing personnel. Because definitions of *casualty* are not all alike, a term such as "twenty casualties" is often unclear; in some counts but not in others a broken toe or a severe strain may make one a casualty.

catalog/catalogue   Two centuries ago Noah Webster advocated simplifying many spellings, including most of those with a final silent *ue*. Today both *catalog* and *catalogue* are SWE, as are *dialog*, *dialogue*, and some others. SANE admires Webster.

catch on fire   *On* is unnecessary.

catch up   This term is now SWE in these senses: **1.** Overtake: "The second platoon tried to catch up with the first." **2.** Bring up to date: "catch up with the news." **3.** Become involved in: "caught up in the excitement." **4.** Discover (and probably point out) minor errors or untruths: "caught his brother up in a fib" (chiefly British).

Catholic/Roman Catholic   SWE uses *Roman Catholic* rather than *Catholic* if any likelihood of confusion exists about whether Roman, Greek, or some other variety of Catholicism is meant. Uncapitalized, *catholic* usually means "wide-ranging, broad, universal": "As a reader, she is catholic in her tastes."

Caucasian   With reference to race SWE prefers *white* to *Caucasian* unless clarity suffers. *Caucasian* is often considered rather pompous, and comparable words for *black*, *brown*, or *red* may be unfamiliar or offensive. Anthropologists no longer use *Caucasian* as a scientific term.

causal   See CASUAL/CAUSAL.

cause/reason   A *reason* gives an explanation: "The reason the storage tank was believed safe was that state inspectors had approved its design." *Cause*, however, deals in some direct way with origin: "The cause of the failure of the storage tank was an improper weld."

46

cavalry See CALVARY/CAVALRY.

cease More pretentious than *quit* or *stop*.

celebrant/celebrator SWE commonly restricts *celebrant* to a priest celebrating a religious rite or any person taking part in such a rite. It uses *celebrator* to mean, for example, someone in Times Square on New Year's Eve.

celebrate/commemorate To *commemorate* is to honor the memory of someone or something. You may *celebrate* your birthday, but only after you are dead can anyone commemorate it or you.

Celtic/Gaelic *Celtic* is the more inclusive term; it does not refer only to the Irish, as some people assume. The Celtic languages are divided by linguists into two branches: the Brythonic, consisting of Cornish, Welsh, and Breton, and the Goidelic, consisting of Irish Gaelic, Scottish Gaelic, and Manx. The ancestors of the speakers of all these languages were Celts, who lived in western and central Europe before settling mainly in the British Isles. A Gael is a Scottish Celt or Highlander, or any Celt who speaks Gaelic. *Gaelic*, as an adjective, means "pertaining to the Gaels or their language."

cement/concrete *Cement* is one of the ingredients of *concrete*. Usually the greater part of concrete is sand or gravel, with cement used as an adhesive. SWE refers to concrete – not cement – sidewalks or roads.

censer/censor/censure A *censer* is an incense burner. To *censor* a book is to forbid its sale or to cut out parts of it for political, moral, or other reasons. To *censure* is to blame. Some persons may censure an author for something he or she has written – possibly a book that was censored.

centenarian/centurion If your grandfather, who fought in World War I, lived to be a hundred, he was a *centenarian*, but he was not a *centurion*, as one small-town newspaper would have called him. A centurion served in an ancient Roman army and was in command of one hundred men.

center (preposition with) It's not logical to say "The argument centered *around* (or *about*) the high cost," for a center is not really around anything. Logic demands centered *in*, *on*, or *upon*. So many reputable writers have written *center around* or *about*, however, that those usages have become SWE, along with *in*, *on*, and *upon*. Language often refuses to be the slave of logic.

center/middle *Center* is usually a more precise term. In a circle, for example, the center is the point equidistant from any point on the circumference. *Middle* may be synonymous with *center*, but is usually interpreted as more inclusive: the area including and close to the center. Sometimes, though, *center* is used in that same sense: "the center (or *middle*) of town." Similarly, a person may be in either the center or the middle of a controversy.

47

cents SWE writes "ten cents," "10 cents" (especially in journalism), or "10¢" (in a table or an advertisement), but not ".10¢," which technically means "a tenth of a cent."

centurion See CENTENARIAN/CENTURION.

century 1. SWE uses context to indicate whether "*the past* (or *last*) *century*" means "the hundred years before this year" (e.g., 1891–1990) or "the century before the present one" (1801–1900). 2. The first century A.D. lasted from A.D. 1 through 100, so the second century began in 101. The twenty-first century will begin January 1, 2001, the twenty-second in 2101, and so on.

ceremonial/ceremonious SWE restricts *ceremonial* to things: "a ceremonial occasion," "ceremonial robes." *Ceremonious* may be applied to either things or persons; it refers especially to the formality and pomp of ceremony, and may suggest a dislike of what appears to be excessive or meretricious, insincere, unwarranted showiness: "the ceremoniousness of a presidential inauguration," "a high-church ceremoniousness," "spoke in the ceremonious tones she considered desirable for a commencement address."

certain Overused by amateurs, who timidly and uncertainly refer to "a certain place," "this certain person," "one certain time." SWE usually deletes *certain* or names the place, the person, the time. An unintentional biblical flavor may come from *certain*, as in "A certain man had a fig tree . . . ." (Luke 13:6). "I know a certain little girl who hasn't washed her face" is arch and condescending.

certainly Often can be omitted. "His account is certainly true" may be less strong than "His account is true," because the latter does not raise any question of certainty.

chafe/chaff To *chafe* is to irritate or annoy: "Armor often chafed parts of a knight's body." To *chaff* is to banter, to tease lightly: "Did I see you staring at that blonde again?" she chaffed.

chain reaction For a *chain reaction* to occur, each action in a group must be caused by (linked to) the preceding one, as in a chain.

chair/chairman/chairperson To *chair a meeting* is SWE. In an attempt to combat sexist language, the National Council of Teachers of English experimented with *chairperson* and then settled on *chair* to signify a person who heads a committee or presides at a meeting. The NCTE considers *chairman* sexist, *chairperson* awkward, and *chairman or chairwoman* too long for repeated use. Many members, however, both female and male, dislike *chair*. NCTE's uncertainty reflects that of the public. Bold writers use whichever they prefer, aware that each choice will offend someone. Timid or cautious writers substitute *presiding officer* or *head*.

chaise longue The plural is *chaise longues* or (French) *chaises longues* ("long chairs"). Popular etymology, lacking a French education, metathesizes *longue* to *lounge*, *longues* to *lounges*. Odds are that the French form will gradually disappear from English; *chaise lounges* already appears, for example, in some catalogs.

character **1.** Sometimes can be omitted: "Incidents of an unpleasant character" are "unpleasant incidents." **2.** SWE uses expressions such as "a suspicious (or *likable, amusing,* and so on) character." **3.** Frequently in FF and occasionally in SWE, *character* is used for "eccentric person": "He's a real character."

character/reputation *Character* is what or who a person really is, deep inside; *reputation* refers to what people say he or she is.

characterized by This expression often seems wordy or high-flown. Instead of "Her knitting is characterized by neatness," SWE says ". . . is neat."

charisma From "blessings bestowed by God" or "a spiritual quality bestowed on a leader," *charisma* moved on to refer to the ability of leaders to attract devoted followers, and has been further extended to mean the attractiveness of some actors, actresses, athletes, and other entertainers such as politicians, and even to that of things: "charismatic jewelry (*clothing,* and so on)." The once rare word, along with its adjective, has thus become overused.

charlady American SWE prefers *charwoman.*

(the) charts Has become SWE in reports on the ratings of currently popular music: "'Clackety-Quack' is still fourth on the charts this week."

chauvinism Nicolas Chauvin was a seventeen-times wounded follower of Napoleon. His enthusiastic and perhaps foolhardy loyalty was enshrined in the word *chauvinism.* Loyalty to a leader became translated into fanatical patriotism, "my country right or wrong," and then to loyalty to any group. Almost any sort of patriotism or loyalty is sometimes miscalled chauvinism. More recently, *chauvinist* has been equated with *male chauvinist pig,* a man accused of regarding women as inferior beings. Often the accusation is accurate, but a few extremists apparently believe that all men are chauvinists – that *chauvinist = man.*

cherub/seraph (plurals of) The Hebrew plurals are retained in the line of the hymn "Holy, Holy, Holy" about *cherubim* and *seraphim,* as well as in other religious references. Elsewhere *cherubs* and *seraphs* are likely. Those rosy-faced, babylike beings that have often been used on greeting cards are cherubs.

chicanery/duplicity Both words refer to deception. However, *chicanery* has a suggestion of trickery and wiliness, and *duplicity* of double-dealing.

Chicano *Chicano* is preferred to *Mexican-American* by many residents of the United States who are from Mexico or of Mexican ancestry. Historically, *Chicano* means "Mexican." However, other such residents prefer *Mexican-American* on the ground that *Chicano* does not show that they are now or expect to become American citizens. Both terms are SWE. SANE prefers *Mexican-American* as parallel to *German-American* and other such terms.

chide *Chide* is a somewhat old-fashioned word for "reprove" or "scold." Its past tense (*chided* or *chid*) and past participle (*chided, chid,* or *chidden*) have never settled down. *Chided* for each might cause least trouble.

Chief Justice The nation's top jurist is technically not Chief Justice of the Supreme Court. He or she is Chief Justice of the United States.

child See BABE/BABY.

childish/childlike/infantile *Childish* or *childlike* behavior is to be expected of children. In adults, however, "childish behavior" is considered immature in a spoiled-brat way. "Childlike behavior" is less likely to be reproached; it tends to be interpreted in terms of a child's innocence and lack of sophistication. Some old people behave in childlike ways.

Chinamen/Chinese Use *Chinese* or *Chinese people.* Singular: a *Chinese.* See also ASIANS/ASIATICS.

chintzy This word, derived from *chintz* ("a bright-colored cloth"), is an SWE substitute for *gaudy, tawdry, excessively ornate, trashy, cheap, inferior, stingy.* Because of such varied meanings, some good writers avoid it.

chiseling Figuratively, *chiseling* is cheating repeatedly in small ways: "chiseling on one's expense account," "chiseling by not reporting tips." Since such a word is needed, the accurate image (a sculptor with a chisel) conveyed by *chiseling* makes it worthy of its SWE acceptance.

choosy See PICKY.

chord/cord The most common use of *chord* is in music, referring to a combination of notes. It may also mean "an emotional response": "a sympathetic chord"; or, in mathematics, "a straight line joining two points on a curve." Most other meanings require *cord*: "tie with a cord," "electric cord ('wire')," "the cord ('raised rib') on a piece of cloth," "vocal cords," "a cord of wood." A cord of wood is not just any load but is 128 cubic feet, usually 8' × 4' × 4'.

Christian name This term may be offensive if applied to non-Christians. *Given* (or *first*) *name* is usually preferable. *Baptismal name* is appropriate if a ceremony of baptism has occurred.

chronic See ACUTE/CHRONIC.

chummy There's no obvious reason why some dictionaries treat *chum* as standard English, appropriate for all stylistic levels, but call *chummy* "informal." With reference to pleasant, continuing, but not deep relationships, *chummy* is useful in SWE.

chutzpah Flesch comments that dictionary-makers have never found a perfect definition for Yiddish *chutzpah,* but that *Webster's Collegiate's* "supreme self-confidence" and *Webster's New World's* "shameless audacity" come closest. It may also mean "a lot of nerve." Because no single English word is equivalent, *chutzpah's* rating is gradually changing from FF (dialectal) to SWE.

circle around Anything that circles goes around. SWE deletes *around.*

circumstances (*in* or *under*)   *In the circumstances* is more logical, but *under the circumstances* is also established.

cite/quote   If we *cite* a passage (e.g., from a book), we refer to its source and possibly either summarize or quote it, especially as reinforcement of what we are saying. To *quote* a passage from something either written or spoken is to use the exact words, unless the quotation is designated as indirect.

cite/sight/site   *Cite*, as a verb, may mean "refer to someone else's words" but also "use as an example" or "accuse formally of a violation." *Sight* has to do with seeing or something to be seen. It may be a noun or a verb. *Site*, a noun but occasionally a verb, refers to location: "The site is a pleasant one." "The houses are sited along a ravine."

CITIES   **1.** It is tautological to say "the cities of Oslo, Copenhagen, and Stockholm" except when writing for children who presumably haven't yet studied geography. SWE just names the cities if the expected readers have passed the eighth grade. **2.** Except in addresses, names of countries may be omitted with names of large cities. Not "Moscow, Russia, and Paris, France," but "Moscow and Paris." But with smaller cities: "Moscow, Idaho, and Paris, Illinois."

citizen/inhabitant/resident   These words are somewhat interchangeable. However, *citizen* carries the connotation of "voter," "one who holds citizenship." People not born in the United States must meet certain requirements to become citizens. An *inhabitant* or a *resident*, however, must merely live in a place (although he or she *may* be a citizen). A person questioned by police is more likely to say, "I'll have you know that I am a citizen" than ". . . I am an inhabitant (or *resident*)."

clad   This is SWE, but perhaps slightly old-fashioned, for *clothed* or *wearing*.

claim (for *assert, declare, maintain*)   Once criticized almost groundlessly when used in sentences such as "The defendant claimed that he was asleep when the assault began," *claim* is now SWE.

clarify   *Clarify* means "to make clear" or "explain further." It does not mean "answer." "I'll try to clarify your question" is not the same as "I'll try to answer your question."

classy   *Classy* is informal SWE for "stylish, elegant," or sometimes for "associated with very rich people."

clean/cleanse   *Clean* usually has the literal sense of "to free from dirt": "clean the stable," "clean house." *Cleanse* may have the same meaning but is often more figurative, suggesting "to free of defilement, to eliminate impure thoughts": "Cleanse my spirit of whatever is vile, O Lord."

clench/clinch   *Clench* is a variant of *clinch* and is generally used with parts of the anatomy: "clench one's fists (fingers, lips)." It may also mean "hold tightly": "clenched the document in her right hand." Normally one *clinches* nails, a baseball team clinches the pennant,

51

pieces of evidence may clinch an argument, and boxers clinch or "go into a clinch" when they hold each other.

clever/ingenious/inventive   All three are words of praise. A *clever* person does well in solving small problems. An *ingenious* person probably combines work with imagination to reach unusual solutions. An *inventive* person is most likely to produce something new, especially something concrete.

cliché   See ADAGE.

climactic/climatic   *Climactic* pertains to climax: "climactic moments in the play." *Climatic* pertains to climate: "excellent climatic conditions."

climax   This word is not used in SWE to mean "lowest point" or "point of lowest intensity." Dubious: "The drop in college enrollments reached its climax in the 1980s."

clinch   See CLENCH/CLINCH.

clippers/pincers/pliers/scissors/shears/tweezers (verb with)   Customarily take plural verbs: *clippers, pliers, shears, tweezers.* Usage divided: *pincers, scissors.* When *a pair of* precedes any of these nouns, however, the verb is singular: "A pair of pliers is on the table."

clone (noun, verb)   Now SWE for asexual reproduction or its results: "The large graduate colleges cloned young Wall Streeters who looked alike, spoke alike, and – worst of all – thought alike."

close proximity   Redundant, so SWE deletes *close.* Instead of *in close proximity to* it chooses *near* or *close to.*

close scrutiny   See CAREFUL (*CLOSE*) SCRUTINY.

close to   With numbers, SWE but more informal than *nearly*: "Close to twenty thousand people attended."

closet   Now SWE for "secret," "private," "secrecy." It's used in such expressions as "closet homosexual" or "came out of the closet."

clout   Now SWE for "influence," "pressure": "President Johnson seldom hesitated to use his clout with Congress." It's also SWE for "a blow, especially with a fist." Sportswriters often call a home run "a mighty clout."

clover leaf (plural)   *Clover leaves* grow on clover plants. For highway intersections of that shape the usual term is *cloverleafs.*

clunker   FF for something almost worthless, especially an automobile.

coach (verb)   Once Someone decided that *coach* shouldn't be used with the name of a sport as the object, as "to coach football," arguing that the players are coached, not the ball or the game. But the substitute expression, such as "to give instruction in football," was so long-winded and high-flown that Nobody listened to Someone. So today men and women happily coach players, teams, and football and other sports. It's simpler – and better – that way.

cockamamie   FF, but now appearing in SWE for "silly, ridiculous, worthless": "a cockamamie plot." Perhaps it's related to *poppycock, cock-and-bull story.*

coca, cocoa, coconut   See CACAO/COCA/COCOA/COCONUT.

codger/curmudgeon A *codger* is an elderly but perhaps strange-acting man sometimes fondly referred to, redundantly, as "an old codger." A *curmudgeon* is not necessarily male or elderly. He or she is a grouchy and probably stingy person. In an obsolete definition a curmudgeon is a miser.

cohort In Latin a cohort was a division of a Roman legion. For that reason conservatives dislike calling one person a cohort, as in "the gangster and several cohorts." AHD labels such language "not appropriate in formal use." The more liberal RHD uses as a legitimate example ". . . followed by his faithful cohort, his son-in-law." SWE usage here agrees most often with RHD.

coiffeur/coiffure A *coiffeur* (feminine *coiffeuse*) is a hairdresser. A *coiffure* is a hairstyle considered suitable for a person and her or his intended image. (But what's wrong with *hairdresser* and *hairstyle*?)

53

cold glass of milk/hot cup of coffee It's usual for the milk to be cold, the coffee hot.

collaborate (or *collect, cooperate, gather*) together SWE omits *together* in such expressions.

collect together See COLLABORATE (OR COLLECT, COOPERATE, GATHER) TOGETHER.

collective *Collective efforts* and *collective strength* make sense, but *collective* works less well with parts of the body. Dubious: "raised their collective hands," "shook their collective heads." The second example suggests heads in a basket, like a farm wife's eggs.

collision See ALLISION/COLLISION.

collude/connive Interchangeable to mean "act together secretly, conspire." *Connive*, however, often adds the sense "pretend ignorance." A governor, for example, may connive by pretending to be unaware of misdeeds of his aides, even though he himself may have profited.

collusion *Collusion* is used in SWE only when the purpose of working together is illegal or evil: "worked in collusion to evade taxes." For a legal or good purpose, *cooperation* is SWE.

colossal, colossally (and the like) Searching for emotional strength, careless or hasty writers frequently use adjectives and adverbs loosely and without strict attention to meaning. Writers of advertising and of "confessions" are among the worst offenders. The words in the following list, as well as their adverbial forms, are all good, respectable, and useful, but they have been employed so frequently and hyperbolically that they have lost much of their intrinsic strength.

amazing	gigantic	miraculous	stupendous
awful	great	petrifying	terrible
breathtaking	huge	remarkable	terrific
colossal	incredible	sensational	thrilling
fabulous	magnificent	spectacular	tremendous
fantastic	marvelous	splendid	wonderful

If a writer uses *colossal*-type words honestly (and seldom), readers will be likely to respect her or his judgment and believe that anything described as colossal or the like really is.

colt/filly/foal/gelding/horse/mare/stallion   A *colt* is a young male horse. Both he and his sister, a *filly*, are also *foals*, a term applied to a newborn horse or to one less than a year old. *Foal* may be used as a verb, too, meaning "to give birth": "The mare will foal in April." The young female horse, the filly, is generally no more than two years old; some races are specifically for two-year-old fillies. *Horse* can be used generically for any equine animal of any age, or more specifically for an adult male horse. A *stallion* is a horse that has not been castrated; a *gelding* has been. (One meaning of the verb *geld* is "to castrate.") A *mare* is a female horse, usually adult.

come aboard   Overused for "become a member of our company (*group, team,* or the like)."

come of age   Although "She will become eighteen in May" is SWE, "She will become of age in May" is not. SWE says *come of age*.

comes time   1. "When it came time for recess" is a dubious expression, if only because it is wordy. SWE says, "When recess came" or "At recess." 2. "There came a time when" and "Comes a time in every woman's life" are SWE but verbose and somewhat affected. "*Come a time* like that again, I'll be happy" and "*Come fall,* we'll be out of debt" are FF (localisms).

comeuppance (also *comeupance*)   This bouncily FF Americanism for "appropriate punishment" or "just deserts" is not ordinarily used for long-term or severe punishment. Sometimes it may be no more than a reprimand or an effective rejoinder. (A clever put-down may give someone else his comeuppance.)

comfy   A pleasant FF shortening of *comfortable* sometimes found in SWE. It may elicit a vision of a couch or soft chairs, somewhat worn rugs, a fireplace, and one or two people in bathrobes and snug slippers.

comic/comical   A *comic* book or opera is not quite the same as a *comical* book or opera. *Comic* means "pertaining to comedy," and *comical* means "laugh-provoking." The two words are sometimes used interchangeably, but *comical* is more likely to refer to something odd or even ludicrous. An actor in a comedy is likely to be called a *comic* actor, but a clown or anyone in a clownish role is probably *comical*.

comity   This word for "mutual civility, courteousness," especially between nations, churches, or other large organized groups, is sometimes misused to mean "league, association." In speech, it may be misunderstood as *comedy*.

commendation   See PANEGYRIC.

comment/observation/remark   All are often used interchangeably. A *remark* is likely to be the most casual, least carefully thought out of the three. A *comment* often is an opinion, but it may add information. So can an *observation*, which is frequently based on the speaker's or writer's experience.

commentate   Not used for an ordinary comment, but is SWE to name what a professional or otherwise qualified *commentator* does. That is more than just comment; it includes or should include research into the background of the topic, interviews with informed persons, and hard thinking.

Commie   *Communist* is a neutral term, and the usually FF *Commie* may be either friendly or hostile, depending on intention, point of view, or tone of voice.

common/mutual   1. In conservative use, *common* refers to something shared by two or more persons, and *mutual* to something felt or done by each of two persons toward the other:

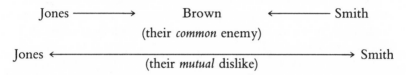

Charles Dickens, however, in his novel *Our Mutual Friend*, did not maintain this distinction. Perhaps he, like others, avoided *common* because of its other meanings. 2. Expressions such as *mutual friendship* (*exchange*, *cooperation*) and *mutually antagonistic toward each other* are redundant.

common   See also AVERAGE/COMMON, ORDINARY.

company   As a synonym of *guests*, *company* has a folksy air, but that does not disqualify it from being SWE.

compare/contrast   To *compare* is to show a way or ways in which two or more things (persons, opinions, and so on) are alike or different. To *contrast* is to point out differences only.

compare to/compare with   Often interchangeable. Many good writers, however, prefer *compare to* for a quick, undeveloped comparison, as in "Burns compared his beloved to a red, red rose." With *compare to*, the things are apparently dissimilar, as a sweetheart and a rose are. These precise writers use *compare with* in more fully developed comparisons, usually involving members of the same category: "The speaker compared the Russian variety of Communism with that of China." In the sense of "worthy of comparison," *compare with* is SWE: "In fragrance, roses do not compare with those of fifty years ago."

COMPARISON OF ABSOLUTES   Some adjectives, such as *complete*, *dead*, *equal*, *final*, *full*, *impossible*, *perfect*, *round*, *total*, *unique*, and *vertical*, represent absolute conditions. If a man is dead, he cannot be deader. If a feat is impossible, another may be equally impossible but not more so. SWE generally avoids comparison of absolutes, saying, for instance, *more nearly round* rather than *rounder*, *more unusual* rather than *more unique*. But the comparative or superlative does sometimes appear, most often in figurative expressions: "the *deadest* party of all," "He's *straighter* than an arrow."

compendium   Not used in SWE for a collection (of ideas, articles, and so on), *compendium* is a condensation or abridgement (e.g., of a speech, article, or book), or a full list or inventory, as "a compendium of the defense lawyer's objections."

complacent/complaisant   A *complacent* person is self-satisfied, probably too contented. A *complaisant* person is amiable, glad to please others (this word is used infrequently).

complected   FF (regional) for *complexioned* – but the region is spreading. Conservatives still prefer *dark-* (or *light-*) *complexioned*, arguing that *complected* means "interwoven." RHD, however, confirms that the word is used "occasionally in edited writing."

complement/compliment   A *complement* is that which *completes* (note the first *e* in each word). Thus the complement of an angle is whatever needs to be added to complete 90°. A *compliment* is a statement made to praise or flatter. *Compliments* is now seldom used to mean "greetings": "Cap'n sends his compliments, Sir."

compliment   See also PANEGYRIC.

compose/comprise   SWE follows only at times the conservative view, which is that *comprise* is similar to *include*, *contain*, or *consist of*: "A baseball team comprises one pitcher, one catcher . . ." The converse is not true. Conservatives do not say "Nine players comprise a baseball team," because the players do not contain or consist of the team. SWE: "Nine players *compose* (or *make up*, *constitute*) a team." The distinction is slightly slippery, and only by a small margin did the conservative usage panel of AHD favor the "rules" just explained. SWE sometimes goes along with them but often not.

comprehend/understand   *Understanding* is usually broader and deeper than *comprehension*. One may comprehend the meaning of a word by knowing its dictionary meaning and its basic uses and applications. But thoroughly understanding the word may necessitate knowing something of its derivation, changes in meaning, appropriateness in given situations, and especially its connotations – its overlay of associations. In addition, *understand* has a kindly, human touch that *comprehend* lacks. It's better to have understanding parents than parents who only comprehend.

comprise   See COMPOSE/COMPRISE.

computerese   This young word refers to the jargon used among computer operators. Much of it quickly became recognized in SWE, and new terms continue to be added.

con man   FF for SWE *confidence man*, "a person who wheedles his way into one's confidence in order to obtain money or otherwise cheat." A *con man* today is anyone who uses fraud to achieve his ends. Con women also exist. *Con man* may eventually supplant the longer term.

conceit See ARROGANCE/CONCEIT/HAUGHTINESS/PRIDE/VANITY.

conceive/conceive of To *conceive* is to create; to *conceive of* is to understand or imagine: "He conceived the idea of extracting milk from milkweed." "I can't conceive of anyone's doing such a thing."

concern See ANXIETY/APPREHENSION/CARE/CONCERN/WORRY.

concerned about/concerned with If you are worried about something (or someone), you are *concerned about* it: "concerned about Jasper's health." A magazine article may be *concerned with* (may *deal with*, may *treat*) children, nuclear power, tsetse flies, or any other subject.

concert/recital Musicians prefer to limit *concert* to group performances (e.g., band, orchestra, chorus), and *recital* to solo performances or possibly those in which two or three persons perform singly and jointly – often called a *group recital*. In popular use, *concert* frequently applies to both group and solo presentations.

concertize SWE now occasionally uses this once condemned word meaning "to give concerts or recitals professionally." But see -IZE.

conclave Not just any meeting, but probably one held in secret by powerful people. Its participants are not a lad and a lass but a larger group with concerns that go beyond the personal: "Striking pro football players have just learned about a conclave of the team owners."

conclude/decide *Decide* is a general word for "choose between two or more alternatives," "make up one's mind." *Conclude* can mean the same thing but implies that considerable thought was expended before the decision. SWE usually prefers *that* instead of *to* after *conclude*: "We concluded that we should make one more attempt," not "We concluded to make . . ."

conclusion See FINAL COMPLETION.

concrete See CEMENT/CONCRETE.

concretize For "make concrete or specific," *concretize* is unpretty, as many *-ize* words are, but it's terse and is sometimes found in SWE. See also -IZE.

condition, conditioned Overused, especially in reference to illness or disease: "She has a nervous (or *muscular*, *intestinal*, or the like) condition." So do well people. SWE tries to be more specific. *Conditioned* is also overworked and may be unpleasant, but it's part of the jargon of many psychologists and educators. Instead of "He was conditioned to missing lunch," ordinary people and SWE say "accustomed to" or "used to," or "He generally missed lunch" or "He didn't mind missing lunch."

congenial/genial *Congenial* is often used when *genial* is more apt. A genial person is pleasant, affable, warm-mannered. Two persons or things are congenial if they get along well together. Thus desert conditions and cactuses are congenial, and many long-married couples live together congenially even though each may have personal quirks usually considered undesirable.

congregation   See AUDIENCE/CONGREGATION/SPECTATORS.

conjure   **1.** Accented on the second syllable, *conjure* means to beg, implore. The heroine in a melodrama sobs, "I conjure you, do not desert me thus!" **2.** Accented on the first syllable, *conjure* means to practice magic. In parts of the South and the West Indies a witch doctor may be called a *conjure man*. **3.** Accented on the first syllable and followed by *up*, *conjure* means to summon or imagine. Charles Lummis, holding a cigarette, overpraised it as a magic wand that "can conjure up tomorrow." Spiritualists supposedly conjure up the dead.

connect together, connect up   *Connect* is enough in SWE, but FF often wastes a word.

connive   See COLLUDE/CONNIVE.

CONNOTATIONS   The denotation of a word is its bare, unadorned, unemotionalized meaning, usually as in a dictionary. But most words other than *an*, *and*, *to*, *for*, and the like have connotations as well. These are fringe meanings. The denotation of *mother* is "female parent," but the connotations are various. They are normally in two not completely separable layers. In the first are one's personal reactions: what *I* associate with *mother*. Someone else, with a different mother, has different associations, and *mother* has different connotations for him. (Both my connotations and his may change as we get older and learn more about mothers.) The second layer consists of more generalized reactions – the associations that most people have. For *mother* the second-layer connotations tend to be favorable, because most people have good memories of mothers. They think of them as kind, helpful, generous.

To influence readers as he or she wishes, a writer or speaker needs to think of the connotations of words, especially the second layer. An able prosecuting attorney chooses nouns, verbs, adjectives, and adverbs that through their connotations make the defendant seem despicable: "Ladies and gentlemen of the jury, this *ex-convict sneaked* down that dark, deserted street, waiting, *lust-driven*, for any *hapless female victim*." Political orators are adept at choosing emotion-laden words, words with "good" connotations for what they favor, words with "bad" connotations for positions held by the opposition.

Insensitivity to connotations makes writing or a speech less convincing and persuasive. The word *socialistic*, for example, in the United States still has a generally unfavorable second layer. Knowing that, no Democrat or Republican will call socialistic a bill he or she is advocating, but may use it as a smear word to attack someone else's bill.

consciously/intentionally   SWE relates *consciously* to *consciousness*, *intentionally* to *intention*. People who consciously brag, for instance, are aware of what they are saying, but perhaps have no intention to be boastful, do not deliberately say to themselves, "Now I'll brag a little."

consensus A *consensus* is an opinion or agreement shared by all or most of the group. Both redundant: *consensus of opinion*, *general consensus*. SWE lets *consensus* do the job.

considerable/considerably SWE says, "She was *considerably* annoyed." "She helped us considerably." In each, a verb form is modified. FF often substitutes *considerable*, as in "She helped us considerable," a word used in SWE only to modify a noun.

considered judgment Any judgment should be considered, or else what good is a judge?

constitute See COMPOSE/COMPRISE.

constrain/restrain To *constrain* is to oblige or impel: "Her upbringing constrained her to tell the truth always." To *restrain* is to hold back: "Fear restrained her from telling the truth."

contact (verb) *Contact* as a verb has been inexplicably condemned by many persons who find no fault with the etymologically equivalent *get in touch with*. Extreme purists still shrink from *contacting* anyone, but despite their opposition the word is SWE. Indeed, it is overused. Frequently *call*, *make an appointment with*, or another specific term is preferable. The noun *contact* in the sense of "someone who can provide help or information" is also SWE: "Her contact was Shirley Rand, 555-4986."

contagious/infectious A *contagious* disease, such as scarlet fever, can be spread only by direct or indirect contact. The word comes from Latin for "in touch with." An *infectious* disease, however, can be spread in other ways, such as germ-bearing air or water.

contemporary This word does not mean "modern" only. Alexander Hamilton and Thomas Jefferson, for example, were "contemporary statesmen" or "contemporaries" – that is, they were contemporary with each other. *Contemporaneous* or *co-existent* may sometimes be more clear, for each means "existing at the same time."

contempt/disdain Both are varieties of scorn. *Disdain* has been defined as "aloof contempt" or "condescending contempt." If I have contempt for mice, I speak nastily of them, but if I disdain mice, I largely ignore them. The noun *contempt* is generally folllowed by *of* with reference to things or abstractions, or by *for* with people: "contempt of mice," "contempt of public opinion," "contempt for the neighbors."

contemptible/contemptuous *Contemptible*: "despicable, worthy of contempt": "To most people a rat is a contemptible creature." *Contemptuous*: "having contempt for": "The rat was contemptuous of our expensive cheese but nibbled on our bacon."

content/contents Often interchangeable: "the content(s) of the package." When the reference is not to anything concrete, however, *content* is more likely: "Read the article for its content, not its style." *Content* is also used for "volume, capacity": "The radiator's content is three gallons."

continual/continuous Sometimes used interchangeably. SWE, however, generally draws these distinctions: *Continual* describes things that go on almost steadily but with occasional and at least fairly regular lapses: "continual traffic on our busy street." *Continuous* means "unbroken, uninterrupted": "The need for continuous operation of a life-support system."

A visual aid: *continual*: --- -- ----- ---- -
continuous: _____

continue/resume A man is digging a ditch. He *continues* ("keeps on") working until noon and then takes an hour off. He *resumes* ("starts again") at one o'clock and *continues* until five.

60 **CONTRACTIONS** Although contractions are regarded as informal, they often appear in relatively serious books and in articles in reputable magazines. They lighten the tone somewhat. For placement of the apostrophe, see APOSTROPHE.

contradict/deny/refute SWE avoids *refute* when *contradict* or *deny* is accurate. For example, a police officer charges that Brown committed a burglary. Brown *contradicts* the officer and *denies* the charge, but he cannot *refute* it unless he can provide proof that he is not guilty.

contrast See COMPARE/CONTRAST.

converse/inverse/obverse/reverse The face of a coin or a statue is the *obverse* side; the back of either is the *reverse* side. In general, *reverse* relates to "back" or "backward." *Converse* refers to the exact opposite of something else: "*Fearful* is the converse of *fearless*." *Inverse* is related to *inverted*, and means "upside down," although it has additional, technical meanings in mathematics and logic.

convince/persuade Sometimes interchanged. However, SWE usually assumes that one may *convince* by reasoning only, but may *persuade* by both reasoning and emotional appeal: "The accountant's figures convinced them that they were near bankruptcy." "Her husband's tearful pleading persuaded her to change her mind." "Her clenched fists persuaded him."

cool (lose one's) "When the bull charged, Glenn lost his cool." Conservatives would prefer "lost his composure," but in the example *cool* is not unlikely in SWE, which may reserve *composure* for more sedate situations, such as a courtroom trial.

coolth Why should this noun be treated as a joke? It follows the pattern of *warmth* and can become as useful. It's rare, though, in both SWE and FF.

cooperate together See COLLABORATE TOGETHER.

cop FF (slang) for "police officer," but also informal SWE. Likely to be used affectionately or neutrally rather than hostilely.

copacetic FF (slang) for "excellent."

cope A small skirmish is going on in SWE. May one cope in general rather than *with* or *against* something specific? Is "I can't cope" or

"He seldom copes very well" satisfactory, or must one say, for example, "I can't cope with my father's sarcasm"? Conservatives argue that undirected coping is like having a boxer in a ring with no opponent. Logic is on their side, but increasingly SWE allows an apparently unopposed *cope*, perhaps assuming that the enemy is all the things out there trying relentlessly to defeat us.

copout Based on an older slang phrase, *cop an out*, which meant "to seize an excuse," *copout* is today FF for "excuse, evasion, conciliatory compromise," or as a verb "to renege." Also, one who "cops out" may informally be called a copout.

copy/recopy See RE- + AGAIN OR BACK.

cord see CHORD/CORD.

corespondent/correspondent One may become a *correspondent* just by writing letters to someone. But one may become a *corespondent* in a divorce case by being accused of illicit relations with someone else's spouse.

corn, corny 1. To Americans, *corn* is a grain that grows on large ears and tall, thick stalks. To the British, it is wheat or oats, with shorter, thinner stalks. 2. *Corn* is FF (slang and outmoded) for "something old-fashioned or too sentimental." The adjective *corny* is an offshoot: "a corny joke."

coronary/heart attack/stroke A *coronary* (short for *coronary thrombosis*) is the closing of a heart artery by a blood clot. A *heart attack* is caused by failure of heart muscle. A *stroke* is a cerebral hemorrhage; a blood vessel in the brain bursts.

corps/corpse "Do your duty! Join the Ground Observer Corpse!" a newspaper advertisement urged. The request would have been more enticing if an *e* had been dropped. A *corpse* is a dead body. A *corps* is some kind of organized group. The plural of *corps* is *corps* (pronounced *cores*; the singular is pronounced *core*).

corpus delicti A Latin term popularly employed to mean "body of a murder victim." To a lawyer, though, it means "material evidence that a crime has been committed." That evidence is often a corpse, but not necessarily.

correspondent See CORESPONDENT/CORRESPONDENT.

corresponding/similar Here is dubious usage: "Robberies are most frequent at similar times in each December." If those times are approximately the same each December, *corresponding* would be more accurate than *similar*. In the example, *similar* suffers from vagueness. Are the times similar in dates, nearness to Christmas, weather, or what?

cosmonaut See ASTRONAUT/COSMONAUT.

couldn't care less Informal and overused for "don't care at all," "am indifferent." *Could care less* is vague but may mean that an unspecified degree of caring does exist. Both expressions are more likely in FF than in SWE.

council/counsel A *council* is an organization, for example, the National Council of Teachers of English, or a meeting such as a council of Indian chiefs. *Counsel* consists of advice or opinion: "Your counsel helped us to decide correctly." It may also be a lawyer, particularly one's representative in court: "Counsel for the defendant will approach the bench."

countless SWE employs this word only to refer to something actually uncountable, such as grains of sand on a beach. Dubious: "The room was filled with countless people."

couple 1. This word is inaccurate for any number other than two. A minister marrying a couple doesn't marry three persons. Especially irksome are people whose "couple of minutes" turn out to be fifteen. 2. Ordinarily *couple* takes a plural verb: "The couple *are* expecting their first child." In some instances, however, as in "This couple *is* next in line," when the word clearly refers to a unit, a singular verb is appropriate. 3. "A couple weeks" is FF. SWE says "a couple of weeks," because *couple* is considered a noun, not an adjective.

(the) course of Can usually be deleted from phrases such as "during the course of the meeting."

courteous/polite Courtesy has more depth than politeness. A *polite* person says "Please" and "Thank you" and "May I help you?" A *courteous* person means them.

covet/envy If you *covet* your neighbor's wife, you probably also *envy* him for having her. To covet is to want something belonging to another, and to envy is to be sorry that someone has something that you desire.

crack down on Informal journalese (and to that extent SWE) for "enforce the laws strictly against (wrongdoers)."

crass Although some writers on usage say that *crass* should be used only as "stupid," in today's writing it almost always means "coarse, unrefined, insensitive, thoughtless." A crass remark, for example, is uttered by someone who pays no attention to the feelings of his or her listeners. In some instances it may have overtones of greed, money-grabbing: "the crass tactics of Wall Street."

crawfish *Crawfish* is what kids wading in a creek call the cretacean known to scientists as *crayfish*. Eaters of the delicacy are likely to look for *crawfish* on the menu. In Louisiana, crawfish lovers might not order at all if it were called *crayfish*, which might connote a high school biology laboratory. The verb *crawfish* ("to back out of an agreement or a position") is FF. But it's a picturesque metaphor suggested by the backward scurry of the creature.

credibility gap

What someone says	(credibility gap)	What we can believe

This is a useful term, and not only in politics, although SWE does often employ it in political contexts. Such gaps are perhaps even more numerous in business dealings. The ancient Romans showed that in their frequent use of *caveat emptor*, "let the buyer beware."

credible/creditable/credulous/discreditable/incredible/incredulous/uncreditable A *credible* story is believable; an *incredible* one, not believable. A *creditable* act deserves credit or praise; an *uncreditable* one does not; a *discreditable* one harms the reputation of the doer. A *credulous* person is too willing to believe anything heard or read; an *incredulous* one prefers to disbelieve.

crescendo Conservatives like the historically accurate definition: "gradual increase in intensity or volume": "Near the end of a long crescendo passage, the sounds of the percussion instruments became almost deafening." The conservatives dislike "The music reached a crescendo," in which the word signifies "peak, intense climax." Most classical musicians probably agree. The use in this sense is not rare in SWE, however.

criminally assaulted Nice-Nellie journalists use the term as a euphemism for "raped, sexually attacked." It's somewhat silly to do so, for almost every physical assault is a criminal act. See also ATTACK/ASSAULT/RAPE.

criterion Almost always the SWE plural is *criteria*, but dictionaries do now also recognize *criterions*. *Criteria* is not SWE as a singular, however. SWE says "criterion," "the only criterion is . . ."

critical When referring to health, a writer of SWE may remember that the word comes from the same distant source as *crisis*. It concerns a turning point, a state in which the patient's physical or mental condition may become either much better or much worse. This is what hospital reports mean when they say, "Her condition is critical." Physicians and good writers distinguish *critical* and *serious*. The same principle applies to figurative uses, as in "The health of the national economy seems critical."

criticism Strictly speaking, criticism may be unfavorable, neutral, or favorable, or a mixture, but in the popular mind, and in most SWE, the word suggests more vinegar than honey. When the usual interpretation is not intended, SWE often resorts to "favorable criticism" or "comment" or another unambiguous term.

critique Increasingly used in SWE as a verb, not just as a noun: "Publishers' readers seldom have time to critique a manuscript thoroughly." Conservatives who dislike the noun-to-verb shift prefer *analyze*, *review*, or *criticize*. *Criticize*, however, is now often interpreted as basically negative, whereas a critique points out both good and bad qualities. See also CRITICISM.

crude/rude A *crude* man probably is too mentally handicapped or uneducated to realize when he is being rude. A rude woman probably

63

knows that she is rude but doesn't care. An English saying: "A gentleman or lady is never rude – unintentionally."

culmination   See FINAL COMPLETION.

cumulative   See ACCUMULATIVE/CUMULATIVE.

curious   Can be ambiguous. "She is a curious person" may mean either that she has curiosity and asks many questions, or that she is odd, peculiar, out of the mainstream. SWE tries to word sentences so that readers can easily determine which meaning is intended.

curmudgeon   See CODGER/CURMUDGEON.

currently   SWE omits this word unless it seems essential. Often a present-tense verb is enough. "She is currently writing a novel" is probably no better than "She is writing a novel."

cursive/cursory   *Cursive* handwriting is flowing, connected writing as contrasted with manuscript writing as taught to many children, who first learn to print letters individually. *Cursory* means "rapid, hasty, superficial, perfunctory": "cursory inspection of our luggage," "cursory reading."

custom, custom-built   Although originally these terms meant "especially built for each buyer," the meaning has gradually shifted to "more expensive than and slightly different from another model." SWE clarifies such terms by defining them or by choosing an unmistakable context, or it may substitute an undiluted, uncheapened expression such as *tailor-made*.

customary/habitual   What "most people" do or say is *customary*: "It has long been customary to avoid wearing bright clothing at funerals." *Habitual* refers to what has become a habit, and it often applies to only one person: "his habitual discourtesy."

cut in half   SWE, but so are the more logical *cut in halves* and *cut in two*.

cute   Overused for "pretty," "delightful," "possessing qualities desirable in an attractive small child." Of late, *cute* has taken on added meanings; "arch," "mischievous," "pretending to be shy": "I'll answer you directly. I'll not be cute about it." Here is a rule followed by one writer of SWE: Use *cute* no more than once a day.

cyclone/tornado   A *cyclone* is any system of rotating wind, ranging in size from a whirlwind to a hurricane or typhoon. A *tornado* (informally a *twister*) is one variety of cyclone. Its funnel-shaped cloud whirls with winds of high velocity and potential destructiveness, but a tornado is much smaller than a hurricane and lasts not nearly so long. In popular usage a tornado is often called a cyclone. That's what it is, but the more specific term is customary in SWE. See also HURRICANE/TYPHOON.

cynical/skeptical   A *cynical* person distrusts people's motives and almost always suspects the worst. A *skeptical* person is less steadily and less broadly negative. He doubts the truth of someone else's assertion but does not make doubting a way of life.

D

dais/lectern/podium A *dais* is a stage or platform where a speaker and perhaps others appear before an audience. A *podium* is a smaller platform, especially that where a conductor stands to be more easily seen by the orchestra. A *lectern* is a reading desk, usually with a slanted top on which a speaker may place notes.

damaged/injured Things are *damaged*; people or animals are *injured*; parts of the body are injured, except for teeth, which are damaged: "damaged car, bicycle, apartment"; "injured boy, cat, wrist, paw."

Dame/Sir In England, *Dame* is approximately the feminine equivalent of the knightly title *Sir*. Just as one refers to Sir Winston or Sir Winston Churchill but not Sir Churchill, one also does not refer to Dame Edith Sitwell as Dame Sitwell. (A once prominent English actress rejected American speaking invitations in which she was addressed as "Dear Dame.")

damsel This once favored word of poets is now seldom used except jocularly: "Prithee, rescue yon damsel in distress."

dastardly A *dastardly* act is not only despicable but also cowardly. The word is sometimes misused to mean despicable and bold.

data (singular or plural) *Data*, a Latin plural, has gradually become treated in English more as a singular ("this data is"). The reason is that the meaning has shifted from "these figures" to "this set of figures." Most conservatives, scientists, and academic writers, however, are still likely to write "these data are." The Latin singular, *datum*, is rare. In its stead SWE generally prefers *this fact* (or *statistic*, or the like). See also AGENDA.

daylight-saving time See SAVING(S).

dead body "Three dead bodies were found in the wreckage of the plane." In such a context, we would be unlikely to say *bodies* unless they were dead. However, *dead* is defensible in "over my dead body" or other contexts in which death is not really meant.

deadbeat Used occasionally in SWE for "loafer, no-good, one who does not pay his bills," *deadbeat* still seems slightly slangy, and for this reason some writers avoid it.

deadly/deathly *Deadly* means "death-causing": "deadly weapon," "deadly carbon monoxide gas." *Deathly* means "like death": "deathly still," "His gray, emaciated face looked deathly."

deal **1.** FF (informal and overused) in expressions such as "Big deal!" and "That's no big deal." **2.** "A raw deal" is also somewhat informal but does appear rather often in SWE. **3.** "A good (or *great*) deal of" appears frequently in SWE, although many writers prefer the shorter *much*. **4.** In SWE one deals *in* things, *with* persons or subjects: "Some brokers deal in junk bonds. They deal with both large and small investors. An article in *Money* deals with the topic."

deathly   See DEADLY/DEATHLY.

debar/disbar   *Debar* ("exclude, shut out, prevent") is giving way to *bar*: "The chairman debarred (*barred*) the topic of finance from the discussion." *Disbar* means only "officially expel a lawyer from the profession or from practice in a particular jurisdiction": "After being convicted of grand larceny, Lane was disbarred."

debut (as verb)   SWE occasionally produces sentences such as "The soprano debuts in Carnegie Hall tonight," although strong conservatives prefer "makes her debut." Unlikely in SWE: "Auto dealers are debuting their new models" or "New-model Fords debut this week."

decease(d)   Except in legal use, *die* is usual in SWE, not *decease*. *The deceased*, meaning "the dead person," is also mainly legal or at least largely impersonal. A person delivering a funeral eulogy, for instance, is likely to call the dead person by name rather than "the deceased." SWE carefully distinguishes *deceased* from *diseased*, "having a disease."

decide   See CONCLUDE/DECIDE.

decimate   Roman military officers sometimes enforced discipline by *decimating* troops – casting lots and killing one man in ten. Purists say that in modern use of the word the one-in-ten ratio should be preserved; if the population is decimated by AIDS, for example, about a tenth die. Modern dictionaries, however, define *decimate* as "destroy or kill a large part of," purposely leaving *large* vague. SWE writers, especially sportswriters, sometimes use the verb in that way. FF says, "The Denver Broncos decimated the hapless Houston team" (Denver did not kill or destroy the Oilers or even a substantial number of them).

declare   See CLAIM.

decomposed/discomposed   Anything *decomposed* is rotten. When things are *discomposed*, they are disarranged, disordered. A discomposed person is upset, agitated, but not quite distraught.

deduce/deduct/induce   To *deduct* is to subtract: "Deduct line 9 from line 8." To *deduce* is to draw a conclusion: "She quickly deduced his motives, as any woman could." Although some dictionaries give *deduce* as a synonym of *deduct*, confusion may arise if no distinction is made. To *induce* is to persuade or to cause or in logic to move from particular instances to a generalization. Some people fail to distinguish *induce* from *deduce*. When you deduce, you start with a broad principle and then reason that certain specific points can be derived from that principle. For example, if the general principle is that most Swedes have blond hair, you may deduce that Lars, a Swede, probably has blond hair. But when you induce, you start at the other end, with a number of specifics from which you attempt to draw a general principle. For example, if you know several hundred Swedes, most of whom have blond hair, you may induce from those specific cases the generalization that most Swedes have blond hair.

defamation/libel/slander *Defamation* is a general term meaning the stating of something harmful to someone's reputation. *Slander* and *libel* are two different kinds of defamation. Slander is always oral. Libel is usually printed but may be in handwriting, pictures, effigies, or even recorded oral language. So if *X* says of *Y* in a speech, "He is a liar and a thief," she may be guilty of slander unless she can prove the truth of her assertion. But if she says it in a recording that is played somewhere, or prints it, or shows it in caricature, she may be guilty of libel.

67

defective/deficient Something *defective* has a flaw of some sort, such as a starting mechanism that does not work or a law that is ambiguously worded. Something is *deficient* if a part is missing. Perhaps a connection is missing in the starter or there is an oversight in the law.

definite/definitive Something is *definite* if it is exact, certain, clearly defined: "a definite answer," "a definite meeting date," "definite steps toward a solution." *Definitive* means "final, best, authoritative." Thus a definitive edition of Poe's poetry is supposedly complete, accurate, and impossible or at least highly unlikely to be improved upon.

DEFINITIONS See CONNOTATIONS; IS WHEN, IS WHERE.

defuse/diffuse To *defuse* is to remove a fuse from, or in some other way make discharge impossible. We hope that a bomb is *defused*, not *diffused*. In diffusion its parts would be widely scattered – probably by the force of the explosion.

deliverance/delivery Although *delivery* has several meanings ranging from "conveying a package" to "giving birth," *deliverance* is restricted in SWE to (1) a rescue from danger or bondage, or (2) (much more rare) a jury verdict or other publicly expressed decision. Example of (1): "In *Huckleberry Finn*, Tom Sawyer concocts an elaborate scheme for the deliverance of Jim from his confinement."

demand/order To *demand* is to ask strongly and peremptorily that an action be taken: "Signers of the document demanded that political prisoners be released." Only a person with authority may legitimately *order* that an action be taken: "The president (*general*, or the like) ordered that political prisoners be released." *Order*, but not *demand*, may have a personal pronoun as an object. Instead of "He demands you to return the money," SWE requires "He demands that you return the money" or "He orders (or *commands*) you to . . ." See also ASK/DEMAND/INQUIRE.

deny See CONTRADICT/DENY/REFUTE.

depend (on vs. upon) Either *on* or *upon* is SWE after *depend*, but *upon* is slightly ponderous. Sometimes the sound or rhythm of a sentence may affect the choice. See also ON/UPON.

dependent on   See ADDICTED TO/DEPENDENT ON.

deplete/reduce   A depletion is normally greater than a reduction. To *deplete* is to use all or almost all of: "Mother Hubbard's cupboard was depleted." To *reduce* is to lessen, to use or eliminate part of: "Our food supply was reduced by a third."

deplore/lament/regret/repent   Both *deplore* and *lament* express higher or more conspicuous emotion than *regret* does. To *deplore* is to regret strongly, but simultaneously to show disapproval: "Elizabeth Barrett Browning deplored the use of children as mine workers." *Deplore* does not take a personal object: you may deplore my actions but not me. To *lament* is to mourn deeply, and often loudly: "The mourners beat their chests and cried, lamenting almost hysterically." To *repent* is to be contrite about one's misdeeds: "Repent, ye sinners!" One who repents hopes to do better in the future.

depraved   See ABANDONED/DEPRAVED/VICIOUS.

deprecate/depreciate   To *deprecate* someone or something is to disapprove, belittle, disparage, make fun of: "She deprecated the usefulness of her own efforts." To *depreciate* is to reduce in value or to make a deduction for wear, age, or the like: "The IRS allowed us to depreciate the property over a five-year period." Confusingly, however, SWE sometimes uses *depreciate* in the sense of "belittle, disparage." Most often, though, SWE keeps the two words separate. See also SELF-DEPRECATION/SELF-DEPRECIATION.

desalinate/desalt   When a long and a short word have the same meaning, SANE and SWE ordinarily choose the short one.

descend down   See ASCEND UP.

descendant   See ANCESTOR/DESCENDANT.

description   SWE tries to avoid vague or ambiguous phrases such as "horses of this description." Is the meaning "such strong horses" or "horses that look like this" or "wild horses," or what?

desegregation/integration   Although the readily apparent results of either process may be the same, the words have different emphases and perhaps different psychological effects. *Desegregation* stresses getting rid of something – a rather negative idea. *Integration* emphasizes developing something – a positive idea. SWE users are aware that neither of these words applies to racial matters only. For example, large companies may integrate (combine) or segregate (separate) parts of their operations, such as sales and consumer relations.

desert(s)/dessert (nouns)   A barren, dry area is a *desert* (pronounced *dez*-urt). What a person *deserves* are his *deserts* (pronounced de-*zurtz*). In "He got his just deserts," *just* is redundant. *Dessert* (pronounced de-*zurt*), with an extra *s*, refers to the last course of a meal – the "extra" course that puts on unwanted weight.

designed/intended   Although the two words are often interchangeable, *designed* is preferred in SWE when some actual designing (drawing, inventing, creating) is involved. Dubious: "The hay was de-

68

signed to feed hungry caribou" (the hay was *intended* for the caribou, but nobody designed it).

desire Sometimes pretentious. "I have a desire for a Seven-Up" means only "I want . . ." or "I'd like . . ."

desperate/hopeless A *hopeless* person has no hope left. A *desperate* person has little hope but feels that there is a slight chance if reckless (desperate) measures are taken. A desperate criminal, for example, may try to drive through a police barricade, but may be less likely to do so if there is no hope of escape.

despite the fact that Wordy. SWE usually shortens it to *although* or *even though*.

dessert See *desert(s)/dessert*.

destroy The old order saith that *destroy* means "ruin completely, eliminate," and that therefore "destroy completely" or "partly destroy" is wrong. But the old order changeth. The distinguished conservative panelists of *Harper's* split their votes almost evenly, with Leo Rosten arguing that *completely* adds emphasis, and with several panelists saying that partial destruction is possible – say, two rooms in a five-room house. SWE also is somewhat split, but generally avoids "destroy completely" and is ambivalent about "partly destroyed the house" vs. "destroyed part of the house." See also AN-NIHILATE, DESTROY, FLAY. . . .

develop/invent To *invent* something is to create it. To *develop* something is to elaborate or improve upon what already existed. Bell invented the telephone, but many later workers have developed the phones that we have today. See also DISCOVER/INVENT.

device/devise *Device* is a noun: "This device
Catches mice.
Ain't that nice?"
Devise is a verb: "We'll devise a plan
To catch a man."

devilry/deviltry To use as a synonym of *mischief*, most British prefer *devilry*, most Americans *deviltry*. *Devilry* sounds more wicked.

devil's advocate In the Roman Catholic Church a *devil's advocate* is a qualified person designated to show why someone should not be canonized or beatified. In other contexts, a devil's advocate presents arguments against a proposal, not necessarily because of dislike but simply to make available the evidence on all sides. More loosely, the term means someone who is hostile to what is generally considered a good cause; SWE seldom follows this definition.

devise See DEVICE/DEVISE.

diagnose SWE says, "The illness was mistakenly diagnosed as malaria," but not "She was mistakenly diagnosed to have malaria." A condition may be diagnosed, but not the person who has it.

dialectal/dialectical *Dialectal* means "pertaining to dialect": "Professor Reeder is studying dialectal differences between North and South Carolinians" (*Dialectical* is occasionally used for this meaning but can cause misunderstanding.) *Dialectical* means "pertaining to dialectics ('methods of argument')": "Philosophers often have dialectical differences."

diaphanous/translucent/transparent   Thin, see-through clothing such as artists assume that houris wear is *diaphanous*. Anything that lets light through but denies a clear view of the houri is *translucent*. Clear glass, being *transparent*, does not interfere with the view. See also OPAQUE/TRANSLUCENT.

dice/dies   In games, the usage is one *die*, two or more *dice*; with reference to machinery, one *die*, two or more *dies*.

diction   Two meanings are usual for *diction*: "choice of words" and "degree of clarity in enunciation." These two meanings, however, may result in ambiguity. Does "Her diction is excellent" mean that she chooses words well or speaks (or sings) clearly? To avoid such ambiguity, some writers choose not to use *diction* at all unless something else in the sentence clarifies the meaning: "Her diction suggested a large vocabulary." "His diction – every word distinct – impressed the audience more than his ideas did." Other writers prefer to limit *diction* to "choice of words," and substitute *articulation*, *enunciation*, or *distinctness* for the other meaning.

die (*from* vs. *of*)   FF "She died *from* cancer." SWE says, "She died *of* (or *as a result of*) cancer."

die (noun)   See DICE/DIES.

differ from/differ with   The more common expression is *differ from*, meaning "to be unlike": "Peas differ from beans." "A child sometimes differs from both parents." "I differ from you in that I prefer chocolate to vanilla." In the sense of "disagree," however, *differ with* is SWE: "Mrs. Raleigh differed with her husband about the principles of child-rearing."

different   Often redundant, as in "They sampled fifteen (different) varieties of cereal."

different from/different than   *Different from* is the usual SWE, although *different than* sometimes appears and is prevalent in FF. When a clause follows, *different than* is SWE: "The quality of asparagus is different than it was last week." Using *from* would here require adding *what*. A beautiful example of differentiation is in this sentence by Adam Clymer in the *New York Times Magazine*: "Americans think of Russians as quite different from themselves, much more different than the British, Germans, or Japanese [are]." British people often use *different to*.

differential   In expressions such as "the differential between *A* and *B*" or "the differential is small," *difference* has the same meaning and is unpretentious. *Differential* is needed in some technical contexts.

diffuse   See DEFUSE/DIFFUSE.

dilemma   Historically, a *dilemma* is a situation in which two choices appear equally satisfactory (or unsatisfactory). More recently, it has been used to mean any troublesome situation: "One of today's greatest dilemmas is drug use." Since many other words exist for *problem* or *trouble*, it would be good (SANE believes) to hold *dilemma* to its historical meaning. The battle, however, seems unlikely to be won; SWE is moving toward the loose definition.

dimensions/proportions SWE often uses the words interchangeably, although many careful writers choose *dimensions* for measurements and *proportions* for comparisons or relationships. If the dimensions of a box are 4″ × 6″ × 4″, the proportions are 1 to 1.5 to 1. Less careful writers may say, "The dimensions of the disaster are unknown," when *extent* or *gravity* is probably better. Or they refer to "the proportions of the Grand Canyon," even though the canyon is measurable; *vast size* or a similar expression may be more accurate. See also DISASTER PROPORTIONS.

diplomacy/tact Sometimes used interchangeably, although *diplomacy* has a connotation of higher importance. Nations, for instance, engage in diplomacy, but individuals have more need of tact. *Diplomacy* also suggests adroit management, but *tact* is more often reflected in choice of words or small deeds. Diplomacy may have great things at stake, even the fate of a corporation or a nation, but the goal of tact may sometimes be only to avoid hurting someone's feelings. And, even though tact is not the same as diplomacy, diplomats must use a great deal of it.

direct/directly The adjective *direct*, like other adjectives, tells something about a noun: "a direct shipment," "a direct answer." The adverb *directly* is used in SWE especially in these senses: exactly – "Aim directly at the bullseye"; immediately, quickly, by the shortest route – "Go directly home"; positively, straight – "Evidence points directly at the butler as the murderer." In a sentence such as "We deliver _____ to your home," *directly* is usual in SWE, but *direct* is not questioned in advertising or other commercial contexts.

disapprove/reject Although SWE may use the words interchangeably, *reject* is stronger. For example, a parent may disapprove of a child's choice of friends but may be wise enough not to reject them.

disassemble/dissemble To *disassemble* is to take apart: "We disassembled the big clock." To *dissemble* is to conceal one's actions, intentions, or feelings: "Not wanting her husband to know where she had been, she dissembled by murmuring something about shopping."

disassociate/dissociate The simpler *dissociate* has almost pushed out *disassociate*.

disaster proportions Journalists sometimes write, "Damage has reached disaster proportions," or the like. The use of a noun as an adjective is often awkward, as it certainly is here. Usual SWE: "a disastrous amount."

disbar See DEBAR/DISBAR.

discerning/discriminating According to SWE, when you look at something with a *discerning* eye, you attempt to see the details. Art appreciation classes, for example, help viewers to discern things normally overlooked in a Rubens or a Monet. If you are *discriminating*, you again look at details but you also evaluate and compare, and especially you reject some things. An art expert may be discriminating enough to distinguish between a Monet and a Monet imitation.

disclose/divulge/reveal SWE uses each only with reference to something that has been hidden, not as a synonym of *say* or *tell*: "The secretary of state revealed (or *divulged*, *disclosed*) today that a secret meeting was held last month with . . ." Dubious: "The secretary of state revealed today that he will hold a press conference next Tuesday." Here *announced* or *said* is preferable unless the official had previously kept secret the upcoming conference.

disclosure/revelation In SWE *disclosure* is a neutral word, meaning "making known what was unknown." *Revelation* is more striking, perhaps even sensational. For example, an officeholder may make a disclosure of his income, but a revelation may occur if someone finds that some of that income derived from illegal activities.

discomfit/discomfort When SWE uses the verb *discomfort*, the idea of loss of comfort is present: "The move into a single room discomforted her." *Discomfit*, however, suggests becoming discontented or dejected: "Word of his cousin's injury discomfited Eric for several days."

discomposed See DECOMPOSED/DISCOMPOSED.

discontinue/disemploy/release Business and government use several such verbs for "discharge, fire." The intent is kindly, and the euphemism may be less damaging to the worker when he or she tries to get another job. In general, though, SWE prefers a more direct word. See also EUPHEMISM/EUPHUISM.

discourage/frustrate In SWE *discouragement* often suggests longer duration than *frustration*, which is usually a temporary or even momentary condition. For example, I may be frustrated but not discouraged by a balky can opener.

discover/invent People have *discovered* gold but *invented* radios. We discover what already exists but invent what was previously unknown. See also DEVELOP/INVENT.

discreet/discrete *Discreet* means "prudent, cautious, tactful": "A discreet editor insists that reporters check names and addresses carefully." *Discrete*, a comparatively rare word, means "separate, distinct": "There are many discrete species of bees."

discriminating see DISCERNING/DISCRIMINATING.

discrimination The emphasis on *discrimination* in references to unjust treatment of minorities has hidden the fact that discriminating people realize that discrimination of other sorts is desirable, for example, discrimination between politicians' words or smiles and politicians' substance and actions.

disdain See CONTEMPT/DISDAIN.

disemploy See DISCONTINUE/DISEMPLOY/RELEASE.

disinterested/uninterested The usual dictionary definition of *disinterested* is "impartial," and conservative editors still follow that. An umpire should be disinterested – fair to both sides – even though he or she has great interest in the game. But *disinterested* is used so widely to refer to loss of interest ("I soon became disinterested") that the battle to preserve the conventional definition seems all but lost. A sentence such as "The umpire was disinterested" is now often understood to mean that the umpire lost interest or had no interest. SWE frequently substitutes *impartial* for *disinterested* and uses *uninterested* in the usual meaning, "not interested." Some editors accept the "loss of interest" meaning for *disinterested*, but others (stubbornly or loyally) reject it.

dismiss against "Both charges against Gray were dismissed" is obviously more logical than "Both charges were dismissed against Gray." SWE realizes that the charges (not the dismissal) were against Gray.

disorganized/unorganized Ordinarily, in SWE, something *disorganized* was formerly organized but no longer is. *Unorganized* means "not organized, not systematically arranged."

disqualified/unqualified A person who has been disqualified was once qualified or was thought to be so. A person who is *unqualified* lacks the education, strength, skill, or other qualifications required for a position.

disremember/misremember *Misremember* is SWE as the equivalent of *remember incorrectly*: "I misremembered the number and touched a 7 instead of a 6." However, it is FF (dialectal) for "forget" or "fail to remember." *Disremember* is FF.

dissect See BISECT/DISSECT.

dissemble See DISASSEMBLE/DISSEMBLE.

dissimulate/simulate You *dissimulate* if you hide your thoughts, feelings, or motives: "She was angry, but had enough self-control to dissimulate." You *simulate* when you pretend: "My father often simulated dislike for my jokes, but he could not repress the laugh lines near his eyes."

dissociate See DISASSOCIATE/DISSOCIATE.

distinct/distinctive Something *distinctive* has an individual touch that differentiates it from most other things in the same category, but it is not necessarily unique: "This pitcher is distinctive because an unusual design has been etched in the Finnish glass." Something *distinct* either may be dissimilar to anything else or may be clear and unquestionable: "Platinum is distinct from silver." "His enunciation is always precise and distinct." The adverbs *distinctively* and *distinctly* are differentiated similarly.

distinctive/distinguished That which is *distinctive* is out of the ordinary (see DISTINCT/DISTINCTIVE). *Distinguished*, used chiefly of people, refers to accomplishments, eminence, or dignified appearance: "Senator Laramie's record is distinguished: he has sponsored much ecologically significant legislation."

dive (noun) FF (slang) for a disreputable place, often one where liquor, narcotics, or prostitutes are available and where robbery and other misdeeds are likely. Increasingly, however, the term appears in SWE: "in a dive in Bangkok."

dived/dove Both are standard, but *dived* is more likely in SWE. It is the older form, *dove* having developed by analogy with *drive, drove*. As a past participle, *dived* is usual, *dove* only occasional: "She had dived from an eight-meter board."

divide off (out, up) *Divide* is usually enough.

divorce (verb with) 1. SWE often draws several distinctions. If Helen was the plaintiff: "Helen obtained (or *got*) a divorce." "Helen divorced Tom." If Helen was the defendant: "Helen was divorced." "Tom divorced Helen." If the divorce was "no fault": "Helen and Tom (or *Tom and Helen*, or *The couple*) were divorced." To indicate present status, regardless of who brought the suit: "Helen is divorced." "Helen is a divorcée." 2. Purists say that *divorce* is only a transitive verb, as in "She divorced him," "He divorced her," "They were divorced." But in recent years sentences such as "They divorced in 1988" have become as common as divorce itself, and modern writing treats the verb as both transitive and intransitive.

divorcée A *divorcée* is "a divorced woman." Some dictionaries and most newspapers print the word without the accent mark. There's also *divorcé*, "a divorced man," but that word is infrequently used because of confusion with *divorce*.

divulge See DISCLOSE/DIVULGE/REVEAL.

do time This term is now SWE for "serve a prison sentence": "He has done time. He did ten years." Note that *do* is standard in many expressions for everyday tasks, such as doing chores, housework, homework, dishes, hair, exercise, problems.

dock/pier/wharf Technically, a *dock* is the space filled with water in which a ship remains when in port. A passenger boat or ship is tied to a *pier*, a freighter usually to a *wharf*. The three terms have been confused so frequently, however, that most dictionaries treat them as virtually interchangeable. Even seamen now refer to *dockworkers*, although such workers labor on a wharf (or *wharfside*) rather than out in the water. Some SWE writers follow the technical distinctions, but probably few people notice when they do not comply. See also HARBOR/PORT.

dog who (or *that*) A longtime controversy: should an animal be referred to as *that* or *who*? For people who have a beloved pet, the answer is clear: their pet deserves *who*-dom as much as a person does, so "our dog, who died last year," but "the cows that are grazing in the pasture" – unless the cows are personal friends.

dogma/tenet Each means "a principle, belief, or opinion." A *dogma* is more likely to emanate from an organized group and so to be regarded as authoritative: "Christian dogma." It may also mean "a system of principles or tenets." *Dogma* is the basis of the adjective *dogmatic*, which suggests unproved and perhaps arrogant assertions. A *tenet* is a firm belief held by either an individual or a group: "One of my political tenets is that . . ." Several or many tenets may be components of a dogma.

dollars SWE avoids the combination of $ and the word *dollars*, choosing one or the other; not any of these: "$45,000 dollars," "$45 thousand dollars," "the dollar-value is $45,000."

domicile Used in law, but in other contexts seems superelegant. Usually *house, apartment*, or *home* – or even *place* – is better. (Does anyone ask, "Your domicile or mine?")

dominating/domineering Both refer to controlling, to exertion of power by a superior. Neither is regarded as kind or gentle, but *domineering* is the more unpleasant term. A domineering person is haughty, arrogant, overbearing, even tyrannical and cruel.

donate SWE uses *donate* especially for charitable giving, not for gifts to friends and relatives: "She donated fifty dollars to the Christmas Basket Fund."

done, done with *Done* in the sense of "finished" is slightly informal but does appear in formal contexts as well: "The work of the committee is now done." SWE is careful, though, to avoid ambiguous sentences such as "The work of the committee will be done next Thursday," in which *done* may mean either "finished" or "performed." *Done with*, meaning "finished with," also hovers between formal and informal, leaning toward the latter: "She declared that she was done with him forever."

donnybrook A part of old Dublin called Donnybrook was the locale of fairs where savage fights often occurred. The word is now SWE for any fierce, no-holds-barred brawl involving several or many combatants. Loosely, it is also applied to angry, loud oral arguments with numerous participants on each side. The word is occasionally still capitalized.

don't **1.** Like other contractions, *don't* is generally informal. However, it often appears in moderately formal SWE, sometimes to lighten the tone slightly, sometimes in imperatives such as "Don't underestimate the influence of letters to Congress." **2.** *Don't* with a third-person singular subject is FF except in reporting conversations: "He (*She, It*) don't." SWE: "He (*She, It*) doesn't." **3.** *Don't let's* is FF for *let's not.* **4.** The plural of the noun *don't* ("a negative rule") is written *don'ts*. See also **CONTRACTIONS**.

dope FF for "narcotics, habit-forming drugs." See also DRUGS.

double entendre   This French borrowing is SWE. It refers to a phrase or sentence that has two possible meanings, one of which is likely to be sexy or improperly suggestive. An old example is Mae West's "Come up and see me sometime."

DOUBLE NEGATIVE   See NOT (AND OTHER NEGATIVES); NOT UN-.

doubtless(ly)   SWE prefers *doubtless*. Oddly, both words often imply that some doubt does exist, as *no doubt* also does: "No doubt (or *Doubtless*) Harry will be late again" is similar to "Probably . . ."

dove (verb)   See DIVED/DOVE.

downplay   Although some dictionary editors seem not to have noticed it, the verb *downplay*, meaning "pay little attention to," or "de-emphasize" is rather widely used in both formal and informal contexts. It is no better, however, than the more conventional *play down*.

drag   The past tense and past participle are both *dragged* (not *drug*) in SWE: "The terrier (has) dragged in a dead opossum."

drama/dramatic   Strong words associated with literature and with high emotion. SWE avoids trivializing them. It chooses other words in, for example, accounts of most Little League baseball games.

drastic   *Drastic* means "extreme, severe, violent." SWE avoids use in matters of relatively small importance: "Just because I misspelled a few words, the teacher lowered my grade from *B* to *C*. That was a drastic thing to do." SWE might rewrite: "That reduction seemed excessive" or "I thought that I still deserved a *B−*."

draw a conclusion   Often can be shortened to *conclude*.

dreadful/horrible   These words are too often used to describe trivial things or events, such as a large but harmless barn spider, misty weather for a picnic, or a sweater of an unstylish color. Something truly *dreadful* should fill us with dread; something *horrible*, with horror. See also AWFUL; COLOSSAL, COLOSSALLY; TERRIBLE, TERRIBLY.

dribble/drivel   When a baby drools or slobbers, it may be said to *dribble* or *drivel*. The saliva is also called *dribble* or *drivel*. (*Drivel* is more likely as both verb and noun, *drool* still more likely.) A person talking stupidly *drivels*, and what he or she says is *drivel*.

drivel   See DRIBBLE/DRIVEL.

dropout   Now SWE for one who leaves school, employment, and so on, earlier than usual or perhaps earlier than desirable: "Even in kindergarten he wanted to be a dropout." "Our dropout rate is lower than most." To use it as a verb, SWE breaks the word in two: "to drop out of the race."

drought/drouth   These alternative spellings are both SWE, but *drought* seems less desirable because in other words (*bought, ought, sought, thought*) *ought* is not pronounced like *out*. SANE pleads, "Don't further complicate English spelling." But SANE may be losing this one.

drowned/was drowned   In a long debate, some persons argued for "Henry was drowned," saying that Henry himself did not perform the act. Opponents said *was drowned* meant that someone drowned him. Today, *drowned* and *was drowned* are interchangeable, with *drowned* more common because it is shorter. Note that *drowned* has only two *d*'s. The pronunciation and spelling *drownded* are nonstandard.

drugs   This is now a standard shortening of "illicit drugs," even though most of the drugs sold in a drugstore are not illicit. If any misunderstanding is likely, SWE substitutes a more specific term, such as *heroin* or *narcotics*. *Drug addict* and *drug peddler* are also SWE, and *drug pusher* often appears in SWE.

drunk   **1.** *Drunk* is FF (informal) in such expressions as "became a drunk," "the town drunk." *Drunkard* is slightly more likely in SWE. **2.** Conservatives prefer "drunken driver" to "drunk driver," but to a victim of such a driver the distinction is unimportant. "Drunk driver *(driving)*" is common in newspaper writing, and there is an organization called Mothers Against Drunk Driving (MADD). **3.** *Drunken* is now used only before a noun: "a drunken woman." *Has drunken* is an outworn form.

due to   An unquestioned usage is "Her hospitalization was due to a fall" (*due* used as an adjective). Conservatives dislike *due to* as equivalent to *because of:* "Due to a fall, she was hospitalized." "She was hospitalized due to a fall." RHD, however, informs readers that *due to* for *because of* has been in use since the fourteenth century and says it is now "standard in all varieties of speech and writing." Most writers of SWE agree.

due to (owing to) the fact that   SWE usually shortens the expression to *because* or *since*. Instead of "The reason is due to the fact that . . . ," SWE prefers "The reason is that . . ."

duel   Dubious: "Four National League East teams are dueling for the championship." A duel involves only two teams, groups, or contestants.

duff   This is FF (slang or highly informal) for "rump, buttocks, seat," but good writers and speakers sometimes use the word publicly. Carl Sagan, in a CBS interview, said, "The world will get better only if we get off our duffs and make it so."

dumb/ignorant/stupid   An *ignorant* person may have only a small supply of general knowledge or have no knowledge in a particular field: "ignorant of the world outside his section of Chicago," "ignorant in music." A *stupid* person is dull, unintelligent, perhaps foolish: "too stupid to learn simple arithmetic." An ignorant person can usually be taught. A stupid person perhaps can be taught only a little. *Dumb* is an FF synonym of *ignorant* or *stupid* or both. In SWE it is ordinarily used to mean "unable to speak": "She is a deaf and dumb child."

duplicity   See CHICANERY/DUPLICITY.

during the course of, during the time that   *While* is usually enough.

dwarf, midget, pygmy   A *dwarf* is a small person, usually one whose growth has been arrested by a pathological condition. Snow White's companions are the best-known dwarfs (or *dwarves*). A dwarf's physical proportions are distorted in some way. A grown *midget*, however, is well proportioned, a miniature man or woman. Tom Thumb was a midget famous in British folklore before someone given that name became a favorite P. T. Barnum attraction. Capitalized, Pygmy (or *Pigmy*) refers to a member of an African or Asian tribe whose heights range from four to five feet. Uncapitalized, *pygmy* (*pigmy*) may mean any unusually small person, and as an adjective may refer to some animals.

dwell/live/reside   An ordinary family *lives* at 1136 Elm Street. A wealthy or pretentious family *resides* at 1101 Elmwood Circle. *Dwell* is old-fashioned, surviving mainly in poetry of yesteryear. Wordsworth's Lucy "dwelt among the untrodden ways."

E

each (verb and pronoun with)   FF: "Each of the girls were trained to do their work well." SWE: "Each of the girls was trained to do her work well." The reason for SWE's preference is that *each* refers to one person or thing, as do the verb *was* (*is*, *walks*, and so on) and the pronoun *her* (*his*, *its*, and so on). The presence of the plural *girls* in the example confuses some writers, but *each* is the governing word.

each and every one   *Each* or *every one* should be enough.

each/either   Here is a dubious usage, from a catalog description: "The handbag has two outside pockets on either side." *Either* suggests "one or the other," but the catalog picture shows two pockets on *each* side. "Two pockets on both sides" would be ambiguous, probably meaning "two plus two" but possibly "one plus one."

each/every   The essential meanings of "Each boy brought his rifle" and "Every boy brought his rifle" are the same, but the emphasis with *each* is on individual action, while *every* stresses that the group was unanimous.

each other/one another   Interchangeable in most usage, although many SWE writers prefer *each other* for two persons, *one another* for more than two: "The boxers battered each other unmercifully." "All the members of the winning team were congratulating one another." SWE possessive forms are illustrated in "The two women admired each other's dresses" and "The three women admired one another's dresses." Note the placement of the apostrophes.

each   See BOTH/EACH.

early beginnings   SWE deletes *early*, or for *beginnings* substitutes *days*, *years*, or the like.

early on   A relatively recent American borrowing from England, now SWE although not in general superior to *early*. It may be a little smoother and clearer as a sentence opener: "Early on, man had no tools at all."

easily/easy   SWE uses *easily* to modify a verb: "He could easily lift two hundred pounds." "She can do most of her work easily, but lifting is difficult." In a few idiomatic expressions *easy* has become SWE where *easily* might be expected: "Take it easy." "Please go easy on me."

Easter Sunday   This term has become SWE even though *Sunday* is unnecessary (Easter is always on a Sunday – the first one after the full moon on or next after March 21). One defense of *Easter Sunday* is that *Easter* is now often taken to include the period before and after the Sunday, as in "Easter vacation."

easterly/eastern   *Easterly* is used especially in "easterly winds" and "in an easterly direction." *Eastern* appears in most other contexts. Similar distinctions apply to the other points of the compass. An east wind comes from almost straight east, but an easterly wind is shifty, although it tends toward one direction. Each of the *-ly* words may also be a noun referring to a wind or a storm: "A northerly hit us hard."

easy money   SWE for money obtained by deception or with little effort – usually the latter.

easygoing   This word is SWE.

eaves   SWE chooses a plural verb: "the eaves are . . ." The form *eave* is rare, although SANE considers it logical when only one is meant. (*Eavesdrop* originally referred to standing under the eaves to hear what was being said inside a building.)

eccentric/erratic   An *eccentric* wheel rotates on an axle that is some- what off center; in consequence the movement, while predictable, is not what is customary for wheels. Similarly, an eccentric person is "off center," not like us well-balanced folks. If there were such a thing as an *erratic* wheel, it would have many notches into which its axle could slip at random. Its rotation would be bumpy, unpredict- able. An erratic person is also unpredictable, causing us to ask, "What on earth will he say or do next?" See also EROTIC/ERRATIC.

ecology/environment   *Environment* means "surroundings," "every- thing within one's surroundings": "The Arctic environment is un- suitable for most plants and animals." *Ecology* is the relationship between organisms and their environment, or the study of such relationships: "The ecology of an area is greatly affected when land is cleared and parts of it are cultivated." See also AMBIANCE/ENVI- RONMENT.

economic/economical   *Economic* is a broad term referring to material wealth, finance, economics, the economy: "economic conditions," "the family's economic well-being." *Economical* means "not waste- ful": "Economical buying is essential for most families." Although *economic* for *economical* does appear, SWE almost always differentiates to avoid possible confusion. See also ECONOMICAL/FRUGAL/THRIFTY. . . .

economical/frugal/thrifty/miserly/stingy In SWE the first three are words of praise for not spending carelessly or foolishly. *Miserly* and *stingy*, however, refer to excessive saving, extreme unwillingness to spend. *Miserly* has the added connotation of hoarding: "Silas Marner was miserly; he buried his gold coins." See also ECONOMIC/ECONOMICAL.

edgeways, edgewise/endways, endwise/lengthways, lengthwise/sideways, sidewise The words in each pair are interchangeable, although SWE usually prefers the form with -*wise*. See also -WISE.

edifice See BUILDING/EDIFICE.

edition/impression, printing A new *edition* of a book involves extensive revision. A new *impression* or *printing*, however, is only a reprint made without alteration (although very minor corrections are sometimes made).

educational/instructive *Educational* is overused and pretentious in the sense of "instructive." Exploration of a cave, for example, or playing with toys, might better be called *instructive*. *Educational* may refer to methods of teaching, a type of philosophy, or a system rather than to something relatively small in extent and effect.

educationese, pedagese These interchangeable disparaging names are applied to the language used by some educators, especially in their speeches and articles. Typically, it includes many passive verbs and vague, abstract, or cumbersome nouns, and is verbose.

educationist SWE seldom uses this word, preferring *educator*. When it does appear, it is as a disparaging term for an educator, or to describe educational policies disliked by the writer.

educator Most likely to be used in SWE for a school administrator or a professor of education. Miss Hanson in the third grade probably insists proudly that she is a *teacher*.

-ee This suffix normally refers to the one done to rather than to the doer, for example, *donee* vs. *donor*, *trainee* vs. *trainer*. Few people like -*ee* words. All the world loves a *lover*, but the word *lovee* may not have been used since 1894. *Hatee* seems never to have been used at all, thank goodness.

e'er/ne'er Contractions for *ever* and *never*, used mainly in poetry of a bygone time.

effect See AFFECT/EFFECT.

effective This word is used as business or military jargon in sentences such as "Effective May 12, these prices will be ten percent higher." In ordinary English, *on* or *beginning* is more likely.

effective/efficient *Effective* describes something that can produce a desired result: "Rat-Rid is effective in killing rats." *Efficient* is similar but suggests that the product can be used with comparatively little effort and perhaps at low cost: "Kill rats with efficient Rat-Rid: no traps, no mess, no odor, no danger to pets."

effeminate/female/feminine/womanly *Effeminate* in SWE is used to describe men whose appearance, actions, or other qualities seem more characteristic of a woman: "an effeminate way of walking." *Female* means only the opposite of *male* and is not at all judgmental: "Female breasts are larger than male." *Feminine*, the opposite of *masculine*, refers in a usually commendatory way to the delicate qualities, mannerisms, and so on of a woman: "He marveled at her softness and her feminine grace." *Womanly* suggests greater maturity than does *feminine* (although feminine qualities are also womanly): "womanly in her understanding."

effete Something strange has happened to *effete* in the twentieth century. It has moved from "exhausted, barren" to "self-indulgent, decadent," and is now most likely to refer to rich people such as those characterized by Spiro Agnew as "effete Eastern snobs." At one time, an unfruitful tree could be effete; hens, people were told in 1774, "after three years become effete and barren." SWE, of course, is unlikely to write about trees or hens as effete. Its effete people are likely to be degenerate or at best lacking in vigor.

efficient See EFFECTIVE/EFFICIENT.

e.g./i.e. *E.g.* means "for example" (from Latin *exempli gratia*). *I.e.* means "that is" (Latin *id est*). Both abbreviations are appropriate in technical writing or reference books but seldom appear in literary works. Punctuation before and after *e.g.* is the same as for *for example*; with *i.e.*, the same as for *that is*.

egoist/egotist Interchangeable, although a shade of difference is worth noting. An *egotist* is more likely to brag about himself; in his opinion he's the greatest. An *egoist* may think just as highly of herself and work selfishly toward her own goals, but she usually doesn't trumpet her abilities or accomplishments. (The term *egoism* is used in philosophy and ethics for the belief that morality is based on self-interest.)

egregious Originally meant "outside the flock, extraordinary," but now it means "unusual in an extremely bad way." Thus egregious lies are likely to be worse than ordinary lies.

either See EACH/EITHER.

either/neither (with more than two) Ordinarily, *either* or *neither* refers to one of two: "Either (*Neither*) of the two coats is satisfactory." For more than two, SWE usually chooses *any one* or *no one* (*none*). In sentences such as "I must buy either oranges, apples, or bananas," however, *either* is SWE even though three or more alternatives are given.

either . . . or/neither . . . nor (verb with) With two singular subjects, SWE uses a singular verb: "Either (or *neither*) Roy (n)or Sue is . . ." With two plurals, it uses a plural verb: "Either (*Neither*) the Poles (n)or the Czechs are . . ." With a singular and a plural, it uses a verb that agrees with the one that comes later: "Either (*Neither*) the boys (n)or Sue *is* . . ." "Either (*Neither*) Sue (n)or the boys are . . ."

elder, eldest/older, oldest   *Older* and *oldest* may refer in SWE to either persons or things, *elder* and *eldest* to persons only. SWE now seldom uses *elder* and *eldest* except in referring to members of the same family or business firm: "the elder Mr. Craig," "the eldest member of the family," "The elder Mr. Lamson is a vice-president, the younger an office manager." Even in these examples, *older* or *oldest* may be used. *Elder* and *eldest* appear to be dying. *Elder statesman*, however, survives.

elderly   No one knows for sure when elderliness begins, but suddenly it's there. *Middle-aged* quietly grays or balds into *elderly*. *Elderly* is a little kinder than *old* and considerably younger than *aged*.

electric/electronic   *Electric* means "pertaining to, producing, derived from, or operated by electricity": "electric lights, vacuum cleaners," and so on. *Electronic* refers to devices or systems in which electrons flow in a vacuum, in a gaseous medium, or in semiconductors: "A computer is an electronic device."

ELEGANT VARIATION   An ironic term coined by Fowler for a needless shift from a noun to its synonym; for example, from *woman* to *lady*, or from *Achilles* to *the son of Peleus* (yes, Homer did it often). Sportswriters may be the greatest American offenders, saying in one line, "Carter hit a home run," in the next that "Schmidt countered with a four-bagger" before "Elster decided the issue when he skied one to left." Perhaps only a close follower of baseball realizes that each of the three hit a home run. In general, SWE avoids such elegant variation.

elegy/encomium/eulogy   An *elegy* is "a poem, especially a lament for the dead." An *encomium* is "a tribute or high praise to someone, usually living." A *eulogy* is "a speech or written prose praising someone, not necessarily a dead person."

elemental/elementary   *Elemental* may refer to forces of nature: "an elemental force, such as gravity," or it may mean "simple but powerful": "the elemental fury of a hurricane," or "essential": "an elemental part of the process." *Elementary* means "introductory, basic, pertaining to basics." An elementary school provides an introduction to formal education, and when Sherlock Holmes said, "Elementary, my dear Watson!" he meant, "basic, simple." An elementary step, sometimes miscalled *elemental*, is a beginning step.

elevated   Often too big a word for "high" or "tall." SWE prefers "high temperatures" and "high (or *tall*) hills." For moving up to a more responsible and better-paying position, "Hawkins was promoted to the vice-president's office" is more appropriate than *was elevated* (which suggests that the Otis Company was involved).

elicit/illicit   *Elicit*, a verb, has the figurative meaning of "draw out" and usually refers to information of some sort: "Officers elicited the admission that Conrad had been drinking." *Illicit*, an adjective, means "illegal" or sometimes "not approved by public opinion": "an illicit love affair."

eliminate/prevent These words are not interchangeable in SWE. Rust can be *prevented*, but it can't be *eliminated* unless it's already there. For example, this is not SWE: "Eliminate formation of rust by using No-Rust." See also AVERT/AVOID/PREVENT.

ellipse/ellipsis An *ellipse* is an oval with both ends alike. Many racetracks are ellipses. In grammar, an *ellipsis* is the omission from a sentence of one or more words that can readily be "understood" by the reader or hearer. In "Call your mother" the elliptical word is *You*. In "I voted, but you did not," it is *vote*. The plural of each word is *ellipses*, but the plural of *ellipsis* is pronounced e-*lip*-seez rather than e-*lip*-suz. Three dots (. . .) to indicate an omission are called "marks of ellipsis." (Four are often used if the omission is at the end of a sentence, but the first is a period.)

elope SWE is aware that a young woman should be careful if a man asks her to elope. An elopement does not necessarily include marriage. When a couple run away together, they are eloping, but marriage may not always follow.

eloquent/grandiloquent/magniloquent An *eloquent* speaker speaks fluently, persuasively, movingly. A *grandiloquent* or *magniloquent* speaker uses too many flowery or polysyllabic words, seems pompous, and is not likely to be convincing even though he or she puts on a good show.

else's SWE uses *somebody else's, nobody else's,* and so on. *Who else's* is also SWE: "Who else's answer is correct?" If no noun follows, either *who else's* or *whose else* is used: "Who else's is correct?" "Whose else is correct?" To obviate a choice, SANE recommends *who else's* in both instances.

emblazon See BLAZE/BLAZON.

emend See AMEND/EMEND.

emigrant/immigrant If your ancestors came to the United States from Ireland, for example, they *emigrated* and were *emigrants* from that country (*e-* means "out"). From the standpoint of the United States, they *immigrated* and were *immigrants* (*Im-*, a variant of *in-*, means "in" or "into").

eminent/imminent *Eminent* means "well-known, prominent, famous." It is more likely to be applied to statesmen or members of a profession than to actors, athletes, or tradespeople. *Imminent* means "coming soon," especially in time: "A flood seemed imminent." "Triumph was imminent."

emolument Highfalutin for "wages, pay."

emote Some dictionaries say that this word for "speak emotionally or theatrically, overact" is only to be used informally, but most do not attach a label. SWE uses it but realizes that it connotes effusiveness or excessive dramatics.

empathy/sympathy The usual meaning of *sympathy* is "sharing the feelings of another – most often feelings of sadness or loss." *Empathy* is a stronger word, suggesting identification with another person or possibly an animal: "His empathy with the deer was so great that he could feel the sharp, cruel arrow in his own side." A less common meaning of *empathy* is pretending that inanimate beings share human feelings and qualities. Statements showing such empathy (also called "pathetic fallacy") include "The clouds began weeping gently" and "This crazy cliff is trying to kill us."

enact into law   SWE deletes *into law* because *enact* means "make into law."

encomium   See ELEGY/ENCOMIUM/EULOGY; PANEGYRIC.

end (come to an)   This expression is wordy: "At last the struggle came to an end." Usually better is ". . . ended." *Put an end to* is similarly wordy.

end result/end product   SWE deletes *end* unless some noteworthy preliminary or intermediate results have been named or at least have existed.

endemic/epidemic/pandemic   An *endemic* disease almost constantly exists in an area or in one part of the population: "Swamp fever was endemic in the marshlands, especially among the white settlers." An *epidemic* strikes many people about the same time but is not customarily prevalent: "the 1918 flu epidemic." *Pandemic* diseases affect everyone or almost everyone in an area: "Tuberculosis became pandemic in the tribe." *Endemic* in the sense given here is almost always an adjective, seldom a noun, but *epidemic* and *pandemic* may be either adjectives or nouns.

ending   See FINAL COMPLETION.

enemy   See ADVERSARY/ANTAGONIST/ENEMY.

enervate   Sometimes mistakenly thought to refer to nerves, and occasionally confused with its near-opposite, *energize*, *enervate* means to weaken, to reduce strength or vigor. An enervated person is debilitated: "Clancy's two months in a military prison camp had enervated him unbelievably."

enough   See AMPLE.

endways, endwise   See EDGEWAYS, EDGEWISE/ENDWAYS, ENDWISE/LENGTHWAYS, LENGTHWISE . . .

engage in/indulge in   Both mean "take part in, occupy oneself with." *Indulge in*, however, means "take part in (something) to a great extent or excessively." The "something" may lead to unpleasant results. Thus two persons in an office may engage in gossip for a few minutes, but if they indulge in gossip for a couple of hours each day, they may lose their jobs.

engine/motor   Steam-powered: engine. Gasoline-powered: engine if large, engine or motor if small. Electric-powered: motor. Nuclear-powered: engine. Liquid-fueled rocket: engine. Solid-fueled rocket: motor.

engineer/scientist/technician   *Scientists* search for principles or scientific truths, and *engineers* and *technicians* apply them. The technicians are especially concerned with day-to-day use and maintenance.

England   See BRITISH ISLES, ENGLAND/GREAT BRITAIN . . .

engraving/etching   Cutting tools are employed in making an *engraving*. For an *etching*, acid substitutes for the tools.

enigma/riddle   Listed in some dictionaries as synonyms. *Riddle*, however, is more often used to mean a trivial or amusing question or problem: "What did the boy angle say to the girl angle?" "You're acute angle." An *enigma* is usually more obscure and is more likely to refer to serious matters. "The enigma is this: 'Why does so much poverty exist in the world's richest nation?'" Sir Winston Churchill's famous statement incorporates both words: "Russia is a riddle wrapped in a mystery inside an enigma."

enigmatic   Not used in SWE to mean "doubtful" or "questionable." The meaning is "puzzling, like an enigma": "The wording of the new tax laws was so enigmatic that even IRS agents differed greatly in their interpretations."

enormity/enormousness   For the meaning "great size," *enormousness* is more common in SWE: "the enormousness of the Sahara." In general, SWE restricts *enormity* to "extreme wickedness, something horribly offensive": "the enormity of this brutal crime," "the enormity of the Holocaust." *Enormity* for "great size" is gaining ground in edited writing. Nevertheless the distinction is worth maintaining, because confusion may arise when the two words are used interchangeably.

enough (*that* vs. *to*)   SWE prefers *enough to*: "They have enough money to live on comfortably." More wordy: "They have money enough that they can live on it comfortably." (In general, a phrase is preferable to a clause if it is shorter and no less clear.)

enough   See AMPLE.

enraged/incensed/infuriated   Each refers to a different degree of anger. *Incensed* describes somewhat controlled anger, often justified: "I realized that my father was incensed by Hugo's insult, but his appearance remained calm." *Enraged* means "strongly angered": "Kate was so enraged that she stamped her foot hard enough to break off the heel of one of her dainty slippers." An *infuriated* person has lost even more emotional control, is "in a fury": "Kate was so infuriated that she threw two of her Royal Copenhagen plates at her husband."

enthuse   A back-formation is usually a verb shortened from a noun. Some writers object to each new one but later may come to accept it, as is true of *edit* (from *editor*) and *reminisce* (from *reminiscence*). At present, *enthuse* (from *enthusiasm*) is still in the transitional stage. It is informal but appears increasingly in SWE: "She enthused every time another volunteer appeared." Many writers may not yet be happy with that sentence, but others prefer it to "She waxed enthusiastic."

entitle/title   In the sense of "give a name or title to," the words are synonymous: "Sarah entitled (or *titled*) her book *Retrieval*." The former is more common.

entomologist/etymologist   An *entomologist* studies insects; the word comes from Greek for "insect." An *etymologist* studies the origin of words. Greek *etumon* means "the true sense of a word." "The etymologist looked into his Latin dictionary to find an appropriate name for the insect that the entomologist had discovered." *Entomology* and *etymology* are the fields associated with each term.

enviable/envious   People who are happy are *enviable*, "to be envied." Those who do the envying are *envious*: "envious of other people's happiness." See also ENVY/JEALOUSY.

environment   A general word, and sometimes pretentious. If *home*, *family*, *neighborhood*, *community*, or *city* will express the meaning clearly, SWE chooses that because of its greater specificity. Pretentious: "In the baby's immediate environment were only his mother and sister." SWE says, "In the house at that moment were only the baby, his mother, and his sister." See also AMBIANCE/ENVIRONMENT; ECOLOGY.

envisage/envision   *Envision* is the more imaginative verb, as its relation to *vision* suggests. One envisions great and perhaps impossible things such as universal peace or a building grander than the Taj Mahal. To *envisage* is usually to form a mental picture that is not excessively unrealistic: "The college president envisaged a science building twice as large as the existing one, and much better equipped."

envy/jealousy   These are not synonyms in SWE. One may be *envious* of another's possessions or qualities but *jealous* of a rival: "Bartram envied the older attorney's poise in the courtroom." "Bartram was jealous of his wife's first husband, who often came to see his child and – Bartram suspected – also his ex-wife." See also ENVIABLE/ENVIOUS.

epic   In SWE this word describes only great events such as might be the subject of epic poetry. It is not applicable to games or anything else not involving truly heroic deeds. A clutch home run or a strikeout that wins a World Series can be exciting or dramatic but is hardly epic.

epicure/epicurean/hedonist   A *hedonist* believes that pleasure is the chief goal of living. The small *-e epicurean* does also but differs from other hedonists in placing most emphasis on food and comfortable living. A capital *-e Epicurean* follows the philosophy of Epicurus, who believed in avoiding pain and worry and rejected most of the religious beliefs and practices of his contemporaries. An *epicure* has refined taste in food and wine.

epidemic   See ENDEMIC/EPIDEMIC/PANDEMIC.

episode/event/incident/occurrence   *Event* is the general term for any happening: "a pleasant event." An *episode* is one in a series of events: "Most novels consist of many connected episodes." An *incident* is a relatively small event: "Little Jerry scratched his finger – only one of the day's many incidents that Alicia would save to tell Tom about." *Occurrence* is often used for *event*, especially when the event is rather ordinary: "a daily occurrence."

epithet Not necessarily an unfavorable word. In "Louis the Sun King" and "Stan the Man Musial," *the Sun King* and *the Man* are favorable epithets; but in "Ethelred the Unready," the epithet at least appears to be unfavorable (it may, however, be translated as "the Cautious"). *Epithet* may also mean "a term of abuse or contempt": "Members of the street gang shouted epithets at us." Today that meaning is probably more frequent than the other, although some conservatives consider it a misuse.

epitome See ACME/APEX/EPITOME.

eponym/namesake An *eponym* is a real or imaginary person from whom a place, tribe, institution, era, and so on, takes its name: "The perhaps mythical Romulus was the eponym of *Rome* and *Roman*." "George Washington was the eponym of thousands of American places." A *namesake* is on the receiving end: "Uncle Henry was very proud of the nephew who was his namesake, Senator Henry Lake." A namesake is a person named for someone else or – less often – a person who by chance has the same name.

equable/equitable *Equable* means "uniform," "relatively unchanging," "unemotional": "States' penalties for the same sexual violation are far from equable, ranging from short sentences to life imprisonment." "She has an equable temperament, seldom showing even traces of anger." *Equitable* means "fair, just, right" but not necessarily "equal." An equitable division of property is one fair to all, even though the claimants may get different amounts.

equal (in comparisons) Although George Orwell's *Animal Farm* told readers that some animals are more equal than others, SWE reasons that equal is equal and can't be any more or less so. See also COMPARISON OF ABSOLUTES.

equally as Generally, one or the other word can be deleted: "The second cake tasted equally (as) good." "The second cake tasted (equally) as good as the first."

equitable See EQUABLE/EQUITABLE.

equivocal See AMBIGUOUS/EQUIVOCAL.

equivocate/lie/prevaricate Each verb refers to deceiving, to telling a falsehood. *Lie* is the strongest, referring to what is definitely untrue: "He lied about his age, saying that he was thirty-nine instead of forty-five." *Equivocate* and *prevaricate* resemble each other in suggesting evasion of the truth rather than outright falsehood. One who equivocates often resorts to ambiguities: "She is thirty-nine, but equivocates by calling herself 'thirtyish.'" "He equivocated by saying

'Mistakes were made' rather than 'I made mistakes.'" *Prevaricate* is closer to *lie*: "He prevaricated, calling himself 'about forty' although he is forty-five."

-er, -est   In general, adjectives of two syllables do not have comparative and superlative forms with *-er* and *-est* if they have any of the following endings:

-al (*formal*)	*-ile* (*agile*)
-ed (*muddled*)	*-ive* (*pensive*)
-en (*rotten*)	*-om* (*random*)
-ent (*lucent*)	*-ose* (*verbose*)
-ful (*sinful*)	*-ous* (*porous*)
-ic (*frantic*)	*-que* (*antique*)
-id (*candid*)	*-st* (*unjust*)
-il (*tranquil*)	*-ure* (*mature*)

Most other two-syllable adjectives do take *-er* and *-est*, although in some sentences *more* or *most* may sound better. Most dictionaries list the *-er* and *-est* spellings when appropriate.

erotic/erratic   A newspaper story reports the following: "Police said that the suspect, John Doe, was walking down the street in an erotic manner." Well, maybe, but Doe's walking was probably *erratic* – stumbling, unpredictable. Male strippers, rather than poor Mr. Doe, are likely to walk in an erotic manner.

erotic/exotic   *Erotic* means "sexually suggestive": "an erotic dance (movie, swaying of the hips)." *Exotic* means "foreign, strange," but has connotations of warmth, beauty, and imagination – like something out of the *Arabian Nights*. An exotic dance is one not native to or customary in our region. Technically, an ugly, barren foreign place can be exotic, but most modern readers will interpret the word to mean "charmingly unusual to Americans." SWE chooses a different word for an unattractive place.

errata (verb with)   The plural of *erratum* ("error, especially in print") is *errata*. *Errata* usually means a list of errors not noticed or corrected before a book was printed. In this sense, like *agenda* and *data*, the word is often followed by a singular verb: "The errata is at the end of the book." Strong conservatives, however, would substitute *are* in that sentence, and SWE uses the plural in clearly plural senses: "Many errata were not corrected in the second edition."

erratic   See ECCENTRIC/ERRATIC; EROTIC/ERRATIC.

error/mistake   Although these words are often interchangeable, *error* is more likely to suggest blame, a failure to follow a course generally believed right or wise: "a serious error in judgment." A *mistake* may result from a rather small misinterpretation or a failure to remember: "a mistake in conjugating a Latin verb." In baseball, *errors* are strictly defined and are counted in the box score. *Mistakes*, probably much more numerous, may result from many small causes, such as throwing the wrong kind of pitch or playing too deep for a hitter. Such mistakes are usually less obvious than errors and do not appear in the box score.

ersatz   See ARTIFICIAL/ERSATZ/FAKE . . .

escalation   Often another word is more exact: *increase, enhancement, growth, invigoration, freshening, intensification, extension.*

especial/special   Interchangeable, with *special* the usual choice. *Especial*, if used at all, generally means "exceptional, superior in some way": "my especial friend," "my especial favorite."

especially/specially   *Specially* means "for a particular reason" or "in a particular way": "specially chosen," "specially prepared." *Especially* means "more than anyone or anything else," "more than ever": "Patience is especially needed now." "Patience is needed now especially." SWE avoids the redundant *more especially.*

espresso   The term is *espresso* coffee (not *expresso*).

-ess   Although no one objects to feminine-gender words such as *lioness* or *tigress*, recent decades have driven into disfavor people-oriented words such as *poetess, postmistress*, and *stewardess*, as well as other forms that for no good reason make gender distinctions: *aviatrix, usherette, salesgirl*, and so on. See also HOSTESS; STEWARDESS.

essay   see ASSAY/ESSAY.

essential/indispensable/necessary/requisite   Almost interchangeable, especially *essential* and *necessary.* To many writers, however, the order from strongest to weakest appears to be *indispensable, essential, necessary, requisite.* In SWE, *more* (or *less, least*) is seldom employed before any of these words, because if something is indispensable, no one can do without it. One thing cannot be more indispensable than another. In FF, however, one frequently says things such as "For her, admiration is more indispensable than food." See also COMPARISON OF ABSOLUTES.

essential . . . must   In "It is essential that children must learn more geography," *essential* and *must* carry the same meaning. *Must* here is omitted in SWE, or the sentence is shortened to "Children must learn more geography."

-est   See -ER, -EST.

-est, -eth (verb endings)   Only feeble humor results from use of archaic verb forms – feeble humor or sometimes pity of the ignorant. A horrendously garbled invitation to a college dance read, "Bringeth thou thine wench or thine squire to ye olde Don Quixote Ball." If it is ever necessary to write in the style of the King James Bible, rereading a few chapters may refresh memory. *Dost*, for example, is second person, *doth* third; *leadest* and *prayest* are second, *leadeth* and *prayeth* third: "thou dost," "thou leadest," "he doth," "he leadeth." *-Est* and *-eth* verbs are not imperative. The following is not King James: "Prithee prayeth thou for all who sinnest thus."

estate-size(d)   This term is used loosely in real-estate ads describing pieces of land. *Estate-size* or *estate-sized* lots may vary from less than a quarter-acre to enough for a small plantation. The small print is generally more precise.

estimate/estimation   Although the words are often used interchangeably as nouns, SWE treats *estimate* as a reasoned guess about profit, cost, and so on, but treats *estimation*, like *estimating*, as the act of making such an estimate: "The assessor's estimate was $20,000." "The estimation took only ten minutes." *Estimation* can also mean "esteem, regard": "His behavior caused him to rise in my estimation."

estimated at about   "The number of casualties is estimated at about thirty." SWE deletes as redundant either *estimated at* or *about*.

-et/-ette   When a choice exists, as in *cigaret*, *octet*, and so on, SWE is inconsistent. SANE chops off the useless *te*.

etc., et cetera   **1.** Since *et cetera* means "and other things," SWE does not duplicate *and* by writing "and etc." **2.** SWE avoids the term unless readers can easily fill in some of the "other things." Poor: "The speaker discussed waste, pollution, etc." Acceptable: "She labeled the displays *A*, *B*, *C*, etc." **3.** *Et cetera* or *etc.* is unlikely to be used of persons. Poor: "Committee members who were absent included Jane Colwell, Marcia Babcock, etc." **4.** SWE avoids frequent use. **5.** Some SWE writers use "et cetera" or "and so forth" in full, disliking the abbreviation, but the shortened form is more common.

etching   See ENGRAVING/ETCHING.

eternal   In SWE this word is not modified by *more* or *most*. Nothing can be more eternal than eternal. See also COMPARISON OF ABSOLUTES.

-eth   See -EST, -ETH.

ethic/ethical/ethics   *Ethic* means "principle, rule of conduct": "The work ethic requires one to work at least enough to support oneself and one's own dependents." *Ethics*, referring to morals or moral choices, ordinarily takes a plural verb: "Her ethics have never been questioned." But with reference to a branch of philosophy, it takes a singular verb: "Ethics is sometimes called moral philosophy." *Ethical* is an adjective: "Is deception ever ethical?" To a doctor, an ethical drug is one that requires a prescription.

ethnic   Actually, everyone is *ethnic* – that is, belongs to several racial, cultural, religious, or national groups. The word is generally limited in SWE, however, to mean "belonging to a racial group other than the one predominant in the area." In that sense, whites in Africa are ethnics. The word is descriptive, not a slur. It may be used as noun or adjective.

etymologist   See ENTOMOLOGIST/ETYMOLOGIST.

eulogy   See ELEGY/ENCOMIUM/EULOGY.

euphemism/euphuism   A *euphemism* is a gentle, kindly expression used instead of a more direct one that might hurt or offend someone: "passed away" for "died." *Euphuism* (often capitalized) is a literary term, from *Euphues* by John Lyly (1579). It is a highly artificial prose style, characterized by elaborate comparisons, balanced sentences, antitheses, and alliteration.

eve Now rarely used for "evening" except in such terms as *Christmas Eve* (December 24), or *New Year's Eve* (December 31), or the *eve of battle* (the evening before a battle).

event See EPISODE/EVENT/INCIDENT.

eventuate This is a fat, pompous word for "happen."

ever so often/every so often Although the two idioms are often used interchangeably, SWE uses *ever so* for "very," as the expression *ever so easy* clearly shows. "He called ever so often" means, then, "He very often called." SWE uses *every so often*, in contrast, to mean "now and then, occasionally," "once in a while": "Every so often the phone rings."

every Since *every* carries a singular meaning (similiar to that of *each one*), a pronoun referring to it should also be singular: "Every private or officer must obey his superiors." Informally, *their* often occurs in such sentences, probably because of the confusion between "every private" and "all privates." Eventually that usage may also become SWE, but at present it appears only occasionally. See also EACH/EVERY.

every day/everyday SWE uses the solid form as an adjective: "everyday clothing," "an everyday event." The meaning is "appropriate for ordinary days, usual, commonplace." When the term is not an adjective, SWE uses two words: "Every day is different from every other." "Every day they rise at dawn."

every other . . . except SWE avoids "every other family except ours" and the like because the meaning is duplicated in *other* and *except*. SWE: Either "every family except (but) ours" or "all other families."

every which way On the edge of SWE. Some writers still consider it an informal way to say "in all directions," "scattered about": "The ball bearings rolled every which way."

everybody/everyone Interchangeable. Since each of these words is singular, a singular verb or pronoun accompanies it in formal context: "Everybody (*Everyone*) in both houses *was* so alarmed that *he* (or *she*, or *he or she*) ran outdoors, fearing an earthquake." "Everybody must bring his (or *her* or *his or her*) own food." (FF uses *their*, which occasionally appears also in SWE.)

everyplace See ANYPLACE.

evidence/proof *Evidence* is data that may be used to show that something is true or false or to lead toward any other conclusion. Sufficient and strong enough evidence constitutes *proof*, which is defined as "conclusive demonstration": "After listening to many bits of evidence, the jury decided that there was no proof of Hardy's guilt."

evident See APPARENT/EVIDENT/OBVIOUS.

evoke/invoke *Evoke* means "elicit, draw or call out": "The speech evoked calls for the governor's impeachment." *Invoke* means (1) "ask for": "Let us invoke the help of God." (2) "put into effect": "Two aldermen requested that Ordinance 2607 be invoked."

exact same   SWE deletes *exact*. However, *exactly the same* may on rare occasions be useful to emphasize the sameness.

exam   SWE prefers *examination* but often uses *exam* in newspaper headlines and in informal contexts.

example/exemplar/ideal/model   Each word may mean "something or somebody worth imitating." An *example* may be good or bad: "set a good (bad) example for the boy." *Exemplar* is in some ways like *example* but stresses worthiness of being followed: "Horatio Alger's boy heroes were held up as exemplars for a whole generation." *Ideal* suggests something or someone that approaches perfection: "an ideal house," "When Sid was a boy, his ideal was George Washington." A *model* may be physical, as in "Visit our model homes," or a pattern worth emulating: "a model office," "His father was his model."

example/instance   For *example* and *for instance* are interchangeable.

example/sample/specimen   An *example* is something used to illustrate or represent a class of things or a principle: "One example of her bravery occurred yesterday, when a bear wandered into camp." A *sample* is usually a physical thing: "Try a sample of our new candy." *Specimen* is most likely to be used in scientific contexts: "urine specimen," "one specimen of crab."

except   See ACCEPT/EXCEPT; BUT (FOR EXCEPT); EXCEPTING.

excepting   In most instances, *except* is SWE but *excepting* is not: "All the claims, except that dated 07/14/90, have been paid." As a verb, *excepting* is possible but rare: "We are excepting ('excluding') the claim dated 07/14/90." "All claims, not excepting ('not making an exception of') the one dated 07/14/90, will be paid."

exception proves the rule   Cliché. The meaning is not "The exception proves that the rule is correct" – a generally ridiculous statement. The actual meaning is "The exception *tests* the rule to help us to discover whether or not it is correct." Some writers substitute *test* in the expression.

exceptional   Often confusing when applied to a child, for some persons think of it as meaning "precocious, unusually talented," and others think of it as meaning "retarded." SWE prefers an unambiguous adjective. The usual definition of *exceptional* is "unusual, extraordinary." Careful writers explain the way(s) in which the thing or person is out of the ordinary.

exceptional/exceptionable   Something unusual is *exceptional*: "exceptional apples that weigh a pound each." Something is *exceptionable* if one may take exception to it, object to it, on some rational grounds: "I found nothing exceptionable in his assertions." (Caution: So few people understand *exceptionable* that the word may be misunderstood.)

excess(ive) wordiness All *wordiness (verbiage, verbosity)* is *excess (excessive)*. SWE deletes the adjective.

exciting/fascinating *Exciting* music may make us dance. *Fascinating* music almost hypnotizes us; it adds depth to our emotions or may make us philosophize. Outside of music, the distinction is essentially the same. See also COLOSSAL, COLOSSALLY; FABULOUS/INCREDIBLE.

exclusive/select Except in certain legal or business expressions, such as "exclusive rights" or "exclusive of sales tax," *exclusive* usually suggests snobbishness. Thus an "exclusive club" excludes as members people who do not meet an arbitrary qualification, such as wealth, and an "exclusive dress design" is one that you and I can probably not afford. The adjective *select*, however, refers to high quality, the sort that even ordinary folks would be likely to choose.

93

excuse/pardon (verbs) Interchangeable in the polite expressions "Excuse me" and "Pardon me."

excuse (noun) See ALIBI.

execute/kill, murder *Execute* is used in SWE with reference to killing only when a sentence of death has been imposed – by a court, for instance: "The convicted murderer will be executed in May." *Gangland execution* is a term sometimes used in newspapers. It is accurate when a "court" of gang leaders determines that someone is to be eliminated. Unless that is certainly the case, *gangland murder* (or *killing*) is preferable.

exemplar See EXAMPLE/EXEMPLAR/IDEAL.

exercise/exorcise One way to *exercise* spirits would be to put them on bicycles. What is more likely is that we would try to *exorcise* them – chase them away.

exhausted/fatigued/tired/weary *Fatigued* implies more weariness than *tired* does, and *exhausted* suggests such weariness that any action at all is impossible. *Exhausted* is sometimes misused of a person who is still working. Not SWE: "Although exhausted, she continued shoveling the snow." *Tired* and *weary* are interchangeable, although *weary* seems slightly bookish.

exhausting/exhaustive *Exhausting* means "making extremely tired, making worn out": "She endured an exhausting daylong physical examination." *Exhaustive* means "thorough, including almost all possibilities": "Her doctors said that an exhaustive examination was necessary."

exhibit/exhibition Often used interchangeably, although sometimes in SWE an *exhibit* is one part of the things displayed in an *exhibition*: "the Tom Thumb exhibit in the exhibition of model trains."

exist/subsist To *exist* is to be, to live. Although *exist* and *subsist* are sometimes used interchangeably, *subsist* followed by *on* indicates what one "lives on" (often something simple or minimal): "That winter they subsisted on cornbread and beans."

exit When *exit* is a verb, it is intransitive (takes no object): "He exited from the room" rather than "He exited the room." Better still: "He left the room," "He hurried from the room," or the like.

ex-murderer   *Ex-convict* is satisfactory, because the person is no longer a convict. But once a murderer, always a murderer. SWE deletes *ex-*, or is kind and calls the person something else – maybe his or her name, or *he* or *she*.

exorcise   See EXERCISE/EXORCISE.

exotic   See EROTIC/EXOTIC.

expatriate/ex-patriot   A book ad says, "Viertel's novel is a drama of ex-patriot high life." This is not SWE. Viertel's characters have not lost their patriotism, as *ex-patriot* suggests. Rather, they are *expatriates* – people who live outside their native land, voluntarily or not.

expect   FF for "suppose," as in "I expect you did well in calculus." In SWE, *expect* is generally used in the context of looking ahead, not back: "I expect that you will do well in calculus" or "I expect you to do well . . ." See also ANTICIPATE/EXPECT.

expectorate/spit   *Expectorate* seems too high-flown for so ordinary an act. Besides, many people would not understand a sign that says "No Expectorating."

expedient/politic   Something *expedient* is appropriate, as well as quickly accomplished: "Obviously the most expedient thing to do was to call the fire department." Sometimes it suggests "done for selfish reasons": "He saved money by doing what was expedient, not necessarily what was wise." The adjective *politic* refers either to what is prudent or to what is shrewd and perhaps artful and ingenious. It does not necessarily concern politics or politicians: "a politic decision, widely applauded for its good sense," "a politic decision, regarded as a clever stratagem," "a politic businesswoman."

expensive   Not SWE: "Prices are too expensive." In SWE, prices or costs are high or low, but not expensive. Cars, food, and other things that are purchased may be expensive.

expert   See QUALIFIED EXPERT.

explicit   A valuable word for "specific, clearly delineated, forthright." Unfortunately, it has been used so frequently in recent years to mean "fully detailed in its portrayal of sex" that some people now equate it with "X-rated." SWE does not abandon the word but shows from context that no sexual inference should be drawn. Possibly subject to misinterpretation: "This book is an explicit portrayal of life in an almost manless small Italian town in World War II" (*detailed, authentic,* or *no-holds-barred* might be better).

explore every avenue   Cliché. Politicians sometimes promise to "explore every avenue" to reduce poverty or correct some other problem. The figure of speech seems odd on the surface, since most people equate *avenue* with a broad, tree-lined street that would require no exploration. However, *avenue* may also mean "a way to a place, an approach."

explosion/implosion An *explosion* is a bursting outward. The related verb is *explode*. An *implosion* is a bursting inward, like that of a dropped light bulb. The verb is *implode*.

expose Because *expose* now often means "show one's nude body, 'flash,'" SWE makes certain that no ambiguity exists when the word is used. Dubious: "He exposed himself for what he was." Clear: "He proved what kind of person he was."

express/expressed An *express* purpose is one that is definite, clear, and perhaps single, exclusive: "The society's express purpose is to help the blind." An *expressed* purpose is one that has been stated. Often the word hints that the statement may not be true: "The expressed purpose is to help the blind, but most contributions are used to pay office expenses and salaries."

extended Some writers on usage object to "extended illness," saying that *extended* means "stretched out" and that probably no one would intentionally stretch an illness; they recommend *long*. However, the conservative AHD includes this definition of *extended*: "continued for a long period of time."

extra 1. SWE avoids overuse in expressions such as *extra fine, extra plentiful, extra easy to operate*. If a modifier is needed, *uncommonly, unusually,* or some other adverb can often replace *extra*. 2. In combinations such as *extracurricular*, no hyphen is needed unless to help a reader, as in *extraactive*, which should be *extra-active*. An *extra-base* hit is not the same as an *extra base* hit.

F

fable/legend/myth A *fable* is a fictitious story, often with animal characters, usually illustrating some principle of human behavior: "the fable of the fox and the grapes." A *legend* is a probably untrue story that usually concerns a real person or persons and that has been passed along for years: "the legend of George Washington and the cherry tree." A *myth* often has to do with gods or superhuman heroes such as Apollo, Juno, or Hercules. To social scientists it is a widely accepted but only partly true belief: "Hitler's myth of Aryan superiority in all things." Loosely, a myth is any made-up story.

fabricate One meaning of *fabricate* is "to speak an untruth, to lie," so it is redundant to say "fabricate falsely" or "fabricate an untrue story."

fabulous/incredible Overused, especially in fiction aimed at the semiliterate, to mean "thrilling, exciting, super," and the like, and to refer to almost anything – most often emotions and the "incredibly" handsome men who arouse them. See also COLOSSAL, COLOSSALLY.

facile May refer either to a task easily done or to anyone who performs a task easily: "facile writing," "a facile writer." The word carries a suggestion of superficiality, since important tasks are seldom easy.

facility   Instead of using *facility* to mean something specific and tangible, such as an airport, a harbor, a building, or a part of a building, SWE usually names the structure: "He used the bathroom" rather than "He used the facility."

(of the) fact   In sentences such as "You can be certain of the fact that this account is accurate," SWE omits *of the fact*.

factious/factitious   *Factitious*, a comparatively rare word, means "contrived, not authentic, produced artificially rather than naturally": "a factitious rise in sugar prices, caused by crooked speculators," "a factitious appearance of thoughtfulness." *Factious* is related to the noun *faction* and means "factional, divisive": "Factious elements may once again split the Democratic party."

factor   Overused by some writers, especially in phrases such as "one factor" and "an important factor." Among possible substitutes are *component, constituent, contributing fact, division, feature, ingredient, installment, integral part, item, member, part, piece, portion, section, sector, segment, share, slice.*

fair/fare   The distinction is made clear in "The public insists that this fare increase is not a fair increase."

fair-trade agreement   Before 1975, if you were on the side of a manufacturer who wanted all retailers to sell his product at a stipulated price, you referred to *fair-trade agreements* or *fair-trade laws*. But if you were a consumer who objected because the product was not available in a competitive market and perhaps at a lower price, you used a different term, *price-fixing*. Fair-trade agreements became illegal in 1975, but accusations of price-fixing still exist.

fairy/gay/pansy   Today, it seems, fairy stories are found mainly in gay magazines. Thus two attractive words have become difficult to use in their earlier meanings. *Gay*, because of its brevity, is apparently here to stay in its meaning of "homosexual," "a homosexual person," and must be considered SWE. However, with increasing awareness and understanding of homosexuality, *fairy* and other ridiculing terms such as *pansy* are used less and less in that context and may yet be reclaimed by folklorists, children, and floriculturists.

fake   See ARTIFICIAL/ERSATZ/FAKE . . .

fallacy   A *fallacy* is an error in reasoning, not just any error. A mistake in judgment, for example, is not in itself a fallacy, although it may be based on fallacious reasoning.

false illusion   SWE deletes *false*. An illusion does not exist and so cannot be true or false. See also ALLUSION/ILLUSION.

famous   SWE doesn't bother to tell readers, unless they are children or uneducated people, that, for example, Napoleon was a famous general. It is perhaps satisfactory, though, to note that Nimrod, much less widely known than Napoleon, was a famous hunter in Old Testament times. See also NOTABLE/NOTED/NOTORIOUS.

fancy/imagination   As the word *fanciful* or the expression *strike my fancy* may suggest, fancy is lighter and more whimsical than *imagination*. Fancy in the sense of "playfulness" may be part of imagination, but the latter may also include recall of past sights and sounds and other experiences, all blended with thought to attain a perhaps unexpected result.

fantastic   See COLOSSAL, COLOSSALLY.

fare   See FAIR/FARE.

farther/further   An attempt has long been made to restrict *farther* to physically measurable distances, and *further* to nonphysical: "Harrisburg is farther from here than Allentown is." "Shall we discuss the question further?" Today *farther* and *further* are used almost interchangeably in sentences such as the first example, but only *further* is customary in SWE in the second and in other such instances as "further argument," "further preparation," "Further, I want to say that . . ." Conservatives still do not use *further* for physical distance. The superlative forms are *farthest* or *farthermost*, and *furthest* or *furthermost*. SANE prefers the shorter words.

97

fascinating   See EXCITING/FASCINATING.

fatal/fateful   A *fatal* event involves death. A *fateful* event has important good or bad consequences but ordinarily no deaths. SWE rarely uses the terms interchangeably. The distinction is worth keeping.

fatigued   See EXHAUSTED/FATIGUED/TIRED . . .

fault (verb)   As a substitute for *criticize* or *blame, fault* has been used occasionally since about 1850 and has finally attained SWE approval. The AHD usage panel split 52–48 in favor, and a 1988 *New York Times* headline read "New York Faulted on Tuberculosis."

favorable   See OPTIMISTIC, PESSIMISTIC; FAVORABLE, UNFAVORABLE.

faze   Note the spelling of this word meaning "bother," "make uncomfortable": "The presence of his ex-wife did not *faze* him." In SWE *faze* occurs mostly in negative statements, not in sentences such as "He was fazed by the presence of his ex-wife." In questions, it may take a form like "Did this faze him?" or "Didn't this faze him?"

feasible/possible   An action is *feasible* if it is not only possible but also sensible, likely to bring the desired results. The action is *possible* if it can be performed, regardless of how sensible or worthwhile it may be.

feel   Despite onetime opposition, *feel* is now SWE for "believe, think": "Senator South felt that the legislation went too far." *Feel*, however, still connotes more emotion, *think* or *believe* more rationality.

feel (good/well; bad/badly)   *Feel badly* is sneaking up on *feel bad* in SWE, but *feel bad* still has a common-sense defense. An apple may taste good or bad, a perfume may smell good or bad, music may sound good or bad, and a person may look or feel good or bad.

Like *look, smell, sound,* and *taste, feel* is a verb referring to one of the five senses. The modifier after such a verb describes the subject: apple, perfume, or the like. Usually, then, in SWE a person feels *bad*, not *badly.* A person, however, may feel either *good* or *well*, because *well* can mean "in good health." There are two SWE exceptions to the *feel bad* generalization: A dog may *smell badly* if illness has decreased its smelling ability, or *smell well* if it is able to follow a faint trail, and people may *feel badly* if something is wrong with their sense of touch. Also, besides feeling well if their health is good, they may feel well if their sense of touch is unusually acute.

feisty Although some dictionaries label *feisty* as regional or slang, this word – meaning "active, spirited, small but lively" – is useful. When Congressman Claude Pepper became an octogenarian, the media frequently described him as *feisty.* The word deserves to be listed with no qualifying label. It is SWE.

feline See BOVINE.

fellow For the meaning "man," *fellow* is FF: "See that fellow over there?" For the meaning "beau, boyfriend," *fellow* is obsolete slang, used extensively in the first third of this century: "Who's your fellow now?" Although President Ronald Reagan sometimes addressed "my fellow countrymen," *fellow* is redundant.

female companion/girlfriend/mistress Newspapers sometimes report that an alleged criminal, a businessman, or someone else has been found in a hotel room with a "girlfriend" or "female companion." They avoid *mistress*, which can be libelous when not provable.

female, feminine See also EFFEMINATE/FEMALE/FEMININE . . .

feminist A person can be a *feminist* without being female. The author of this book is a reasonably good husband, a good-natured father, and a feminist. "I am proud to be a feminist," actor Paul Newman reportedly said.

(on the) fence Cliché. It is perhaps overused to mean "not yet having decided" but still a quick and rather picturesque phrase.

fever/temperature Dictionaries record *fever* as one synonym of *temperature.* Minority report: It would be good to preserve a distinction. Each of us has a body *temperature*, even if it is only 90°. We have a fever only if our temperature is above 98.6°, so there is a difference. If our temperature is 102.6°, we have a fever of 4°. Everybody, even a dead person, has a temperature, but only occasionally do most living people have fevers.

few(er) in number SWE deletes *in number*, just as it omits the *in*-phrases in "small(er) or large(r) in size," "circular in shape," "taller in height," and so on.

fewer/less In FF, *less* is used almost exclusively for both countables and uncountables: "less vehicles," "less sugar." SWE, however, ordinarily requires *fewer* for countables: "fewer vehicles," "fewer members than last year." Apparent exceptions are references to time: "less than four months"; distance: "less than ten miles"; money: "less than twenty francs"; weight: "less than twelve ounces"; and percentage: "less than three percent." The reason for each exception is that the unit (e.g., four months) is considered a collective — a single period of time, a single amount.

fiancé, fiancée   Masculine and feminine, respectively. The accent mark is increasingly disregarded outside France.

fictional/fictitious   A *fictional* person is someone, such as Scarlett O'Hara, who exists in fiction but not in real life. A *fictitious* person is also unreal but is not in a novel, short story, or other fiction. For example, many children have fictitious (imaginary) playmates. A false name is also fictitious, and if you lie about having money in the bank, you are referring to a fictitious bank account.

fiddle/violin   Itzhak Perlman and other great violinists may refer affectionately or humorously to their *fiddles*, but you and I had better call them *violins*. All of us, however, may refer to the fiddles and fiddlers at the old-time barn dance or its modern equivalents. There are violins in the New York Philharmonic and fiddles in the Grand Ole Opry.

field   **1.** Overused. If all the traveling salespeople and educators who talk about spending time *in the field* were laid end to end and side by side, they would cover 8,732 acres. If *the field of* were omitted before every reference to chemistry, photography, and so on, scientists could do more work and photographers could take more pictures. **2.** SWE is wary of ambiguity in using *field*. The newspaper of a small college for teachers ran this item: "Professors Henry Eastman and Hilda Bogue spent last week together in the field." No, there was no hanky-panky. The professors were off campus visiting student teachers — the jargon for which was *in the field*.

fight with   Ambiguous: "Jones fought with the English." Did he help them or try to hurt them? Unless the context clearly answers that question, SWE replaces *with* by choosing *against, beside*, or some other unambiguous preposition.

figuratively/literally   "I was so tired after the long hike that I was literally dead." Only a ghost could honestly say that, because *literally* means "actually." Possible substitutions: "figuratively dead," "almost dead," "thought I was dying." *Figuratively* is related to *figure of speech*. Anything said figuratively is not to be considered a reflection of actuality. It may exaggerate or draw a comparison that is not to be interpreted as true except in a somewhat poetic sense.

figure   FF for "predict," "conclude," or "believe" in sentences such as "He figured that the enemy soldiers would avoid the top of the ridge." *Figure* in SWE means "to calculate": "I figure the distance to be eighty miles."

figure out   Overused by writers too lazy to figure out whether to say *understand, invent, solve, compute, calculate, decide, determine, contrive, comprehend, reason out*, or something else.

figurehead   SWE says, "Although Rankin held the title of Chairman of the Board, he was actually a mere figurehead." As this example shows, a *figurehead* is only nominally important – conspicuous but little more powerful than the carved figurehead on the prow of an old-time ship. SWE does not use the word to mean "chief," "leader," or the like.

final analysis Often wordy or pretentious. "In the final analysis one must conclude that the procedures were ineptly chosen" may be better stated, "An observer must conclude that the procedures were inept" or "The procedures were inept."

final completion (conclusion, culmination, ending, upshot) SWE omits *final*.

finalize Although criticized by some writers on usage, *finalize* is listed without comment in most modern dictionaries. It appears mainly in business or political contexts: "finalized the deal." See also –IZE.

find/locate *Find* is the broader term, applicable to coming upon something either by chance or by intention: "While exploring the area farther west, Giles found a large, bubbling spring." "Drillers found oil near here." *Locate* emphasizes the place or location of something being searched for: "They finally located the missing child, still alive, in an abandoned cistern."

fine As an adjective of praise (a fine day, sweater, woman, boy, rain, or the like), *fine* is both vague and overused. A writer usually has time to think of a more specific word. *Fine* is also used excessively as an adverb, although that use seldom appears in SWE. Instead of "doing fine," "it works fine," "I can hear fine now," SWE chooses *well* or, when feasible, a more definite adverb.

fire (verb) SWE for "dismiss, discharge" but more likely to be found in informal contexts. See also DISCONTINUE.

firmly entrenched Although a cliché, the metaphor is clear and useful. *Firmly* is often deleted.

first and foremost An established idiom, but SWE omits *and foremost* unless the writer wants to stress the special importance of the point.

first annual This term is sometimes too optimistic. Maybe the "first annual" celebration (or whatever) will be so unsuccessful that it will never be repeated.

first-rate *First-rate* as an adjective meaning "of the finest quality" is SWE. In the sense of "in good health," however, it is more likely FF: "He feels first-rate today." The adverbial use, as in "He does his work first-rate," is FF.

first two/two first Today "the first two pages" and "the two first pages" are sometimes used interchangeably. Some writers dislike "the two first pages," however, arguing that there can be only one first page. SANE agrees. Similar comments apply to *last two* and *two last*.

firstly, secondly (and so on) These are SWE, but usually *first, second,* and so on are enough and are not pretentious. (Old-time preachers sometimes got at least as far as *fourteenthly*; the record-holder is unknown.)

fish/fishes   Both are standard plurals, but the usual SWE choice is *fish* except with reference to different kinds or species: "caught a few fish," "Fishes of these waters include yellowtail, pompano, and grouper."

fishy   Flesch lists eighteen definitions of *fishy*, including "suggestive of deception" and "casting doubt or suspicion." He asserts that "the word, with its unique blend of smelliness and slipperiness, simply can't be replaced by another." Consider it standard, he says, because "it's one of the great treasures of the English language." *Great* is probably an overstatement, but the word is indeed useful enough that it appears occasionally in SWE.

fit/fitted   Interchangeable as the past tense, although when the verb is transitive, many writers prefer *fitted*: "The tailor fitted the jacket carefully," in contrast to "The jacket fit well." *Fitted* is the usual choice for a passive: "Each rod must be fitted precisely to its opening."

fix   This is an overused word, both as noun and verb. For one of the noun meanings, *predicament*, *dilemma*, and *embarrassing position* are among the more specific substitutes. For the meaning "injection of an opiate," *fix* seems informal, but no short equivalent is available. In using *fix* as a verb, SWE checks context to be sure that the meaning is clear. "I fixed it" may mean, among other things, that I repaired it, made it immovable, made a chemical substance nonvolatile, prevented its discoloration, prepared it, prearranged its outcome, or castrated it.

flab   Related to *flabby*, this word for "soft body tissue" is now SWE: "This rowing machine will get rid of your flab."

flabbergast   This eighteenth-century synonym of *astound* sounds humorous, but modern dictionaries treat it as standard because it does occur in SWE, although infrequently.

flagrant   See BLATANT/FLAGRANT.

flair/flare   SWE: "Rosemary has a *flair* for politics." "The marooned sailors lighted a *flare*." *Flair* means "natural aptitude"; *flare*, "a burning light, such as a torch." (If Rosemary had a flare for politics, she might set the voters ablaze.)

flak   In World War II *flak* was coined to refer to antiaircraft fire: "The planes encountered heavy flak over Berlin." Today the meaning is broadened to include "hostile criticism": "Senator Barnes has taken much flak because of his stand on abortions." Because of its vigor and brevity, the word is useful, and it does occur in SWE, usually in informal contexts.

flammable/inflammable   SWE prefers *flammable*. *Inflammable* was once favored but was sometimes misunderstood to mean "not burnable." This misinterpretation could cause a serious problem. More drivers may be reluctant to cut in front of a truck labeled "flammable" than one labeled "inflammable." Figuratively, *inflammable* is frequent: "an inflammable temper."

flap FF (slang) for "commotion," "dispute," "disorganization."

flare See FLAIR/FLARE.

flaunt/flout To *flaunt* is to show off, display ostentatiously: "He flaunted his wealth by purchasing a 150-foot yacht." To *flout* is to ignore or disobey in a scornful way: "Alec flouted the dormitory regulations by openly bringing in booze and girls from the town."

flay A strong word, with the primary meaning "strip off the skin, for example by whipping." The secondary meaning, "criticize vigorously," is also SWE but ordinarily applies to extraordinarily harsh, even cruel remarks. See also ANNIHILATE.

flied **1.** SWE as baseball talk. We can hardly say that a batter "flew out to left field" even if he is a Cardinal or a Blue Jay. So, "He flied out." **2.** In a theater, parts of the scenery may be flied (raised into the flies, the space above the stage).

flipflop, flip flop Dictionaries treat either form as standard in the sense of "handspring" or "back somersault" but informal for "change of mind." It's a vigorous word, useful in vigorous prose, and deserves to be considered standard.

flotsam/jetsam/lagan The legal difference is sometimes important to shipping and insurance companies. *Flotsam* is wreckage or cargo left afloat after a ship has sunk or been badly damaged. *Jetsam* is equipment or cargo thrown overboard to lighten a ship in trouble. The less familiar *lagan* refers to jetsam to which a buoy has been attached as a marker.

flounder/founder A just-decapitated chicken or a live fish on shore *flounders*, "moves about wildly." A boat or ship that sinks because it's filled with water, or a business, marriage, or other enterprise that fails (figuratively sinks), *founders*.

flout See FLAUNT/FLOUT.

folks An SWE but informal ("folksy") word for "people," "relatives": "Folks around here will never believe this." "We went to visit my wife's folks."

following In referring to quite ordinary events, *following* is a little high-flown for "after": "Following the meat and potatoes, we ate vanilla ice cream." It's better in more important contexts, such as "Following the debate on highway funds, the legislature turned to school appropriations."

foot, hour, mile, pound (in measurements) An SWE writer refers to a twelve-*foot* ladder, but a ladder twelve *feet* long; a three-*hour* wait, but waited three *hours*; a two-*mile* walk, but walked two *miles*; a ten-*pound* weight, but weighs ten *pounds*.

foot speed Sports analyst: "The fullback lacks foot speed." In contrast to what other kind of speed? SWE omits *foot* or calls the fullback "slow-moving."

for free Widely used, and treated as standard in some dictionaries, although *for* adds nothing to the meaning, and the adjective *free* is needlessly used as a noun. Why waste space? Usual SWE is "This is free."

for the purpose of   Usually can be replaced by *to*: "Such a map is drawn for the purpose of showing differences in barometric pressure." SWE says, ". . . drawn to show. . . ."

for the reason that   SWE prefers *because*.

for . . . to   Not customary in SWE: "Jansen wanted for his son to become a lawyer." SWE says, "Jansen hoped that his son would . . ." or "Jansen wanted his son to . . ."

for   See also BECAUSE/FOR.

force   SWE avoids using *force* as a verb unless the implication of power or strength is intended. Dubious: "They were forced to choose between cake and pie." Better: "Their only choices were . . ."

forced/forceful/forcible   *Forced* means "caused by something outside one's control." For example, a pilot may make a forced landing because of engine trouble or ice on the wings. It may also mean "strained, unnatural": "a forced attempt at cheerfulness." *Forceful*, often used figuratively, means "giving the appearance of strength and energy": "a forceful courtroom pleader." Something is *forcible* if it is done through physical force: "forcible entry," "forcible rape."

foregoing/forgoing   *Foregoing* means "going before, preceding": "as the foregoing example suggested." *Forgoing* means "abstaining, doing without": "Her forgoing lunch was extraordinary."

FOREIGN EXPRESSIONS   Purposeless use of foreign terms is mere exhibitionism. Sometimes, however, a foreign expression is justifiable because it is the precise one a writer needs and has no exact English equivalent. The Spanish *simpatico*, for example, is variously equated with *attractive, congenial, compatible,* and *friendly*, but it comes closer to being all of these rather than one. Foreign words that have not become thoroughly anglicized are underlined (italicized), but those common in English, such as "laissez-faire," usually are not. Accent marks, the cedilla, the tilde, and special foreign uses of capitals are retained in formal writing until the terms are accepted as English.

foreseeable future   Strictly speaking, no part of the future is foreseeable. Nevertheless, *in the foreseeable future* is a rather useful equivalent of "to the extent that is predictable."

foreword/forward   Part of the front matter in a book or long essay may be a *foreword*. Note the spelling. Uses of the adjective or adverb *forward* are illustrated in "a forward cabin," "a forward girl," "walk forward," "forward-looking."

foreword/introduction/preface   A book may have one, two, or (rarely) all three of these. Usually *foreword* and *preface* are interchangeable, although a foreword is sometimes regarded as less formal. Some publishers prefer *preface* if the book's author wrote it, *foreword* if someone else did. An *introduction* is usually but not always written by the author. Although a preface or foreword normally consists of some background information and gives credit to various people, an introduction actually gets into the subject matter of the book, presenting basic information to clarify or pave the way for what comes later.

former, latter Most SWE writers use these words in referring to one of two things. For three or more, they use *first* and *last,* or if necessary repeat a noun. Some writers try to avoid *former* and *latter,* considering them stiff.

formulate Often *form, devise,* or *invent* may be more suitable. *Formulate* is most useful if in some way a formula is involved: "to formulate a medicine that will be both effective and palatable."

fortuitous/fortunate Something is *fortuitous* if it is entirely unplanned; it may be either good or bad but more often good. A one-day drop in stock market prices, for example, may not be due to anyone's machinations and may help some investors, harm others; it is a fortuitous drop. Something *fortunate,* however, is attributable to good luck, not bad; it brings good fortune. A fortuitous meeting may or may not be a fortunate one.

forward See FOREWORD/FORWARD.

founder See FLOUNDER/FOUNDER.

founding fathers Careful, informed writers remember that founding mothers existed, too. Women's roles in the American Revolution were considerable; in fact, a number of women took part in actual fighting. So *founding fathers and mothers* may often be more appropriate.

FOUR-LETTER WORDS AND PROFANITY Only rarely do writers of SWE use four-letter words and profanity except in quotations and, in fiction, when in keeping with the narrator or the character being depicted. The reason for the general avoidance is not that there is anything inherently "bad" or "wrong" about them or the actions they depict. The letters and sounds in *piss* and *goddam(n)* appear unchallenged in thousands of other words, and the bodily functions named in the four-letter words are not objected to when their Latinate versions are employed: *urinate, defecate, copulate,* and the like. The SWE stance is based on the fact that, with or without justification, large segments of the public do consider the four-letter words and the profanity vulgar or sacrilegious. Most SWE writers believe that giving offense alienates many readers and listeners rather than convinces or persuades them. FF, used mainly with a small and familiar audience, shows less restraint.

fraction In an expression such as "a fraction of the time," meaning "a small part," *fraction* is not entirely logical because $^{19}/_{20}$ as well as $^{1}/_{20}$ is a fraction. Nevertheless the expression is generally accepted in SWE, although many writers substitute something more specific, such as "less than half the time."

Frankenstein In Mary Shelley's story, Frankenstein was a scientist who created a monster. So many people have confused the two that some dictionaries now define *Frankenstein* as both the scientist and the monster. Most SWE writers, though, avoid risk of ridicule by saying "created a Frankenstein monster" or the like.

fraught   Old-fashioned for "filled" or "laden," as in "fraught with pain."

free gift   Obviously a gift is free. SWE omits *free*.

free rein   Horses are sometimes given "free rein," with the reins relaxed so that they can go at their own pace in the direction they choose. The term should not be confused with *reign* or *rain*.

frequently/regularly   Dubious: "Chickadees appear regularly at our feeder." *Regularly* means "at regular intervals, on schedule." Chickadees may appear *often* or *frequently*, but few birds except the swallows of Capistrano or the buzzards of Hinckley, Ohio, do much on a precise schedule. *Regularly* may be equally faulty in other contexts.

friable/fryable   *Friable* has nothing to do with frying. It describes soil that is easily crumbled or powdered. *Fryable* means "capable of being fried": "a chicken too old to be fryable."

friar/monk   With some exceptions, *monks* live in self-supporting monasteries and through meditation and prayer strive to make themselves morally and spiritually better. *Friars* normally live on alms, often move from place to place, and try to improve the lives of others.

friendlily   Standard but awkward in expressions like "behaved friendlily toward us." SWE generally chooses *friendly*, which is standard as both adjective and adverb, or uses a phrase such as "in a friendly manner."

from . . . to   In expressions such as "walks from eight to ten miles a day," SWE deletes *from*.

from where/from which   *From which* makes good sense if a noun is present to serve as the antecedent of *which*: "This was a spot from which he could watch the entire valley" (*spot* is the antecedent of *which*). SWE uses *from where* when no antecedent is explicit: "From where he sat he could watch the entire valley."

frugal   See ECONOMICAL/FRUGAL/THRIFTY . . .

frustrate   See DISCOURAGE/FRUSTRATE.

fryable   See FRIABLE/FRYABLE.

-ful (plurals)   If you need two containers of flour, you probably fill one cup, empty it, and refill the same cup. So the plural is *cupfuls*, not *cups full* as it would be if you used two cups. Similarly, the plural is *spoonfuls, basketfuls, bucketfuls, armfuls*, and so on. However, if you actually use two or more containers, the model is "We raked up three *baskets full* of leaves." Many writers prefer *cups, baskets*, and so on to avoid a choice.

fulsome   A somewhat risky word to use. Most dictionaries define it as "exaggerated, excessive, overdone": "Her compliments were so fulsome as to be unbelievable." Some dictionaries add a second definition (which is about 750 years old but is now often criticized): "abundant, copious, generous": "Her fulsome compliments were obviously heartfelt." A reader may not know which meaning the writer intends.

fun (as adjective)   "A fun time," "a fun game to play," and the like are relatively new expressions, with *fun* corresponding in meaning to *enjoyable*. The usage is still mainly FF but may become SWE because of its brevity and expressiveness.

function (noun)   Suitable name for a ceremonious event such as an inauguration or a formal dinner but rather high-flown for a club meeting or most parties.

funny   In the sense "strange, odd, unexpected, coincidental," *funny* is often considered informal: "It's funny that you and he arrived in town on the same day." Both AHD and RHD, however, consider this meaning standard. Nevertheless in SWE *funny* is usually associated with humor.

furlough   Now called *leave* by the U.S. armed forces.

further   See ALL THE FARTHER; FARTHER/FURTHER.

future plans   See ADVANCE RESERVATIONS/FUTURE PLANS.

fuzz   see COP.

FYI   A useful abbreviation in business correspondence is often penciled at the top of a note, letter, or copy of something. It means "for your information," and it brings the overworked recipient the messsage, "Here's one thing that probably won't cause you any labor, but you may find the contents useful, interesting, or amusing. No response is necessary."

G

Gaelic   See CELTIC/GAELIC.

gallon   A U.S. gallon is 231 cubic inches (3.785 liters). A British imperial gallon is 277.42 cubic inches (4.545 liters). A gallon of petrol will take you farther than a gallon of U.S. gasoline.

galore   Most dictionaries and writers on usage classify *galore* as informal. 'Tis a pity that this word, derived from Old Irish *co* + *leór*, "enough," is not generally recognized as standard in all contexts, for it adds a lively tone to statements about abundance: "chances (neckties, corned beef, shamrocks, and so on) galore." It does appear fairly often in SWE.

gambit   Conservatives prefer to use *gambit* in a sense comparable to that in chess: an opening in which a player sacrifices one or more pieces for the sake of a favorable position: "Often Lincoln's gambit was to grant the validity of one or more of his opponent's most credible or least important arguments and then to say, 'But the point really at issue is . . .'" SWE often uses the word to refer to any kind of strategic opening, however, even when no sacrifice is made: "His gambit was to win his listeners with a broad smile and an appropriate joke."

game (adjective) 1. SWE for "plucky," "resolute": "a game young man." 2. It's also SWE for "considered suitable for hunting": "The pheasant is the leading game bird of South Dakota." 3. FF for "willing" (especially if some risk is involved): "Are you game for some ice-fishing?"

gaping hole That's what most holes are. SWE omits *gaping*.

garbage in, garbage out (gigo) Perhaps overused by computerists, this term is still helpful as a reminder that computer (or word-processor) results are almost invariably wrong, poor in quality, or useless if the input is inaccurate, incomplete, or badly chosen.

gargantuan Unlike *gigantic* or *enormous*, *gargantuan* does not refer to size in all its varieties. Named for a character invented by Rabelais, it suggests unusually large capacity for food or pleasure: "a gargantuan appetite," "gargantuan lust."

gas/gasoline After almost three quarters of a century of being labeled "informal" in most dictionaries, gas (for *gasoline*) finally reached unlabeled dignity in the conservative *AHD*. SWE makes sure, however, to avoid any possible confusion between the liquid fuel (gasoline) and the airlike substance (gas). There's a difference between *gas lamp* and *gasoline lamp*, for example, and *gas-burning equipment* is ambiguous.

gather together See COLLABORATE . . . TOGETHER.

gay see FAIRY/GAY/PANSY.

gem/jewel With regard to precious or semiprecious stones, *gem* and *jewel* are interchangeable. Also, an extraordinarily likable or helpful person may be either a gem or a jewel: "My wife's husband, I believe, is a gem (or *jewel*)."

gender Used chiefly to refer to the sexual classifications "male" and "female," *gender* in grammar does not necessarily refer to sex at all. In some languages, word forms vary in gender to show differences in size, age, closeness of relationship, or almost anything else. In other instances the classification may seem to mix sexes, as in references to a no-sex ship as "she." The German *Mädchen* ("girl, maiden") is grammatically neuter in gender.

general consensus See CONSENSUS.

general public *General* is unnecessary unless you have just been discussing one part of the public and now want to compare or contrast that part with the whole. Satisfactory: "The racetrack owners objected to the new tax, but the general public raised no outcry."

generally always FF. Because these two words contradict each other, SWE prefers *almost always*.

genial See CONGENIAL/GENIAL.

genie A supernatural being that supposedly will perform for its master any task, workaday or miraculous. The word is also spelled *jinn, djin(n), djinni, djinny.* In the *Arabian Nights* it is associated with a magic lamp. In other fiction it may remain patiently in a bottle until released.

genius (plurals of)   Plural *geniuses* except in regard to guardian spirits in Roman mythology or to demons in Moslem mythology. In those two senses, *genii* is standard.

genius/talent   *Genius* is regarded as the higher of the two qualities and is not used in SWE as equivalent to mere "skill" or "high ability." It usually implies extraordinarily great intellectual and creative power. *Talent* may be mental or physical and (unlike genius) is not necessarily inborn but may be acquired. An athlete may have great physical talent, and a musician a talent for playing well, but neither is ordinarily said to have genius unless he or she demonstrates it through intellectual or creative activity. Talent, however, can apply the products of genius. Marie Ebner Eschenbach said, "Genius points the way; talent pursues it."

genre   Use of this word (pronounced *zhahn*-ruh) for "variety" or "kind" is restricted in SWE almost entirely to the arts. Thus novel is a literary genre, sonata a musical genre, surrealist painting a genre in art. Basketball, however, is a game but not a sports genre, and the term is equally unlikely to be used in business or science.

genteel   Now rarely used for "fashionable, polite, refined" or "prudish." When it is used, it often seems sarcastic and implies artificiality and old-fashioned behavior.

Gentlemen: Feminists may be driving out this conventional salutation of business letters, yet few women are enthusiastic about *Ladies and Gentlemen:* and certainly not *Gentlepersons:* or the cold and legalistic *To Whom It May Concern:*. Frequently, today's letters to recipients not identifiable by name have no salutation at all. William Safire recommends *Greetings:*.

genuine   See AUTHENTIC/GENUINE.

genus   Plural *genera*. A genus is part of a family and usually consists of several or many species. *Homo sapiens* indicates that human beings belong to the genus Homo; the self-congratulatory *sapiens* identifies us as a thinking species. See also SPECIE/SPECIES.

geographic, geographical; geometric, geometrical   In each pair, take your choice. SANE, of course, recommends the shorter.

geometric progression   See ARITHMETIC PROGRESSION . . .; AVERAGE. See also GEOGRAPHIC, GEOGRAPHICAL . . .

gerund   See -ING; -ING (CASE PRECEDING).

gesticulation/gesture   As nouns, these words are sometimes used interchangeably, although *gesticulation* is more abstract, referring to the use of certain bodily movements rather than to the movements themselves: "He is fond of gesticulation (or *gesturing*)." "His gestures are numerous and sometimes almost violent."

get   A prominent American grammarian, the late C. C. Fries, had access to thousands of letters written to a governmental agency by

Americans of varying backgrounds. One of his findings was that less literate writers used forms of *get* much more frequently than others did. OED devotes five pages of small print to *get*, and other dictionaries define scores of phrases using it. *Get* is thus a valuable word, but SWE avoids using it unnecessarily or inappropriately. SWE is unlikely to employ, for example, *get it* for "receive a scolding," *get his hooks into* for "take control of," *get with it* for "become aware of or alert." Other uses of *get* may be intelligently questioned, although a fair proportion of them are worth keeping. See also GET/OBTAIN/SECURE; GOT.

get/obtain/secure   Not quite synonymous. To *get* something, you may or may not exert any effort, but to *obtain* or *secure* something, you must ordinarily work, scheme, or take some other action. You can get a cold without effort, but you don't obtain or secure a cold. You may get money either by earning or stealing it or as a gift, but if you obtain or secure money, usually you must perform some act.

GI   World War II slang, corresponding to the *doughboy* of World War I. It first meant "galvanized iron," some historians say, then "general issue" or "government issue," and finally "an enlisted person" in one of the U.S. armed forces. Not applied to commissioned officers. The term became SWE but now is used less and less except with reference to World War II.

gibe/jibe   To *gibe* is to make fun of, to ridicule lightly: "He gibed her about her new hairdo." "Maybe that's a new hairdo," he gibed, "but I think it's a hairdon't – your hair don't look good." An alternative spelling is *jibe*. The other *jibe* is a nautical verb referring to a shift of a fore-and-aft sail, but more recently it has come to mean "harmonize, agree": "The account he gave the arresting officers did not jibe with what he said today." Some dictionaries call this use informal, but it appears fairly often in SWE.

gift   "Sam said that he had gifted her with a new Porsche." Both Sam's language and his intentions may disturb her if she is doubly a purist. SWE does not use *gift* as a verb, especially because it necessitates using *with*. It chooses the appropriate form of *give*.

gimmick   Nobody knows where this word came from, but it's useful for a trick or device to catch attention, sell something, or attain some other end in an uncommon way. It has become SWE.

gimpy   A somewhat unkind or jocular FF (slang) word to describe someone who limps.

girlfriend   See FEMALE COMPANION/GIRLFRIEND/MISTRESS.

give the cold shoulder   Cliché. Fairly widely employed to mean "ignore, slight, pay no attention to." The cliché is more meaningful if writer and reader both know that in medieval castles the welcome guests were treated to choice hot roast beef and the less welcome ones were given cold shoulder of mutton – tallowy and unpleasant.

given   Mathematical and, less often, scientific problems may begin, "Given (or *Given that*) A > B, how . . . ?" This use of participial *given* is SWE. In the 1980s the use of *given* as a noun equivalent became frequent, as in "It is a given that . . ." The meaning is "what is granted, what is true, what must be admitted." Although relatively new, this usage has also become SWE.

gizmo   Also spelled *gismo*. FF for "gadget" or for some whatchamacallit whose name is unknown or temporarily forgotten. *Widget, thingamajig,* and *doohicky* are among the other FF synonyms.

glance/glimpse   Fowler and Nicholson best expressed the difference: "The glimpse is what is seen by the glance." For example, if you take a *glance* at a store window, you get a *glimpse* of what is in it. The verb *glance* means to look quickly; it takes no object: "She glanced in his direction." *Glimpse* does take an object: "She glimpsed a slight grin on his face."

glean   Gleaners used to follow reapers (and in impoverished places still do) to pick up grains that were missed. The idea of gathering a small amount at a time is still implicit in the verb, which is seldom used as a substitute for *gather, collect, acquire, obtain, find,* or the like, except when the gathering is indeed done bit by bit.

glimpse   See GLANCE/GLIMPSE.

glitch   A word from outer space – or at least derived from American space ventures. Flesch says that Germans who aided our early efforts (Wernher von Braun and others) used the German *glitschig* ("slippery") in referring to certain pulsars, and that *glitch* came from that. It means "rather unaccountable interruptions, speedups," and the like. The useful word has become standard and has expanded from pulsars to mean any of the many mysterious little things that can go wrong in any operation. The sputters, pings, and other automobile eccentricities or the occasionally inexplicable behavior of a computer are examples. Authors and editors know that glitches in publishing are not infrequent.

glittering   SWE uses this word as the equivalent of *sparkling* – the sparkles being either literal or figurative. Glitter, like sparkles, is evanescent and may suggest gaudiness rather than intrinsic beauty. Users of SWE are dubious about "the glittering wedding ceremony of Prince Andrew and his bride," because *glittering* hints at cheap glamor.

glitzy   Related to *glitter*, German *glitzern* "glitter," and perhaps *ritzy*, *glitzy* describes something showy, shiny, expensive – like Hollywood movies based on Judith Krantz novels. It started as slang and is now SWE.

glorious   A strong word, associated with *glory*. Not used in SWE if *delightful* or *unusually pleasant* is more honest.

glutton/gourmand/gourmet   The *glutton* emphasizes quantity of food; the *gourmet*, quality. The glutton goes back for second helpings of roast beef while the gourmet is still savoring the *potage cressoniére* with the chef's special croutons. The *gourmand* ranks between the two. He enjoys food but is more choosy than the glutton, less so than the gourmet.

go all out FF for "do wholeheartedly," "give one's best," "try with enthusiasm and hard work."

go him one better FF or borderline SWE for "outdo him," "outperform him," "excel him in some way."

gobbledygook The coiner of this pejorative name for "officialese, language of bureaucracy" (probably a former congressman, Maury Maverick) said that much of that language reminded him of the gobbledy-gobbling of turkeys, which usually ends in a "gook." It is characterized by long but vague words, passive voice, lengthy and convoluted sentences, and often uncertain meaning.

God rest ye merry, Gentlemen That comma is in the right place – no comma after *ye*. The meaning is "God keep you merry, Gentlemen."

goes by the name of Appears in SWE but less frequently than *is named*, *is called*, *is popularly called*, or (most likely) *uses the alias*.

(it) goes without saying, needless to say Although the first reaction to either phrase may be "Then why say it?" each is a short way of telling the reader, "Presumably you are already familiar with the following bit of information, but you should keep it in mind in reading this passage." Occasional usage is found in SWE.

gofer An FF (slang) term more picturesque than *errand-boy* or *errand-girl* but equivalent in meaning. It's not likely to rise high among users of SWE; puns seldom do.

going (modifier) SWE for "current, prevailing, present": "the going rate of interest."

going on A CBS television reporter was not illustrating SWE when, in telling of a fire in Yellowstone Park, she referred to "the plight that is now going on." SWE does not use *go on*, *occur*, *happen*, or other verbs of movement when the subject is a noun that suggests the status quo. A plight, condition, situation, or status, for example, *exists* but does not *go on*.

going-over (noun) SWE, although most frequent in informal contexts, for (1) "inspection," (2) "scolding," (3) "rehearsing, repeating": "Give it a quick going-over." "Her mother gave her a real going-over." "Your story needs another going-over."

goings-on (noun) FF, used disapprovingly for "behavior, conduct": "I won't put up with such goings-on."

gold/golden As a rule, *gold* refers to the physical substance: "a gold coin." *Golden* is ordinarily figurative: "her golden hair," "a golden sunset."

good and ready SWE omits *good and* in most writing, although the phrase is widely used in FF for "completely ready."

good and sufficient reason One of the adjectives is usually enough, but both may sometimes be justifiable.

good benefit, good success   Are there any bad benefits or bad successes? SWE customarily omits *good*.

good long time   In expressions such as "a good many people" or "a good long time ago," *good* is equivalent to the adverb *very*. It only rarely appears in SWE.

good/well   The use of *good* and *well* may be one touchstone by which some employers may judge candidates for positions in which making a good impression on the educated public is important. Maybe not so much should hinge on two little words, but a candidate who explains lateness by saying, "My car wasn't running good this morning," may have not one but two strikes against him. The distinction is simple. If the word describes the subject, *good* is standard: "Her work was good." "The report looks good." But when the verb shows action and a word is needed to describe that action, *well* is standard: "My car wasn't running well." "She plays the piano well." See also BAD/BADLY; FEEL (GOOD/WELL).

goodly   Old-fashioned for "attractive" or "rather large": "a goodly appearance," "a goodly sum of cash."

goodwill   It's one word: "a message of goodwill," "a goodwill message." Obviously, two words are necessary in "No good will come of this" or the old-fashioned "He worked with a right good will."

goof   **1.** FF for "blunder, mistake, error," but it's moving toward SWE because none of its synonyms are equally good-natured, forgiving, and rather humorous. **2.** *Goof off* is FF (slang) for "waste time, loaf, do nothing of any importance": "Are you goofing off again?" **3.** *Goof up* is also FF (slang) for "bungle, make a mess of": "I goofed up. I goofed up the whole job."

goofy   This FF (slang) word describes rather affectionately a somewhat stupid person or silly mistakes of the sort that he or she may make.

gorgeous   Overused for "resplendent, brilliant, splendid, delightful," and the like, this word may be restricted by purists to decoration or outward appearance. They may say, for example, that a dress is gorgeous but that some other word should describe the girl wearing the dress. Bernstein approved of "gorgeous peacock," however, saying that the adjective is understood to refer to the plumage. Nonpurists, including many good writers, seldom bother about the distinction. They use the word sparingly, though, because of its strength.

got   A pseudonymous author in 1789 concocted a paragraph of about 150 words in which he used *got* 22 times and other forms of *get* six more. He started like this:

> I GOT on Horseback within ten minutes after I GOT your letter. When I GOT to Canterbury, I GOT a chaise for town. But I GOT wet through before I GOT to Canterbury, and I

HAVE GOT such a cold as I shall not be able to GET rid of in a Hurry.

Some teachers have foolishly ordered students never to use *got*. Instead of proscribing, they should prescribe: "For Occasional Use." See also GET; GET/OBTAIN/SECURE; GOT/GOTTEN.

got/gotten In British English the past participle of *get* is *(have) got*; *gotten* is rather rare. In American English *(have) got* and *(have) gotten* are both used but are not always interchangeable. "They've got enough food" is informal for either "They have enough food" or "They have obtained enough food," but "They've gotten enough food" has only the second meaning. In many other sentences, Americans use either word: "They've got (or *gotten*) together on several occasions." *Gotten* is less common in SWE than *got*.

gourmand/gourmet See GLUTTON/GOURMAND/GOURMET.

graduate (verb) FF says, "She graduated college." SWE says, "She graduated from college" or, now less likely, "She was graduated from college." The argument favoring the last example is that the institution does both the admitting and the graduating, but the reasoning has not convinced everyone. SANE favors "She graduated from college."

graffiti In Italian, *graffiti* is the plural of *graffito* ("crude drawing or inscription"). Theoretically, then, we should say, "The graffiti *were* ugly and offensive." Usage, however, is divided. Members of the Harper panel voted 51–49 in favor of *were*. Take your choice. Only seldom is there a need for the singular, "A graffito was . . ."

grammar school Used in the British Isles for a secondary school for academically superior students, but often in the United States for an elementary school. Most U.S. teachers and school officials, however, prefer *elementary school* to *grammar school*. There is a National Association of Elementary School Principals – not "Grammar School."

grand This was a strong word until weakened by overuse. Most "grand openings" are not really "noted for grandeur," "rich and sumptuous," or "stately, regal." A "grand time" is often no more than a pleasant evening. *Grand* deserves more grandeur than it is usually accorded. It has fallen into plebeian surroundings.

grandiloquent See ELOQUENT/GRANDILOQUENT/MAGNILOQUENT.

grandiose *Grandiose* started out well in life. For example, a writer in 1850 used it in describing Greek amphitheaters. But the word has sunk in reputation and now suggests pomposity, affectation, garish display, size but not solidity.

grateful/gratuitous Not related in meaning. A person who feels gratitude is *grateful*: "Ogden Nash said that if you are grateful for anything, it will probably be gone tomorrow." Something is *gratuitous* if it is freely given and probably unwanted: "gratuitous advice (*information, assistance,* or the like)."

gratuity/tip If your dinner costs more than most people can afford, you leave a *gratuity*; if less, a *tip*.

graze See BROWSE/GRAZE.

great Bernstein coined the term *atomic flyswatter* to describe unnecessarily powerful adjectives. *Great* is one of these. In SWE it is reserved for the "truly great" – something important, large, extraordinarily noteworthy, and probably even rare. SWE avoids *great* hairdos, detergents, ice cream bars, bird-calling devices, or even boyfriends.

Great Britain See BRITISH ISLES/ENGLAND/GREAT BRITAIN.

greenhorn Follett called *greenhorn* a "fine English coinage." Originally, it meant "a young animal with horns not fully developed" and was so used as early as the fifteenth century. Today it is an SWE synonym of *novice, inexperienced person*, or *recent immigrant* but is used most often as ridicule.

green house/greenhouse A *green house* has green paint. A *greenhouse* has green plants inside its glass walls and roof.

grind to a halt Criticized as a cliché, but what other rather dramatic way is there to suggest a slow, unpleasant process of stopping, like that of most trains?

grisly/grizzly *Grisly* means "horrible, gruesome, repugnant." Maybe that's how a grizzly bear looks to someone it is endangering. (In fact, its scientific name is *Ursa horribilis*.) *Grizzly*, however, really means "grayish, flecked with gray," and the grizzly bear's brown hair usually has gray or silver tips. A man's hair may be described as grizzly (or *grizzled*), but it is unlikely to be ugly enough to be called grisly.

groom Informal for *bridegroom*, but found sometimes in SWE. Some people don't like *groom* because of its association with stables. *Bridegroom*, incidentally, means "bride('s) man."

ground/grounds Usually interchangeable when the meaning is "reason, basis": "no ground(s) for making that statement." Lawyers generally use *grounds*: "grounds for legal action."

groupie Kings and other potentates have often traveled with entourages consisting of servants, friends, sycophants, advisers, lovers, and family. Modern entourages, most often the followers of popular music stars, may consist in part of *groupies* – a term most frequently applied to young persons of the opposite sex who believe they enjoy their dim share of the starlight. The word lingers on the boundary between FF and SWE.

grouse (verb) FF for "grumble, complain": "He groused about the too-soft boiled eggs."

grow smaller Sometimes condemned as a contradiction, this expression is SWE nevertheless. The reason: *grow* may mean "become," as in "grow tired," "grow faint."

guess Informal in the sense of "suppose, expect, believe," long regarded by the British as one of the most typical Americanisms but is now used often by them, too. In fact, Chaucer some six hundred years ago used "I guess" about as Americans do, except that he spelled it *gesse*. Perhaps partly because of British ridicule in the nineteenth century, *guess* in this sense still makes only occasional appearances in SWE.

guesstimate (also guestimate)   Although not yet listed in some dictionaries, *guesstimate* (or *guestimate*) is a valuable word for something more careful than a guess but less precise than an estimate.

guest   Needed: a word that means "paying guest," as in a hotel, because *guest* may now refer to one who pays or to one, such as a houseguest, whose food and lodging are provided without charge. "Be our guest" can be ambiguous in some contexts. SWE does what is needed to clarify the intended meaning.

guest host   Perhaps starting as a title for any of the numerous replacements for talk-show master of ceremonies Johnny Carson, *guest host* is an oxymoron (a union of contradictory terms, such as "the cheerful crapehanger"). It has been ridiculed and mocked, but applauded by a few who said, in effect, "OK, but what would *you* call the substitute host?" One answer: *substitute host* or, more informally, *substitute MC*.

guests   See COMPANY.

guilt feelings/guilty feelings   Interchangeable, with psychologists generally preferring the former. Linguistic conservatives advise *guilty feelings* or *feelings of guilt* to avoid using the noun *guilt* as a modifier. SWE uses both.

gumption   This useful word is most likely to be found in informal contexts. It means not so much "intelligence" as "enterprise" combined with "shrewdness," a dash of "imaginativeness" and a little bit of "chutzpah." It appears now and then in SWE.

guru   In Hinduism, a *guru* is a spiritual teacher, a holy man. In American, a (usually) respected leader who advocates rather specific points of view concerning finance, political science, ethics, or other serious and somewhat abstract fields: "Milton Friedman – the guru of the monetarists." The word is used in SWE – often, for example, in the Business section of the *New York Times*.

gut feeling, gut issue, gut reaction   FF and unattractive synonyms for "deep feeling," "basic issue," and "quick or instinctive reaction." The SWE *visceral* is unfamiliar to many people, so SWE often chooses *deep feeling* or the like.

guts   Although intended as praise indicating bravery or boldness in an expression such as "He's got guts," the word carries unpleasant connotations of disemboweled rabbits. Except in references to entrails and the like, it is generally FF but occasionally SWE.

guy   FF for "man" or less often "man or woman" or even "woman": "See those guys over there? The tall fellow and the blonde girl?"

H

hail/hale In stories such as Westerns an old-timer may ask, "Where d'ye *hail from*, stranger?" This old-fashioned expression obviously means "come from." *Hail* may also mean "call, summon," as in "hail a cab." *Hale*, in a rather rare use, may mean "cause to come," used especially in the expression "hale into court." More frequently, it is an adjective for "healthy, vigorous," as in the phrase *hale and hearty*, which usually describes an old person, even though young ones are likely to be haler and heartier.

hairy FF (slang) when used to mean "difficult, dangerous, harrowing,": "Driving for hours on icy roads is a hairy experience."

half It is redundant to use both *a* and *an* (or two *a*'s) with *half*: not "We waited a half an hour" but "We waited a half hour" or "We waited half an hour."

half-mast/half-staff With reference to a position of a flag, the terms are interchangeable.

handgun See AUTOMATIC/PISTOL/REVOLVER.

handle in routine fashion SWE prefers the shorter *handle routinely*.

hang in there Because of the "moral sustenance" it may provide, Flesch calls *hang in there* "one of the great creative idioms of the English language." Probably Flesch is exaggerating, but this expression, although still somewhat slangy, has been increasingly used to lend encouragement to a skier in a crevasse, a patient in a hospital, a couple contemplating a divorce, and countless other people in harrowing circumstances. It is increasingly used in SWE.

hanged/hung For the sense "executed legally by hanging," many SWE writers prefer *hanged*: "The murderer was hanged at dawn." The legal phrase is "hanged until dead." FF and often SWE use *hung* as both the past tense and past participle of *hang*, in all its meanings. "He hung himself" is standard, because legal execution is not involved.

hang-up 1. An imprecise informal term and perhaps for that reason not listed in the *Dictionary of Behavioral Science*, this term may mean "inhibition, fear, worry, concern, emotional disturbance, overenthusiasm," or any possible cause of any of those. Because of such vagueness, SWE either avoids *hang-up* or else makes it explicit. It is much more common in FF. 2. It is SWE in the sense "something that can be hung from something else": "One of the hang-ups was a small mobile."

happening (noun) Starting perhaps in the 1960s in Woodstock, Greenwich Village, and then at other celebrations that hippies called *happenings*, the term spread to television, often as a synonym for "variety show," and then sometimes shrank to designate a family gathering or even a birthday party. The peregrinations of a word are often fascinating to follow. This one has seldom been given the sanctity of an SWE context unless between the protective arms of quotation marks.

happiness/pleasure Although we often speak of "a moment of happiness," in general happiness is more lasting than pleasure. For that reason we refer to "a happy life" when we are talking about a lifetime, but "a pleasant life" when referring to a shorter period. In addition to having greater duration, happiness also is likely to be less sensual, more quiet and contented. The Founding Fathers did not write about "life, liberty, and the pursuit of pleasure."

harangue/tirade Each is a noisy speech. A *harangue* is usually delivered to several or many persons, but a *tirade* may have an audience of one or a few. The harangue is likely to be vociferously and unpleasantly argumentative, the tirade bitterly, almost uncontrollably assertive and angry.

harbor/port Often used interchangeably, although to a sailor a *harbor* is any place that provides safe or sheltered anchorage, and a *port* is in a harbor, but is equipped for the loading and unloading of freight or passengers. See also DOCK/PIER/WHARF.

hard hat Because hard hats are required in much construction work, *hard hat* is often used in both FF and SWE to mean a worker who needs such protection. The word is also used as a modifier: "a hard-hat job."

hard put An SWE idiom in such sentences as "The Democrats will be hard put to win the majority of Senate seats" (meaning that they will have great difficulty). The odd expression may come from equestrian competition and relate to "putting" a horse to a jump.

hardly no/hardly none Double negatives. SWE substitutes *hardly any, almost no,* or *very few. Scarcely* appears in similar FF double negatives: *has scarcely none, scarcely no money, didn't scarcely find any;* or even triple negatives such as *didn't scarcely find none.*

hardly . . . than, scarcely . . . than SWE prefers *when* to *than* in sentences such as "She had hardly *(scarcely, barely)* entered the house when (not *than*) she heard Clara sobbing softly." Because the relationship is one of time, *when* is more logical.

hard-nosed In sports, a *hard-nosed* player is one who is tough, fearless, determined, and perhaps merciless. From sports the term has spread to politics, business, and other fields. Like many other metaphorical terms, it is still classed in dictionaries as informal, but it is not infrequent in SWE.

hardware/liveware/software In computerese, *hardware* consists of the equipment itself – keyboard, monitor, printer, and the like. The *liveware* (an infrequently used term) is the operator. The *software* is the programs, instruction books, and so on used by the liveware as he works with the hardware. In education, hardware is again equipment – projectors, recorders, radios, television sets, and the like – and software is slides, films, tapes, manuals, or other items used in or with the hardware.

hardwood/softwood A *hardwood* tree (oak, maple, cherry, and so on) is deciduous, with broad leaves that fall annually. The term *softwood* is used less often. It applies to coniferous trees (pine, spruce, and so on), which bear cones, have needle-shaped leaves, and are commonly called "evergreens."

hardy/hearty Sometimes confused because of similarity of sound. *Hardy* means "robust," "long-lasting," "able to endure inclement weather": "hardy outdoor man," "a hardy perennial." *Hearty* means "pleasantly warm, outgoing" as in "hearty greetings"; "strong," as in "hearty support"; "nourishing," as in "a hearty lunch." (What would a *hardy* lunch be?)

harebrained Since the meaning is "stupid like a rabbit," *harebrained* is preferable to *hairbrained*, given as a variant in some dictionaries. (*Hair-triggered* is standard, though: it suggests a trigger so sensitive that the weight of a hair can move it.)

harmony/melody The *Oxford Dictionary of Music* explains the difference as "vertical" vs. "horizontal." Notes that are simultaneously blended, as in a chord, are in *harmony*, but the succession of musical sounds constitutes a *melody*.

hassle Now becoming standard for "disagreement, small fight," *hassle* ordinarily is not used for a major confrontation.

haste/hasten *Haste*, a noun, as in "Make haste!" is no longer used as a verb: "Haste!" The verb is now *hasten*, although *hurry* is much more common: "The butler hastened to bring in the tea." "The butler hastened the maid on her way."

haughtiness See ARROGANCE/CONCEIT/HAUGHTINESS . . .

have reference to Not always avoidable, but in unnecesssarily wordy expressions such as "the story I have reference to," SWE substitutes something like "the story I mean."

he (the _____) "The clerk reported to the manager that he (the clerk) had unintentionally overcharged a customer." SWE tries to recast such a sentence to eliminate the awkward *he (the clerk)* or, of course, *she (the clerk)*. In the example, since no misunderstanding is likely, *(the clerk)* may be deleted. If misunderstanding might occur, one solution is to recast as "The clerk reported an unintentional overcharge to . . ." Another is to use direct address: "The clerk told the manager, 'I unintentionally . . .'"

he, him, his/she, her, hers/it, its/they, them, their, theirs SWE tries to make sure that the reader immediately understands the antecedent. (Editors sometimes ask "Who he?" in margins of manuscripts. They may also do that when a named person should be further identified.) SWE avoids sentences like these: "Mrs. Claire Prior will be the hostess. He is the president of the Nu-Times Company." (Substitute *Mr. Prior* or *Her husband* for *he*, or omit the whole sentence as irrelevant.) "The Tim Ranch family have faith in education. She is a graduate of Wellesley." (Who she? Mrs. Ranch? A daughter?) "The lawyer told the doctor that he had made a mistake." (Who he?) "The fireplace was roaring because it was windy." (A windy fireplace?)

he is a man who . . . , she is a woman who . . . It's usually not necessary to identify or describe a person as a man or a woman. SWE omits four of the five words.

he or she Many feminists who disliked a historically standard sentence such as "Everyone should solve *his* own problems if *he* can," saying that it left women out of consideration, have now decided that there are more important battles to fight in order to attain completely equal rights. One reason for abandoning the skirmish is that a good revision is hard to find. Awkward: "Everyone should solve his or her own problems if he or she can." Ungrammatical but widely used: "Everyone should solve their own problems if they can." Changing the subject to *People* will work, but not if the writer wants to concentrate on individuals. One solution: Use *he* unless it is important to emphasize that both sexes are meant. Another: Alternate, sometimes using *he*, sometimes *she*. Of course, use *she* for a member of an all-female group, *he* when each is male. (I once used *heshe, himer,* and *hiser* on a trial run in a book, but they were stillborn. The book was distributed by two major book clubs, but nobody liked my pronouns.)

119

He, She SWE capitalizes a pronoun referring to God: "Our Heavenly Father, He who . . ." "Our Heavenly Mother, She who . . ." Some writers, but apparently not most, capitalize *He* and *She* in referring to Jesus and the Virgin Mary.

head up In "Ms. Grove will head up the committee" and the like, *head* is enough, or *chair, lead, direct,* or (for an investigation) *conduct.* SWE deletes *up.*

headquarter(s) 1. "The expedition headquartered near St. Louis." Conservatives ordinarily disapprove of a shift that makes a noun a verb, especially if the result is cumbersome, as this seems. But the alternative, "set up headquarters" or "located its headquarters," is longer. Some dictionaries and some authors of histories treat the verb as standard. 2. The verb with *headquarters* as its subject is usually plural, but sometimes SWE uses a singular.

healthful/healthy Probably the battle is lost, but there's a good reason for keeping *healthful* instead of making *healthy* do two unlike jobs. Conservatives say that *healthful* describes something that promotes health, *healthy* something (or someone) that has health. If we write, "These vegetables are healthy," the meaning is uncertain. Are we saying that the vegetables are vigorous or that they are good for us? Using *healthful* for the second sense would prevent misinterpretation. SWE sometimes but not uniformly differentiates between the words.

heap SWE for "a somewhat disorderly pile": "a heap of trash." When Edgar A. Guest wrote, "It takes a heap o' livin' / To make a house a home," he was using *heap* in the FF (informal) sense meaning "lots, a great deal." The plural is sometimes used similarly: "heaps of good wishes." *Heap* for "an almost worn-out car: is FF (slang).

hear/listen In a world filled with sounds, many strike our eardrums – are *heard* – but pass unnoticed. When we *listen* to any of these abundant sounds, we pay attention, trying to interpret or otherwise make sense of them. Obviously, then, we hear much that we do not listen to. Less frequently, we listen but cannot hear because our hearing apparatus is not sharp enough or because an expected sound does not materialize: "She listened for the friendly ring of the telephone, but it was inexplicably silent."

hear tell FF (dialectal) for "hear, be told": "I heard (or *heerd*) tell you was with Zeldie last week."

heart-rendering Sorry, but a movie (or anything else) is never *heart-rendering* unless a heart can be rendered ("clarified by melting") as lard is. SWE would describe the movie as *heart-rending*.

hearty See HARDY/HEARTY.

heavy Because *heavy* has more than a score of legitimate meanings, it can easily be overused. One way to avoid the problem is to substitute a different word in modifying an intangible, for example, *ponderous* style, *substantial* losses, *severe* cutbacks, *pungent* odor, *grave* matters of state, *oppressive* taxes.

Hebrew/Israeli/Jewish/Yiddish (language) *Hebrew* is the language of the Old Testament and (in a modern version) of many people in today's Israel. These people are *Israelis*, but there is no Israeli language. We may speak of *Jewish* customs, Jewish life, and the like, but there is no Jewish language. *Yiddish* is a blend of languages long spoken by many European Jews, including large numbers who emigrated to the United States. It is basically a German dialect to which some Hebrew and Eastern European words have been added. See also ISRAELI/JEW.

hectometer *Centimeter, meter,* and *kilometer* are widely known, but the useful *hectometer* (100 meters) is rarely seen or heard.

hedonist See EPICURE/EPICUREAN/HEDONIST.

heist Once slang, now called informal in dictionaries for "steal, rob, hijack," or, as a noun, "theft, robbery, hijacking." It's rare in SWE, except in newspapers.

helicopter (verb) Although the Germans manage long verbs in addition to their sometimes immense nouns, verbs of more than three syllables occur infrequently in English and so are likely to seem awkward. Sentences such as "We helicoptered from Midway to O'Hare" do exist in SWE, probably because "We flew by helicopter" is more wordy. *Chopped* would be ambiguous, and *choppered* is uglier than *helicoptered*.

hell of a As in "a hell of a lot of trouble." Informal for "serious."

Perhaps not suitable for a letter to Great-Aunt Matilda, but publications as highly regarded as *Time* and *Harper's* may occasionally comment on the "hell of a mess" somebody thinks the world, or at least part of it, is in.

helm/rudder/tiller In a boat a *helm* or a *tiller* is used to move the *rudder*, which is a metal or wooden plate under the stern. The movement causes the vessel to alter its course. The tiller is in the shape of a bar or heavy rod, but the helm, especially on a ship, is probably a wheel. Figuratively, *taking the helm* and *taking the tiller* are interchangeable for "taking charge."

help Once criticized when used to mean "avoid, refrain from," as in "Many drunkards don't like drinking, but they can't help doing it," *help* in this sense is now SWE, even though the meaning is far from the usual one. See also CANNOT BUT.

helpmate/helpmeet Interchangeable. The King James version of Genesis 2:18 says that God, looking at the lonely Adam, declared, "I will make an help meet [an old word for 'suitable'] for him." When *meet* was no longer understood to mean "suitable," ministers and others interpreted *an help meet* as *a helpmeet* ("helper"). But that, too, seemed to make little sense, so *helpmate* developed. Now both words are SWE.

hemlock Some Americans have wondered how a drink made from hemlock could have killed Socrates, since their own ancestors drank hemlock tea. The two hemlocks are of different genera. The European one is a poisonous plant of the parsley family, but the American one is a coniferous tree.

hence/thence/whence *Hence*, meaning "from here," *thence*, "from there," and *whence*, "from where," have an archaic flavor, reminiscent of "Get thee hence" or "Whence he came I know not." A writer of SWE who is not bothered by the old-fashioned air at least avoids using *from* with any of these words.

henceforth/thenceforth Seldom used today except in legal documents.

hereditary/innate A *hereditary* trait is inherited from earlier generations. This may also be true of an *innate* quality, but usually *innate* means simply "present at birth." Perhaps because it is not possible to tell exactly what was inherited and what was not, SWE does not invariably try to differentiate the two words, although geneticists say, for example, that eye, skin, or hair color is hereditary, not innate.

hereof/heretofore/hereunto/herewith/theretofore Legalese for "of this," "before this," "to this," "with this," and "before that," respectively.

heroic 1. *A*, not *an*, usually precedes it. 2. *Heroic*, not *heroical*, is usual in SWE.

heroics Requires a plural verb, is now often used mockingly: "Such congressional heroics should be told in song and story!"

her's Never in SWE. See APOSTROPHE.

hew *Chop* or *cut (down)* is usual, but *hew* is now rare in the United States.

hex *Hex* comes by way of Pennsylvania German from German *Hexe* ("witch") and now is an SWE synonym for "magic spell, bad influence, nemesis" or as a verb "bewitch, cause bad luck." Most modern Pennsylvania Germans laugh good-naturedly at the old superstitions, but many take commercial advantage of them.

high/lofty/tall *High* is the general term and often can be used for either *tall* or *lofty*. Unlike *tall*, *high* may be applied to abstractions: "high ideals." *Tall* means "higher than average" or "high in relation to breadth": "a tall woman," "a tall grandfather's clock." *Tall* is more likely than the others in references to living things: "tall trees" (although *lofty* is aptly applied to the giant redwoods). *Lofty*, seldom used, refers to impressive height: "Lofty Mt. Denali," "lofty ceilings." It is applied, often rather unbelievingly or semihumorously, to abstractions: "lofty ideals," "lofty thoughts."

high noon In SWE, ordinarily used only for "precisely 12 M.," not 11:59 A.M. or 12:01 P.M.

highbrow/lowbrow/middlebrow Although *middlebrow* is seldom seen or heard, *lowbrow* and *highbrow* are not rare, even in SWE. The alternatives are wordy locutions such as "a person of high intelligence and considerable culture."

highfalutin (also *hifalutin*) An unpretentious word for "pretentious." It knocks the pomposity out of users of high-flown language, the glitz out of purchasers of hundred-dollar perfumes. From frontier slang of the sort used to discombobulate stuffed shirts it has moved up the stairway to a dictionary rating of "informal" and to occasional SWE use.

highlight (noun and verb) Established for centuries as a noun, *highlight* is now widely – perhaps too widely – used as a verb: "highlighted today's news stories," "highlight the eyelashes," "highlights the congressional hearings today." Sometimes *emphasize, feature, stress, play up, are most prominent, add color to*, or something else may be substituted.

hijack, hijacker, hijacking These words sound slangy, but since no short synonyms exist, they are now listed as standard in most dictionaries. *Highjack* is an alternative spelling.

hike Now SWE for "increase," as in "wage hike." Most useful to writers of headlines.

hilarious A strong word. A *hilarious* movie is not merely amusing, funny, humorous, witty.

hillbillies Don't call us that when we can hear you!

hinder/prevent To *hinder* is to present difficulties, to delay: "A few fallen branches hindered our progress along the road." To *prevent* is to stop completely, to keep (something) from happening: "Fallen trees prevented our driving farther."

hindsight/retrospect(ion) *Retrospection* is thoughtful recall, review, or evaluation of past decisions and events. (*Retrospect* is rarely used except in the phrase *in retrospect*.) *Hindsight* also refers to looking back but carries the connotation of critical evaluation often tinged with regret: "Hindsight told him that he should have resigned earlier."

hippie An SWE word, but now seldom used except nostalgically by former "flower children," most of whom have changed from long-haired, free-loving, pot-smoking idealists to kempt, married, relatively abstemious pragmatists.

historic/historical A *historical* event can be any in history, whether important or not. A *historic* event is an especially memorable one. A place, such as a battlefield, may be historic, is associated with historical events, but is not itself likely to be called historical. SWE uses either *a* or *an* before both words, with *a* perhaps moving ahead because the *h* is rather distinctly pronounced.

123

historic/momentous Both words are overused by sports announcers in describing a contest a little more important than most. Perhaps the very first World Series game or the ones postponed in 1989 by a California earthquake were historic or momentous or both, but the words are trivialized if used with regard to every World Series or Super Bowl. *Momentous* differs from *historic* mainly by especially emphasizing the consequences, the later impact, of the event. See also EPIC.

hit over the head This idiom is established, but *hit on the head* is more logical.

hither, thither, whither All three are bookish, obsolescent words, usually avoided unless an archaic flavor is desirable. One exception is "a come-hither smile," never out of date.

hitherto SWE prefers *previously, earlier,* or *up to that time.*

hobnob *Hobnob* is an SWE word. It was associated hundreds of years ago with companionable drinking and now means "to talk with companionably," "to mix with in friendly fashion."

hock SWE but informal for "pawn" (verb) or "state of being pawned" (noun). In recent years the image of the pawnshop has faded somewhat, so that someone who claims to be "in hock" simply means that he or she is in debt – probably not to a pawnbroker.

hocus-pocus 1. An SWE word for "trickery, magic, nonsense." 2. The verb *hocus* is also standard, although rarely used. It means "deceive," "cheat," "adulterate," or "conceal as a drug in food or drink": "He hocused me again." "She hocused the coffee with vodka." ". . . the vodka with water."

hog (verb) In such expressions as "trying to hog the show," "hog the camera," or "hogging the time of other speakers," *hog* means "use more than a fair share of." It dates back to as early as 1887 and is now SWE, though informal.

hoi polloi Since the expression means "the common people," SWE doesn't write "*the* hoi polloi." In fact, since the term is condescending, many writers avoid it.

hokey   Probably derived from *hocus-pocus*, this adjective means "contrived," "unrealistic," or "too sentimental": "His first short story was a hokey account of bank robbers with hearts of gold," "a hokey movie about children who are never even mischievous." It is usually FF but does appear in informal SWE. See also HOCUS-POCUS.

hold (steady vs. steadily)   It's usually *hold steady* in both FF and SWE. The meaning of "Hold it steady" is "Hold it so that it remains steady." *Hold steadily* is rarely seen, but it's possible in the sense of "constantly": "He held the pose steadily for an hour." Similar comments apply to *hold firm* vs. *firmly*.

holdup   See BURGLARY/HOLDUP/ROBBERY . . .

hollow tube   Has anyone ever seen an unhollow tube?

holocaust   Capitalized, *Holocaust* has come to mean Hitler's attempt to exterminate the Jews, especially in the cinerators of concentration camps. Uncapitalized, *holocaust* most often means a tremendously destructive fire, but – in a use sometimes questioned – it may mean any great disaster. The derivation, from a Greek word for "entirely burned," suggests that the implication of fire should be retained (although admittedly many words have strayed from their historical meanings).

home/house   Follett illustrates a distinction that real-estate agents ignore: "Homes are not bought and sold, houses are." A *house*, conservatives like Follett say, is a physical structure. A *home* is not merely a structure but also a place of kindness, affection, and shared work and play, a place where memories – both pleasant and less than pleasant – gradually accumulate. Follett and his friends have lost to commercialism.

homely   Has different meanings in Great Britain and the United States. A woman called *homely* in London may be pleased, especially if she is proud of her homey charm – the sort of wife a man would be glad to come home to. A woman in New York may feel insulted, because she interprets *homely* as "unattractive."

homicide/manslaughter/murder   *Homicide* includes both manslaughter and murder, as well as almost any other killing of one person by another (unless as a result of war, court action, or – debated questions – abortion or euthanasia). *Manslaughter* in U.S. law is the illegal killing of one person by another without intent to do injury – for example, by a negligent driver. *Murder* is like manslaughter but involves "malice aforethought," interpreted as a desire – perhaps a plan – to do injury even if not to kill.

homosexual   Either a male or a female can be *homosexual*, although the word increasingly is applied to males only. The language needs a male equivalent of *lesbian*.

honkey, honkie, honky   An FF (slang) word used by some blacks to disparage whites; the reverse equivalent of *nigger*. All such offensive expressions are generally avoided in SWE except in direct quotation.

hooked This is still FF (slang) in the sense of "addicted." The addiction need not be to drugs; it may be to gambling, computers, or classical or rock music.

hooker This word appears to be more widely used, in most kinds of context, than *whore, harlot, prostitute*, or any other such word. It may still be called slang or informal, but it is much less so than a hundred or so clearly slang words with the same meaning. It frequently appears in well-edited publications.

hope Fowler lists three problem constructions and includes examples parallel to these: **1.** Double passive, as in "A better result is to be hoped to be attained tomorrow." Better: "The designers hope to attain . . ." **2.** Analogy with *expect*: "We hope him to do well." Better: "We hope that he does well" or "We expect him to do well." **3.** Omission of a needed *it*: "Plans for what is hoped will be the city's greatest parade have been completed." Better: Insert *it* before *is hoped*.

hope I remember "I hope I remember (*find, see*, and so on) it" is a standard Americanism in which a present-tense verb is used for future time. Conservative British speakers are likely to say, "I hope (that) I will remember it" or "I hope to remember it."

hope, hopeful/optimism, optimistic *Optimism* and *optimistic* suggest a higher probability of a favorable outcome than *hope* and *hopeful* do. A person can be hopeful about winning a lottery without being optimistic.

hopeless See DESPERATE/HOPELESS.

horn To classical musicians, *horn* means "French horn." To others it may include any brass instrument, or possibly even woodwinds. Modern dictionaries treat both definitions as standard. An English horn is technically a woodwind, somewhat similar to an oboe.

horrible, horribly Like the similar *dreadful, horrible* has degenerated in meaning from "filling with horror" to the much weaker "very bad" or "highly unpleasant": "a horrible day at the office." Its substitutes, including *horrid, horrifying, ghastly*, and perhaps *grim*, are following the same downward path. Today, to express the idea that the sight of a bloody accident filled you with horror, that's probably the way you have to say it, unless you choose to substitute specific details. "Horrible accident" has been demeaned to signify (in some FF) no more than a scratch or a broken fingernail.

hostess Despite the gradual disappearance of *poetess, sculptress*, and other such words often considered sexist, *hostess* is still an active noun. The occasional verb use, however, as in "hostessing a party," seems to be vanishing.

hot cup of coffee See COLD GLASS OF MILK/HOT CUP OF COFFEE.

hot-water heater *Hot* is unnecessary.

hour See FOOT.

house See HOME/HOUSE.

housewares SWE retains the *s*. Although *silverware, earthenware,* and several other such words are standard without the *s*, each of those refers to a single variety of "ware," but *housewares* includes several kinds.

how come Usually considered informal for "Why?" in sentences such as "How come the medicine has lost its effectiveness?" In a rare reversal, RHD calls the expression informal, but the conservative AHD defines it without comment. It's infrequent in SWE.

how ever/however Written as two words in sentences such as "How ever did you stay so calm in that emergency?" The fact that two words are essential is indicated by the alternative phrasing, "How did you ever . . . ?" When the meaning is "no matter how" or "nevertheless," *however* is standard: "However wise they are, they cannot solve every personal problem." "However, they will try to help you."

hubris OED gives an 1831 citation for the adjective *hubristic* ("insolent, contemptuous"), but the noun *hubris* ("arrogance, presumption") has been in wide use only since about 1960. Now it is fully established, although still not familiar to some readers.

huddle A good word for a brief conference on the football field, but probably executives and other high officials *meet, confer,* or *hold a discussion,* even though journalists may say that "the three prime ministers huddled." Other SWE items use the word occasionally.

huge throng Nobody has ever seen a small throng. SWE omits *huge*.

huh-uh Some writers confuse the negative *huh-uh* with the affirmative *uh-huh*.

human (noun) Is *human* a noun as well as an adjective? *Human* or *human being*? The argument has long continued, and differences of opinion still exist. Most dictionaries now treat both *human* and *human being* as standard. Some writers avoid a choice by using *person(s)* or *people*. See also BOVINE.

human/humane Although once the same word, *human* and *humane* are now differentiated. *Human* refers to any characteristic – good or bad – of people: "That's only human." *Humane* has only good connotations. It means "kind, helpful, sympathetic, compassionate": "humane treatment of animals."

humanist/humanitarian A *humanist* is a student of the humanities, often with emphasis on the classics, or a student of humans and their well-being. A *humanitarian* deals more with concrete cases than with theory. While a humanist makes a study of charity, a humanitarian leads the local food drive on behalf of the poor.

humble 1. Usually preceded by *a*, not *an*, because most people pronounce the *h*. 2. "In my humble opinion" is seldom said by a truly humble person, who (as Roy Copperud wittily notes) most likely will "humbly adopt the views of others."

humbug An example of how a colorful word sometimes ascends from slang to complete acceptance. A boost from Ebenezer Scrooge helped. The word now means not only "nonsense," the Scroogean application, but also "hoax" or, referring to a person, "charlatan, impostor": "He's a humbug."

humongous FF (slang) based on *huge* and *tremendous*: "At the top of the beanpole was a humongous giant." "I've got a humongous idea."

humor/wit *Humor* is usually more kindly than *wit*. A humorous person looks with amusement on human foibles and on the absurdities that characterize much in life. Although "black humor" reflects an almost hopeless view of life, most humor is much more tolerant. The eighteenth-century humorist Joseph Addison, for example, poked gentle fun at coquettes, empty-headed young men, and many others. *Wit* is often more biting than humor and is based largely on verbal cleverness. Ambrose Bierce was the American wit who said that *belladonna* in Italian means "a beautiful woman" and in English "a deadly poison." That proves, he said, the identity of the two languages. See also BLACK HUMOR/SICK HUMOR.

hunch *Hunch*, as in "having (or *playing*) a hunch," may sound like modern slang, but it has been common in American English since about 1900, and in different senses ("a thrust" or "a lump") in British English for several centuries.

hung See HANGED/HUNG.

hurl SWE uses *hurl* only when such a powerful verb is appropriate. Most people *throw* stones instead of *hurling* them. And a remark or even a curse that is hurled must be uttered with great vehemence. A strong-armed baseball player may justifiably be called a *hurler*.

hurricane/typhoon A *hurricane* has spinning winds exceeding seventy-five miles an hour. It originates in the Caribbean or the warm waters of the Atlantic. A *typhoon* has the same description, but it occurs in the China Sea or the western Pacific. See also CYCLONE/TORNADO.

hurting Now SWE even with subjects that can have no feelings, such as "Efforts to aid Bangladesh are hurting because most Americans know little about the country." Many writers, however, would substitute *being hurt* or *hampered*.

hype Some hypodermic injections are stimulants. The shortened form of *hypodermic, hype*, has existed since about 1960 with the meaning "something that stimulates sales." Hype may be "socially accepted fraud," as Flesch defines it, but often it is only high-powered or gimmicky salesmanship. The word is slang or informal but sometimes finds its way into serious discussion, including SWE. It may be either a noun or a verb.

hyper-/hypo- One way to remember the difference between these prefixes is to recall familiar words to remind you that *hyper-* means "above" and *hypo-* "below." For example, a hyperactive child is *above* average in activeness, and a hypodermic needle goes *below* the skin.

hypnotic   Refers to hypnotism, not to normal sleep. A drug that assists falling asleep may be described as *sleep-inducing* or (at the risk of incomprehension) *soporific*.

I

I   In most scholarly and scientific writing and in official corporate reports, news stories, or the like, use of the first person is not permitted or, at best, is unorthodox. In other writing *I* is usually preferable to *the author, the writer,* or *the present writer.* See also PRESENT WRITER.

I don't think   This idiom, as in "I don't think the chief will consent," has been attacked because obviously the speaker *is* thinking. Purists insist on "I think (or *believe*) the chief will not consent," and obviously logic is on their side. But the idiom is firmly established.

-ic/-ical   Many adjectives have both -*ic* and -*ical* forms with the same meanings, for example, *strategic, strategical; tyrannic, tyrannical.* Unless the longer word improves the rhythm of a sentence, SANE favors the shorter. See also GEOGRAPHIC, GEOGRAPHICAL . . .

ice water (*tea*, and so on)   Purists ask for *iced water*, in a restaurant, believing that *ice water* can be only melted ice. But Americans have so persistently ordered *ice water* that the term is now standard. A battle is still going on between *ice* tea (or coffee) and *iced*, with *iced* ahead. *Iced drinks* is also SWE.

-ics   Names of sciences ending in -*ics* are treated as singular: "Ethics is a branch of philosophy." "Acoustics is important to many architects." Some of these words may be used other than as names of sciences and then are usually treated as plurals: "Her ethics are questionable," meaning her standards of conduct. See also ACOUSTICS; ETHICS/ETHICAL/ETHICS.

idea   A word broad enough to encompass almost any thought, any product of the mind. Often, however, a more precise word is preferable. Among the choices: *assumption, belief, conception, conviction, fancy, feeling, image, impression, notion, opinion, plan, principle, scheme, significance, solution, theory, view, viewpoint.*

ideal   See EXAMPLE/SAMPLE/SPECIMEN.

IDENTIFICATIONS (PILING UP)   "Well-known Sioux City soft-drink bottler Herman Schmidt" is journalese for "Herman Schmidt, a well-known soft-drink bottler from Sioux City." Certainly, journalists must identify people they write about, but putting two or more identifications before the name, or putting four or more of them in the same sentence, often results in awkwardness.

identified with   Dubious for "in the employ of," as in "Mr. Rasmussen was identified with the Crown Corporation for thirty years."

SWE substitutes *was employed by, worked for, was an officer of,* or something similar.

identify with "Some young people try to identify with favorite fictional characters." Conservatives ask for *themselves* after *identify,* but psychologists use the verb without an object (this applies even to conservative psychologists). SWE accepts both versions.

idiot/imbecile/moron The *Dictionary* of *Behavioral Science* says that an *idiot* has an IQ below 25 and cannot learn to speak, read, or write. An *imbecile* has an IQ between 25 and 50, a mental age between two and seven years. A *moron* has an IQ between 50 and 70 and can usually perform simple tasks under supervision. In the United States, the term *feebleminded* includes all three groups, but in Britain it's synonymous with *moron.* All four of these terms are SWE, but because they unfortunately are often used by the unkind or unwitting as terms of ridicule, many writers prefer a euphemism such as *mentally retarded person* or *slow learner.*

idle (verb) Long established as SWE in sentences such as "The strike has idled 350 workers."

idle rich Some are idle, others not. Some may work harder than you or I. SWE generally tries to be fair and to avoid stereotypes of the rich, the poor, or anyone else.

i.e. See E.G./I.E.

if and when Usually either *if* or *when* will suffice.

if I were/if I was More frequently needed is *were,* as in "if I were you," "if Janice Smith were president." The reason is that the statements are contrary to fact: I am not you, and Smith is not president. The subjunctive *were* is customary in *if*-clauses that refer to such unreality. However, in one instance *if . . . was* is standard: when the statement is *not* definitely contrary to fact. For instance, assume that we are not certain whether Pauline was or was not at a meeting. We say correctly, "If Pauline *was* at the meeting, she may have an answer for us." Another example: "If I was crazy, I'm not crazy now."

if need be SWE, but sounds old-fashioned. *If necessary* is more likely today.

if that were the case Wordy for *if so.*

if/whether Either word is used in SWE as an opener in an indirect question. "Mrs. Thatcher asked whether (of *if*) the Conservative majority would agree." *Whether* is more likely than *if* to introduce two or more possibilities: "Whether we lose, tie, or win, we intend to play well."

iffy A word often used by Franklin D. Roosevelt to mean "uncertain, problematic, doubtful, questionable, hypothetical." If it was good enough for him, it should be good enough for most of us. Dictionaries, however, insist that it is suitable only for informal contexts.

ignorant/illiterate *Illiterate* basically means "unable to read and write" but is often used to mean also "uneducated, lacking in culture." The relatively recent term *functionally illiterate* means "not well enough educated to perform more than menial tasks." *Ignorant* is a broader term, although lack of formal education is usually a contributing cause of ignorance. All of us are mainly ignorant: most of the world's knowledge is unknown to us. On the other hand, as William Cobden said long ago, if a plowman "knows how to plow, he is not to be called an ignorant man."

ignorant See DUMB/IGNORANT/STUPID.

ill/illy Comparative forms are *more ill* or *worse*, superlative *most ill* or *worst*. Although usually an adjective, as in "an ill person" and "She is ill," the word may also be an adverb, as in "ill defined." *Illy* is rare and not needed: "an ill-defined (not *illy defined*) task." (Both Thomas Jefferson and Washington Irving, however, did use *illy*.)

ill/sick Interchangeable in the United States, although in England *sick* almost always means "nauseated." Some Americans feel that *ill* is for some reason a "nicer" word.

illegal/illegitimate/illicit/unlawful *Illegal* and *unlawful* both mean "forbidden by law." *Illegitimate* may have that meaning, too, but earlier meant "born out of wedlock," as it still does. Its meaning has expanded, though, to "fake, spurious," as in "illegitimate claims for reimbursement." *Illicit*, too, though synonymous with *illegal*, often adds a note of shame, as in "an illicit romance." Such a romance may be contrary to custom, law, or both.

illegal operation Not many years ago journalists euphemistically referred to an abortion as an *illegal operation*. Now *spayed* is called *spayed* and *abortion* is called *abortion*.

illegible/unreadable Not quite the same. A letter or document may be *unreadable* because the handwriting is *illegible*, "impossible to decipher," but in addition it (or even a printed book) may be unreadable because it is badly worded, too polysyllabic, poorly organized, extremely boring, or offensive, even though all parts are legible.

illicit See ELICIT/ILLICIT; ILLEGAL/ILLICIT.

illiterate See IGNORANT/ILLITERATE.

illusion See ALLUSION/ILLUSION.

image Now an SWE word for "public impression," *image* was not widely used in this sense until after 1950: "The president's aides try to protect and enhance his image."

imaginary/imaginative An *imaginary* child is an unreal, perhaps dreamed-of or hoped-for child. An *imaginative* child is a real child with a lively, creative mind.

imagination See FANCY/IMAGINATION.

imagine/suppose In theory, *imagine* should be the verb-companion of the noun *imagination*. However, it also has been used for centuries in the sense of *suppose*, even in such unimaginative sentences as "I imagine you're hungry, John." As a result, some dictionaries give *suppose* as one of its synonyms. In scientific or other technical writing and other SWE, however, *suppose* is the more likely choice for "assume to be true."

imitation   See ARTIFICIAL/ERSATZ/FAKE . . .

immature/premature   Evans says that all babies are *immature* but only 6 percent are *premature*. An immature mind is not fully developed. A premature baby is born before the usual nine months are up. A premature plan is made before such a plan is needed. An immature plan is not thoroughly developed.

immediately   Sometimes needs to be followed by *after* for clarity. "Immediately he fired the shot he was sorry." Without *after, Immediately he fired the shot* may be momentarily misunderstood to mean "Quickly he fired . . ." Note the different meaning when *after* is added.

immigrant   See EMIGRANT/IMMIGRANT.

imminent   See EMINENT/IMMINENT.

immoral   See AMORAL/IMMORAL.

impact   **1.** This noun for *effect* is sometimes too strong. Many writers of SWE reserve it, for example, for head-on collisions, not sideswipes; for momentous influence, not for a tag in sandlot football. **2.** The verb *impact* for "have an effect on" became a vogue word in the 1980s, appearing tiresomely in sentences such as "The holiday season impacts the lives of everyone."

impeach   Often misused to mean "remove from office." In actuality an impeachment hearing is comparable to a grand jury investigation to determine whether charges should be brought. For a president or other officeholder to be removed from office, he or she must first be formally impeached and, after that, be tried and convicted. A second meaning, not necessarily defined in a legal sense, is "discredit, degrade, attack verbally": "Layton repeatedly impeached his former friend, calling him a liar and a thief."

impecunious   Most poor people call themselves "poor." Some poor people with college degrees call themselves "impecunious." *Impecunious* shouldn't be confused with *penurious* ("stingy").

impel/incite/induce   To *impel* is to drive something or someone forward: "Greed impelled the Hunts to try to corner the silver market." To *incite* is to urge on or to stir into action. It is often associated with a socially undesirable outcome: "incited to riot." To *induce* is to persuade, often to use sweet reason to lead someone to a decision or action: "Henry needed an hour to induce Joel to accompany him."

imperial/imperious   Today these two words are quite different in meaning. *Imperial* is used in expressions such as "the imperial palace, robes, decrees" and means "relating to the emperor or the empire." *Imperious* means "commanding, demanding, domineering": "an imperious tone" ". . . gesture," or the like.

impertinent/impudent/insolent   All three words refer to inappropriately rude words or action. *Impertinent* suggests lack of respect for one's elders or superiors in rank: "Private Lewis spoke impertinently to the captain." Although impertinence may sometimes be forgiven because of the immaturity of the offender, *impudence* is less likely to be. It is stronger, brasher than impertinence. *Insolence* is still more rude. It suggests open dislike and may come close to insubordination: "'You sure you want me to do that, Cap?' Lewis asked insolently."

impressive See ARRESTING/IMPRESSIVE/STRIKING.

implant/inculcate/inject/instill (passive voice) SWE seldom says, "Young Jefferson was implanted (*instilled* or the like) with the knowledge that . . . ," because Jefferson was not implanted at all. Instead, "The knowledge that . . . was implanted in the young Jefferson" or "Young Jefferson's father inculcated (*implanted*) in his son the knowledge that . . ."

implement (verb) Used in SWE for "provide the tools or other means" to accomplish something: "The House funding bill would implement construction of the dam." In some contexts *provide, accomplish, execute, achieve* or simply *make* will be more accurate.

implement/instrument An *instrument* is ordinarily more delicate, complex, or precise than an *implement*. Doctors and musicians, for example, use instruments, but farmers, carpenters, and tractor repairmen more often use implements or tools, although on some occasions they need instruments.

implosion See EXPLOSION/IMPLOSION.

imply/infer SWE uses *imply* to refer to the sending end: "The speaker implied that Congress should provide military aid." The movement is speaker → listener, or writer → reader. On the receiving end, the listener or reader *infers* that Congress should provide the aid.

important/importantly Both are SWE in sentences such as "More important(ly), the jurors seemed impressed by the defendant's manner." SANE votes for *more important* and suggests that it is short for "what is more important."

impossible "Jill is impossible!" Not really. If Jill exists, she must be possible. *Impossible* as used here is FF (slang) for "too funny (*serious, unpleasant,* or anything else)." Only someone who knows Jill and the speaker well can guess what is meant.

impression See EDITION/IMPRESSION, PRINTING.

impracticable/impractical Something *impracticable* cannot be done or is foolish: "It is impracticable to mix two quarts of lemonade in a one-quart pitcher." Something is *impractical* if it is unwise to do, especially as a regular thing: "It is impractical to prepare two term papers during the last week of the semester."

in (adjective) On the edge of SWE but possibly faddish for "popular, stylish": "Short skirts are in," "the in thing to do." Sometimes *in* makes a phrase a little hard to read. It's impossible to say how long *in* will be in. *In* can be a noun, too – again on the SWE edge: "In politics the ins keep trying not to become outs."

in addition to See ALONG WITH, AS WELL AS, IN ADDITION TO . . .

in back of See BACK OF/IN BACK OF.

in/into "Mavis danced into the kitchen" means that she entered dancing. "Mavis danced in the kitchen" means that she danced while she was in that room. Informally, *in* is often used where *into* is the usual SWE, but sometimes that usage may be ambiguous.

***in* phrases** Writing can often be tightened by reducing a phrase to one or two words. Examples starting with *in*:

> *in addition to* – besides
> *in all probability* – probably
> *in a* _____ *manner* – solemnly, quietly, and so on
> *in any shape or form* – Omit?
> *in connection with* – concerning, about
> *in height* – tall. Omit?
> *in most instances* – often, frequently
> *in number* – Omit?
> *in order to* – to
> *in question* – Omit?
> *in regard (respect) to* – on, about, concerning
> *in spite of the fact that* – although, even though
> *in terms of* – about. Omit?
> *in that time frame* – then (see also POINT IN TIME)
> *in the area (vicinity) of* – about, in, near
> *in the belief that* – believing
> *in the course of* – during, while, at
> *in the event that* – if
> *in the final (last) analysis* – finally, I conclude that
> *in the majority of cases* – often, most often
> *in the midst of* – in, within, during, amid, among
> *in the nature of* – like, such as
> *in view (light) of the fact that* – since, because

in re Meaning "in regard to," *in re* or *re* may be used in legal documents or a business letter to notify the reader of the subject matter. It is underlined (italicized). SWE seldom uses it for other purposes. In many business letters, the word *subject* is used instead.

in receipt of Outmoded business phrase, as in "We are in receipt of your recent shipment, but . . ." Modern: "We have received . . ." or "Thank you for filling our recent order, but . . ." or "In checking your recent shipment we . . ."

in the shape of Objectionable if what is discussed has no shape. Possible: "in the shape of a T." Illogical: "in the shape of a letter to the editor."

in the wake of Needed in "smaller boats were rocking in the wake of the yacht," but usually replaceable by *after* or *following* in figurative expressions such as "in the wake of the disaster."

in to/into We walk *into* a building, turn into a frog, fall into a creek, crash into a tree. In each instance, *into* carries the notion of movement from one place or condition to another. We walk *in to* see a friend, turn *in to* get some sleep – using *in* followed by the infinitive *to see*, and so on. Instances without an infinitive are rare. Copperud gives the example "We dropped in to coffee with the Smiths," which would be ridiculous as "We dropped into coffee . . ." See also IN/INTO.

inasmuch as, insofar as These are the standard ways to write the two expressions – which, by the way, can often be shortened to *because* and *so far as*, respectively.

inaugurate SWE avoids use for trivial occasions. Although one definition is "to begin or start officially," *inaugurate* is a bit strong for an added bus route or a new perfume counter. *Open, begin, start,* or *commence* will do.

incapable/unable *Incapable* suggests an inborn lack of ability, but *unable* more often means only a temporary lack. Most of us would rather be unable to answer the phone rather than incapable of answering it.

incensed See ENRAGED/INCENSED/INFURIATED.

inchoate *Inchoate* means "just beginning, developing, immature." Because of confusion with *chaos*, it is sometimes misused as "disorganized, chaotic." In reality a fetus – an inchoate baby – normally is well organized, each part where it belongs and of appropriate size for its current stage.

incident Defined as "a relatively minor occurrence," but used rather oddly in some newspaper stories: "Members of the youth gangs met at First and Sudbury and exchanged epithets and brandished weapons before police intervened, but no incidents occurred." (No blood, no incidents!) See also EPISODE/EVENT/INCIDENT . . .

inclined to In the sense of "favorable toward," most logically applies to animate beings. A person or a dog may be inclined to be lazy, but a stone has no inclination to be anything; not "This kind of stone is inclined to flake off in strips." SWE prefers *has a tendency to* or *often flakes off.*

include Questionable: "The membership of the Budapest String Quartet included Joseph Roisman, Alexander Schneider, Boris Kroyt, and Mischa Schneider." Ordinarily *include* implies "among others," but here, obviously, all four are named. Better: "The members . . . were . . . ," or "Joseph Roisman [et al.] comprised . . . ," or "The Budapest String Quartet was composed of . . ." SWE also says, "The membership . . . included two Schneiders." See also COMPOSE/COMPRISE.

incognita SANE favors discarding *incognita*, a feminine form, along with *aviatrix, poetess,* and the like. *Incognito* can serve both sexes.

incomparable/uncomparable Although few people ever use *uncomparable* (accent on *par*), statements carrying the literal meaning of "not capable of being compared" would often be clearer if that word were chosen instead of *incomparable*. The latter could then be reserved for "matchless, unsurpassed": "Sales figures for the two years are uncomparable (or *not comparable*) because different methods of tabulation were used," but "The beauty of Helen of Troy is said to have been incomparable."

incredible! A vogue word for "Great!" "Wonderful!" An interviewer said to a young actor, "And so you two married and now have a baby?" "Yes." "Incredible!" It wasn't at all unbelievable. That sort of thing happens frequently. See also COLOSSAL/COLOSSALLY.

incredibly fantastic After tiring of this vogue term, some people have discovered *fantastically incredible* – no improvement.

indefinitely A catalog stated that an adjustable wrench was "guaranteed to last indefinitely." Since an indefinite time can be a second or almost forever, the manufacturer need never make amends for defective wrenches. *Indefinitely* does not necessarily mean "a very long time." *Almost indefinitely* or *somewhat indefinitely* is meaningless.

indexes/indices Take your choice. SANE recommends anglicized plurals (*indexes*) except for firmly entrenched foreign forms.

indicate Follett says rightly that *indicate* is often used when a more specific verb is preferable. He lists about thirty possible substitutes, including *hint, insinuate, imply, announce, specify, proclaim, propose, urge, point out, report, admit, declare*. He also understandably dislikes such passive-voice usages as "A good stiff drink is indicated."

indict/indite Pronounced alike, but quite different in meaning. A person who is *indicted* is charged with a crime (note that the indictment does not prove guilt). Most people never need *indite*. It's a stiff old word for "write."

indispensable See ESSENTIAL/INDISPENSABLE/NECESSARY . . .

individual (noun) Usually SWE prefers *person* (or *dog, cat,* and so on) to *individual* except in singling out one or a few for special attention. Dubious: "Several individuals were injured." Possible: "Study of two individuals in the group is not enough to justify a generalization."

indoor(s), outdoor(s) SWE uses *indoor* and *outdoor* before a following noun: "an indoor pool," "an outdoor party." Otherwise it uses *indoors* and *outdoors*: "walked outdoors," "stayed indoors," "the great outdoors."

induce, induction See DEDUCE/DEDUCT/INDUCE.

indulge in See ENGAGE IN/INDULGE IN.

ineffable A seldom-needed word meaning, in effect, "with no words sufficient to describe." Adequate words almost always exist; the problem lies in finding them.

ineffable/unspeakable Although both words mean "impossible to express," they are quite different in usage. Something is *ineffable* if it seems too splendid to be described: "the ineffable joy of a mother who can once more hold her kidnapped child." *Unspeakable*, in contrast, often connotes something too unpleasant or vile to be talked about: "an unspeakable crime," "the unspeakable filth of Rio's slums."

inept/unapt   *Inept* usually means "clumsy" or "foolish": "played an inept game at shortstop," "an inept remark." Rather rarely it means "inappropriate." *Unapt* means "unlikely" or "inappropriate": "She is unapt (or *not apt*) to follow such a suggestion." "In those circumstances, his comment was unapt." (Rarely, *inapt* substitutes for *unapt*, but it is even more likely to be confused with *inept*.)

inequity/iniquity   SWE is careful with these. *Inequity* is "unfairness, inequality of treatment": "The inequity of some tax regulations." *Iniquity* is "sin, wickedness, moral offenses": "Sons should not be judged by the iniquity of their fathers."

infant   See BABY/CHILD/INFANT.

infantile   See CHILDISH/CHILDLIKE/INFANTILE.

infectious   See CONTAGIOUS/INFECTIOUS.

inferno   Described in the *Inferno*, part of Dante's *Divine Comedy*, in which it represents a place of torment for lost souls, *inferno* can mean "Hell, a Hell-like place, or the fiery place that Hell is rumored to be." From these definitions has derived the use of *inferno* for a tremendous conflagration such as the skyscraper fire shown in the movie *The Towering Inferno*. SWE does not cheapen the word as some writers of modern "romances" do. Some stories describe a woman's heart or desires as "an inferno of emotions" or "a roaring inferno of passion." (Sounds painful!)

infinite(ly)   *Infinite* means "having no knowable limits, immeasurably large." SWE avoids "the infinite heights of the Rockies" or "the infinite reaches of the prairies" unless trying to reflect a child's perceptions. A thesaurus offers several dozen substitutes besides the obvious *immense* and *far*. Similar comments apply to *infinitely*.

inflammable/inflammatory   We refer to *inflammable* (or *flammable*) materials, but almost never to *inflammatory* materials except figuratively: "Thomas Paine's inflammatory articles sparked many Colonists' anger against the British." A second meaning of *inflammatory* is related to *inflammation* ("bodily heat or swelling"): "Several anti-inflammatory drugs are available." See also FLAMMABLE/INFLAMMABLE.

informal(ly)   When context by itself suggests informality, this word is not needed. Redundant: "Lounging beside the pool, Sylvia Heartthrob spoke informally with reporters for several minutes."

informant/informer   Often interchangeable. However, a person who supplies information to a pollster or researcher is usually an *informant*: "Thousands of informants supplied data for Professor Cassidy's monumental study of American dialects." *Informer* has as one of its meanings "one who informs on others (perhaps for pay)" or the slang "squealer": "a police informer."

information/knowledge Not synonyms. *Knowledge* refers to a body of facts and inferences, especially but not necessarily carried in one's head, as "Dickens's thorough knowledge of London." *Information* refers particularly to facts – many or few – sometimes gathered at random and not necessarily systematized mentally. It may be contained in one's head or in a book or other place. Information is the basis of knowledge but is less broad, deep, and patterned than knowledge itself.

infrastructure In a city the infrastructure is the system of streets, sewers, electric and telephone conduits, and the like on which smooth functioning depends. In a large business it may be both the physical necessities and the system of governance. It is SWE, not just a "vogue word," as Morris calls it.

infuriated See ENRAGED/INCENSED/INFURIATED.

-ing Verbs, which are usually action words, often enliven sentences. Nouns, being names, keep them standing still. Many writers suffer from noun-itis – relying too much on nouns. One cure is to make more use of *-ings*, which of course are verb forms. Examples:

> gradual reduction of excess weight – *gradually losing pounds*
> a disinclination toward payment of additional taxes – *hating tax hikes*
> approach to the point of saturation – *nearing saturation*
> calls for modification of – *calls for modifying*
> movements of wings – *flutterings*

-ing (case preceding) When an *-ing* word such as *dancing* is used as a noun, is *you* or *your* preferable before it? In FF it makes little difference. In SWE a possessive (*your, my, the boy's, Linda's,* or the like) is usual: "We enjoyed watching your dancing again," meaning that it was the dancing that we enjoyed. But suppose that the dancer has just recovered from a long illness. We are likely to say, "We enjoyed watching *you* dancing again," meaning "watching *you* able to dance again." In short, the choice of modifier can result in conveying a slightly different meaning.

ingenious/ingenuous An *ingenious* person is clever, but an *ingenuous* one is usually naive and artless, or possibly a little too frank and revealing. See also CLEVER/INGENIOUS/INVENTIVE.

in-group/out-group Both are SWE words, popularized by sociologists. Members of an *in-group* share beliefs, interests, and activities, but persons in an *out-group* differ from them in one or more significant ways. Many out-groups, such as Christian sects or denominations, become new in-groups, which develop new out-groups, which . . . , perhaps almost *ad infinitum*, illustrating multiplication by division.

inhabitant See CITIZEN/INHABITANT/RESIDENT.

inhibit/prohibit Sometimes interchangeable, but *inhibiting* usually is a slow process whereas *prohibiting* may be as quick as a vote by a city council. Also, a prohibition usually comes from an outside authority, as in "an ordinance prohibiting parking." But an inhibition generally comes from within; for example, a person may be inhibited from sexual intercourse by fear of disease.

inhuman/unhuman *Inhuman* means "brutal": "inhuman treatment of captives." *Unhuman* means "not like a human being." For example, a sound not like any normally produced by humans may be described as unhuman; such a sound may be pleasant or unpleasant.

injured See DAMAGED/INJURED.

in-law (plural and possessive) Examples of SWE plurals are *sons-in-law, mothers-in-law*; SWE singular possessive, *my son-in-law's opinion(s)*; SWE plural possessive, *my sons-in-law's opinion(s)*.

inmost/innermost These are interchangeable, so why not use the shorter?

innards Standard since about 1815 for "the inner parts of a body or a machine." Derived from *inwards*, which today is rarely used in that sense.

innate See HEREDITARY/INNATE.

inner man Once meant "soul," but now is a feebly humorous cliché for "stomach, digestive tract": "keeping the inner man happy."

innocent bystander Sometimes another word is more appropriate than *innocent*, which means "not guilty." If guilt is not in question, *chance bystander, coincidentally a bystander, a bystander by mischance, uninvolved bystander*, or something else may be more accurate.

innocent/not guilty A defendant in court may plead "not guilty" but not "innocent." American law does not require a person to prove innocence – only lack of guilt of specified charges.

innovation Not preceded in SWE by *new* or *old*. An innovation is necessarily new, cannot be old. *Modern* or *recent* may be defensible, however.

innumerable/numerous The grains of sand on a seashore are *innumerable* ("countless"). Gulls along a seashore may be *numerous* ("great in number"), but they probably are not actually innumerable, although a count is unlikely.

inoculate/vaccinate Often used interchangeably, although *vaccinate* is customary for smallpox.

input/output SWE, but the words are ugly and quickly become tiresome. Perhaps they're essential in computer work or other special fields.

inquirer/inquisitor An *inquirer* asks questions. An *inquisitor* asks penetrating, often harsh, unfair, or unreasonable questions for a prolonged period. Because of its association with the Spanish Inquisition, the word suggests cruelty, relentlessness, and often a predetermined conclusion.

insoluble/unsolvable These words are interchangeable for "incapable of being solved": "an insoluble ('unsolvable') problem." Only *insoluble* is used for "incapable of being dissolved."

instance See EXAMPLE/INSTANCE.

instant/minute/moment/second Some people use time words more accurately than others do. To careful souls, *instant, moment,* and *second* each refer to a single tick of a clock, and *minute* to sixty ticks. Other people, however, not only fail to distinguish *minute* from the other words but also from *quarter hour. Second* implies a more precise measurement than does *instant* or *moment.*

instinct, instinctive, instinctual/intuition, intuitive *Instinctive* and *instinctual* are interchangeable. An *instinct* is an inborn manner of behavior: lemmings' instinctual journey to the sea, birds' nest-building and migrations, babies' reactions to differing tones of voice. Instincts reveal themselves especially in physical acts. *Intuition* is likewise untaught. It refers to making a judgment or decision or taking an action on the basis of "feeling" that it is correct, without following the usual processes of reasoning. One may have an intuitive knowledge or belief (not inevitably correct) that a personal or governmental decision is unwise, or feel intuitively that something pleasant or dreadful will soon happen (although it doesn't always).

institution of higher learning Note the position of *higher.* It is the learning, not the institution, that is higher.

instructional/instructive *Instructional* materials are used in instruction, especially in schools. Those materials are supposedly also *instructive* ("informative"). However, many instructive things are not necessarily used in schools or in other intentional teaching-learning situations. Good newspapers or magazines, novels, trips, discussions, or even a night in jail can be instructive without being intended as instructional. See also EDUCATIONAL/INSTRUCTIVE.

insufferable Not clearly related to *suffer* in the usual modern sense, *insufferable* means "intolerable, not endurable": "an insufferable tyrant," "The wait for the bus was almost insufferable."

integration See DESEGREGATION/INTEGRATION.

intelligent/intellectual An *intelligent* person has a quick and retentive mind and as an adult can grasp the abstract, not just the concrete. An *intellectual* person must first be intelligent, but he or she likes to focus that intelligence on literary or political theory, philosophy, scientific theory, or other subjects (or combinations) requiring considerable abstract thought. (It must be recognized, though, that an intelligent longshoreman – such as Eric Hoffer – or an athletic coach can be or become an intellectual; lack of academic degrees in theoretical subjects does not rule out intellectualism.)

intend See AIM TO.

intended See DESIGNED/INTENDED.

intense/intensive *Intense* means "extremely high in degree, size, or strength," "felt deeply": "The strain was intense." "She is an intense person who can mourn the death of a pigeon." *Intensive* has some of the significance of *intense* but suggests greater concentration. For example, an "intensive care unit" in a hospital concentrates attention on a small number of patients – possibly only one. Fowler uses as an example *intense* vs. *intensive* bombardment. Both kinds are heavy, but the intensive sort delivers most of the bombs to a small area.

intentionally   See ADVISEDLY/INTENTIONALLY; CONSCIOUSLY/INTENTIONALLY.

intents and purposes   Wordy: "To (*For*) all intents and purposes, the feuding has stopped." The first five words may be replaced by *apparently, essentially,* or (before *stopped*) *almost* or *nearly,* or by whatever word best conveys the meaning.

intercourse   Some people automatically think of sex when they see *intercourse.* That fact should not necessitate abandonment of the basic meaning: "Communication, interchange between persons or groups." Context usually shows quickly what the writer intends.

interesting   A namby-pamby word, sometimes unavoidable. When possible, SWE is more specific, designating what the kind of interest is.

interface   Although *interface* is older than computers, it has thrived with them. Defined only as a noun in older dictionaries, it is now even more often an intransitive or transitive verb. Operators interface with computers, computers with one another or with a network, a space suit with the cabin, a woman's dress with its accessories – almost anything with anything else. A meeting on a street corner can be an interface; perhaps even a lover's tryst can be. People who overinterface should start to deinterface.

interject/interpolate   In a conversation one person – quickly or sometimes rudely – may *interject* a remark of his or her own. Less often the softer *interpolate* is used in the same way – usually to suggest a remark intended to clarify or strengthen what the other person is saying. An interpolation frequently occurs in writing; for example, a writer may interpolate a new sentence or paragraph within a passage composed earlier.

interpersonal   Often can be deleted, as in *interpersonal friendships* (or *enmities, relationships*). Sometimes *mutual* can be substituted for clarity: "mutual ill feelings." See also COMMON/MUTUAL.

interpretative, interpretive/preventative, preventive   The SANE refrain: Choose the shorter. SWE increasingly does so.

into   Since the 1960s many people have been *into* things: into karate, philosophy, mud-wrestling. Apparently, the hippies were into things when they weren't laid-back. The word at least carries a suggestion of hippiedom. Many specific SWE substitutes are available, depending on what one is "into." See also IN TO/ INTO.

intrigue (verb)   "The contradictions in the girl's account intrigued us." As a synonym of *fascinate* or *arouse interest, intrigue* has been criticized as too vague. But it is stronger than *interest*, and it appears frequently in reputable book-review magazines, among others.

introduction   See FOREWORD/INTRODUCTION/PREFACE.

inured   See ACCUSTOMED/INURED.

invaluable/priceless   *Invaluable* and *valuable* both mean "having considerable value" (one of the many confusing things about our beloved language). Something *priceless* also has value, this time so great that it cannot be measured in money: certain heirlooms, for example. (It puzzles some foreigners that a *worthless* thing, in contrast to *priceless*, has no value at all.) *Priceless* is obviously a strong word, not to be used of most household items, a 1930 Ford, or other things to which price tags may indeed be attached. Things of great sentimental value, however, are properly described as *priceless*. Modifiers such as *absolutely, perfectly, simply, more,* or *less* are redundant.

invent   See DISCOVER/INVENT.

inventive   See CLEVER/INGENIOUS/INVENTIVE.

inverse   See CONVERSE/INVERSE/OBVERSE . . .

invite   FF as a noun: "We received an invite to the dance." SWE: ". . . an invitation . . ."

invoke   See EVOKE/INVOKE.

inward(s)   SWE uses *inward* when a noun follows: "an inward path." It uses either *inward* or *inwards* after a verb: "driven inward(s)." In such an adverbial use, *in* often serves equally well. See also INNARDS.

ipse dixit   See **FOREIGN EXPRESSIONS**.

IQ, I.Q.   Both forms are SWE for the abbreviation of "intelligence quotient." The term refers only to an often-questioned specific manner of measuring intelligence by use of a test. A person's IQ should not be treated as a true indicator of knowledge, practicality, common sense, wisdom, creativity, or anything else not claimed by the test constructors. What constitutes intelligence is still debated.

iron/steel   *Iron*, one of the elements, occurs in an impure ore. Its most easily forged form, *wrought iron*, contains a very small amount of carbon and impurities. *Steel* is an alloy of iron and from 0.2 to 1.5 percent carbon, possibly with other constituents added. It is normally hard, malleable, and durable. *Stainless steel* has more chromium than most.

ironic, ironically   Both are so overused in so many contexts that the meanings are often vague or incomprehensible. They appear to mean "odd(ly), incongruous(ly), (by) chance, coincidental(ly), disappointing(ly)," or nothing at all. Usually a word like one of those just listed is more precise.

In a literary sense, *irony* means saying the opposite of what is meant: "Lovely day!" when the rain is pouring down. Jonathan Swift was writing ironically when he seemed to be advocating that poor Irish children be fattened and sold to rich English people for food. In drama a situation is ironic if the audience but not the characters understand the incongruity in a situation. *Socratic irony* is a pretense of ignorance, a tactic that Socrates often employed in conversations with his disciples.

irregardless FF. Technically a double negative (*ir-* and *-less*). SWE uses *regardless.*

irreparable/unrepairable Although dictionaries call these words synonyms (as well as their antonyms *reparable* and *repairable*), *unrepairable* is ordinarily used of physical things, *irreparable* of abstract ones: "This clock is unrepairable." "The administration has done irreparable harm to the economy."

is (are, was, were) to A sentence like "He is to leave tomorrow" is ambiguous if not clarified by the context. It may indicate simple future, "He will leave tomorrow," or it may represent an order equivalent to "I demand that he leave tomorrow." SWE rewrites when the context is insufficient.

is when, is where Often used in FF definitions: "Enteritis is when the intestines are inflamed." That construction is too illogical for SWE use, since nothing is a when or a where. SWE says, "Enteritis is inflammation of the intestinal tract." Note that a good definition of a noun shows the general class to which it belongs (e.g., "inflammation") and then the way(s) in which it differs from other members of the class (e.g., "of the intestinal tract").

ism Because *-ism* is the ending of many nouns related to beliefs or systems (*atheism, Protestantism, Americanism,* and so on), *ism* is often used, even in fairly sedate writing, instead of *belief* or the like. In using it or its plural, *isms,* an SWE writer is aware that it may connote a slur, as in "She keeps switching from one ism to another."

Israeli/Jew An *Israeli* is not necessarily a *Jew,* for many followers of other religions also live in Israel. Israelis are the inhabitants of Israel. Similarly, not all Jews are Israelis. Although interpretations differ, in general any adherent of Judaism or descendant of biblical Hebrews is a Jew, and Jews live in many countries. See also HEBREW/ISRAELI/ JEWISH . . .

issue Seldom if ever is *controversial* or *noncontroversial* needed with this word. If something is an issue, it is by definition controversial. If it is noncontroversial, it is not an issue.

it As a sentence opener, *it* is often needed but can be overused. Only occasional sentences should begin with "It is true (*certain, probable,* and so on) that . . ." As for "It is believed," SWE usually tries to tell who the believer is, or chooses *probably, perhaps, possibly,* or *may.*

it stands to reason that A smug expression that may irk someone whose reasoning differs from that of the writer.

iterate/reiterate Interchangeable, although *reiterate* seems more forceful and is generally chosen.

its No apostrophe when used to show possession: "The dog ate its chow (*lost its patience, hid its bone*)." "Romanticism was losing its appeal." See also **APOSTROPHE**; IT'S.

it's The apostrophe shows the meaning to be "it is" or "it has": "It's ('It is') going to snow. In fact, it's ('it has') already started." See also **APOSTROPHE**; ITS.

it's I/it's me Standard formal usage is "It is (*was*) I," "It is (*was*) he (*she, we, they*)." Informal is "It's me (*him, her, us, them*)." Because in English we are accustomed to having an object after a verb, as in "John hit me," the tendency to use an objective pronoun is strong. For that reason it is probable that "It is me (*him, her, us, them*)" will eventually become accepted in all contexts. (Winston Churchill often wrote "It was me," and an earlier prime minister declared, "The navy is us.") "It was me" sometimes appears in American SWE in informal contexts.

-ize An unbeautiful verb ending, often criticized by writers on usage, yet frequently necessary, as *criticize* itself illustrates. It is least objectionable when it reduces wordage: *hospitalize* is short for "place in a hospital." Dubious: *secretize*, no fewer syllables than *make secret.* When tempted to use a word ending in -*ize*, some writers try to find a substitute with no more syllables. Thus *make final* may replace *finalize*, and *give priority, prioritize.* But they may keep *democratize* because each alternative is longer.

J

jail/prison A distinction is not quite fixed but is worth making. In general, a *jail* is a relatively small place of confinement for rather short periods of time: "the town jail," "overnight in jail," "in jail for vagrancy," "held in jail while awaiting sentence." A *prison* is usually larger, and its inmates normally are serving longer sentences and for more serious crimes: "a state (or federal) prison," "a prison sentence of ten years for armed robbery."

Japanese The adjective and the singular and plural nouns are the same: "Japanese customs," "a Japanese is," "several Japanese are." Many Japanese and others regard *Jap* as insulting or at best derogatory.

jealousy See ENVY/JEALOUSY.

jerk (noun) FF (slang) for "a foolish, incompetent, unreliable person."

jet lag Now SWE for the temporary psychological or physical discomfort or disruptions caused by crossing several time zones in a few hours.

jet set Informal term, but often used in SWE for persons financially, emotionally, and mentally equipped to travel long distances to attend insignificant social affairs. The term is used enviously by some writers, noncommittally by most, and pejoratively by others.

jetsam See FLOTSAM/JETSAM/LAGAN.

jew down "Bargain to reduce a price." Offensive not only to Jews. If a term like *german down* or *italian down* existed, it would be equally offensive.

jewel See GEM/JEWEL.

Jewess Considered derogatory, like many other nouns with *-ess* to indicate females.

Jewish See HEBREW/ISRAELI/JEWISH . . .

jibe See GIBE/JIBE.

job action An inclusive name is needed that covers strikes, slow-downs, absenteeism, and any other way to impede production. Unless a more descriptive term is coined, *job action* will have to do, although supposedly anything that one does on the job could also be called a job action.

job/position No clear difference. *Job* most often connotes relatively low-paying, although not necessarily menial, work: "a job as a clerk (*laborer, welder, police officer,* and so on.)" *Position* supposedly connotes white-collar work. Nevertheless many executives speak of their "jobs," although probably few ditchdiggers talk about their "positions."

jobless Interchangeable with *unemployed,* this term is preferred by headline writers.

jock This is FF (slang) for "male athlete" or, more recently, "man who flaunts his maleness."

john This word is a euphemism for "toilet, bathroom" or (sometimes capitalized) for "man who patronizes a prostitute."

join together A traditional wedding ceremony – with occasional small differences in wording – includes, "Those whom God hath joined together, let no man put asunder." There's no reason to tinker with that tradition; the phrasing has a fine resonance. In less sublime contexts, SWE omits *together.*

joint recital See CONCERT/RECITAL.

jocose/jocular/jolly/jovial *Jolly* is associated with broad smiles, an outgoing nature, good humor, and often large bellies like that of the "jolly old elf," Santa. *Jocose* and *jocular* come from the same Latin source as *joke,* and people so described do like to tell jokes. They exude informal cheerfulness. A *jovial* person is again hearty and good-natured, but his jests are likely to be more meaty, with an undercurrent of seriousness. The jovial person is often better educated than the jolly person.

judge/jurist *Jurist* is a designation for an eminent or somewhat eminent lawyer, a person unusually learned in the law, but not necessarily a judge. A *judge,* if well qualified, may deserve to be called a jurist, but that title is a little high-flown to be applied to everyone who gets elected to a minor judgeship.

judicial/judicious A *judicial* action (or judicial anything else) is related in some way to courts: "judicial branch of government," "judicial chambers (*decisions, issues*)." *Judicious* means "thoughtful, sensible, showing good judgment" and is not necessarily related to courts at all. For example, many parents try to give judicious advice and to behave judiciously and encourage judicious behavior in their children.

juncture   A juncture is a point in space or time at which two things meet. "At this juncture" is rarely used in SWE for "at this time" unless the reference is to a crisis or a turning point, perhaps like that in Robert Frost's "The Road Not Taken" – a moment of choice or decision that can make "all the difference."

junket   Although a junket can be any tour or trip for business or professional purposes, the term has so often been used to refer to costly and sometimes fun-filled excursions by politicians that it has acquired an unfavorable connotation. SWE usually avoids it unless it intends ridicule or denigration of a trip or the travelers.

junkie   FF (slang) for "drug addict" and more recently "person with extraordinary enthusiasm for one thing." So we have television junkies, basketball junkies, and others for politics, Latin, humming-birds, or you-name-it.

jury-rigged   Mainly a nautical term, *jury-rigged* sometimes is erro-neously thought to refer to "'fixing' a jury," or is confused with *jerry-built,* which means "built cheaply and flimsily." To *jury-rig* is to make temporary repairs, usually during an emergency.

just exactly   *Just* isn't needed, but the expression is so widely used that *exactly* may appear naked without it. SANE approves that kind of nudity. *Just merely* is undesirably redundant. SWE deletes *just.*

juvenile/puerile   *Juvenile* refers to girls and boys below voting age or possibly before some other specified age: "juvenile offenders (*pastimes,* and so on)," "juvenile books" (i.e., suitable for juveniles). *Puerile* is generally slightly derogatory and applies to boys only: "a puerile, ill-considered remark." As in that example, behavior by a man may be described as puerile if it seems immature.

K

karat   See CARAT/CARET/CARROT . . .

kibitz, kibitzer   An old German name, *Gibiz,* for a bird with an erratic flight and a strange cry, followed a devious path through Yiddish for "unwanted adviser of cardplayers" to useful, cheerful, but still informal English words for "meddle" and "meddlesome person." It is sometimes SWE.

kick   FF (slang or highly informal) for each of these meanings: com-plain – "I won't kick about that"; contribute (with *in*) – "Can you kick in a few dollars?"; stimulating power – "This whiskey's got a real kick!"; die (with *off* or *the bucket*) – "He kicked off (*kicked the bucket*) last night." *Kick off* is also informal, mainly but not exclusively journalese, for "begin," as in "The charity drive will kick off (or *be kicked off*) at a dinner tonight." Also there's "a kick-off banquet." These uses may be derived from the SWE football term: "The Giants will kick off."

kickback If a person illegally withholds or is given for his or her own use part of the wages or salary of an employee, the amount is called a *kickback,* especially if without such payment some privilege (or even the job itself) might be removed. A rebate is also called a kickback, but usually only if given for suspect reasons. Some dictionaries label *kickback* informal or slang, but the length of the definitions proves that it is needed. Consider it SWE.

kidding Should be SWE, although most dictionaries do not treat it as standard. No other carries quite the same combination of meanings: "teasing" plus "playfulness" plus "harmless deceit," tied together as in "You must be kidding!" The word itself is playful, like a capering young goat.

kids This is a pleasant informality for "children, young people," not rare in SWE. Formally a kid may be a young goat, a small wooden tub for a sailor's mess, a kind of seed pod, or a bundle of twigs or heather.

kidult The *New York Times* has used the word to mean "the child-adult whose capacities and interests are fixed at an early age." The word isn't widely used yet, but it deserves to be. It implies, for example, a person like John Updike's Rabbit, a grown man whose interests remained stuck in the period when he was a star high-school athlete. Movies aimed at kidults, says Vincent Canby of the *Times*, "render even basic reasoning skills superfluous."

kill (figurative) Several figurative uses of *kill* have become SWE, or close to it, as illustrated by these expressions: "kill the engine," "kill a bottle of gin," "kill the taste," "kill a story" (journalism), "kill the ball" (tennis), "kill the lights," "My back is killing me."

kill time/pass time/spend time All are SWE. *Spending time* is generally more worthwhile and profitable than *killing time* or *passing time*. When you are fighting against boredom, you are killing time. When you are amusing yourself but not completely wasting time, you are passing time. The distinctions are useful but not always observed by copy editors.

kill See also EXECUTE/KILL, MURDER.

kilt A man may wear *a kilt*. He is not wearing *kilts* unless he has on more than one kilt.

kin Together, all your relatives are your *kin*. Infrequently, the word is used to refer to only one person, equivalent to *kinsman*. More often we find "one of my kin (or *relatives*)" "my cousin," or the like. *Kin* and *akin* may both be used as adjectives following a verb: "She is kin (or *akin*) to me." *Kinsfolk, kinfolk,* and *kinfolks* are all SWE variants of the same word, although some dictionaries call the last two informal. *Kissing kin* are cousins or other fairly distant relatives whom one knows well enough to kiss in greeting or farewell. See also KITH AND KIN.

kind of, sort of These classifications apply to both *kind of* and *sort of*: **1.** FF for "rather," as in "kind of short." **2.** FF: One kind of *a* cloud is the cumulus. SWE: One kind of cloud . . . **3.** FF: Those (*These*) sort of cloud (*clouds*) . . . SWE: That (*This*) sort of cloud (*clouds*) . . . SWE: Those (*These*) sorts of *clouds* . . . **4.** FF: That (*This*) kind of clouds *are* . . . SWE: That (*This*) kind of cloud is . . . SWE: What kind of clouds are those?

kind See VARIETY.

kindly Old-fashioned for "please": "Kindly remit the amount due."

kingly/regal/royal Often interchanged, although the words convey subtly different emphases. That which is *kingly* is especially suitable for or characteristic of a king (as *queenly* is of a queen): "kingly attire," "a kingly hauteur." *Regal* and *royal* apply to both kings and queens and sometimes to their immediate families. *Regal* refers to more outward, more visible manifestations of the office: "regal pomp," "assumed his proud regal posture." *Royal* is usually the most favorable of the three and can imply greatness of spirit, generosity, and the like; "royal family," "royal munificence," "royal welcome."

kinky FF (slang or informal) for "highly unusual, bizarre." When applied to sex, some people equate it to almost anything sexual except the position approved by early missionaries. T. S. Eliot used *kinky* in *The Cocktail Party* to refer to slightly uncommon emotionalism. The word is likely to become SWE in one or more of its senses. It is needed – increasingly.

kith and kin Old-fashioned but still used occasionally. *Kith* means "friends and neighbors" but is not seen except with *kin*. See also KIN.

knave/rascal/rogue/scoundrel *Knave* is an old-fashioned word for the other three. All four are now used mainly in fun or even with more or less affection, as when a proud father calls his mischievous small son "you little rascal." A *scoundrel* is perhaps the worst of the four, most likely to behave criminally or to play dirty tricks. A *rogue* has few worthy principles and will probably cheat if given a chance. A *rascal* is sly and scheming but probably steals no more than a few chickens unless the farmer's daughter happens to show up.

knee-jerk Without the hyphen, an SWE noun for the little kick you make when a physician taps your knee. With the hyphen, it is an informal adjective for "involuntary, automatic." A *knee-jerk* conservative, for example, is one who automatically and unthinkingly takes a conservative stance on almost every issue. *Knee-jerk* is seldom used to describe things or people approvingly. Since no other word has precisely the same meaning, it appears increasingly in SWE.

knocked up In the United States, FF (vulgar) for "made pregnant." In England, it is often used to mean "awakened," as in "I knocked her (*him*) up at seven this morning," or "very tired," as in "He (*She*) seems knocked up." The expression should be used cautiously on both sides of the Atlantic.

knot (unit of speed)   SWE: "a speed of ten knots through the bay." FF: "knots an hour." A speed of ten knots is about 11.5 statute miles an hour. *Knots* is used only for speeds across (or under) water. Sailors do not use *knot* as a measure of distance. They do not say, for example, that a place is seven knots from here.

know as   FF (regional or dialectal) for *know that* or *know whether,* sometimes followed, but not improved, by *how*: "I don't know as (how) I believe you."

know-how (also knowhow)   The word is disliked by many conservatives, who prefer *knowledge, skill,* or *understanding the way to perform* (a task). But that last phrase is too long, *knowledge* is a broad term that pertains more to "know what" than to "know how," and *skill* refers to performing rather than understanding how to perform. SWE uses *know-how* when it fits the intended meaning. Useful but rare: *know-what, know-when.*

knowledgeable   Some people object to the word, preferring *well-informed.* SWE uses both.

kudos   This word for "acclaim, praise, fame, glory" is from a Greek word of the same meaning and spelling (the *s* is pronounced as *s,* not as *z*). It is singular: "His kudos is deserved." *Kudo* developed as an alternative early in this century but is often disapproved of. Caution: Few people know the meaning of either *kudos* or *kudo.*

L

labyrinth/maze   Often interchangeable, although *maze* is conventional for a kind of paper-and-pencil puzzle or a network of hedges. *Labyrinth* is more common for confusing caves or the intricate passageways in the dungeon areas of old castles or monasteries, or even in the Pentagon.

laconic/reticent/taciturn   President Coolidge reportedly summarized for his wife a sermon on sin by saying, "He was agin it." Coolidge was a *laconic* man. He liked to use as few words as possible. A hermit, however, more than likely prefers to remain completely silent if possible. A hermit may be described as *reticent,* which does not mean "reluctant" as some people believe. Somebody equally silent but possibly also a bit uncheerful is *taciturn.*

lady/woman   In years gone by, most American females were glad to be or hoped to be *ladies,* partly because of the high regard in England for lords and ladies. Gradually, though, *lady* came to vacillate between a suggestion of excessive primness and the great un-primness of "lady of the evening." Today, except in a few contexts such as "Ladies and Gentlemen," *woman* has largely replaced *lady.*

ladylike/womanlike, womanly Comparatively rare, *ladylike* suggests refined femininity, the qualities and decorum once taught in "finishing schools." *Womanlike* is literally "like a woman," similar to *womanly,* but sometimes is used unfavorably to indicate supposed weakness: "her womanlike fear of mice and snakes." See also FEMALE, FEMININE.

lagan See FLOTSAM/JETSAM/LAGAN.

lama/llama One difference is in the number of legs – two vs. four. The *lama* is a high-ranking Buddhist priest or monk of Tibet or Mongolia. The *llama* is a South American beast of burden.

lame duck SWE, though somewhat informal, for an elected official completing a term of office to which he or she will not be returning.

lament See DEPLORE/LAMENT/REGRET . . .

languid/limpid *Languid* means "spiritless, lacking in energy." After an illness a person often feels languid. *Limpid* is not related to *limp.* It means "clear, transparent," and by extension "calm, untroubled, at ease": "a limpid pool," "the relaxed, limpid singing of Perry Como," "limpid prose." See also LANGUOR/LASSITUDE.

languor/lassitude Can be used as synonyms, but *languor* is the somewhat softer word associated with laziness, quietly doing nothing, lacking much energy. *Languid* is obviously related. *Lassitude,* slightly harsher, often is associated with numbness or exhaustion.

large (or small) number of *Many* and *few* are obviously shorter. For *a large portion of, much of* or *most of* can usually be substituted, and for *a small portion of, little* saves a dozen keystrokes.

lascivious/lecherous/licentious All three refer to immoral or excessive sexual thoughts or behavior. A *lascivious* person is lustful, and lascivious dress (or undress) is intended to incite lust. Only a man is usually described as *lecherous.* He is considered excessively desirous of sex and frequently yields to that desire. *Licentious* refers to commission of acts (usually sexual) that are considered both immoral and illegal. The sexual fondling of a young child, for example, is licentious because it is clearly immoral and also can be punished by law.

lassitude See LANGUOR/LASSITUDE.

last/later/latter 1. In referring to the person or thing named at the end, SWE uses *latter* if only two names were given, *last* for three or more. 2. *Latter* and *later* may sometimes be used almost interchangeably: "the latter (or *later*) part of her life." However, *later* refers specifically to time (not position) and implies a comparison not involved in *latter*: "later, during the night," "a later plane," "happened later." Also, *later* but not *latter* may be used as an adverb.

last/latest Often used interchangeably in SWE, as in "the last (*latest*) issue of *Newsweek.*" Conservatives choose *latest* when the meaning is "most recent": "the latest issue," not *last* unless the magazine has ceased publication.

last two   See FIRST TWO/TWO FIRST.

late   Not "the late William Shakespeare." The term refers to someone who died in the recent past – *recent* being imprecisely defined. It is most useful in reminding or informing readers who may not be sure whether or not the person is still alive.

   Not "the widow of the late . . . " Having left a widow, the poor fellow must be dead. See also WIDOW/WIFE.

later on   SWE omits *on* unless it helps the rhythm or clarity of the sentence.

later, latest   See LAST/LATER/LATTER; LAST/LATEST.

latter   See FORMER; LAST/LATER/LATTER.

laudable/laudatory   When Mary says that Herbert is *laudable* or has laudable qualities, she is making a *laudatory* remark. The one who praises is being laudatory; the one who is praised is said to be laudable. The verb *laud* is bookish for "praise."

lawful/legal   Synonyms, although *legal* always pertains to man-made law, and *lawful* sometimes is concerned with the higher law – that of God. See also ILLEGAL/ILLEGITIMATE/ILLICIT . . .

lawman   A term used mainly in Western fiction or movies to refer to a sheriff or other law-enforcement official, *lawman* is not listed in some dictionaries. It can be useful in the plural to indicate several kinds of such officials, however, or in the singular when the exact title is unknown.

lawyer   See ATTORNEY/ATTORNEY AT LAW/LAWYER.

lay/lie   A college president once remarked that he could gauge roughly the amount of education a person has had by observing his use of *lay* ("to place") and *lie* ("to recline"). The distinction is simple and can be mastered in a few minutes by composing and saying aloud repeatedly several sentences like these: "*Lay* it on the table. I *laid* it on the floor. You had *laid* it in the wrong place. Now you are *laying* it in the right place." "*Lie* down, Rover. Rover is *lying* here. He *lay* (past tense) here yesterday. He has *lain* here every day. Why does he *lie* in this spot? He enjoys *lying* here. Yesterday I *lay* beside him. I have often *lain* there."

leading question   A leading question is not intended to entrap, as is the familiar "Have you stopped beating your wife?" Rather, it is a question so worded as to suggest the desired answer, such as a court lawyer for either side often asks. A prosecuting attorney may ask the defendant, "Then you opened the door to the closet where the gun was, didn't you?" The attorney for the defense may phrase the question, "Next, did you open the closet door to hang up your coat?"

leak   Both as noun and verb, *leak* is SWE for "anonymous and usually unauthorized disclosure of information": "a leak from the administration," "an aide may have leaked the news." The brevity of the word is in its favor.

least, less/littler, littlest/smaller, smallest *Littler* and *littlest* are rare but do occur in SWE. A well-known Christmas narrative is "The Littlest Angel." In most contexts, however, *smaller* and *smallest* are used with reference to size. *Less* and *least* refer to quantities. See also FEWER/LESS.

leastways/leastwise *Leastways* is FF (dialectal) for *leastwise,* which is informal for "at least, anyway." See also ANY WAY/ANYWAY/ANY-WAYS; -WISE.

leave/let **1.** Both "Let me alone" and "Leave me alone" are SWE for "Do not bother me," although many argue that "Leave me alone" is ambiguous because it can also mean "Leave me by myself." **2.** For the meaning of "allow, permit," only *let* is SWE, as in "Let me do that," "Let it stay there."

leave/lief *Lief* has an old-fashioned tone and is associated with nineteenth-century expressions such as "I'd jest as lief go squirrel huntin'" or "I'd liefer set right cheer." As *lief* was dying, nonstandard *leave* replaced it in some dialects: "I'd just as leave work on my car." SWE: *just as soon.*

lecherous See LASCIVIOUS/LECHEROUS/LICENTIOUS.

lectern See DAIS/LECTERN/PODIUM.

led One of the most often misspelled words is *led,* the past tense of *lead:* "We led the horse to water." The word seems to be widely confused with the name of the metal.

lee/port/starboard/windward The *lee* side of a ship (or of anything else) is the side sheltered from the wind – opposite the direction from which the wind blows. *Windward* is an antonym of *leeward* and *lee.* The *port* side of a ship or plane is on one's left when one is facing forward. A familiar mnemonic device is "We left port." The *starboard* side is to the right. The name comes from an old word for "steerside": the rudder on an old Teutonic ship was on the right side.

leery SWE, though informal, for *suspicious, hesitant, doubtful, wary, fearful, distrustful,* or *somewhat afraid.* It is less specific than any of those near-synonyms. An infrequent variant is *leary.*

legal See LAWFUL/LEGAL.

lend/loan Dictionary makers now classify "to lend money" and "to loan money" as interchangeable. Conservatives, however, prefer not to use *loan* as a verb. The noun use, as in "ask for a loan," is SWE. To obtain something as a loan is expressed in SWE by *borrow,* not by *loan:* "May I borrow some money from you?"

lengthways, lengthwise See EDGEWAYS, EDGEWISE/ENDWAYS, END-WISE/LENGTHWAYS, LENGTHWISE . . .

lengthy/long A conversation may be described as either *lengthy* or *long. Lengthy* is seldom used except with reference to time, but *long* is more versatile. For example, we are unlikely to refer to a "lengthy board" or a "lengthy distance." *Lengthy* sometimes, but not always, carries a suggestion of tediousness, as in "lengthy congressional debate."

lens   SWE: "A lens is broken," "Both lenses are broken." FF: *a len, two lens.*

less/lesser   As comparatives of *little, less* generally refers to quantity and *lesser* to degree of importance: "less ammunition (or *daylight,* and so on), "a lesser reason," "the lesser man." See also FEWER/LESS; LEAST, LESS/LITTLER, LITTLEST/SMALLER, SMALLEST.

lest   A bookish word, usually for expression of doubt or fear, as in "He was fearful lest he be found guilty" (note the subjunctive *be,* customary after *lest*). More likely today: "He was fearful (*afraid*) that he would be found guilty."

let   See also LEAVE/LET.

let/net (tennis)   A ball that hits the net and goes over is technically a *let* or a *let ball,* not *net.* Here *let* has the meaning "obstacle," as it has in the legal phrase "without let or hindrance." Most professional tennis players use *let.*

let's   1. As in "Let's you and me talk it over alone," *me* is SWE. Expanded, the sentence is "Let us – that is, you and me – talk it over alone." 2. *Let's not* is standard. *Let us not,* unless in very formal context, sounds like James Fenimore Cooper. 3. *Don't let's* and *let's don't* are FF. 4. In *let's us, us* is redundant, because here *'s* signifies "us."

level with   Now SWE for "speak frankly with": "She leveled with her employer about what really happened."

lexicographer/linguist/philologist   A *lexicographer* writes, edits, or helps to prepare dictionaries. A *linguist* specializes in linguistics and may or may not speak several languages. A *philologist* has wide interest in and knowledge of words and their literary use – often extending into classical scholarship or other languages such as Old Norse or Old High German.

liable   See APT/LIABLE/LIKELY.

libel   See DEFAMATION/LIBEL/SLANDER.

license   Singular. "My license is lost. I don't know where it is."

licentious   See LASCIVIOUS/LECHEROUS/LICENTIOUS.

lie   See LAY/LIE.

lief   See LEAVE/LIEF.

lightening/lightning   "Thunder and *lightning,*" "It lightninged (or, rather ambiguously, *lightened*) in the west." SWE avoids both the awkward *was lightninging* and the ambiguous *was lightening,* substituting perhaps "Lightning was flashing . . . " One meaning of *lightening* is illustrated in "They were lightening the donkey's load." Another: "Although the sun was not yet up, the east was lightening."

like   Overused, as in "The place was like, you know, like you've never seen before, like a – even like a nightmare, like, you know." Rare in writing of any kind, this *like* is equivalent to "er" or "uh" in speaking.

like for   FF (dialectal) in sentences such as "We'd like for you to come along." SWE omits *for*.

like   See also AS/AS IF/LIKE.

likes of   "People the likes of you should be in jail." Writers on usage differ, some approving *likes of,* others both *like of* and *likes of,* still others neither. Probable in SWE: "People like (or *such as*) you . . . "

likewise   *Likewise* has a somewhat formal tone but does occur also in ordinary speech. Its standard use is as an adverb: "do likewise," "answered likewise." It is not standard as a substitute for *and* or *together with.* Unlikely in SWE: "His sister, likewise his aunt, met him at the airport."

limit/limitation   Usually interchangeable. In law, however, *limitation* is often a technical term for a time limit beyond which legal action is not possible: "statute of limitations." In general use, *limitation* is customary in the sense of a handicap: "mental or physical limitations." To refer to specific conditions, *limit* is likely: "reached the limit of his strength."

limited/Ltd./small   1. *Limited* and *small* are not synonyms. The powers of the U.S. president are limited but not small. 2. *Ltd.,* following the name of a British company, signifies that in financial matters the liability of each shareholder or officer is limited to a specified maximum.

limpid   See LANGUID/LIMPID.

linage/lineage   For clarity, SWE writes *linage* (pronounced *line-ij*) when referring to the number of lines: "The linage of the news story." *Lineage* (pronounced *lin-ee-ij*) refers to heritage, ancestry: "Some American women were seeking husbands who claimed noble lineage."

line   SWE tries to avoid overuse and vagueness. For example, "He is in the cosmetics line" may be changed to "He sells (*manufactures, speculates in*) cosmetics," "I don't like his line" to whatever is meant by *line. Along these lines* may become *like this, in a similar way,* or *similarly.*

linguist   See LEXICOGRAPHER/LINGUIST/PHILOLOGIST.

liquid refreshment   Ordinary people serve coffee, tea, milk, beer, whiskey, or maybe just "drinks."

lion's share   This term is hackneyed but more colorful than *largest portion.*

listen   See HEAR/LISTEN.

litany/liturgy   A *litany* is a prayer or incantatory recital in which a phrase or sentence uttered by a leader is responded to by a congregation. By extension, such things as a sometimes repeated conversation between parent and child, or any familiar, tedious recital, may be called litanies. The *liturgy* of a church is the form followed in a worship service. It may also mean the Book of Common Prayer or the Rites of the Eucharist.

literally See FIGURATIVELY/LITERALLY.

literature "Write for free literature," an advertisement invites us. When the "literature" arrives, it is a colorful leaflet extolling the merits of an insurance plan or . . . The term is so widely used in this sense of "advertising" that dictionaries list it without comment. But conservatives, at least those who revere Euripides, Virgil, Racine, John Milton, or even John Updike, shudder at what they regard as desecration. Many writers of SWE avoid cheapened use of the word.

littler/littlest See LEAST, LESS/LITTLER, LITTLEST/SMALLER, SMALLEST.

liturgy See LITANY/LITURGY.

live audience Except in a graveyard, this appears redundant. Radio and television people use the term, however, usually in the phrase "recorded before a live audience," to mean that laughter or applause we hear does not come from a re-recording of a laugh track.

live See DWELL/LIVE/RESIDE.

liveware See HARDWARE/LIVEWARE/SOFTWARE.

livid Most members of a class of college juniors and seniors misdefined *livid* as "bright red," "reddish," or something similar. Dictionaries define it as "discolored, as from a bruise," or "pale, as with rage."

llama See LAMA/LLAMA.

lo and behold See BEHOLD.

loan See LEND/LOAN.

loath/loathe Note the spellings. *Loath* is an adjective meaning "unwilling, hesitant": "loath to disagree" (the *th* is pronounced as in *thin*). *Loathe* is a verb meaning "hate, despise, abhor": "Some people loathe squash, but I like it" (the *th* as in *this*).

locate See FIND/LOCATE.

long See LENGTHY/LONG.

lose See MISLAY/LOSE.

lot/lots 1. In "a lot (*lots*) of food," "lots of fun," "a lot of birds," *a lot* (two words) and *lots* are SWE, although slightly informal. However, conservative writers prefer *many, much, large quantities* (or *numbers*), or the like. 2. When *a lot* or *lots* is used as an apparent subject, as in "A lot of corn *was* spilled," the noun following *of* determines whether the verb is singular or plural: "A lot of apples *were* spoiled." "Lots of flour is left." "Lots of flowers are left." The explanation is that *a lot* or *lots* is not a real subject but a modifier of the subject.

loud speaker/loudspeaker A *loud speaker* is a person who speaks in a loud voice. A *loudspeaker* is an instrument for amplifying sound: "Music came booming from a nearby loudspeaker."

lousy This means "louse-infested." In the sense of "bad, inferior, unpleasant," *lousy* is FF (slang). An old joke:

Teacher: "Two words you should never use. One is *swell* and the other is *lousy*."

Student: "What are the two words?"

love   Historically, *love* suggests intense affection, but the word has been cheapened not only by its frequently being limited to sexual activity, as in "making love," but also by its use with relatively trivial objects, as in "I love persimmons." Obviously, the numerous senses of the word cannot be thrown out, but many careful writers tend to restrict it to such senses as God's love for humanity or the strong and often enduring affection between man and woman or parent and child.

lovely   Overused to describe almost anything that a person likes.

low profile   Philip Howard, an Englishman, calls *low profile* "Pentagonese, or American defence jargon." The Pentagon, for example, favors tanks that have a low profile, that is, are difficult to see from a distance. So far so good. But the expression has become too widely employed in too many contexts. Some corporation officers (even tall ones) are urged to maintain a low profile, and so (very often) are school administrators and teachers and anyone else not likely to be helped by publicity.

lowbrow   See HIGHBROW/LOWBROW/MIDDLEBROW.

Ltd.   See LIMITED/LTD./SMALL.

luggage   See BAGGAGE/LUGGAGE.

lunch/luncheon   Interchangeable, but *luncheon* is more probable for a planned, formal or semiformal occasion. Hamburgers are more likely for lunch, Salisbury steak (glorified hamburger) or even London broil for a luncheon.

lusty/lustful   In modern usage, *lustful* is largely restricted to sexual appetite or desire: "He looked at her with lustful eyes." *Lusty,* however, although it does not rule out sexuality, means "vigorous, robust, active": "He looked athletic, lusty." It may also be used to describe a vigorous way of doing something: "lusty singing."

luxuriant/luxurious   The usual meaning of *luxuriant* is "growing abundantly": "the luxuriant plant life of the tropics, "luxuriant hibiscuses." Unusually fertile soil on occasion is called luxuriant. A spin-off definition is "elaborately ornate": "a luxuriant, even florid room with colorful rugs, bright tapestries, and geegaws galore." *Luxurious* is related to *luxury*. It suggests riches and probably comfort and good taste: "the Queen's luxurious bedroom."

M

machismo/macho   *Macho,* Spanish for "male, masculine," is usually an adjective but sometimes a noun equivalent to *machismo. Machismo,* a vogue word in the United States from the 1960s on, means "overtly expressed maleness," including exhibition of boldness or courage, aggressiveness, and (often) domination of women.

macro-/micro- These are combining forms with opposite meanings: *macro-* "large," *micro-* "small." For example, the *macroclimate* is the climate of a large geographical area, such as the Antarctic; the *microclimate* is that of a relatively small area, such as Chicago, in comparison with the climate of Illinois or the macroclimate of the Midwest.

mad See ANGRY/MAD.

magic/magical Sometimes interchangeable, *magic* as a modifier serves mainly to identify: "magic show," "magic lanterns." *Magical* describes things as being "like magic": "a magical change," "The effect of her words was magical."

magniloquent See ELOQUENT/GRANDILOQUENT/MAGNILOQUENT.

magnitude In most instances *size, significance,* or *importance* is preferable, especially if the topic is inconsequential. This sentence from a sports commentary illustrates dubious use: "The fact that the loss plunges the Chiefs into last place shows the magnitude of the defeat." When two teams are battling for next-to-last place, the "magnitude" of a loss or a victory cannot be very great.

maintain See CLAIM.

major SWE generally uses *major* in serious, important contexts. Dubious: "a major disagreement in the village council," "Are you faced with a major decision about tonight's dinner entrée?" *More major* and *most major* are even more questionable, because, at least historically, *major* (as well as *minor*) is already a comparative.

majority/plurality In an election no candidate with fewer than half of the votes may claim a *majority*. If 5,000 votes are cast, a minimum of 2,501 is a majority. In some circumstances a two-thirds majority or other large fraction may be required. If in the election with 5,000 votes *A* received 2,000, *B* received 1,600, and *C* received 1,400, *A* has a *plurality* of 400. No one has a majority. (In many elections only a plurality is required.)

make As a synonym of *earn* ("Mrs. Landon makes forty thousand a year"), *make* was long opposed by purists but has become so widely used that dictionaries now list it without comment. Color it SWE.

make a pass Now SWE, although somewhat informal, for "make a sexual overture." In transportation, it is standard for "make an approach": "The little plane made a pass at the runway but went up again without touching down."

make an investigation into SWE shortens to *investigate*. SANE notes that other phrases with *make* can also be reduced. Examples: "make a comment" – *comment*; "make a report" – *report*; "make a study of" – *study*; "make use of" – *use*.

make do SWE for "get along with a somewhat insufficient or otherwise unsuitable or unsatisfactory amount or variety": "The family had to make do with forty dollars a week." "She made do with her fraying coat for another year."

MALAPROPISM   This book is about appropriate words. A malapropism is not appropriate. It is a word confused with another of similar sound or spelling. *Malapropism* dates back to 1775, when Richard Brinsley Sheridan's play *The Rivals* introduced Mrs. Malaprop. Her name, from French *mal à propos* ("not right for this purpose"), suggests her problem. She urges her niece Lydia to "illiterate" (obliterate) Beverley from her memory. She does not like a young woman to be a "progeny (prodigy) of learning" but thinks that a well-bred girl should "be mistress of orthodoxy" (orthography), and that she should "reprehend" (apprehend) the true meaning of what she is saying. She hopes that Lydia will be courted by a captain who will find her "not altogether illegible" (ineligible). In her own love affair she hopes to find "joy infallible" (ineffable). Mrs. Malaprop is a humorous character, quite unaware that she is making herself ridiculous. She has not learned that simple words which one is sure of are much safer and saner than polysyllables wrongly used.

male chauvinist pig   See CHAUVINISM.

malevolent/malicious   Sometimes interchangeable, but *malevolent* stresses intention, "wanting bad things to happen," while *malicious* more often refers to the hostile act itself: "malicious mischief."

maltreat/mistreat   Although each word means "to treat badly," *maltreat* implies a higher degree of roughness and cruelty.

mammoth (adjective)   Best restricted to huge things. The sales advertised by small-town department stores seldom qualify. Macy's sales – maybe.

man and wife   Although long used in many English and American wedding ceremonies, in other contexts *husband and wife* is more appropriate because both words refer to marital status.

man (woman) of letters   Pretentious and unspecific term for *writer, author, poet, literary critic,* and the like.

mandatory   Perhaps because of executive privilege, former President Gerald Ford was entitled to say (and did say) "absolutely mandatory." The rest of us should be satisfied with *mandatory*.

manhandle   See ANNIHILATE, DESTROY, FLAY . . .

-mania/-phobia   The combining form *-mania* refers to an extreme eagerness or passion for doing something, either bad or good: *kleptomania* ("urge to steal"), *bibliomania* ("enthusiasm for using or collecting books"). The form *-phobia* refers to obsessive fear: *claustrophobia* ("fear of small enclosed areas"), *triskaidekaphobia* ("fear of 13").

mankind   After a time when a few feminists wanted to eliminate all such words as *chairman, foreman,* and *mankind,* most modern women grant that *mankind* includes women, too, and need not be replaced by *people, humankind,* or something else.

manly/mannish   *Manly* is a term of praise. The person described, often a boy, has qualities considered especially desirable in a man, such as bravery, strength, and courtesy. *Mannish* now usually applies to women or things associated with some women: "Women's suits this year have a mannish look."

man-made artifact   See ARTIFACT.

manner born (to the)   *Manner* is SWE, not *manor*. When Hamlet said that he was "to the manner born," he meant that he had spent his childhood learning the customs or "manners" of his native land. The spelling *manor* would have implied a boast about being born in a manor. If that had been Hamlet's intention, he might have used *palace* or *castle*.

manslaughter   See HOMICIDE/MANSLAUGHTER/MURDER.

margin/score   Football announcer: "The Saints lead by a margin of twenty to fourteen." No. The *score* is twenty to fourteen. The *margin* is six points.

marks of ellipsis   See ELLIPSE/ELLIPSIS.

marriage/nuptials/wedding   Many brides and some bridegrooms prepare elaborately for their *weddings* or their *nuptials* – a more highfalutin name for the ceremonies. Not nearly so many brides and bridegrooms prepare adequately for their *marriages* – in the sense of lasting unions.

marry/be married to   When it was customary for a man to woo and the maid to accept or reject, society reporters and Aunt Harriet wrote that "John married Anne" or "Anne was married to John." But now that many women woo and many weddings are reached by alternating the role of pursuer, the distinction in form is not regularly observed. Now Anne may marry John, and John may be married to Anne.

martyr/victim   A *martyr* accepts suffering or death willingly – may even seek martyrdom for a cause in which he or she passionately believes. A *victim*, in contrast, is usually unwilling, unacceptive. Some outside force brings suffering or death, and while still alive the victim struggles to avoid or overcome it. One exception: A person who endures great suffering – say, from cancer – is often called a martyr to the disease but obviously is also a victim.

marvel/miracle   A *marvel* is an oddity, something to wonder at: "The Taj Mahal is an architectural marvel." The word ordinarily refers to a thing rather than an event. A *miracle*, although it, too, is something to wonder at, has qualities of the superhuman, the supernatural. We speak, for example, of the miracle in which Christ fed thousands with a few loaves and fishes. It is most often an event.

massacre   See ANNIHILATE, DESTROY, FLAY . . .

massive   Originally used to refer to physical mass, *massive* spread to include abstractions such as "massive campaigns," "a massive plot," "massive affirmation," and so on. Such a shift is legitimate and often occurs in SWE, but *massive* does seem overused.

masterful/masterly   These two words are sometimes used interchangeably, but many people preserve this distinction: *Masterful* means "strong, demanding": "The overseer's masterful voice and dire threats frightened the workers." *Masterly* means "skilled, expert in a craft": "This cabinetwork is indeed masterly."

material/matériél Almost anything can be called *material*, but *matériel* is most often military gear. It also means "apparatus or machinery" (not personnel) used industrially.

materialize Pretentious for "happen." *Materialize* means "assume actual form, become real": "Their dream house was finally materializing." Dubious: "The feared accident materialized the following morning." (An accident itself is not a material thing, even though things are involved in it.)

matinee performance SWE omits *performance* because *matinee* means "daytime performance."

matutinal ablutions No, SWE wouldn't write that for "morning bath." But whenever inclined to use a polysyllable (whoops! big word) instead of an equally pertinent short one, a would-be writer of SWE may think about *matutinal ablutions*.

maudlin/mawkish *Maudlin* carries the connotation of tearfulness, sometimes mingled with sentimentality. It is based on (Mary) Magdalene, a symbol of tearful repentance: "The drunk became maudlin each time he mentioned his wife." *Mawkish* sentimentality is so effusive as to be nauseating. The word is derived from a Middle English word for "maggot."

mausoleum/morgue/mortuary A *mausoleum* is a large, stately tomb. A *morgue* is a place, often under police supervision, in which persons found dead are kept until identified or buried or cremated. The term is also used for a newspaper's reference library. A *mortuary* is a funeral home, once called an "undertaking parlor," where bodies are kept until time for burial.

maven (also mavin) Introduced from Yiddish as slang in the middle of this century, *maven* is now sometimes used in SWE for "expert, connoisseur," and often refers to things more commonplace than those shown in the Metropolitan Museum or heard in Lincoln Center: "a rhinestone maven," "mavens of Elvis Presley souvenirs."

mawkish See MAUDLIN/MAWKISH.

maximize/minimize To *maximize* an effect (or anything else) is to increase it to the greatest extent possible. *Minimize* has the opposite meaning. The definitions make clear that these verbs cannot logically be modified by such words as *somewhat*, *greatly*, or *considerably*, although *nearly* or *almost* is possible.

may possibly be See POSSIBLE/POSSIBLY.

may See CAN/MAY.

may/might *Might* started as the past tense of *may*, but the time distinction is now not emphasized. *May* suggests slightly greater probability than *might*, as illustrated in "We may (*might*) call you tomorrow."

maybe/perhaps Interchangeable, with *perhaps* a shade more formal.

mayn't See CAN'T/MAYN'T.

maze See LABYRINTH/MAZE.

meander/wander Each means "to wander idly and aimlessly." *Meander*, however, often has the sense of "winding." A meandering stream, for example, is very crooked. Unlikely: "Where is my meandering son tonight?"

meaningful Some writers assert that *meaningful* isn't meaningful, but lexicographers define it as "significant" and attach no label. Appears often in SWE.

meant to be In the advertising exhortation "See these islands from small boats, as they were meant to be seen," the reader wonders about who "meant them to be seen" in any specific way. Similar is a cereal manufacturer's claim "Breakfast as it was meant to be."

mechanization See AUTOMATION/MECHANIZATION.

media (verb with) Is *media* to be treated as singular or plural? The battle goes on. Conservatives favor *are* rather than *is*, on the ground that the media are newspapers, magazines, radio, television, and so on, and not a single entity. Liberals say that *data* and *agenda* have switched from plural to singular, so why not *media*? The conservative rebuttal is that *data* can mean one set of figures, *agenda* one list, but *media* does not mean one single thing. The conservative argument seems stronger. One more vote for *media are*. FF says *medias*.

mediate See ARBITRATE/MEDIATE.

medic Now SWE, although infrequent, for "physician, surgeon." Long established in the armed forces.

mediocre This word has worsened or weakened in meaning (a process called "pejoration"). What conservatives call its "true meaning" is "average, neither good nor bad," but it has been used so often to mean "below average, not good" that anything or anyone now described as mediocre is faintly damned. Too bad, because the language needs a word for "in the middle range, intermediate in degree of excellence." (The now rare *middling* has suffered the same pejoration.) See also AVERAGE/COMMON, ORDINARY.

meet/meet (up) with "I'll meet with you tomorrow" suggests a longer get-together than does "I'll meet you tomorrow." *Meet with* is standard when referring to experiences: "meet with disaster," "meet with unexpected opposition (or *offers of help*)." SWE deletes the useless *up* in *meet up with*.

melodic/melodious Although they are sometimes interchangeable, *melodic* is a somewhat more technical term. It means "pertaining to melody," and thus is differentiated from *rhythmic* and *harmonic*. *Melodious* is more often the word needed by the layman. It means "pleasant-sounding, tuneful, containing an agreeable succession of sounds": "the melodious anthems of our church choir."

melody See HARMONY/MELODY.

melt/thaw The basic distinction is that when something *melts*, it changes from a solid to a liquid, but when something *thaws*, it changes from a frozen to an unfrozen state. Thus heated lead melts, but we thaw a frozen turkey. Snow melts during a spring thaw. Figuratively, *melting* may refer to a softening of attitude: "Joyce's heart melted when the baby smiled up at her." *Thawed* would suggest that Joyce's earlier attitude was extremely hostile.

memorandum Standard usage is "one *memorandum*," "two or more *memorandums* or *memoranda*." SWE uses either form. Historically, the trend has been toward anglicizing plurals of foreign nouns.

memories of the past SWE deletes *of the past.*

mendacity/mendicity *Mendacity* is what a liar is guilty of, and *mendicity* is what a beggar engages in. *Mendicant* friars lived by begging. *Mendicancy* is a synonym of *mendicity.*

mental telepathy *Telepathy* is by definition "thought transference." SWE omits *mental.*

meretricious Not related to *merit*. Something meretricious is showy, tawdry, deceptive, and possibly conducive to evil: "the meretricious allurements of a circus sideshow."

Messrs. Americans seldom use the plural of *Mr.*, preferring "Mr. Brown and Mr. Lavel," but may use *Messrs.* before a long list or omit titles entirely.

meteor/meteorite/meteoroid A *meteoroid* is a tiny-to-large body that wanders the solar system and may happen to enter our atmosphere. Friction makes it burn, and we exclaim, "There's a meteor!" or "There's a shooting star!" If any of the meteoroid survives the fiery passage, the stony or metallic piece that strikes the earth's surface is a *meteorite.*

method/methodology *Method* is usually rather narrow, applied, for example, to a procedure in a chemistry class. *Methodology* can pertain to the set of principles and methods followed in an entire field of knowledge, such as chemistry, or in an elaborate scientific study. When in doubt, SWE tries *method* first.

meticulous/punctilious/scrupulous All refer to being careful about details. To be *meticulous* is to be unusually precise and painstaking – often anxiously so. *Punctilious*, from Latin for "point," means paying great attention to small points, even unimportant ones. For example, a punctilious person obeys even small rules of etiquette and insists on "approved" forms in wedding invitations. A *scrupulous* person has scruples about possible mistakes or misconduct, is especially conscientious about behavior: "a scrupulously clean politician, making no promises that she is unlikely to keep."

Mexican-American See CHICANO.

micro- See MACRO-, MICRO-.

middle-age(d)/teen-age(d) 1. Should a person be described as *middle-age* or *middle-aged*, *teen-age*, or *teen-aged*? Answers are not consistent. SWE uses both forms. 2. *Middle age* (no hyphen) as a noun is variously defined as the period in a person's life between ages forty and sixty, or forty-five and sixty-five. In a life span of seventy years, the middle third would be from twenty-three through forty-seven, but apparently no one accepts that as middle age. See also ELDERLY.

Middle English/Old English Even some college English majors say that Chaucer and Shakespeare wrote in "Old English." Those authors wrote "old" English but not "Old." Language historians say that Old English ended and Middle English began about A.D. 1100. Chaucer wrote in Middle English, which lasted until about 1500, when Early Modern English, used by Shakespeare, began.

middle See CENTER/MIDDLE.

midget See DWARF/MIDGET/PYGMY.

midnight Tuesday is ending, and Wednesday is beginning. The time is exactly twelve o'clock. Should we say "Tuesday midnight" or "Wednesday midnight"? Because the night started on Tuesday, the former is SWE.

might See MAY/MIGHT.

mighty Informal adverb for "very," as in "mighty happy," was more popular in the nineteenth century than it is now. It is rare in SWE as an adverb.

mile See FOOT, HOUR, MILE . . .

miles square See SQUARE MILES.

million (plural) As is true of *dozen, score, thousand,* and *billion,* the singular form is used when the number is specified: "eight million unemployed," "several million (or *millions*) of them." Otherwise the plural is customary: "millions of cicadas."

miniature Not a synonym for *small, miniature* is best restricted to a scaled-down version, as "a miniature plane, twelve inches long." Ordinarily, there is no "miniature lake," ". . . forest," and so on.

minimize See MAXIMIZE/MINIMIZE.

minister/pastor/preacher/priest/rector The first three are used interchangeably in many Protestant churches. *Minister* is the inclusive term. *Pastor,* from Latin for "shepherd," emphasizes caring for "the flock" by making pastoral calls, helping the poor and the unhappy, and so on. *Preacher* emphasizes sermon delivery. Episcopalian ministers are *rectors.* (This term is used in other senses by Anglicans, and also by Roman Catholics, whose ministers are called *priests.*)

minus As in "Because of the accident he is minus two fingers," the usage is unlikely in SWE.

minutia "A detail, a trivial thing." The word is generally employed as a plural, *minutiae.*

miracle See MARVEL/MIRACLE.

miserly See ECONOMIC/ECONOMICAL.

mishap See ACCIDENT/MISHAP.

mislay/lose If you *mislay* your keys, you have merely left them in an unaccustomed place, but if you *lose* them, your chances of getting them back are much smaller. See also MISS/LOSE.

misremember See DISREMEMBER/MISREMEMBER.

miss/lose In expressions such as *miss his opportunity* and *lose his opportunity*, *miss* sounds a little less serious than *lose*. *Miss* may have a subliminal association with shooting: if one misses a shot, he probably can take another. But *lose* has an air of finality. See also MISLAY/LOSE.

mistake See ERROR/MISTAKE.

mistreat See MALTREAT/MISTREAT.

mistress See FEMALE COMPANION/GIRLFRIEND/MISTRESS.

mob Has been SWE for years, although eighteenth-century authors such as Jonathan Swift and Richard Steele opposed this shortening of the Latin *mobile vulgus* ("fickle crowd"). Brevity often supersedes length.

mode/mood Interchangeable as grammatical terms: "subjunctive mood (or *mode*)." They are not synonymous otherwise.

model See EXAMPLE/EXEMPLAR/IDEAL . . .

modern/modernistic In general, SWE uses *modern* – shorter and less judgmental. *Modernistic* is related to *modernism*, which like many other isms is sometimes held in low esteem. To many people, including some who profess to like modern art, modernistic art is thought (mistakenly) to refer mainly to distorted figures, strange angles, and utter meaninglessness.

mom-and-pop (also *mom-'n'-pop*) An informal but often accurate way to characterize a small store or other business owned or directly managed by a couple or a family. It is rare in SWE.

momentous See HISTORIC/MOMENTOUS.

monastic/monkish *Monastic* means "pertaining to monks or to the monasteries in which they live": "monastic life," "monastic architecture." *Monkish* is a usually unfavorable term for "like a monk." It suggests narrowness, unworldliness, excessive piety, a withdrawn quality.

monk See FRIAR/MONK; MONASTIC/MONKISH.

monkey (verb) Informal SWE intransitive verb for "play idly, manipulate unsystematically," generally followed by *with*, *around*, or *around with*: "I was monkeying with my computer." A seldom used, although SWE, transitive verb, *monkey* means "imitate, ape": "She monkeyed her grandmother's limping walk."

monolog(ue)/soliloquy A *soliloquy* is talking to oneself, especially in a play, as Hamlet does. A *monolog* (or *monologue*) is a one-person discourse, generally humorous, addressed to others. In his television talk show, Johnny Carson over the years has delivered thousands of monologs.

mood See MODE/MOOD.

moonlight (verb) Dating back to the mid-1900s, *moonlight* has now become SWE for "earn additional income from a second job."

moot The usual SWE meaning is "debatable, undecided." A *moot question* is one about which considerable evidence can be presented on each side. Sometimes, confusingly, *moot* is used for "unimportant," "unnecessary," or "hypothetical." That usage makes *moot question* uncertain in meaning. SANE recommends against *moot* with any of those three definitions.

moral/morale *Moral* (adjective or noun) has to do with the goodness or badness of human actions: "moral conduct," "the moral of the story." *Morale*, only a noun, refers to mental or emotional condition, spirits, willingness to work or to obey orders: "After the victory, the morale of the troops was improved."

moral/moralistic A *moral* person is one who believes in and practices conduct that the general public considers "right." A *moralistic* person can accurately be described in the same way. However, the word has come to be associated with narrow definitions of "rightness" and with preachiness in attempting to induce others to accept those definitions. Polonius in *Hamlet* was a moralistic person but not necessarily moral.

morality/mortality *Morality* pertains to moral standards or moral behavior: "No one questioned the morality of her views." *Mortality* refers to the fact that all things that live must someday die: "the mortality of man." The opposites are *immorality* and *immortality* ("living forever"). The importance of distinguishing is shown in the notorious distortion of the title of Wordsworth's "Ode on Intimations of Immortality," which a student called "Ode on Imitations of Immorality."

moratorium This resounding word for "deferment, delay" is used in SWE only for consequential matters, such as granting a nation a moratorium in paying its debts. Dubious or humorous: "The coach called a time-out – a welcome moratorium in the trouncing by the Tigers."

morbid Football announcer: "The punter has had a morbid afternoon." Probably he meant "unsuccessful," "poor," or "mistake-filled." *Morbid* means "diseased," "psychologically unhealthy," or "too preoccupied with unwholesome thoughts."

more preferable SWE omits the redundant *more*.

more than See also ABOVE/MORE THAN; BETTER THAN.

more than one (verb with) Logic demands "more than one were," but logic is frequently defeated by usage. The SWE usage is "more than one was" but "more than two were."

more than/over Interchangeable in such expressions as "more than (*over*) five dollars," "more than (*over*) a foot long."

mores This word (pronounced more-*ayz* or mo-*rayz*) means "accepted views and customs" of a group. The spelling is an unchanged borrowing from Latin.

morgue See MAUSOLEUM/MORGUE/MORTUARY.

mortality See MORALITY/MORTALITY.

mortgagee/mortgagor It may seem odd, but the *mortgagee* lends the money and the *mortgagor* borrows it. The explanation is that the mortgagor puts a mortgage on his or her property.

mortuary See MAUSOLEUM/MORGUE/MORTUARY.

most (for *very*) *Most*, as in "our most gracious hostess," is SWE even though no comparison is intended.

most number TV reporter: "The picture receiving the most number of Oscar nominations is . . ." SWE says "largest (*highest*) number" or "the most Oscar nominations." Although *most number* is not standard, its opposite, *least number*, is. Also standard: *smallest (lowest, greatest, smaller, greater, lesser) number*.

most See also ALMOST/MOST.

mostly FF (dialectal or highly informal) for "most of the time": "Mos'ly, he jes droops aroun' the house."

motif/motive SWE prefers *motif* for these meanings: (1) "recurrent theme in a literary or artistic work," (2) "recurrent phrase in music," (3) "repeated decorative or architectural figure or design." *Motive* for any of these meanings sometimes appears but may be confusing.

motor See ENGINE/MOTOR.

moving violation Police jargon for breaking the law while driving a vehicle; for example, disregarding a stop sign, driving left of center.

Ms. Unquestionably, the language needs *Ms.* It designates a female without regard to her marital status, just as *Mr.* serves for either a married or an unmarried male.

much in evidence SWE, but *conspicuous* or *apparent* is more direct.

muchly Not listed in most dictionaries. *Much* serves as both adjective and adverb.

mucus/phlegm *Mucus* is the useful lubricant that coats body channels. (The lining of the channels is *mucous membrane*. Note the different spellings: noun *mucus*, adjective *mucous*.) *Phlegm* is, in effect, worn-out or morbid mucus, such as may be coughed up or expelled through the nose.

mugging See BURGLARY/HOLDUP/ROBBERY . . .

munch A crunching sound accompanies munching. One can *munch* popcorn, but not most sandwiches other than crisply toasted ones.

murder See EXECUTE/KILL, MURDER; HOMICIDE/MANSLAUGHTER/MURDER.

murderer See ASSASSIN/MURDERER.

mushmelon FF (dialectal) for *muskmelon, cantaloupe*.

mushroom (verb) Real mushrooms grow with amazing speed. The verb has become SWE for almost anything that grows or expands rapidly: "A tent city mushroomed, soon covering several acres."

must (noun) "Flowered blouses are a must this spring." *Must* with the meaning of "an absolute requirement" dates back a couple of centuries. Some conservatives, however, prefer to use it only as a verb. In SWE the noun use is occasional and somewhat informal.

must needs See NEED.

mutual cooperation SWE deletes *mutual*. See also COMMON/MUTUAL.

my dear In the salutation of a letter, *My dear* may be variously interpreted as supercilious, affectionate, prissy, or old-fashioned. Used today less frequently than in 1910.

myriad Either a noun or an adjective: "A myriad of stars," "the myriad stars of the heavens." The original Greek meaning was "ten thousand," and dictionaries still list that as one English definition, but that sense is now only figurative.

myself SWE as a reflexive: "I hurt myself"; and as an intensive: "I myself saw it." Otherwise FF for *I* or *me*, frequently so used by the grammatically unsure: "My father and myself stayed up all night" (SWE: *I*). "It was a terrifying ordeal for my father and myself" (SWE: *me*).

myth See FABLE/LEGEND/MYTH.

N

nab The reputability of a word is often hard to predict. *Nab* ("to grab, catch a wrongdoer, arrest, snatch") has been used by reputable writers, including Dickens and Thackeray, since the seventeenth century, but dictionaries still list it as slang or informal. SWE now uses it as a light synonym for "capture, arrest."

nadir/zenith Some people write *nadir* when they mean its antonym, *zenith*. One who thinks of the words together is likely to recall that *zenith*, not *nadir*, refers to the highest point in the sky. Both terms are also used figuratively: "the nadir of her despair."

naked/nude Usually interchangeable, although obviously painters paint "nudes" and not "nakeds." One may refer to an unsheathed sword as "naked" but not "nude." A legal document still needing some additions to be complete is "nude" but not "naked." For the human body, *naked* is the more frank, honest, and shameless word. Some people regard *nude* as "nicer"; it often suggests careful posing rather than careless and accustomed intimacy.

name of the game, what it's all about Both expressions have been popularized by sports announcers and have spread, often in contradictory statements: "Defense (*Offense, Scoring*) is the name of the game (or *what it's all about*)." "Making (*Saving, Spending*) money is . . ." SWE writers try to write what they really want to say about defense, saving, and so on.

namely SWE writers may ask themselves, "Is *namely* needed?" It is not, for example, in "My sisters, namely Faye and Dorothea, were . . ."

NAMES OF PEOPLE When first using a person's name in an article or a book, SWE normally identifies him or her not as Patterson or L. Patterson but as L. N. Patterson, Louise N. Patterson, Louise Patterson, Dr. L. N. Patterson, and so on. Often a further identification is desirable: "of the Harvard Medical School." Subsequent references, unless far removed, may be only Patterson or Dr. Patterson, although the *New York Times* always uses a title – *Mr., Mrs., Miss, Ms., Dr.,* and so on.

namesake See EPONYM/NAMESAKE.

nary FF (dialectal, old-fashioned) for "no, neither, not a, not one": "I didn't have nary a drop to drink." *Nary* may still be heard in secluded Appalachian and other areas, as (more rarely) may its companion *ary,* for "any, some, either": "I don't like ary one." "Have you got ary apples?"

national (noun) Increasingly used, especially as in "a Mexican national," to show that a person's nationality is not American. *National* is not the same as *citizen*: the Mexican national is not necessarily a citizen of Mexico. See also CITIZEN/INHABITANT/RESIDENT.

native A *native* of San Francisco (or any other place) was born there. The term *natives* has largely lost the earlier connotation of illiterate, half-naked denizens of some largely unexplored area. In some U.S. tourist areas, *native* is used to differentiate permanent residents from transients, even though the residents may have been born elsewhere. The transients are often given uncomplimentary informal names such as "snowbirds."

naturalist/naturist A *naturist* is anyone who enjoys and wants to preserve the joys and beauties of nature; he or she may also be a nudist. A *naturalist* presumably enjoys nature, too, and conceivably may be a nudist but ordinarily is a botanist, zoologist, or other student of nature. To a literary critic a naturalist is a writer of naturalistic fiction.

nature **1.** A more specific word is often desirable. For example, if a woman writes about nature, the reader needs to know whether her chief subject is owls, forests, wildflowers, human nature, or . . . **2.** A phrase such as *in nature* or *by nature* can often be omitted, as is true in "Bobsledding is dangerous (in nature)" and "(By nature), Jens is shy."

naught/nought Variants for "zero" or "nothing," both words seem old-fashioned. "Went for naught" survives but is not thriving. See also AUGHT/NAUGHT.

nauseated/nauseous Traditionalists have a good reason for trying to preserve a distinction between these words because, if used in the standard way, they prevent misunderstanding. In SWE "I am nauseated" means "I am sick to my stomach," but "I am nauseous" means, "I make people sick (by my appearance or actions)." The boundary between the words, however, is rapidly disappearing.

naval/navel *Naval* means "pertaining to a navy." *Navel* is standard for "belly button."

n.b. This abbreviation of Latin *nota bene* ("note carefully") is seldom used today except in business correspondence and reports; even there, *Note* or *Note especially* seems more frequent.

Near East   Now usually called "Middle East" or, less often, "Mideast."

near-record   Bernstein criticizes a statement that voter registration "set a near-record," saying that that was like saying, "The team scored three near-touchdowns." For that example, the criticism is justified, for near-records are not set, and near-touchdowns do not appear on the scoreboard. However, "Temperatures reached a near-record high" is different, comparable to "almost matched the record."

near-miss   Widely used even in SWE, although illogical. If a bullet strikes a tree three feet from you, isn't it really a *near-hit?*

necessary requirement (or *requisite*)   SWE omits *necessary.* See also ESSENTIAL/INDISPENSABLE/NECESSARY . . .

necessity   Sometimes a contributor to wordiness. "The necessity of hurrying annoyed her" might be better worded "Having to hurry annoyed her" or even "Hurrying annoyed her."

nee   Now written without the French accent mark. "Lucy Snodgrass, nee Walker" means "Lucy Snodgrass, whose family name (or unmarried name) is Walker." Dubious: "Lucy Snodgrass, nee Lucy Walker," because *nee* means "born as," and the only name Lucy was born with was *Walker.*

need   Some constructions with *need* have an archaic flavor, although they are still used occasionally: "He need not do (*agree, retire,* and so on)" means "He does not need to." "Need she have chosen (*decided, asked,* and so on)" means "Did she need to?" "If need be" means "If it is (*becomes*) necessary." *Needs must,* as in "She needs must heed her mother's words," is archaic. SWE omits *needs.*

need for/need of   In some sentences *need of* is ambiguous. In "The need of nurses is well known," are the nurses needy or are they in short supply? Clear: "Nurses' low pay . . ." or "The shortage of nurses . . ." When not ambiguous, *need of* can be satisfactory: "Ann's need of (or *need for*) money was becoming acute."

needless to say   See (IT) GOES WITHOUT SAYING/NEEDLESS TO SAY.

ne'er   See E'ER/NE'ER.

negative   See AFFIRMATIVE/NEGATIVE.

neglect/negligence   *Neglect* usually appears worse than *negligence,* which may result from mere carelessness. A child suffering from parental neglect is more likely to be cold and hungry than one suffering from negligence.

negligent/negligible   A *negligent* person is careless about something or fails to do something desirable. *Negligible* most often applies to things or actions; it means "not important, not worth attention": "a negligible sum of money (*contribution to the discussion, breeze,* or the like)." On rare occasions it may apply to persons: a negligible tennis player is one considered highly unlikely to win a tournament. More than likely, however: "his negligible chances of winning."

negotiate   Fowler and his American reviser, Nicholson, say that *negotiate* in the sense of "tackle successfully" is so bad that it "stamps a writer as literarily a barbarian." Modern American dictionaries, however, accept "negotiate a sharp curve" as unquestioningly as "negotiate a union contract." SWE.

Negress Regarded by many as offensive, perhaps because no comparable "Whitess" exists.

neighborhood/vicinity Both words refer to a small area, but a *neighborhood* is usually smaller. In addition, the word suggests neighborliness or even warmth. The size of a *vicinity* is indefinite but sometimes is rather large: "in the vicinity of Omaha."

neither See EITHER; EITHER . . . OR/NEITHER . . . NOR; NOR; NOT ONLY . . . BUT ALSO.

nepotism Some medieval church officials euphemistically called their illegitimate sons "nephews" and helped them to get good jobs – a practice called *nepotismo* in Italian. Since that time, the English *nepotism* has acquired the meaning of favoritism toward not only "nephews" but also other relatives and even friends. The "patronage" given by politicians to their supporters is not much different.

net (tennis) See LET/NET.

nether Old-fashioned adjective for "lower" or "beneath the earth's surface": "her nether lip," "the nether regions."

never had it so good This phrase is FF (informal) for "was never so prosperous (*well fed, comfortable,* or the like)." The uncertainty about what *it* is and the vagueness of *good* may exclude this expression from most SWE contexts.

nevertheless See BUT/HOWEVER; NEVERTHELESS.

new beginner If someone joins an existing group of beginners, he may legitimately be called "a new beginner." Otherwise, SWE omits *new*.

new/novel *New* refers to time or condition: "The new version seems stronger." "Your coat looks new." *Novel* emphasizes creativeness, unusualness: "a novel interpretation of *The Mikado*," "novel decorative effects."

New York City SWE uses all three words whenever *New York* can be misinterpreted to mean the state. (The legal name is *The City of New York*.)

newfangled Perhaps because of its strange sound, *newfangled* is often considered slang or colloquial. However, it has long been established in SWE. Unlike *new*, it is uncomplimentary, meaning "needlessly or excessively new, faddish."

news (verb with) An anecdote about the great newspaper editor Horace Greeley asserts that when he came into the office he customarily asked, "Are there any news?" A smart-alecky cub reporter once responded, "No, sir. Nary a new." If Greeley really did treat *news* as a plural, today's editors would disagree. To them *news* is always singular. The *New York Times* slogan is not "All the news that *are* fit to print."

nice Strunk and White call *nice* "a shaggy, all-purpose word, to be used sparingly in formal composition." Probably everything that somebody likes has been described by someone as "nice." SWE chooses the most appropriate of the hundred or more substitutes, such as *tasty, aromatic, kind, well-proportioned, moral, friendly, lovable, likable, wise, precise.*

nicely Overused. Some alternatives, to be chosen according to context, are *attractively, carefully, cleverly, evenly, pleasantly, precisely, satisfactorily, suitably, thoughtfully, well.*

nicety A nicety is not usually "something nice." It is most often a subtle point, a detail: "a nicety of grammar," "niceties of diplomatic (or *social*) manners."

nigh The word is seldom used in today's English.

nimrod It's no longer considered clever – certainly not original – to call a hunter a "nimrod." The term got its start in Genesis. Noah's great-grandson, Nimrod, was "a mighty hunter before the Lord."

nitty-gritty This FF (slang) expression means "details, basic but possibly unpleasant facts."

no. This abbreviation for *number* (Latin *numero*), useful in commercial descriptions such as "Part No. 426-B," is not standard in most other contexts. (The symbol # is also used for *number*: "Part #426-B.")

no-good Informal, but found occasionally in SWE, as an adjective: "a no-good loafer." In the sense of "worthless," *no good* is found sometimes in SWE: "This poem is no good." SWE generally prefers *not good, worthless, poor,* or a more specific word.

no later than See BEFORE/NO LATER THAN.

no problem Short for "There is (*was*) no problem (*difficulty*) in doing what is (*was*) asked" or "It will cause no problem for me to do that." The shortcut is used mainly in conversation but appears sometimes in business and other contexts: "XYZ Company wants Friday delivery of 4,800 widgets. No problem."

no sooner Followed in SWE by *than*, not *when*: "No sooner had Flo arrived than the party began to sparkle." An *as soon as* construction may save a word or two: "As soon as Flo arrived, the party . . ."

no such a As in "No such a story is credible," SWE usually omits *a*.

no thinking person A sentence such as "No thinking person will conclude that . . ." not only puts down many other people but also indirectly praises the writer, who seems to be boasting of his or her own thinking ability.

no use SWE in "There's no use arguing" or "It's no use to argue," in which the meaning is "There is no need for . . ." or "It will do no good to . . ." It is FF in the sense of "useless"; "His bicycle is no use" (*of no use* is possible here, but seems unnatural).

no way Now overused. A vogue expression that started as a shortening of "I see no way to do that" but broadened to other negative ideas: "Not at all," "Not essential," "Not now," "Not today," and so on. It has been worked, if not to death, at least to exhaustion.

nohow   FF (dialectal) in sentences such as "They couldn't raise the money nohow," in which it is part of a double negative. Questionable but possible although infrequent, in such sentences as "They could nohow raise the money," in which it is equivalent to "in no way."

noisome   SWE, but rarely used because many readers misinterpret it as "noisy." It means "harmful" or (especially with regard to odors) "offensive, putrid." It derives from the same root as *annoy*.

nom de plume   Unless referring to a pseudonymous French author, SWE is likely to choose *pen name*.

nomenclature   "A system of names or naming": "botanical nomenclature." SWE writes, "The society took its name from . . . ," not "its nomenclature."

171

nominal   Not the same as *low*, a *nominal* fee is so low that it is a fee in name only – for example, a fee of $1 for services worth $100. Sometimes for legal or other reasons someone sells property for a nominal amount (e.g., $5) when it may be worth thousands.

NON SEQUITUR   Latin for "it does not follow," this term is generally used in English for a statement or a part of a statement that has no apparent relationship to what preceded it: "A woodsman since his youth, he plays the violin in the local orchestra."

NONCE WORD   *Nonce* dates back to Middle English for *then one(s)*, meaning "for once." A nonce word is coined to fit a particular occasion and may possibly never be used again. For example, when Joe Louis was heavyweight boxing champion, one of his knocked-out opponents was said to have been sent on "a Louisana hayride." A writer who is lucky enough to think of a nonce word that fits the situation, is clear, and is clever or funny or both, should use it – even in moderately formal writing. Some nonce words should become standard, for example, that of the child who, not wanting to walk farther, said, "I don't feel walkative any more."

nonstandard/substandard   Many linguists prefer to call, for example, "he don't have none" *nonstandard* rather than *substandard*. They define *nonstandard* as "not ordinarily used *at this time* in edited writing." They realize that usage changes and that a double negative, for example, was once "correct" and may become so again. Because there are no permanent standards in language, they assert, *substandard* is illogical.

noon luncheon   SWE usually omits *noon*. However, it indicates the time if the luncheon is scheduled at a somewhat unusual hour, such as two o'clock. See also LUNCH/LUNCHEON.

nor   SWE if *neither* is its teammate, but ordinarily not in sentences such as "She does not want fame nor riches," where *or* is standard. Exception: In some sentences the fact that the second part is negative may not be clear unless *nor* is used, as in "The skater showed none of her usual grace or maintained her customary relaxed air" (SWE says, ". . . nor did she maintain . . ."); "Players on four teams have not voted, or is a vote expected before Monday" (SWE says, ". . . nor is a vote expected . . .").

nor none An FF double negative, as in "No sales tax was added in Florida, nor none in Georgia." SWE says, ". . . nor was any . . ." Also SWE: ". . . nor was any in Georgia either" (not *neither*).

normalcy/normality Interchangeable. *Normal* may also be used as a noun, as in "back to normal."

northerly See EASTERLY/EASTERN.

northward(s) Interchangeable, but *northward* has a strong lead over the *s* form, as is true of *southward, eastward, westward.*

nosh FF (slang or dialectal) noun or verb, from Yiddish for "snack."

nostalgia Once referring only to homesickness, and sometimes still so defined, *nostalgia* has broadened its meaning to "fond recollection of persons or places in one's past." Often suggestive, too, of a wish to revisit or relive parts of one's "good old days."

not (and other negatives) Only one negative is customary in SWE in each of these sentences:

> FF: "He did*n't* take *none* of it." SWE: "didn't take any," "took *none.*"
> FF: "She does*n't scarcely* (or *hardly*) have time." SWE: "She *scarcely* has time."
> FF: "We did*n't* buy any, *neither.*" SWE: ". . . either."
> FF: "I would *not* be surprised if she did*n't* decide to go home." SWE: ". . . if she decided . . ."

not (placement) (1) Not all of them are guilty. (2) All of them are not guilty. (3) They are all not guilty. Sentence 1 means "some are, some are not"; sentence 2 is ambiguous; and sentence 3 means that all are innocent. These examples show why SWE is careful about placement of *not.*

not about to/not all that FF (informal, wordy): "I'm not about to tell the judge that I'm not all that certain about what happened." SWE says, "I'm reluctant (*unwilling*) to tell the judge that I'm not sure about what happened."

not anything like/ nothing like These expressions are SWE in "Not anything like (or *Nothing like*) that had ever been seen in Dubuque." FF for "not nearly": "This brand costs nothing like as much."

not . . . but In sentences such as "Don't take but one" and "I didn't see but six of the buffalo," the *not . . . but* construction is frequent in conversation. "Take only one" and "I saw only six" are more likely in SWE.

not only . . . but also In SWE, constructions following *not only* and *but also* are grammatically similar. In
   The union

> not only *insisted on higher wages*
> but also *shorter working hours*

the italicized parts are obviously not grammatical equals, are not "parallel." In this revision they are:

The union insisted on

> not only *higher wages*
> but also *shorter working hours*

The same principle of parallel construction applies when the conjunctions are *both . . . and* or *neither . . . nor.* In conversation we may not have time to attain such parallelism consistently, but in writing we generally can take enough time to make one side balance the other.

not that tired (Also *not that much, . . . little, . . . strong,* and so on)
Conservatives object to using *that* as an adverb, and also to its indefiniteness; how tired is *that tired*? The expressions are firmly entrenched in FF but seldom seen in SWE. See also NOT TOO BAD OF A.

not to exceed Appropriate in business and legal documents, but in other writing *no* (or *not*) *more than* is usual.

not to worry Frequent in British speech, occasional in prose, this short substitute for "There is (or *was*) no need to worry" has gained popularity in the United States. It is rare in SWE.

not . . . too Radio interviewer: "You haven't been in Chicago too long, have you?" Smart-alec interviewee: "No, it just seems too long." *Not . . . too,* if used for *not . . . very,* can be ambiguous. SWE either omits *too* or substitutes *very.*

not too bad of a FF *not too bad of a* and its variants with other adjectives (*good, strange,* and so on) are based on the standard idiom illustrated in *too much of a good thing.* However, it's not too bad of an idea to delete the *of.* In fact, it's a good one, according to SWE custom. Similar is *not that bad of a.*

not un– The *not un–* combination represents one of the few widely accepted double negatives. (Another is much more rare: "Nobody doesn't like Sara Lee" or "I can't endure not playing golf this week.") A *not unusual* occurrence may happen 10 to 50 percent of the time, but for a *usual* one the frequency is certainly above 50. A *not unlikely* story is fairly believable, but less so than a *likely* one. See also NOT (AND OTHER NEGATIVES).

notable/noted/notorious Most often misused of the three is *notorious,* which means "infamous, well-known for evil-doing." SWE: "John Dillinger was a notorious bank robber." FF: "Saint Francis was notorious for his kindness." The noun form of *notorious* is *notoriety.* *Notable* means "worthy of mention, important": "one of the notable events (*women,* and so on) of the late nineteenth century." *Noted* applies mainly to people and means "famous, eminent, celebrated": "James Baldwin was a noted author." You might conceivably be sued for calling someone "notorious" but not for "noted" or "notable."

notable/noticeable Something *notable* is likely to be important, prominent, newsworthy. Something *noticeable* can be seen but may not be of much size or significance.

notary/notary public Often used interchangeably, but conservatives prefer the full title, *notary public*. The SWE plural is generally *notaries public*, but *notary publics* is gaining.

notate Not a substitute for *note* or *annotate*. However, a composer who writes the notes that represent the music in his or her mind may be said to notate – even when using a computer to do so.

nothing, nothing but *Nothing* takes a singular verb even if a plural follows: "Nothing in the packages was (not *were*) what she had ordered. Nothing in them *was* almonds." In "Nothing but bull's-eyes ___ counted," should the missing verb be *is* or *are*? Because the subject appears to be *nothing*, conservatives argue for *is*. Most people, however, automatically say *are* because of the proximity of *bull's-eyes*. The more sophisticated of them argue that here *nothing but* means "only." Because both choices seem awkward, SWE often substitutes "Only bull's-eyes were counted" or "Nothing was counted but (or *except*) bull's-eyes."

NOUNS UPON NOUNS The Germans call it *Substantivseuche* ("the noun disease"). Most common in American headlines but present even in prose needing less compression, it is the tendency to string several nouns together, each modifying what follows: "The teacher lesson-preparation number decrease demand will probably not be granted." To comprehend that string of nouns a reader must start with *demand* and work backward to *teacher* to untangle the mess, perhaps emerging with "The teachers' demand for a decrease in the number of lesson preparations will probably not be granted." In general, SWE looks with concern at more than two nouns strung together, although occasionally the string is clear or unavoidable: "the Michigan State University Research Foundation." See also -ING.

novelty See REAL NOVELTY.

novice See AMATEUR/NOVICE.

now pending SWE omits *now*.

nowhere near As in "The new tank will cost nowhere near (or *not nearly*) so much," this is SWE.

nowheres This word is FF (dialectal) for *nowhere*.

no-win This term is often used in FF, but increasingly in SWE, as adjective or noun: "The president finds himself in a no-win situation." "This is certainly a no-win." Because of its shortness, the expression is useful. Contrast it with the wordy "The president finds himself in a situation in which victory is impossible."

nth degree *N* is not synonymous with *infinite* or *large*. SWE, however, occasionally uses *nth degree* to mean "an indefinitely (or *infinitely*) large degree or extent."

number (verb with) SWE: "The number of errors was small." Here the writer is referring to an actual number – say, six. That number is small. The subject is *number*. SWE: "A number of errors *were* overlooked." Here a *number of* means "several" or "many": "Several errors were overlooked." The subject is *errors*, not *number*. (Columnist James Kilpatrick has campaigned against such use of *a number of*, arguing that it can mean "one" or "a million." He is obviously right, but the phrase is so widely used even in the "best" prose that his campaign has had no visible effect.)

number See also AMOUNT/NUMBER.

NUMBERS (UNNECESSARY) "Our two children, Anne and Paul, were with us." Most people will realize that Anne + Paul = two. "Iran, Iraq, and Saudi Arabia are the three nations that will be most helped by the decision." The SWE writer deletes *three*, and then, thinking further, deletes *are the three nations that*.

numerous Not a noun. SWE changes "Numerous of the new traffic regulations are still unfamiliar" by deleting *of the* or by starting with *Many of the new* or *Several new*.

numerous/populous A newspaper story reports, "The populous Kansas alumni are mostly an affluent group." This is not SWE. Kansas alumni are *numerous*. The usual meaning of *populous* is "densely inhabited": "populous Mexico City."

nuptials See MARRIAGE/NUPTIALS/WEDDING.

O

obligate/oblige Usually interchangeable. When you are under compulsion to do something, you may say either "I am obliged" or "I am obligated" to do it. When you feel gratitude toward someone, you are more likely to choose *obliged*: "I am obliged to him for his kindness." (An old way to say "Thank you" is "Much obliged.")

obscene American courts so far have not been able to agree on a satisfactory definition. It is unsafe to assume that most people will readily accept whatever one's own definition is. (In some societies kissing is regarded as obscene.) Although ordinarily the term is related to sexual behavior, one dictionary definition is "loathsome," and on that basis many people argue that cruelty, violence, terrorism, profiteering, or war is more obscene than display of sexual activity.

obscenity/profanity *Obscenity* in speaking or writing is the use of "indecent" expressions referring to sexual or excretory functions – often but not always four-letter words. *Profanity* is use of expressions that seem to show contempt or irreverence toward God or sacred things.

obscure See ABSTRUSE/OBSCURE.

observance/observation *Observance* refers to (1) celebrating a holiday or a religious rite: "observance of Veterans Day, Hanukkah, and so on"; (2) complying with law or custom: "observance of her

175

family's traditions." *Observation* is "seeing, watching, noticing": "to make weather observations," "a patient kept under observation," "Observation through a telescope revealed . . ." See also COMMENT/ OBSERVATION/REMARK.

obsolescent/obsolete   *Obsolescent* means "going out of style or use," and *obsolete* means "now out of style or use." Many of today's fashions in women's clothing may be obsolescent in a few months and obsolete in a year or two.

obverse   See CONVERSE/INVERSE/OBVERSE.

obviate   Means "make unnecessary," as in "My mother's telephone call obviated our planned visit." Although that meaning is the same as "removed the need of," *obviate* is not used in SWE to mean simply "remove."

obvious   See APPARENT/EVIDENT/OBVIOUS.

occasional/sometime   Use of *sometime* in sentences such as "Gladys is a painter and a sometime (*an occasional*) sculptor" appears to be growing. Conservatives point out that *occasional* does well enough, and that *sometime*, in its rather rare use as an adjective, ordinarily means "former." Confusion may arise: Is Gladys now occasionally a sculptor, or is she a former sculptor? Here SANE sides with the conservatives.

occupation/profession/trade   *Occupation* is broadest in meaning. It is any activity by which one earns a livelihood. *Profession* is usually restricted to an occupation requiring advanced study in a specialized field, such as law or medicine. The distinction is not firm, however. Not nearly everyone in the acting profession, for example, has taken advanced courses in acting. A *trade* normally involves skilled labor or buying and selling. Plumbing and shopkeeping are examples. See also AVOCATION/VOCATION.

occur/take place   Generally interchangeable, but some stylebooks advocate restricting *take place* to prearranged events: "The concert took place on May 9, as scheduled." SWE often follows that usage. *Occur* most often means "happen," but it also occurs ("appears") in sentences such as "The word *placidly* occurs three times on one page."

occurrence   See EPISODE/EVENT/INCIDENT . . .

o'clock   See BELLS/O'CLOCK.

octopus (plural)   If you meet two of these, call them *octopuses* if you speak English, *octopodes* (*oktopoda*) if you speak classical Greek, or *octopi* if you speak no known language.

oculist/ophthalmologist/optician/optometrist   An *oculist* and an *ophthalmologist* are the same, a physician (M.D.) specializing in treatment of the eyes. The professionals prefer the longer word. An *optometrist* also examines eyes and may prescribe glasses but is not an M.D. An *optician* makes or sells glasses and other optical goods.

odd/peculiar/quaint/queer/strange   Often interchangeable, but these connotations are frequent: *Odd* – "not fitting in": "He was an odd student, not interested in sports or girls." *Peculiar* – "having qualities not shared by others": "His gait is peculiar." *Quaint* – "old-fashioned but not unattractive": "When Rip Van Winkle returned from his twenty-year nap, his clothing seemed quaint." *Queer* – "eccentric; (possibly) homosexual": "Her speech is queer – full of uncommon grunts and gurgles." *Strange* – "unfamiliar, inexplicable"; "strange behavior."

-odd SWE avoids *some* (or *about, approximately*) *twenty-odd*, in which either the modifier or *-odd* is redundant. SWE uses the hyphen. "Twenty-odd people" and "twenty odd people" are not necessarily the same.

of (as part of verb) *Of* is FF for *have* in "could of" "might of," and the like. The standard *have* sometimes sounds like *'ve* when spoken and so is misunderstood and miswritten as *of*.

of between/of from With numbers, as in "a deficit of between (or *from*) ten to fifteen thousand dollars," SWE deletes the redundant *between* or *from*.

of course Copperud's advice is usually followed in SWE: "Every *of course* should be weighed critically with a view to striking it out." SWE preserves it only if the reader definitely needs to be assured that the writer is aware that the reader knows. It is equivalent to *as is widely known*.

of/'s SWE: "John's brother," "a brother of John," "a brother of John's"; "the college's president," "the president of the college." The following are SWE but different in meaning: "A photograph of John won the prize." "A photograph of John's won the prize." (Bryant points out that "a dog's bone" and "a bone of the dog's" have essentially the same meaning, but that "a bone of the dog" does not.)

off from, off of SWE omits *from* and *of*.

offer/tender The verbs are often interchangeable, but *tender* is starchy in its formality: "I hereby tender my resignation," "tendered his services (or *regrets*)," but "offered a better deal." SWE: "They tendered all their stock certificates to be cashed in."

offhand/offhanded/offhandedly *Offhand* and *offhanded* are interchangeable as adjectives, and *offhand* and *offhandedly* as adverbs. If that's hard to remember, SANE says, choose *offhand* for either: "an offhand remark," "He commented offhand that . . . ."

officer Should a patrolman who is not yet a sergeant, lieutenant, or captain be called an "officer"? A long battle over that question has been waged. The ayes apparently have won, mainly because the person on the beat is indeed an officer of the law. Besides, *officer* makes unnecessary any concern about whether to say *policeman, policewoman,* or (heaven forbid) *policeperson*.

official/officious The adjective *official* means "pertaining to a governmental or other authoritative post": "Her official duties include checking expense accounts." *Officious* means "bustling, overeager to help": "His officious manner annoyed the visitors."

offputting An unpleasant-sounding word of various meanings, including "ugly," "objectionable," "disconcerting," "distressing." Sometimes confused with *putting off* ("delaying"). SWE prefers a more precise word.

offspring Both singular and plural: "an offspring," "several offspring."

oft Once used by poets who needed a shorter word than *often* or *frequently*. Now regarded as affected, although it occasionally appears in compounds such as *oft-heard* or *oft-told*. *Ofttimes* has been largely replaced by *oftentimes*. *Often* may usually serve as well, although *oftentimes* adds the connotation of "repeatedly."

-og/-ogue See CATALOG/CATALOGUE.

OK *OK* (plural *OK's*) is the most common of the several spellings, although *O.K.* and *okay* are not infrequent. Verb forms: *OK'd, O.K.'d,* or *okayed*; *OK'ing, O.K.'ing,* or *okaying*. SANE, always seeking compactness, recommends *OK, OK'd, OK'ing*. Regardless of its spelling, *OK* is considered informal by most dictionaries – an oddity for the American word most widely used in the whole world. RHD says, "It occurs in all but the most formal speech and writing." And George Will, usually as conservative linguistically as politically, wrote in his *Newsweek* column, "OK, some of those numbers may involve overreaching . . ."

old adage, old cliché See ADAGE.

Old English See MIDDLE ENGLISH/OLD ENGLISH.

older See ELDER, ELDEST/OLDER, OLDEST.

old-fashioned SWE doesn't forget the *-ed*. The term is increasingly written without the hyphen.

oldster SWE for "elderly person." Considered derogatory by some, affectionate by others.

on account of *Because of* usually works as well, but doesn't shorten the expression very much. *On account of* followed by a clause is FF, sometimes considered illiterate: "She worked all summer on account of she needed money to start college." SWE prefers *because*.

on Sunday (and the like) Before names of days, *on* may usually be dropped: "Our guests will arrive (on) Tuesday."

on the basis of SWE finds that *because of, by, for*, or *on* will often suffice.

on the lam FF (slang) for "in flight, especially from prison or fear of prison."

on (or *in*) the order of "The estimate of the fire damage was in the order of about $25,000." SWE deletes *five* words.

on the part of In a sentence such as "More accurate shooting on the part of the team is essential," SWE replaces the phrase with *by*. Even *by the team* is not needed here if the context shows that meaning.

on the whole   See AS A WHOLE/ON THE WHOLE.

on to/onto   In "John walked on to Covington," John was obviously not on top of Covington. But in "John stepped onto the ladder" (or *stage, table*, and so on), John moved to a position on the ladder or whatever. Both sentences are SWE. Grammatically, the difference is that in the first example, *on* is an adverb: "John walked on." In "stepped onto the ladder," *onto* is a preposition.

on/upon   Often interchangeable, although some people try to reserve *on* for a position at rest and *upon* for when motion is involved: "The cat leaped upon the mouse." SWE prefers *on* when possible. When *up* can stand alone (as an adverb) and happens to be followed by *on*, two words are used: "The bear stood up on its hind legs." The difference is noticeable in speaking. Contrast the difference in sound between *up on* in that example and *upon* in this: "The bear was standing upon a large rock."

one (impersonal)   (1) You may feel ambivalent about impersonal *one*. (2) I feel ambivalent about impersonal *one*. (3) One may feel ambivalent about impersonal *one*. Sentence 3 illustrates the use treated here. It appears mainly in formal prose, and to some people appears affected, stilted. Both 1 and 2 are more natural, but sometimes 3 is needed to maintain detachment and impersonality, as in a business or scientific report. In British use, if one starts a sentence with *one*, one must continue using *one* until one reaches the end of one's sentence – or one's patience. In American use, the initial *one* may be followed either by *one* or by *he, him, his, she, her*, or *hers*, as appropriate.

one and the same   SWE generally omits *one and*.

one another   See EACH OTHER/ONE ANOTHER.

one of the   When tempted to write "one of the (questions, answers, catfish, or what-have-you)," the SWE writer asks, "Can I dispense with *of the*?"

one of the only   Awkward: "Ferguson is one of the only, if not the only, legislators favoring the increase." SWE says, "Ferguson is one of the few legislators favoring the increase, if not the only one."

one of those who (verb with)   In "Idaho is one of the states that (is, are) certain to support the Lambo bill," opinion about the verb choice is divided. Logic says that several states *are* certain, and that Idaho is one of those that are certain. But the singular *Idaho* is the focus of the sentence, and Idaho *is* certain. Most TV news people seem to prefer *is*. SWE is ambivalent, although conservatives and all who believe that language should be as logical as possible prefer *are*.

oneself/one's self   SWE uses both. SANE prefers *oneself* for its simplicity – seven keyboard strokes vs. ten.

one-upmanship   Now SWE for "the practice of keeping a little ahead of someone else." It's great to pack all of that into one word!

ongoing   Less bad than Strunk and White consider it, no better than *present, existing*, or *existent* for the meaning "now in operation": "The ongoing (or *present*) program is bringing better results than its pred-ecessor." Often, however, either word is superfluous.

only (as connective)   As in "He would have offered John a beer, only John's wife would have objected." Although *only* sometimes appears in such sentences in SWE, either *but* or the too wordy *if it were not* (*for the fact*) *that* is more frequent. Logically, *only* makes little sense.

only (placement of)   Should you write "Smith only wanted one" or "Smith wanted only one"? A study by Bryant reported in 1962 that 86 percent of magazines placed *only* as in the second sentence. Logic supports that placement: it was *only one* that Smith wanted. Bryant added that in spoken English, sentences like the first predom-inated. Her findings, although dated, still appear valid.

only too   In sentences such as "I'll be only too happy to help," *only too* adds nothing and indeed is nonsensical. SWE generally omits it.

onward(s)   *Onwards* never is needed, although not "wrong" as an adverb: "The troops moved onwards." SANE recommends, and SWE usually prefers, *onward* as both adverb and adjective: "moved on-ward," "the onward movement."

opaque/translucent   Blame glassmakers' labeling for the occasional confusion. Some of them call glass "opaque" if it lets a small amount of light through. *Opaque*, from Latin for "dark," means "not pen-etrable by light." What the glassmakers mean is *translucent* ("letting light through but not permitting clear perception"). See also DIAPHANOUS/TRANSLUCENT/TRANSPARENT.

open up   See UP.

operate   In a hospital, a person is operated *on* or *upon*. FF: "My father was operated yesterday." A factory may be operated, but not a father.

operative word   Overused for "key word, important word."

ophthalmologist   See OCULIST/OPHTHALMOLOGIST/OPTICIAN . . .

opine   Although SWE for "hold or express an opinion," *opine* has somehow acquired a slightly humorous or derogatory connotation.

opinion/theory   A *theory* is more solidly based and carefully reasoned than an *opinion*. Dubious: "My theory is that the Giants are the best team in baseball this year." SWE refers to Einstein's theory of relativ-ity but not to his opinion of or about relativity.

opponent   See ADVERSARY/ANTAGONIST/ENEMY . . .

opt for   SWE for "choose, select, take this action rather than that."

optician   See OCULIST/OPHTHALMOLOGIST/OPTICIAN . . .

optimism, optimistic   See HOPE, HOPEFUL/OPTIMISM, OPTIMISTIC.

optimistic/pessimistic; favorable/unfavorable   People, but not things, can be *optimistic*, because optimism is mental and emotional. So SWE prefers "a favorable economic outlook" to "an optimistic outlook." The same comment applies to *pessimistic* vs. *unfavorable*. See also HOPE, HOPEFUL/OPTIMISM, OPTIMISTIC.

optimize   Somewhat pompous for "use (or *do*) as efficiently as possible." But it *is* relatively short: "Robinson Crusoe optimized the few things he salvaged from the wrecked ship." See also -IZE.

optometrist   See OCULIST/OPHTHALMOLOGIST/OPTICIAN . . .

opulent   See AFFLUENT/OPULENT/RICH . . .

or   See AND/OR.

oral/verbal   SANE recommends that for clarity a distinction between these words should be observed; *oral* for "spoken," *verbal* for "in words, whether spoken or written." Why? Because, for example, "verbal contract (or *agreement*)" is ambiguous, but "oral contract" or "written contract" is not. *Verbal* is useful in contrast to *physical*, *financial*, and probably other words: "Brown's attack was verbal, not physical." "Green's response was both verbal and financial. He publicly criticized Brown and also raised his rent." SWE's use of *verbal* is inconsistent.

oral   See AURAL.

orate   To *orate* is not necessarily to give an oration; it suggests an oratorical, pompous method of speaking. Telling someone that he or she orates may damage a friendship.

orchestra   See BAND/ORCHESTRA.

order   See ASK/DEMAND/INQUIRE.

ordinal   See CARDINAL/ORDINAL.

ordinance/ordnance   An *ordinance* is a regulation or a law, usually in a city or town. In the Old Testament, it refers to a religious ceremony. *Ordnance* comes to English from the same French source but has a quite different meaning: "military weapons, ammunition, and equipment."

ordinary   See AVERAGE/COMMON, ORDINARY.

orient (verb) orientate   Both are SWE. The longer is no better than the shorter, which SANE prefers.

-oriented   As in "business-oriented." Strunk and White call it "a clumsy, pretentious device," but in avoiding it they use an example with one-third more words. SANE says, "Use it, but not excessively. Avoid it in vague expressions such as 'a goal-oriented school.'" (All schools should have goals.) The term appears often in SWE.

ornery   An old variant of *ordinary*, *ornery* is treated in some dictionaries as standard for "unpleasant in disposition, short-tempered, (perhaps) criminal," but it is rare in SWE. It has an old-timey or down-home touch, and is unlikely to be used to describe a corporation president or anybody who might be seen at a society ball.

oscillate/osculate   To *oscillate* is to waver, vacillate, or move back and forth like a pendulum. *Osculate* is a mildly humorous substitute for the verb *kiss*. "He oscillated for a while, but then he osculated her."

ostensibly/ostentatiously   Not at all similar in meaning. *Ostensibly* means "apparently but not certainly": "His testimony was forceful and ostensibly honest." *Ostentatiously* means "in a showy, pretentious way": "Some popular singers dress ostentatiously even when not performing." The adjectives *ostensible* and *ostentatious* are similarly differentiated.

other   Needed after *any* in a sentence such as "Marie is taller than any (other) girl in her class." *Other* refers to persons or things in the same category. Since Marie is in the class, she must be compared not with *any girl* but with *any other girl* in the class. But *other* is not to be used in "Marie is taller than any girl on the opposing team."

ought   FF usage includes *had ought, hadn't ought, didn't ought. Ought* suffices.

ourself   1. An SWE writer uses *we ourself* only if he or she is a king or queen. The plural *ourselves* has no such limitation. 2. *Ourselfs* is FF, as are *themselfs* and *hisself.*

out loud   Slightly more informal than *aloud*, but both are used in SWE.

outcome (verb after)   Questionable: "The outcome may become dangerous." More likely: "The outcome will be dangerous." Questionable: "The outcome may lead to long delays." More likely: "The outcome may be long delays."

outside (of)   *Outside of* is more likely in conversation: "Spot was barking outside of the fence." *Outside* is probable in SWE: "That action was definitely outside the law."

outstanding   Sometimes, as in the following phrases, a more specific substitute for this word of praise can be found: a *world-class* athlete, a *below-four-minute* miler, a *wealthy* businessman, a *philanthropic* businessman, a painter *favorably compared with Monet*. Note that *outstanding* is a feeble substitute for any of the italicized terms.

outworn/worn-out   Often interchangeable, but in reference to what is out of date, *outworn* is more likely: "an outworn belief." Clothing, machinery, and other tangible things more often become *worn out*, although in some families outgrown clothing is also called *outworn*.

over (in comparisons)   Illogical: "The unemployment statistics show a slight decline over last month's figures." A decline, drop, or reduction can hardly be "over." In the example, SWE chooses *from*; in other sentences, perhaps *below* or *down from*. Or sometimes rewriting is preferable: "This month's unemployment figures are below those for March." An advertising claim reads, "Save 20 percent over the regular price!" What does that mean? SWE may substitute *of* for *over*, or write, "Now 20 percent below the regular price!"

over again   FF (redundant): "Sing the chorus over again." SWE deletes either *over* or *again*, or says, "Repeat the chorus."

over (or *under*) my signature   Most things – letters especially – are written *over* ("above") one's signature. In law, however, *written under my signature* means "attested to or authorized by me."

over with   SWE deletes *over*.

over   See also MORE THAN.

overall   SWE checks to see whether *overall* is needed. It often can be deleted. For example, "the overall total," "our overall conclusion," "the overall result of the trial."

overavailability   This is bureaucratic jargon for "glut, surfeit, surplus."

overexaggerated   SWE deletes *over*.

overlay/overlie   The uses are similar to those of *lie* and *lay*. To *overlay* is to apply a covering; to *overlie* is to lie upon. These examples illustrate SWE usage: "The cabinetmaker overlays (*is overlaying, overlaid, has overlaid*) the wood with cherry veneer." "Rich black soil overlies (*is overlying, formerly overlay, had overlain*) a mixture of sand and clay." A similar distinction exists between *underlay* and *underlie*.

overlook/oversee   Dictionaries give *supervise* as a synonym of both words. Theoretically, then, "The supervisor oversees the laborers" and ". . . overlooks the laborers" have the same meaning. The second, however, may be ambiguous, for *overlook* usually means "ignore, pay no attention to." Because of such ambiguity in *overlook*, SWE uses *oversee* for "supervise."

overly   An unnecessary word, *overly* for *over* doesn't increase clarity. *Overoptimistic* and the like have long been standard.

owing to   "Owing to a blizzard, Sally missed two examinations." Conservatives would replace *owing to* with *because of* in this sentence, although they approve of it in a sentence in which *owing to* is used as an adjective: "Sally's missing two examinations was owing to a blizzard," where the expression is equivalent to *attributable to* or *caused by*. Despite the conservatives, sentences like the first example are frequent in SWE as well as in FF. See also DUE TO (OWING TO) THE FACT THAT.

OXYMORON   See GUEST HOST.

P

pad   FF (slang, probably fading) for "a place to live." In the 1960s it was chiefly hippie talk, but it spread to include anything from one corner of a crowded room to a luxurious apartment, and so became increasingly vague.

pail/pale   A *pail* is a bucket. The most common meaning of *pale* is "whitish."

pair   Although "five *pairs* of slacks (or *socks*, and so on)" is usual, *pair* sometimes appears in SWE in similar phrases. When two people (or *animals, insects*) are performing as individuals, *pair* takes a plural verb: "The pair of tame rabbits were frolicking." See also SLACKS.

palate/palette/pallet   Illustrations of differing meanings: "The hot soup burned my tongue and palate." "You made a palate-pleasing dessert." "The artist is mixing colors on her palette" (*pallet* is a seldom-used alternative spelling). "This part of the watch is the pallet." "A potter's paddle is a pallet." "Lay the pallet on the floor here." "Bookbinders use a pallet for artistic work." "The bricks were loaded on a wooden pallet to be hauled away."

pale See BEYOND (OUTSIDE) THE PALE; PAIL/PALE.

paltry/petty/trivial All mean "unimportant, insignificant, slight." *Petty* and *trivial* are almost synonyms, but *petty* carries a note of contempt less evident in *trivial*. *Paltry* is the strongest of the three, expressing deep contempt. It is often used of small amounts of money: "A paltry sum to pay for murder!" However, it may show contempt of quality as well as quantity: "a paltry, imitative pedant" (Jonathan Swift).

panacea/remedy SWE reserves *panacea* for a so-far imaginary cure for *all* diseases or evils. FF: "a panacea for gout." *Universal panacea* is a redundancy. In contrast, a *remedy* is intended to cure or relieve a single disease or evil, or a related group of them.

pandemic See ENDEMIC/PANDEMIC.

panegyric Too formal and high-flown for ordinary "praise," *panegyric* usually refers to a speech or a written tribute. *Encomium*, also formal, is a synonym. Another, which may be slightly less formal, is *eulogy*. On most private or semiprivate occasions, *praise, commendation*, or *compliment* is more suitable. See also ELEGY/ENCOMIUM/EULOGY.

pansy See FAIRY/GAY/PANSY.

paradise Capitalized for the place where many hope to live after death, but not in sentences such as "This is a paradise." SWE uses context to make clear which place is meant: (1) the Garden of Eden, (2) a place where the righteous await the second coming of Christ, (3) a place where the righteous will spend eternity, (4) any especially delightful earthly place, (5) an extraordinarily blissful emotional state. Of the several attempts to form an adjective, *paradisal* is probably best – certainly better than the more common *paradisaical*. Fowler evades the issue, preferring *heavenly*.

parameter Howard offers an excellent discussion of this word, which he says is misused 99 percent of the time. He has coined the term *hyperparametritis* for addiction to its use and has explained the seven highly technical definitions (in conic sections, mathematics, astronomy, crystallography, music, medical writing, and statistics). The eighth, he says, is "usually no more than a grand and showy substitute for boundary, limit, framework, or condition." The word is apparently often confused with *perimeter*. It does appear sometimes in SWE in that sense, but some readers then lose respect for the writer.

paraphrase/summary A *summary* is shorter than the original; it usually presents the main points but omits most examples and other elaboration. A *paraphrase* may be shorter or longer than the original, although usually shorter. It is a restatement, generally intended to clarify or simplify.

pardon   See EXCUSE/PARDON.

partake   In "partook of a delicious repast," the verb and the words for the meal both have an old-fashioned flavor. With regard to social or athletic activities, *participate* or *take part* is usual, not *partake*: "participated in the fun."

partiality   See BIAS/PARTIALITY/PREJUDICE.

partially/partly   Dictionaries draw a distinction, saying that *partly* refers to physical things and the meaning is "in part," but that *partially* refers to conditions and the meaning is "to a certain degree." Because the dictionary distinctions are not easy to make, SWE inconsistently follows them.

particular   May contribute to wordiness. SWE deletes seven words from "on this particular occasion that I am telling you about."

parting of the ways   This is a cliché.

party   "A party of one?" the maitre d' asks in supercilious disbelief. "Please meet your party at the United ticket counter," an employee intones over the airport public-address system. Despite years of dictionary insistence that *party* and *person* are not interchangeable, usages like these remain in FF but are rare in SWE.

pass away/pass on   These expressions, like other euphemisms, are intended kindly. They are certainly not objectionable with reference to family members, friends, or anyone else regarded with affection. For other deaths, the forthright *die* is customary in SWE. See also EUPHEMISM/EUPHUISM.

pass-fail   Now a standard term in academia in expressions such as "a pass-fail course," "I'm taking it pass-fail," the term was at first received questioningly. However, it is less cumbersome than "for credit but without a specific letter or number grade."

pass out   FF for *faint*.

pass time   See KILL TIME/PASS TIME/SPEND TIME.

pass up   More informal than "refuse to accept" (an offer, opportunity, or the like), *pass up* is used frequently in SWE.

passed/past   *Passed* is only a form of the verb *pass*: "A car passed slowly." *Past* is used differently, as in "the past decade" (adjective), "in the past" (noun), "hurried past" (adverb), "walked past the house" (preposition). See also PAST EXPERIENCE/PAST HISTORY.

PASSIVE VOICE   Passive: "She *was given* a huge basket of red roses by her admirers." Active: "Her admirers *gave* her . . ." Although either version may appear in SWE, most good writers prefer the active voice, which follows the natural order of telling who did what to whom. The passive is useful when the doer is unknown, unimportant, or obvious: "Clark was murdered in 1987, but detectives failed to find enough evidence to arrest anyone." "Both winners were elected by comfortable margins." Scholarly writers, instead of saying "I did so and so," still often say "So and so was done" (or the active "The researcher did so and so"). Even in their writing, the passive seems less frequent than it once was.

past experience/past history *Past* is clearly redundant in *past history*, because by definition history is past. It is redundant, too, in *past experience* if the context indicates past time; however, experience may also be present or future. Redundant: "Past experience has shown us . . ." Satisfactory: "Past experience is not a sure forecaster of future experience." *Past* can be omitted as a modifier of *accomplishments*, *records*, or other words clearly referring to past time. See also RECORD.

pastor See MINISTER/PASTOR/PREACHER . . .

PATHETIC FALLACY See EMPATHY/SYMPATHY.

patsy, pushover No single standard word carries quite the meaning of these two words customarily considered slang: "a gullible person; one who is easily deceived, imposed on, or cheated; one who is too softhearted for his own good." Unless a "better" word comes along, *patsy* or *pushover* will continue in occasional use in SWE.

pavement/sidewalk **1.** To many English people and some Americans, *pavement* means the (often concrete) path where pedestrians walk beside a street. The usual American term for that, however, is *sidewalk*. These same Americans may refer to a paved road or other paved area as "the pavement" or sometimes "the concrete." Both words are SWE, but the context must clarify the intended meaning. **2.** *Pound the pavement* is FF (slang) for "walk the streets in search of work or some other objective."

pay boost/pay hike *Boost* and *hike* are good journalistic words that fit well into many headlines. Sedate writers not responsible for writing headlines prefer *increase in pay*. SWE is not always sedate.

peace/piece Columnist James Kilpatrick quotes from a West Virginia newspaper: "The residents there deserve a little piece and quiet at night." Probably the intended word is *peace* ("tranquillity, absence of hostilities or turmoil"). The basic meaning of *piece* is "a part of."

peaceable/peaceful A *peaceable* nation, such as Switzerland, is inclined toward peace and tries to promote it. A book called *The Peaceable Kingdom*, by Elizabeth Coatsworth, describes a place where "the child can walk unafraid in beauty and contentment." A *peaceful* nation is one that is not now at war. It may or may not always be peaceably inclined.

peculiar See ODD/PECULIAR/QUAINT . . .

pedagese See EDUCATIONESE, PEDAGESE.

pedal/peddle You *pedal* a bicycle, and *peddle* cosmetics or fresh fruit from door to door.

peer, peerless A *peer* is one's equal, not one's superior. Confusion arises because in England *peers* are the nobility, the *peerage*. A *peerless* person is so remarkable in some way that he or she has no equal.

pen name See ASSUMED NAME/PEN NAME/PSEUDONYM . . .; NOM DE PLUME.

Pennsylvania Dutch See DUTCH, DUTCHMAN.

penurious Has gradually shifted its meaning from "poverty-stricken" to "miserly." Although dictionaries include both definitions, most readers will interpret the word as equivalent to *stingy*. See also IMPECUNIOUS.

people/peoples/persons A rough distinction: If a count can be easily made or is important, SWE uses *persons*: "Only five other persons were in the house at the time of the murder." Otherwise, *people*: "Many people believe . . . ," "About forty people were present," "the people of Sweden." In some in-between instances, either word is appropriate: "a dozen or so people (*persons*) in the audience." *Peoples* is in a sense a plural of a plural. It refers to nations or other more or less homogeneous groups: "the peoples of Indo-European ancestry," "the peoples of Asia."

per each FF: "The fee is ten dollars per each enrollee." SWE prefers *per enrollee* or *for each enrollee*. See also A, AN/PER.

percent (110) Sports announcers and coaches like to say that an athlete "gave a hundred and ten percent." Impossible, says SWE, because no one can exceed his potential. Probably most of us perform at no more than 50 percent of potential, so maybe the announcer could say that the athlete "gave sixty (or even *one hundred*) percent."

percent/per cent/percentage SWE has a choice of *percent* or *per cent*. SANE recommends *percent*, which is similar in form to *percentage*. Examples of SWE: "7 percent" (not *seven*, except to start a sentence or report conversation). "Seven percent was considered a high rate." "Thirty percent of the people were poor" (note the plural verb). "A high percentage of the estate is taxable." "A high percentage of the children are in school." Note: *A high* (or *low*) *percentage of* is frequently only a wordy way of saying *many*, *much*, *few*, or *little*.

perfect Logically, nothing can be more perfect than perfect. For example, if a perfect score is 100, no score can be higher or "more perfect." The framers of the U.S. Constitution, however, referred to a "more perfect union," so insistence on banning that expression would be unconstitutional. In most minds, *perfect* means no more than "extraordinarily good," and dictionaries include one definition like "unusually delightful or excellent: 'a perfect day'." It is sad, though, that English has no single word that means "without blemish, fault, or error." Many writers of SWE do restrict *perfect* to that sense. SANE applauds. See also **COMPARISON OF ABSOLUTES**.

perhaps See MAYBE/PERHAPS.

persecute/prosecute To *persecute* is to harass persistently over a long period of time: "For years the Romans persecuted the Christians." *Prosecute*, a mainly legal term, means "to take action against, especially in court": "A prosecuting attorney leads the action against the defendant."

-person Words such as *chairman*, *fireman*, and *policeman* are misleading, because many women serve in such positions. But the once recommended *chairperson* is no better (try *chair*), and *fireperson* and *policeperson* are much less desirable than *firefighter* and *police officer*. See also CHAIR/CHAIRPERSON; PEOPLE/PEOPLES/PERSONS.

personal, personally SWE usually omits *personal* and *personally* from expressions like these: "I personally believe," "my own personal opinion," "during my personal visit to them," "my personal friend," "I myself personally," "personally, I think . . ."

persons See PEOPLE/PEOPLES/PERSONS.

perspective/prospective *Perspective*, a noun, means "point of view": "From my perspective, the Supreme Court's decision appears wrong." The word also has technical meanings in art, architecture, and other fields. *Prospective*, an adjective, means "in prospect, expected": "Prospective profits were in the thousands."

persuade See CONVINCE/PERSUADE.

peruse If you *peruse* a document, you read it more carefully than you do, say, today's paper.

pessimistic See OPTIMISTIC/PESSIMISTIC; FAVORABLE/UNFAVORABLE.

petty See PALTRY/PETTY/TRIVIAL.

phenomenal Too strong a word for occurrences or things that are merely strange or unusual. For example, despite the hyperbole of sports announcers and writers, only a few athletic accomplishments are *phenomenal*.

phenomenon The SWE plural is *phenomena*, which FF sometimes then treats as a singular. SWE: "A phenomenon is . . . ," "Several phenomena are . . ."

philologist See LEXICOGRAPHER/LINGUIST/PHILOLOGIST.

philosophy "Coach Ramsay likes the gang-tackle philosophy." *Philosophy* is too intellectual a word here. SWE uses *strategy*, *tactic*, *system*, *method*, or other down-to-earth words for such a down-to-earth result. *Philosophy* refers essentially to thoughtful analysis and classification of fundamental principles of human life.

phlegm See MUCUS/PHLEGM.

-phobia See -MANIA/-PHOBIA.

phony Once regarded as slang for "false, not genuine, pretentious," *phony* has moved to SWE.

picky Most dictionaries call *picky* informal. But "picky eater" has existed for over a century, and such terms as *fastidious* and *excessively meticulous* are too high-sounding for the things that people are usually picky about. SWE uses *picky* or *choosy* for small things such as scraping off the anchovies and refusing to eat any cheese other than Brie. For matters of greater moment, such as selecting a new car, a bigger word may be appropriate.

piece See PEACE.

piece of the action This is FF (slang) for "chance to make a profit," "chance to take part in a (possibly illegal) activity": "Deal me in, boys. I want a piece of the action."

pier See DOCK/PIER/WHARF.

pig This is a hostile FF (slang) term for *police officer*.

pincers See CLIPPERS/PINCERS/PLIERS . . .

pinch hit, pinch hitter Standard in baseball, and broadened occasionally in other SWE to mean "substitute, temporarily replace."

pistol See AUTOMATIC/PISTOL/REVOLVER.

pizza pie SWE omits *pie*, because a pizza is a kind of Italian pie.

place **1.** In SWE one *goes to* a place. FF: "We went many strange places." **2.** In SWE, one places a thing *in* (or *inside*) another, seldom *into* it: "Place the folders in the cabinet."

place/put *Place* implies greater meticulousness than *put*. We carefully place pieces of crystal on shelves in a breakfront, and we put everyday glasses in a cabinet above the kitchen sink.

play down See DOWNPLAY.

play (it) by ear A figurative way to say "improvise": "She did not know what arguments her opponent would use, so she had to play it by ear." It appears in informal SWE. To a musician the meaning is different: "play music after hearing it but without reading a score": "My fiddler uncle couldn't read a note, but he played by ear dozens of country tunes." It is not uncommon in SWE.

189

playwright Like *shipwright* or *wheelwright*, this word ends in *wright*. (A *wright* is a person who makes or builds something. The word is not related to *write*.)

pleasantry A *pleasantry* is a light, often joking or bantering remark. The word is not a synonym of *pleasure* or *pleasantness*.

pleasure See HAPPINESS/PLEASURE.

plenteous/plentiful Interchangeable, although *plenteous* is less common and sounds like a word from old-fashioned poetry.

plenty In SWE use, *plenty* is a noun: "She has plenty of money." "Eden was a land of plenty." Not likely in SWE is "She has plenty money," or "The day was plenty hot."

plethora A *plethora* of something is not merely enough or even plenty. It is an excess, an overabundance, a superfluity, a supererogation, an overkill – like the plethora of words in this list.

pliers See CLIPPERS/PINCERS/PLIERS.

plight/predicament/quandary A *predicament* is an embarrassing or troublesome situation, sometimes with a slight element of danger: "My predicament was that my wife had already made a firm dinner engagement before my boss invited us to have dinner with his family." A *plight* is usually more serious, as the expression "a sorry plight" suggests: "Because of the fire and their lack of money, John's parents' plight worried him." A *quandary* is a state of uncertainty, often with several ways out, none of them pleasant. A satisfactory solution may require much thought or even be impossible. See also DILEMMA.

plurality See MAJORITY/PLURALITY.

plus **1.** Overused in advertising for "besides": "Plus, you will receive at no extra charge . . ." The extensive use is attributable to the favorable connotation. **2.** Note the singular verbs in "One plus one equals two" and "His boldness plus his strength endears him to hero worshipers." In the first the meaning is "One added to one is two." The second *plus* is equivalent to *in addition to*. But note the plural verb in "His good looks plus his strength *endear* him to women," in which the subject is *good looks*.

+ (plus sign)/and/& (ampersand)   SWE avoids using a plus sign or an ampersand as a substitute for *and*.

P.M.   See A.M.

podium   See DAIS/LECTERN/PODIUM.

poet laureate   The SWE plural is *poets laureate*, but *poet laureates* is gaining.

poetry/verse   Although *poetry* and *poem* are widely used for anything that is not prose – especially if it has rhymes and short lines – the terms are usually applied in SWE to writings of high artistic quality. *Verse* is what many of us write as children, or as adults who like to see our literary efforts printed in a weekly rural newspaper or other publication whose editor uncritically calls our stuff "poetry."

point in time   In the Watergate hearings several witnesses repetitively said "at this (or *that*) point in time" instead of the more compact *today, now, at this (that) moment, then*, or the like. Although ridiculed in the press, the expression became widely used and still may be heard (less often seen) with annoying frequency. SWE generally abstains. See also AT THE PRESENT TIME/AT THIS TIME.

point of view   Sometimes wordy. SWE often shortens "My point of view is . . ." to "My opinion is . . . ," and "From my point of view, it seems . . ." becomes "I believe . . ."

point out   SWE employs *point out* when a statement is known to be factual or definitely provable: "The defendant pointed out that he was in Pocatello at the time of the murder." This is correct if evidence is available to prove the defendant's alibi. Otherwise *said, stated, asserted, declared, swore*, or the like is the SWE choice.

pointy   Slightly informal for "pointed": "a dog with a pointy tail." *Pointy head* is FF (slang) intended to ridicule someone whose intelligence or common sense is questioned.

poke   See BAG/POKE/SACK.

police (verb with)   *Police* is plural: "Our police are usually courteous." But *police force* is singular: "Our police force is the best in the state."

polite   See COURTEOUS/POLITE.

politic   See EXPEDIENT/POLITIC.

politician/statesman   A *politician* is anyone involved in politics, particularly party politics. Less frequently, it is anyone unusually knowledgeable about government. A politician may be or become a statesman, but statesmen are few. Most politicians are active on local and state levels. A *statesman* usually has national or international perspective. Another difference is that the statesman traditionally works for the public good rather than for personal or partisan benefit.

politick This verb for "engage in political activity" or "attempt to influence by political maneuvers" is now SWE.

politics (verb with) Singular when referring to the science or art of government: "Politics is his greatest concern." It is plural when equivalent to *political beliefs*: "My politics are of no significance to anyone else."

polyandry/polygamy/polygyny *Polyandry* means "having more than one husband or male mate at a time"; *polygyny*, "having more than one wife or female mate at a time"; *polygamy*, "having more than one husband, wife, or mate at a time."

pooch Flesch says, "A dog is a dog, but a pooch is a beloved friend." The *pooch* may be a mongrel or an animal with a dozen AKC champions in its pedigree. It's the affection between dog and person that makes a dog a pooch. The word is most likely to be used in conversations with family, friends, or the pooch, and so it is FF. See also DOG WHO.

poorly FF (dialectal) for "ailing, unhealthy, in poor health, not feeling well (at this time)": "Pa's real poorly now."

popular Not used in SWE with reference to only one person. FF: "Walter was never very popular with Susan." SWE says, "Susan was never very fond of Walter." However, Walter may or may not have been popular in his class or some other group.

populous See NUMEROUS/POPULOUS.

pore/pour When you *pore* over a book, you study it carefully. If you *pour* over a book, you may be putting water, coffee, or syrup on it.

port See HARBOR/PORT; LEE/PORT/STARBOARD . . .

portray Sometimes misused for *exemplify* or *illustrate*. To portray is to describe or picture: not "This gaunt child portrays the many now starving in Bangladesh." SWE chooses *exemplifies*, *typifies*, or *represents*.

position See JOB/POSITION.

possess This is sometimes a bit stiff. Would you rather "possess charm" or "be charming"? *Is possessed of* is usually only a wordy way to say *has*: not "He was possessed of a small upstate farm" but "He had (or *owned*) . . ." *Possessed by* (or *with*) is similar in meaning to "obsessed or dominated by": "possessed with a demon," "possessed by the age-old urge of the do-gooder." *Possessed* may also mean "calm, self-possessed": "Through the whole storm, Adele remained possessed, apparently unconcerned."

possible SWE avoids "We thank the Stiver family members who made this reunion possible." It would have been *possible* without them. Instead, SWE says something like "who did all the hard work." Dubious: "Two possible suspects are . . ." Every suspect is possible. Illogical: "The firemen damaged the premises no more than possible." SWE chooses *necessary*.

possible/possibly 1. Logic argues that such *possible*'s as these should be *possibly*'s: "a possible broken arm," "a possible serious (or *fatal*) accident," "a possible dangerous encounter." **2.** *May possibly be* is redundant. SWE deletes *possibly* or writes *is possibly*. See also FEASIBLE/POSSIBLE.

postal card/postcard *Postal cards* are printed by the government and sold in post offices. *Postcards* (or *post cards*) may be purchased in many places, require stamps, and often have pretty pictures.

posted Informal for "informed": "Keep me posted about events in Keokuk." Found occasionally in SWE.

pot Sometimes used in SWE as an informal substitute for *marijuana*.

potluck "My wife isn't expecting company for dinner, but we'd both be delighted to have you take potluck." Although a cliché and not highly formal – probably because the meal isn't – *take potluck* is more compact than "eat with us but realize that no special preparations for guests have been made, so that the food, although nourishing, may be lower in quality than you would expect at the Four Seasons." It is SWE, as are *a potluck, potluck supper*, and so on.

pound the pavement See PAVEMENT/SIDEWALK.

pound See FOOT, HOUR, MILE . . .

practicable/practical If an idea is *practicable*, it is physically possible to carry it out. If it is also *practical*, it is sensible to do it. It may be practicable, but not practical, to build a bridge across the English Channel. It is both practicable and practical to lay the carpet before bringing in the grand piano.

practically/virtually Usually interchangeable, with *virtually* slightly preferred for "in effect" or "nearly." However, *practically* but not *virtually* may carry the meaning "in a way that is practical": "Practically, this task will be difficult, but theoretically it is simple."

praise See PANEGYRIC.

preacher See MINISTER/PASTOR/PREACHER . . .

precedence/precedents *Precedence* refers to priority in rank: "Automakers now assert that in their factories quality and safety take precedence over everything else." *Precedents* are acts or instances that may serve as examples or models when similar situations or legal cases arise: "Lawyers seek precedents that have bearing on the case now being tried."

precipitate (adjective)/precipitous *Precipitate* means "moving rapidly and recklessly," "impulsive, hasty": "Precipitate decisions are not characteristic of the Supreme Court." *Precipitous* is associated with *precipice* (cliff): "A precipitous area has several or many precipices." "A precipitous road or path down a mountain is dangerously steep."

predicament See PLIGHT/PREDICAMENT/QUANDARY.

PREDICATE NOMINATIVE See IT'S I/IT'S ME.

predict See PROPHECY/PROPHESY.

predilection A *predilection* is always in favor of someone or something, never against. It is equivalent to *preference*. Washington Irving referred to "her predilection for my powerful rival." See also BIAS; PREJUDICE.

preface See FOREWORD/INTRODUCTION/PREFACE.

prefer (*rather than* vs. *to* or *over*) When followed by an infinitive, usage is "I prefer to watch golf *rather than* to play it." When followed by anything else: "I prefer tennis *to* (or *over*) golf." "I prefer swimming *to* (or *over*) hiking."

preference See PREDILECTION.

pregnant Before this age of sexual frankness, *pregnant* was almost as taboo a word as *intercourse*, except in talking with one's doctor or good friends. Kindly euphemisms such as "in a family way" were numerous, and coarser expressions such as the Americanism "knocked up" were not uncommon. Today squeamishness is regarded as absurd, and some pregnant women wear shirts boasting "Baby soon" or providing the information "It all started one night."

prejudice See BIAS/PARTIALITY/PREJUDICE.

premiere (verb) Formerly condemned, but now SWE in expressions such as "The play will premiere in April" or "They premiered the play in April."

premise, premises The singular means "basis underlying an argument": "His major premise is . . . ," "Your premise is incorrect." The plural refers to land or buildings: "These premises are closed to the public." (*This premise* is not used in SWE for this sense.)

premonition/presage/prescience/presentiment A *premonition* is a feeling which warns that something unpleasant may happen. Since it is a warning, action may yet be taken to avoid the trouble. A *presentiment* is similar but may lack the element of warning. It is a feeling that something (perhaps good) will occur and is unavoidable. *Prescience* is ordinarily based more on knowledge than on feelings. A stockbroker with prescience can often interpret clues showing what the market will do next. *Foresight* is a synonym. *Presage* may be a noun or, more often, a verb. Anything presaged is unpleasant – a foreboding, premonition, bad omen.

prepared to admit (or *deny*) Lawyer: "My client is prepared to admit (or *deny*) being in the room." That shouldn't require much preparation. SWE recommends "My client admits (or *denies*) . . ." or ". . . will admit (or *deny*) . . ."

PREPOSITION AT END When an aide dared to question one of Churchill's sentences that ended with *of* or *with*, Sir Winston reportedly roared, "This is the sort of nonsense up with which I will not put." Questions such as "Where did he come from?" or "What did she work with?" are SWE because the alternatives are awkward. So are alternatives to many SWE statements, such as "That is what he hopes you will talk about." Two sorts of final prepositions are avoided in SWE: (1) Redundant: "Where is she going *to*?" "Where is it *at*?" (2) Resulting in weak endings: "That is the question that he hopes to find an answer *to*." SWE: "That is the question he hopes to answer."

PREPOSITIONS (OTHER TROUBLE SPOTS) **1.** Pronouns as objects: In SWE a pronoun as object of a preposition is in the objective case. Confusion sometimes arises, however, when a noun or a second pronoun is near the first. Actually, the added word makes no grammatical difference and should be ignored in choosing the case form. So *with Jim and me* and *from her and him* are standard, as is *between you and me*. Good teachers ask, "What pronoun would you use if *Jim and* were not in your sentence? That's the one you still need."
2. Redundancy: Examples of redundant prepositions besides those in the entry above are "off *of*," "remember *of*," "opposite *to*," "inside *of*," "amount *up* to." SWE omits each italicized preposition.
3. Verbiage: Some prepositional phrases, rather long and ungainly, are avoided in SWE; for example, "antecedent to" (*before*), "in connection with" (*concerning*), "in the case of" (*as to*), "previous(ly) to" (*before* or *earlier*), "with the intention of" (*intending to*). **4.** Omission: Often two or more words are to be related to another word. Logic determines whether more than one preposition is needed. In "They fired from the tower and the parapet," the preposition *from* may logically serve both *tower* and *parapet*. But in "The children played in the water and the beach," since the children did not play *in* the beach, the missing *on* should be supplied. There is a tendency in FF to omit a preposition after some verbs with which it is required in standard usage; for example, SWE prefers "She graduated *from* college," "He was operated *on* yesterday," "Our minister officiated *at* the ceremony." **5.** Strung-together phrases. Poor: "In theory, at the conclusion of an investigation of this sort made during unusual circumstances of stress and with immoderate delays, an investigator of normal honesty and with due regard to the ethics of his position . . ." Although sentences with six or eight prepositional phrases are not uncommon, stringing together as in this example makes for hard reading. SWE condenses and often divides.

prerogative/privilege A *prerogative* is a privilege officially granted to someone because of rank or accomplishment. An absolute monarch, for example, has or assumes some prerogatives that an ordinary king or a mere president does not have. A *privilege* is an advantage, consideration, or benefit that may be permitted with or without reason, fairly or unfairly. In school, some of a child's privileges may be withdrawn because of misconduct. Doing so is the teacher's or an administrator's prerogative.

present incumbent An incumbent is a person at present holding an office or position. SWE deletes *present* as redundant.

present writer "The present writer first saw this rare moth in Costa Rica." As a minimum, SWE deletes *present*. Unless for good reason it is necessary to avoid first person pronouns, it changes *the present* *writer* to *I*. In a scientific paper, the passive voice is frequent: "This rare moth was first observed by the investigator in Costa Rica." See also **PASSIVE VOICE**.

presidential/president's SWE reserves *presidential* for reference to a president's official roles, acts, or demeanor, not to his or her private life: "a presidential pardon (or *decision, task*)." "The presidential daughter" becomes "the president's daughter."

presume See ASSUME/PRESUME.

pretense/pretext Although it is possible to use the words interchangeably, *pretense* in SWE generally means "the act of pretending, a bit of make-believe, affectation." It implies some sort of action: "the child's pretense that she is a great dancer." A *pretext* is an excuse; it is words, not acts: "His pretext for his absence was that his brother had needed help in moving."

PRETENTIOUSNESS Some writers hide little thoughts in big words. They distrust the simple and straightforward, admire the high-flown and the circumlocutious. Perhaps their houses are decorated with gingerbread; anyhow, their prose is. They say *due to the fact that* for *because, in company with* for *with* or *along with*. They *shed gobbets of perspiration* when other people *sweat*, their *lachrymal glands become active* when others *cry*, and they *keep an engagement at the studio* when others *go to get a picture taken*. They put on thick wigs and long cloaks to hide their littleness. See also MATUTINAL ABLUTIONS.

pretty (adverb) As in "pretty good," "pretty reasonable," *pretty* means "rather, somewhat." It is now SWE except in highly formal writing.

prevaricate See EQUIVOCATE.

prevent See AVERT/AVOID/PREVENT; ELIMINATE/PREVENT; HINDER/PREVENT.

preventative, preventive See INTERPRETATIVE, INTERPRETIVE/PREVENTATIVE, PREVENTIVE.

previously to/prior to Both are somewhat stilted for *before*, but they seem less so in references to important events and considerable periods of time: "Even prior (or *previous*) to the Civil War, disagreements between North and South had involved many issues besides slavery." (With *previously*, *to* can often be omitted.)

price (adjective with) In SWE a price is *low* or *high*, not *cheap* or *dear*. *Dear* is now seldom used with reference to cost. An item, but not its price, may be described as *cheap*: "a cheap pair of shoes," "a low price for these shoes."

pride See ARROGANCE/CONCEIT/HAUGHTINESS . . .

principal/principle *Principle* is always a noun. Some writers associate its *-le* with the *-le* of *rule*: "The principle underlying the operation of this machine is . . . ," "a woman with firm principles." *Principal* is an adjective or a noun. As an adjective it means "main, most important": "the principal reason (or *difficulty, player*)." As a noun, it still retains the idea of "most important": A school principal is the principal teacher. In banking, a principal is the principal sum of money, in contrast to the usually smaller interest.

printing See EDITION/IMPRESSION, PRINTING.

prior to See PREVIOUSLY TO/PRIOR TO.

prison See JAIL/PRISON.

privilege See PREROGATIVE/PRIVILEGE.

pro Informal for *professional*, *pro* someday may replace the longer word in most contexts. Headline writers are preparing the way.

proceed **1.** SWE doesn't use *proceed* when *go* is meant. It's highfalutin in "Let's proceed to the shack for a sandwich." Normally *proceed* means "to move on after a stop, to go on": "The next morning the soldiers proceeded toward Arras." "After the judge admonished counsel for the defense, the trial proceeded." **2.** SWE uses *proceed*, not *proceed on* (*ahead, onward*).

procure This is pompous for *get*; besides, it may carry a sexual connotation because of its kinship with *procurer, procuress*. (A university that had a sign saying "Procurer's Office" soon changed it to "Purchasing Office.")

prodigal Although the biblical prodigal son wandered around while spending his money foolishly, *prodigal* means "squandering" rather than "wandering." It refers to waste, extravagance, being a spendthrift: "Throughout our history we have been prodigal of our resources."

profanity See OBSCENITY/PROFANITY.

profession See OCCUPATION/PROFESSION/TRADE.

progenitor It is not accurate to say that clavichords and harpsichords were *progenitors* of pianos; they were precursors or early forms. Nor was the builder of the first true piano its progenitor; he was an inventor. A progenitor is an ancestor of something animate. Among your progenitors are your parents and grandparents. A progenitor of the modern horse was the eohippus.

progressive *Progressive* is ordinarily what semanticists call a "purr-word" (in contrast to a "snarl-word"), a vaguely commendatory word that seldom defines "progress" or indicates its features. Most politicians want to be considered progressive or "modern" – certainly not reactionary – but each defines the word for himself. SWE users of the word try to make clear the goal toward which they or someone else hopes to progress.

promptitude *Promptness* is a virtue.

prone/prostrate/supine *Prone* means "lying face down"; *prostrate*, "lying face down," but suggesting weakness, helplessness; *supine*, "lying face up" (the *up* in *supine* may be a reminder).

PRONOUNS (PERSONAL) See various entries for I, ME, WE, US; YOU, YOUR(S); HE, SHE, IT, HIM, HER, THEY, THEM.

proof The label on a liquor bottle says "Eighty proof." That does not mean that 80 percent of the liquor is alcohol. Divide by two. "Eighty proof" is 40 percent. See also EVIDENCE/PROOF.

propaganda   Although *propaganda* may be anything used to gain support for a belief or doctrine, it now almost always is interpreted to mean that the belief or doctrine is "bad" or at least is opposed to what we "good" people support. We say that the enemy spreads propaganda but that our side offers facts or information or "the truth."

prophecy/prophesy   *Prophecy*, a noun, means "a prediction": "The unbelievable prophecy was coming true." *Prophesy*, a verb, means "to predict": "The witches had prophesied that Macbeth would become king." *Predict* is preferable to *prophesy* for statements based on fact or logic rather than inspiration or supernatural help. Weather forecasters *predict* or *forecast*; they do not *prophesy*. Old Testament prophets, often claiming to be inspired by Jehovah, prophesied.

proponent/supporter   *Proponent* may mean either "one who proposes" (e.g., a legislative bill) or "one who advocates." A *supporter*, ordinarily less active, seldom proposes anything and usually makes few or no public statements. His or her support more likely comes from contributing money or small amounts of time, making statements to family and friends, or perhaps being just one face in a crowd that shares similar feelings or beliefs. See also PROTAGONIST.

proportions   See DIMENSIONS/PROPORTIONS.

proposal/proposition   It is useful for a woman (or, today, a man) to know the difference: a *proposal* of marriage vs. a *proposition* for a merely sexual relationship. In business a proposition is normally more detailed and specific than a proposal. Thus a proposal may suggest that two companies share the cost of developing a new product, but a proposition specifies the responsibilities of each partner. In FF, *proposition* may mean almost anything: "Baseball is sometimes a funny proposition." No, but it can be a funny game, says SWE.

prosaic   Although *prosaic* in its early uses meant merely "in prose rather than in verse," the word has pejorated to suggest dullness, lack of imagination. Even though novelists write prose, they do not want their creations described as prosaic.

prosecute   See PERSECUTE/PROSECUTE.

prospective   See PERSPECTIVE/PROSPECTIVE.

prostate/prostrate   The *prostate* gland, surrounding part of the male urethra, is often miscalled *prostrate*. *Prostrate* means lying face down, usually after an attack of some sort. See also PRONE/PROSTRATE/SUPINE.

protagonist   There can be only one protagonist ("leading figure") in a novel, play, or other activity. So "two protagonists" and "the main protagonist" are unlikely in SWE. SWE distinguishes *protagonist* from *proponent* or *advocate*. See also PROPONENT/SUPPORTER.

protestant The word associated with religion is capitalized and pronounced *Prot*-us-tunt. An identical word, with small *p* and pronounced pro-*tes*-tunt, means "protester," but it has almost died out because of confusion with *Protestant*. Let it die, says SANE.

prototype See ARCHETYPE/PROTOTYPE.

proved/proven Interchangeable as past participle: "Botanists have proved (or *proven*) that . . ." *Proved* is more frequent. SANE asks, Why perpetuate unnecessary irregular and therefore confusing forms?

proverbial A football announcer reports that "Smith is in the proverbial doghouse of Coach Paterno." Who has ever heard a proverb about that doghouse? Possible: *well-known*, *infamous* (or no modifier at all). Unless *proverbial* refers to an actual proverb, it is of little use.

provided that/providing that Interchangeable, although conservatives prefer *provided*, without *that*. Often *if* carries the same meaning. When that is true, SWE generally chooses *if*.

PRO-WORD Sometimes called a "counterword," and seldom listed in dictionaries, a pro-word is a readily available but vague word used instead of a precise term. Many slang words, much profanity, and some standard words are pro-words: "*lousy* weather," "a *cute* dress," "*damn(ed)* hot," "cold *as hell*," "great," "super," "neat," "some deal," "case," "aspect," "factor."

prude Not necessarily a woman.

pseudonym See ASSUMED NAME/PEN NAME/PSEUDONYM; NOM DE PLUME.

psyche/psych *Psyche*, standard as a noun, is pronounced *sy*-kee and means "soul or spirit but not body" (psychiatrists have a more technical definition). From the noun an FF (slang) verb *psych* (pronounced *sike*) has developed. Alone, it means "use psychology on": "He psyched me." With *up*, it means "increase readiness or excitement": "I was psyched up about my vacation." With *out*, it means "bother emotionally or mentally": "She psyched me out by claiming to be pregnant." Although *psych* and *psych up* or *out* occur rarely in SWE, their brevity makes them candidates for greater use.

psychedelic A relatively new word, now SWE, that became entrenched in the 1960s. The drug subculture defined this adjective as "consciousness-raising, mind-expanding, mind-blowing, mood-enhancing." The medical profession defined it as "causing hallucinations, distorted vision, and possibly psychotic states."

psychiatrist/psychologist Both study the mind. A *psychologist*, usually a PH.D., may give people personal advice or therapeutic help. A *psychiatrist*, usually an M.D., specializes in diagnosis and treatment or prevention of mental illness.

psychological moment Although the *Dictionary of Behavioral Science* has no entry for this term, other dictionaries define it to this effect: "the time when a person's mental [and emotional] state is especially likely to produce the desired effect." In this sense the term is useful. SWE does not employ it, however, when no one's mental or emotional state is involved. This is not SWE: "The factory had reached the psychological moment when almost half of the equipment needed replacement."

public (verb with) Today the verb is almost always singular, but earlier writers made a subtle and worthwhile distinction. They used a singular to refer to the whole group: "The public is wiser than the wisest critic" (historian George Bancroft). The plural was used to signify the many individuals: "The public have neither shame nor gratitude" (essayist William Hazlitt). See also GENERAL PUBLIC.

puerile See BOYISH/PUERILE; JUVENILE/PUERILE.

pull one's weight Cliché, but still SWE. The extended meaning of this rowing term is "do the amount of work that is fair in proportion to the amount of compensation." It is better to write "pull one's weight" instead of about fifteen words.

punch-drunk For "acting in a dazed manner," *punch-drunk* has been listed as standard in American dictionaries for twenty years or more.

punctilious/punctual A *punctilious* person is precise and careful, especially with matters of conduct and etiquette: "Martin kept his procedures manual always at hand and adhered punctiliously to every regulation." A *punctual* person is exact in timing, being especially careful not to be late: ". . . arrived punctually for her nine o'clock interview." see also METICULOUS/PUNCTILIOUS/SCRUPULOUS.

pupil/student As ordinarily used by most teachers, a *pupil* is a child enrolled in elementary school, or anyone studying music or another art under a master: "Franz Liszt was a pupil of Antonio Salieri." *Student* also has two chief definitions: (1) a person enrolled in a secondary school, college, or university, and (2) anyone studying a subject independently. Even an octogenarian can be a student – in either sense.

purebred/thoroughbred Used interchangeably by most people, although some stock raisers prefer *thoroughbred* for horses, *purebred* for other animals. On rare occasions, a person of high integrity or courage is called a "thoroughbred," but probably never a "purebred."

puritanic/puritanical SANE recommends *puritanic*. The word is capitalized only when referring to the specific group known as Puritans.

PURPLE PASSAGE Also called *purple patch*, this term refers to a short section of prose or poetry that exhibits a noticeably heightened style. An author who perhaps has been writing almost ploddingly comes to something that moves him deeply, and he flings himself through his whole show of rhetorical tricks: highly figurative language, emotionality, complicated parallelism and inversion, five-dollar words. True, a heightening of style or change in rhythm or manner of expression is often desirable for a special effect. If overdone, though, heightening becomes a purple patch that distracts the reader and lowers the quality.

purposefully/purposely *Purposely* means "intentionally": "Craig purposely tripped an opponent"; *purposefully*, "having a strong purpose," "with determination": "Knowing that the peaches must be picked in one day, the crew worked purposefully, with almost no time out."

pusher Dictionaries label *pusher* slang for "seller of illicit drugs." But what standard word carries that meaning? The frequency of drug sales has resulted in more–than–occasional use of *pusher* in SWE.

pushy Occasional in informal SWE for "too forward or aggressive."

pushover See PATSY, PUSHOVER.

put up with SWE for "endure," "accept (something unpleasant) with resignation": "She learned to put up with her drunken husband."

put down FF (slang) for "demean, deprecate, suggest inferiority": "Why do you always put me down in front of your friends?" The informal noun *put-down*, meaning "a belittling statement," is related: "He said she looked OK – a real put-down, she thought." *Put-down* is SWE for "the landing of an aircraft."

put (someone) on FF (slang) for "tease, mock, deceive": "You must be putting me on." The related noun *put-on* means "hoax, deception."

put See PLACE/PUT.

pygmy See DWARF/MIDGET/PYGMY.

Q

quaint See ODD/PECULIAR/QUAINT . . .

qualification(s) SWE makes sure that readers can immediately understand which of two definitions is intended: (1) "reservation(s)," as in "I accepted the offer but with some qualifications," or (2) "background, experience, training, ability," as in "This candidate's qualifications are unusually good." Ambiguous: "Voters should cast their votes for this true son of Texas, George Jones, without any qualifications."

qualified expert One cannot be an expert if not qualified. A similar comment applies to *trained expert*. SWE deletes the modifier.

qualitative Does not mean "of high quality." "Qualitative tests" are not necessarily good tests; they are tests of quality – whether high, mediocre, or low.

quandary See PLIGHT/QUANDARY.

quartet *Quartet*, as well as *trio* and other such words, is used in SWE mainly when members of the group are trained to act together: "a string quartet," "the championship (basketball) quintet from Indiana," but not "the trio of escaped convicts," who probably had not received specific training.

queer See ODD/PECULIAR/QUAINT . . .

question as to whether Many sentences with this phrase should be shortened. For example, "Some Japanese legislators raised the question as to whether social science textbooks did not lean too far left" could be reduced to "Some Japanese legislators asked whether social science textbooks leaned too far left."

quick/quickly All modern dictionaries say that *quick*, like *slow*, is standard as either an adjective or an adverb. The adverb is most likely in short, conversational sentences: "Come quick!" but seldom occurs in SWE. *Quickly* is more common in longer, less conversational sentences: "Congress is moving quickly toward adjournment."

quieten Some British writers prefer *quieten*, but the verb *quiet* is more likely in the United States.

quite A few conservatives still insist that *quite* should be used only for "entirely, altogether," as in "quite correct." But a different meaning, "rather, fairly, moderately," has been added: "quite warm, quite studious." Unfortunately, the result is sometimes ambiguity. For example, is a "quite satisfactory report" altogether satisfactory or only moderately so? How low is a "quite revealing décolletage"? The damage has been done but is being somewhat repaired by the gradual decrease in use of the older definition. SWE makes sure that readers can understand which definition is meant.

quite a **1.** SWE usually selects more specific expressions than *quite a while, quite a game, quite an exciting time.* **2.** *Quite a few,* oddly, means "a lot." Because of the oddness, some writers dislike it, but it is established idiom, listed as standard in leading dictionaries. Like other *quite a* expressions, however, it is not very specific.

quiz Standard noun among students for "a short test." Standard verb, perhaps overused by some journalists, for "interrogate, question at length." It occurs occasionally in SWE.

quotation by SWE avoids "The United States is a society 'where it is safe to be unpopular.' This quotation by Adlai Stevenson suggests . . .'" The sentence is not a quotation by Stevenson, because he wrote it – he didn't quote it. It is a *statement* by him, and as used here it is a *quotation from* him.

quote/quotes *Quote* is informal for "quotation": "Did you get a quote from the candidate?" *Quotes* is informal for "quotation marks": "You forgot to put quotes around this." For each, SWE generally uses the complete term. See also CITE/QUOTE.

q.v. Abbreviated from Latin *quod vide* ("which see"). Less used than before to indicate a cross reference; today *see* or *see also* is usual, even in much scholarly writing. A few reference books retain it: "Because of the Treaty of Utrecht (*q.v.*) . . . ," but others substitute an asterisk or other symbol.

R

rack/wrack SWE customarily uses *wrack* in *wrack and ruin*, and with the meaning "a tangle of seaweed," but *rack* for all other meanings.

radical Not necessarily an unfavorable word, *radical* in its original sense means, as a noun, "one who attempts to get at the root of a problem"; a radical solution may be an attempt to dig down to the roots. Some uninformed readers, it is true, will misinterpret the word to mean "left wing."

raise/rear Older convention decreed that one raises animals, poultry, or grain, but rears children. Today most Americans *raise* children, although *rear* is still sometimes retained in SWE.

rambunctious The word may have started as Irish slang or may have been derived from the Latin word for "robust." It became American slang and then informal American and is now also humorous SWE.

range "A wide range of people" is almost meaningless. Is the range in age, income, health, geographic location, eye color, or what?

rap FF (slang or dialectal) for "talk."

rape See ATTACK; CRIMINALLY ASSAULTED.

rare/scarce As a rule, only items of value and high quality are *rare*: "as rare as undiscovered Rembrandts." Things normally more common may become *scarce*: "Pork chops are scarce in the market right now." "Bargains in shoes are scarce."

rarely ever, seldom ever FF (informal, illogical). SWE: *rarely, rarely if ever, rarely or never, hardly ever, almost never; seldom, seldom if ever, seldom or never.*

rascal See KNAVE/RASCAL/ROGUE.

rate For "deserve" as in "He rates a high mark for such a performance," or for "have influence" as in "He really rates in this office," *rate* hovers between informal and SWE. It is unlikely in highly formal contexts.

rather Use of this word always – intentionally or not – reduces the strength of whatever is modified. A "rather pretty girl" is less attractive than a "pretty girl." With some words the weakening is so great that illogicality results: "a rather superb performance." *Had rather* and *would rather* are interchangeable.

rather than What is on the right side of *rather than* in SWE ordinarily is grammatically parallel to what is on the left. So: "tried to *dodge* the question rather than *answer* it" (not *answering*); "tried *dodging* the question rather than *answering* it" (not *answer*). If awkwardness results from such parallelism, SWE rephrases. SWE avoids the combination of *more* with *rather than*: not "She tried more for financial success rather than for integrity in her writing." SWE omits either *more* or *rather*. See also PREFER . . . RATHER THAN.

rational/rationale *Rational*, an adjective, means "able to reason," "sane," "able to talk rather sanely," "logical." *Rationale*, a noun, means "a logical basis": "She has a rationale for everything she does"; or "an expression of reasons or principles": "Where is the rationale underlying this decision?"

rattle (verb) Long considered slang, *rattle* is now SWE, although informal, in the sense of "unnerve, fluster": "The mishap with the food processor rattled him."

ravage/ravish To *ravage* is to destroy, devastate: "The invading army ravaged the crops and the farm buildings." Infrequently, *ravish* has the same meaning; historian John L. Motley wrote, "The Spaniards had ravished the city." Ordinarily, however, it means "to rape," "to carry away," or "to enchant, to entrance." So a criminal may conceivably ravish a woman in any of three ways, although *entrance* is least likely. If we say that a woman is a ravishing beauty, we mean that she is entrancing.

re See IN RE.

re- + again or back A student writes a rough draft of a paper, copies it, and – perhaps because of some smudges – recopies it. He does not *recopy* it *again* unless there is a second recopying. Similarly, one does not *repeat again* or *redo again* unless one has previously repeated or redone. *Back* is redundant in expressions such as *return back* and *revert back*; usually also in *refer back*, but in that expression *back* may sometimes aid clarity.

reaction/response In careful use, a *reaction* is usually quicker, more automatic or more emotional, and less thoughtful than a *response*. A response often offers a reasoned opinion, but when a reaction is an expression of opinion, it is generally one that is preconceived or echoed.

real 1. Informal as an adverb: "real tired, (*happy, pleasant,* and so on)." SWE usually omits it, or substitutes *really, very, greatly, highly,* or another suitable adverb. 2. In *real facts, actual facts,* or *true facts,* SWE deletes *real, actual, true.* See also VERY.

real novelty Is *real* needed? Sometimes yes, sometimes no. If something is actually a novelty, nothing like it has been seen before.

realistic 1. *Realistic* means "true to life, seeing or describing things as they really are." It does not mean "ugly, sordid, unpleasant." Things that are ugly may of course be described realistically, but so may beautiful things. 2. In bargaining sessions, the proposals we favor are always "realistic," but obviously those we dislike are "unrealistic."

realm, sphere, world If tempted to write "in the realm (*sphere, world*) of business (or *sports,* and the like)" an SWE writer checks to see whether "in business (*sports*)" will suffice.

Realtor By no means can all real-estate agents legitimately be called "Realtors." As a registered trademark, it applies only to members of the National Association of Real Estate Boards, which prefers also that the word be capitalized. Members of the public are more likely to misuse the term than are representatives of real-estate firms.

rear (verb)   See RAISE/REAR.

reason/cause   See CAUSE/REASON.

reason is because   Disliked by conservatives, this expression is gaining favor. The usual SWE is "The reason for the delay was that (not *because*) a train was blocking the street."

reason why   Concerning "that is the reason why," conservatives correctly point out that *why* is unnecessary. Yet Tennyson, a poet respected by many conservatives, wrote about the soldiers called "the six hundred": "Theirs not to reason why, / Theirs but to do and die." If it's good enough for Tennyson . . . ? *Reason why* is established in sentences such as "The reason why the secretary of state made the comment is that . . ." SWE with or without the *why*.

reasons   SWE dislikes a construction in which a noun modifies *reasons*: "for courtesy reasons," "for politics reasons." SWE substitutes "for reasons of courtesy" or, better, "to be courteous"; "for reasons of health" or "because of his poor health"; "for political reasons."

rebellion/revolution   A *rebellion* is an uprising or revolt designed to effect a change of rules or even of government. If the rebellion succeeds and does indeed bring about large changes, it is called a "revolution." A *revolution* often enlarges the scope of the original rebellion.

rebound/redound   *Rebound* ("to bounce back") is sometimes misused for *redound* ("to have a good or bad effect"). SWE says, "A politician's name-calling sometimes redounds to his opponent's advantage by building sympathy."

rebuff   Headline: "Governor's Proposal Rebuffed." This is possibly SWE, but ordinarily a person rather than a thing is rebuffed, and the verb carries a suggestion of contempt or scorn that may not have existed when the governor's proposal was rejected.

recap   1. SWE as noun or verb referring to a tire: "A recap is cheaper." "We cannot recap all tires." 2. It's informal but useful for *recapitulation* or *recapitulate*: "Here's a recap of the news." "Let me recap the story."

recapitulate/repeat/summarize   To *repeat* is to say or do something again. To *recapitulate* or to *summarize* is to repeat in a shorter form. The word is based on Latin for "head," and a recapitulation gives basically the "headings," the main points. *Summarize* may mean the same thing but instead may refer to some other method of presenting a concise version, such as combining several points in a sentence or two.

receive   Sometimes pretentious: "I got a bicycle for my birthday" is usually better than "I received . . ." "I received some cracked ribs in the accident" sounds silly. "Some of my ribs were cracked . . ." is more likely in SWE.

receptive   See ACCEPTIVE/RECEPTIVE.

recital See CONCERT/RECITAL.

recollect/remember Usually considered interchangeable, *recollecting* may require more effort than *remembering*: "I am trying to recollect what was said." Also, you may remember people in your will, but you do not recollect them.

recommend FF: "We recommend you to watch this program" (we are not recommending *you*). SWE says, "We recommend that you watch . . . ," "We recommend this program to you."

recondition/renovate Interchangeable, although *recondition* generally suggests mechanical items (cars, vacuum cleaners), and *renovate* often refers to nonmechanical things (sofas, fur coats, rooms). *Remodel*, *reconstruct*, and *restore* imply more thorough treatment than either of the other words.

recopy See RE- + AGAIN OR BACK.

record (noun) Although several writers on usage say that modifiers such as *new* should not be used with *record*, so many records are kept today that qualification is often needed. For example, we may have a February, seasonal, or all-time record; a local, county, state, national, or world record; or an old record that has just been supplanted by a new one. Of course, if *new* or another modifier is not needed for clarity, SWE avoids it. See also NEAR-RECORD; PAST EXPERIENCE.

rector See MINISTER/PASTOR/PREACHER . . .

redound See REBOUND/REDOUND.

reduce See DEPLETE/REDUCE.

refer See ALLUDE/REFER.

reform/re-form To *reform* is to make better, to reduce or eliminate flaws. To *re-form* is to form again: "She re-formed the clay to alter the shape of the nose." Words in which a hyphen makes a similar large difference include *re-claim*, *re-collect*, *re-cover*, *re-creation*, *re-dress*, *re-fuse*, *re-lay*, *re-mark*, *re-move*, *re-place*, *re-pose*, *re-present*, *re-search*, *re-sign*, *re-solve*, *re-sound*, *re-strain*, *re-treat*, *re-trench*, and some rare ones such as *re-tail* ("to re-tail a kite"). Some people prefer to write "claim again" and so on instead. See also RE- + AGAIN OR BACK.

refute Not the same as *deny*. In court a defendant may deny guilt, but denial alone cannot refute charges brought against him or her. Refuting requires proof. See also CONTRADICT.

regal See KINGLY/REGAL/ROYAL.

regret See DEPLORE/LAMENT/REGRET . . .

regular(ly) Not ordinarily required when another word in the sentence shows regularity: *hourly*, *daily*, *monthly*, and so on. See also FREQUENTLY/REGULARLY.

REIFICATION In allegory, characters such as "Good Deeds" put on human clothing and walk around for all to see. In old-fashioned poetic invocations, Inspiration was addressed as a living thing. In some metaphors, such as the familiar "Happiness is a warm puppy," an abstraction is again translated into something tangible. *Reification* (literally "the making of things") is the name given to any such alteration into something concrete. Reification is often a useful way to explain something difficult to grasp. One effective user of it is Robert Krulwich, who on television news programs clarifies economic concepts by showing such things as piles of thousand-dollar bills, partly filled containers, or people with funny hats or odd behavior. They may represent such abstractions as capital, scarcity or shortage, or greed.

rejoinder See ANSWER, REPLY, RESPONSE . . .

relatively Implies a comparison. In "Only a relatively small number of passengers can be accommodated," the smallness (or the number) is relative to what? SWE deletes *relatively* or (not helpfully) substitutes *rather*. More specific: "No more than twenty passengers can be accommodated." A satisfactory use, showing a comparison, is "After yesterday's frigid blasts, today's weather will be relatively warm and calm."

release See DISCONTINUE/DISEMPLOY/RELEASE.

religious (noun) Although a monk or a nun may accurately be called "a religious," the term may baffle some laypersons, as in "Several religious were in the audience." *Nuns* would be less likely to confuse.

relocated "They relocated from Albany to Syracuse." Pretentious for *moved*.

remainder/rest If *rest* is as clear as *remainder*, SWE prefers the shorter word. *Remainder*, suitable in business correspondence, elsewhere may have a rather cold, mathematical connotation. See also BALANCE.

remains (noun) **1.** Outmoded (and unpleasant) for *corpse*: "His remains were dug up again." **2.** It is still used for "items left over": "The remains of her meal were (or *was*) still on the table." Not used with a specific number, such as "three remains," but is possible with *a few, some, many*.

remark See COMMENT/OBSERVATION/REMARK.

remediable/remedial "The problem is *remediable*" ("correctable"). "The child needs *remedial* instruction" ("intended to serve as a remedy").

remedy See PANACEA/REMEDY.

remember See RECOLLECT/REMEMBER.

remembrance/reminder/souvenir A *remembrance*, when physical, is a token of a person generally recalled with affection: "She kept her aunt's Bible as a remembrance." A *reminder* is likely to be of temporary service: "She set the microwave oven for ten minutes, so that its beep would be a reminder to call Jerry." A *souvenir* (French for "memory") is usually a small item that serves to recall a place, occasion, or experience, now and then a person.

remunerate SWE for "pay back, compensate for": "He will remunerate you for your loss." The word may also mean "pay," but here the shorter word is generally preferable: "I will remunerate (*pay*) you for the fruit tomorrow."

renaissance/renascence Each means "rebirth." However, *renaissance* (often capitalized) is the usual form for the "revival of learning" of A.D. c. 1300–1600, and *renascence* is usual for any other sort of rebirth or revival.

renovate See RECONDITION/RENOVATE.

renowned In the adjective, *-ed* is essential: "a renowned clarinetist."

reparable/repairable See IRREPARABLE.

repartee See ANSWER, REPLY, RESPONSE . . .

repast See PARTAKE.

repeat See RE- + AGAIN OR BACK; RECAPITULATE/REPEAT/SUMMARIZE.

repeat the same Redundant: "He repeats the same anecdotes whenever we see him." SWE prefers either "He tells the same anecdotes . . ." or "He repeats his anecdotes . . ."

repent See DEPLORE/LAMENT/REGRET.

repertoire/repertory Interchangeable. The French form is more likely in music: "Mehta's amazingly large repertoire."

replace This word is sometimes ambiguous. What does "Colonel Jordan replaced Major Armstrong" mean? Did the colonel take a post formerly occupied by the major? Did he give the post to another officer, or did he put Armstrong back on the job? In using *replace*, SWE tries to provide clarifying context.

replace/substitute (preposition with) One player, ingredient, and so on may be *replaced by* or *substituted for* another, but SWE does not interchange the prepositions: "Gray has been replaced by Johnson." "Johnson has been substituted for Gray."

replete Not just "full," but "abounding" or even "overflowing": "The kitchen was replete with the aromas of Christmas morning."

reply in the affirmative (or negative) Pretentious for *say yes* or *say no*.

reply See ANSWER, REPLY, RESPONSE . . .

reportedly "Over two hundred people reportedly died in the storm." This is standard journalese for "are reported to have died." Follett asks, "How does anyone reportedly die?" To avoid answering that difficult question, many careful writers say "may have died," or better, "Local officials estimate that over two hundred people died in the storm."

represent "Passenger pigeons represented a large part of the total bird population of North America." No. The pigeons did not represent anything. SWE is likely to choose *composed*, *constituted*, or even *were*.

reprisal/retaliation Both involve getting even, but *reprisal* is getting more than even. A *retaliation* may be a tooth for a tooth, but a reprisal adds a broken nose. Neither, of course, needs to be physical. For example, one nation may decide to impose higher tariffs on another as a retaliation for something, or impose even higher tariffs as a reprisal.

reputation   See CHARACTER.

requisite   See ESSENTIAL . . . MUST.

research   Too often used for a simple action such as looking up a topic in an encyclopedia. Most high school or college "research papers" are, more accurately, "source papers" or "library papers." Research is scholarly or scientific investigation or inquiry. Only occasionally do young students' endeavors qualify.

reside   See DWELL/LIVE/RESIDE.

resident   See CITIZEN/INHABITANT/RESIDENT.

respectively   "Ford, Mager, and Lamont live in Idaho, Wyoming, and Montana, *respectively*" means that Ford lives in Idaho, Mager in Wyoming, and Lamont in Montana. *Respectively* is sometimes meaningless and often unnecessary: "Her three daughters are Alice, Lucille, and Doris (respectively)." "The parrots flew to their (respective) perches."

response   See ANSWER, REPLY, RESPONSE . . . ; REACTION/RESPONSE.

rest easy   *Rest easy* has become SWE, not *rest easily*: "At last he could rest easy about money."

rest on one's laurels   This is a cliché, but it is certainly more colorful than the equivalent "be satisfied without trying to accomplish anything more."

rest   See REMAINDER/REST.

restive   In earlier centuries *restive* meant only "obstinate, resistant to control": "a restive horse." In this century the word has come to signify mainly "restless, fidgety." Conservatives dislike the change, but it is here to stay.

restrain   See CONSTRAIN/RESTRAIN.

resume   See CONTINUE/RESUME.

retaliation   See REPRISAL/RETALIATION.

reticent   See LACONIC/RETICENT.

retire   1. Slightly prim or stiff for "go to bed." 2. *Retire back*, as in "The soldiers retired back from the outpost," is redundant.

retort   See ANSWER, REPLY, RESPONSE . . .

retrospect(ion)   See HINDSIGHT/RETROSPECT(ION).

return back   See RE- + AGAIN OR BACK.

reveal   See DISCLOSE/DIVULGE/REVEAL.

Revelation   The name of the last book in the Bible is "The Revelation of St. John the Divine" – not "Revelations."

revelation   See DISCLOSURE/REVELATION.

revenge   See AVENGE/REVENGE.

Reverend   Much disagreement here, but these classifications describe fairly well the present status: very formal – the Reverend Henry Blue; formal – Reverend Henry Blue, and Reverend Blue (for a later reference); FF – the reverend, the Reverend, Rev. Blue, the Rev. Blue; formal – the Reverend Blue and the Reverend White, the

Reverend Blue and White; informal or FF – the Reverends Blue and White; moving fast toward SWE – Rev. Henry Blue, Rev. Blue. In addressing a minister orally, Mr. or Dr. (when the title fits) seems to be replacing *Reverend* but not *Father*: "Good morning, Dr. Blue." "Good morning, Father Brown."

reverse See CONVERSE/REVERSE.

revolution See REBELLION/REVOLUTION.

revolve/rotate Our moon *revolves* ("circles") around our planet, and Earth itself *rotates* ("turns on its axis") once in each twenty-four hours. The distinction is useful, but *revolve* is frequently used, both orally and in print, for both meanings.

revolver See AUTOMATIC/PISTOL/REVOLVER.

reward See AWARD/REWARD.

rhyme/rime In the sense of "identity of sound," although *rime* is a variant of *rhyme*, most literary folk prefer the longer spelling. Both are SWE.

rich See AFFLUENT/OPULENT/RICH . . .

riddle See ENIGMA/RIDDLE.

right (adverb) 1. SWE for "precisely": "right here," "right now." 2. FF for "very": "right good," "right smart." 3. FF as a modifier of an adverb and with the meaning "somewhat" or "very": "right suddenly," "right sensibly." *Suddenly* or *sensibly* can do the job alone. 4. Sometimes found in SWE is *right away* for "soon" or "at once." FF for the same meaning: *right off*.

rile Formerly regarded as a provincial pronunciation of *roil* ("to make angry, to vex"), *rile* now occurs occasionally in SWE: "Her frequent absences riled her employer."

rime See RHYME/RIME.

Rio Grande river Since *rio* means "river" in Spanish, SWE omits *river*.

rip-off This slang noun or verb referring to robbery, fraud, profitable deception, illegal exploitation, and the like has moved from the underworld to the *Wall Street Journal* and the *New York Times*, where it generally refers to cheating by brokerage houses and big corporations. Dictionaries still call it slang, but it deserves at least a label of informal, and unless moneyed executives stop ripping people off, it will almost inevitably increase its presence in SWE.

rites Any kind of ceremony, especially if solemn and religious, is a rite. The word is not a synonym of *funeral*: not "Rites will be held in the Baptist church," but "the funeral service," "obsequies" (a good nineteenth-century word), "funeral rites," or "last rites." *The service* or *services* also is not fully adequate as a synonym of *funeral*.

rob/steal A person, bank, or store is *robbed*, but the money, clothing, or whatever is taken is *stolen*.

robbery See BURGLARY/HOLDUP/ROBBERY.

rock/stone   *Rock* and *stone* have a few specialized meanings, as in *bedrock* or *grindstone*. A diamond may be called a stone, but only in slang is it a rock. In general, however, the two words are interchangeable. There is no agreement, for example, about which is larger. Boys throw rocks at tin cans, but in the New Testament people threw stones at the woman taken in adultery.

rogue   See KNAVE/RASCAL/ROGUE . . .

role/roll   SWE: "a role in a play," "one's role in life"; "a roll of tape," "call the roll."

romance (verb)   Informal in the sense "woo, make romantic love": "He romanced her with the usual flowers and jewelry." Its use is occasional in SWE.

rotate   See REVOLVE/ROTATE.

round   **1.** (adverb) Interchangeable with *around*, but the latter is more common: "stood around (less likely *round*) without talking." **2.** (preposition) Interchangeable with *around*, but perhaps slightly more informal: "sat round (or *around*) the campfire," "The earth moves round (or *around*) the sun." **3.** *Round* is written with no apostrophe. See also ABOUT/AROUND/ROUND; ALL-AROUND/ALL-ROUND; BULLET/CARTRIDGE/ROUND.

routine training exercise (or *mission*, and the like)   Usually, *routine* can be deleted.

row (noun)   For "a dispute, a quarrel," *row* is generally used for small altercations, not for major disagreements: " a family row" but probably not "a row between France and Germany." See also RUCKUS; SPAT.

royal   See KINGLY/REGAL/ROYAL.

ruckus   FF, occasionally SWE, for "a noisy disturbance." It refers to small commotions such as loud family quarrels or back-fence disputes. See also ROW; SPAT.

rudder   See HELM/RUDDER/TILLER.

rude   See CRUDE/RUDE.

rudimentary/vestigial   A *rudiment* is the beginning stage of something: "Buttonlike projections on the young buck's head were rudimentary antlers." A *vestige* is a remaining trace of something that was once more fully developed: "The human vermiform appendix is a vestigial digestive organ."

rules and regulations   One of the nouns is often enough.

rural/rustic   *Rural* is a neutral word for "pertaining to the country or country people": "rural route (*atmosphere*, *life*)." *Rustic* has the same meaning but may carry either favorable or unfavorable connotations. Many people like rustic furniture, speak of "rustic charm," and believe that they would enjoy supposedly uncomplicated rustic life. But *rustic* is also used pejoratively to suggest backwardness, lack of education and sophistication, lack of awareness of "real life"; a person called a "rustic" is often regarded as a bumpkin.

S

Sabbath To most Christians: Sunday. To Jews and Seventh-Day Adventists: Saturday. To Muslims: Friday.

sack See BAG/POKE/SACK.

safe/vault A *vault* for safekeeping of valuables is ordinarily large enough to walk into, but a *safe* is almost always much smaller. Some hotels that promise to keep your jewelry in a vault have a safe instead.

sagacious/sage A *sagacious* person is shrewd, practical in judgment: "sagacious reasoning about the effect on the stock market." *Sage* comes from a different Latin source. It means "wise" and is often associated with the wisdom of age. (A sage is a wise old person): "Her grandfather offered sage advice about the worth of monogamy."

Sahara desert *Sahara* is Arabic for "desert." When you've seen one *desert*, you've seen enough.

said As in "the said contract," is appropriate mainly in law, less frequent than before in business. "Those wrenches were shipped last week" is more modern than "Said wrenches."

salary/wages Not clearly differentiated, but in general a person is paid *wages* for any manual work or any other in which payment is by the hour, day, or (perhaps) week. One is paid a *salary* for what is customarily called a white-collar position, and the salary is often quoted for a year, although sometimes for a month or a week. See also EMOLUMENT.

same Redundant in expressions such as "This is the same one I mentioned before." It is legalistic in "They found the Christmas tree they wanted and cut same." Outmoded: "Your order has been received and same will be filled at once." SWE uses *it*. See also REPEAT THE SAME.

same as SWE in expressions such as "Your answer is the same as mine." It is FF in "I solved the puzzle the same as you did," for which SWE would usually substitute "the same way you did" or "in the same way that you did." Also FF as the equivalent of *just as*: "He came out shooting, same as you said he would."

sample See EXAMPLE/SAMPLE/SPECIMEN.

sanction It is unfortunate that *sanction* as a noun has two almost opposite meanings: (1) "authorization, permission, or encouragement to do something" and (2) "penalty for doing something." If a synonym will not work, SWE makes sure that the context reveals the meaning intended. The verb *sanction* poses the same problem. It may mean "to encourage, permit, or encourage" or "to impose a penalty."

Follett quotes this example of lack of clarity: "The field of sanction law as we understand it is the entire process of sanctioning."

sanguinary/sanguine *Sanguinary* means "bloody," "bloodthirsty": "a sanguinary battle," "Many pirates apparently were sanguinary fellows." *Sanguine* is quite different. It may mean "having a ruddy complexion" or "cheerful, optimistic": "He seemed always to be smiling and happy – sanguine about his family's future."

sans The French *sans* is used by show-offs instead of the English *without*.

sate/satiate Interchangeable. Each indicates full satisfaction, having an abundance or even an excessive amount, usually of food or sexual pleasure.

save Obsolescent or obsolete for *except*, as in "All save honor was lost." Many modern readers may not understand such a sentence.

saving(s) SWE prefers *saving* in "a saving of five dollars," "an annual saving," "daylight-saving time." It prefers *savings* in "a savings account (*bank, bond*)," "a savings and loan association."

say In reporting a conversation SWE often repeats *say* or *said*. Switching to a different verb with each change of speaker may annoy readers more than repetition does. However, SWE changes when good reason exists for telling readers that someone shouted, insisted, whispered, declared, and so on. (A verb such as *asseverated* may be a reader-stopper.) Frequently, a conversation requires no more than occasional identification of the speaker and consequently few verbs of saying. See also **ELEGANT VARIATION**.

say/state SWE reserves *state* for important people saying important things, or ordinary people saying anything firmly and quietly.

scam This underworld slang for "dishonesty, fraudulent scheme, confidence game" rose rapidly to higher levels in the 1970s and 1980s, when some members of Congress and prominent businessmen were found guilty of scams. Enough of them cooperated, in fact, that the word became SWE.

scan/skim 1. Each may mean "to read hurriedly, superficially": "She scanned (*skimmed*) the help-wanted ads." But *scan* may also mean the opposite: "read carefully," so "She scanned the ads" may also mean that she read them with care. For this reason many people use *skim* for the first meaning, *scan* for the second. Others avoid *scan*, substituting *scrutinize* or *read with care*. 2. To *scan verse* is to make a metrical analysis of it or to read it aloud with emphasis on each stressed syllable.

scarce See RARE/SCARCE.

scarcely See HARDLY NO/HARDLY NONE; HARDLY . . . THAN/SCARCELY . . . THAN.

scenario The meaning of "a plot outline" is often extended to mean "an imagined or hypothesized chain of events": "One possible scenario for the next few years is for our company to open stores in . . ." The word is obviously useful but appears so often as to be tiresome.

schlock   From Yiddish, this noun or adjective for "inferior or trashy merchandise, fashion, art, or almost anything else" is widely regarded as FF (slang), but is useful and often now appears in print, especially in metropolitan newspapers and artsy magazines, thus approaching SWE status. The adjective can be *schlock* or *schlocky*, and the spelling *shlock* is sometimes used.

scholar   Although dictionaries still include as one definition "a pupil in elementary or secondary school," that meaning is almost passé. Today a scholar is usually a mature person regarded as highly educated and a specialist in a branch of the humanities. Anyone who holds a scholarship is also a scholar.

score   See MARGIN/SCORE.

Scot (and the like)   Most Scots prefer these forms: A *Scot* or *Scotsman* rather than a *Scotchman*; (plural) *Scots* or *the Scotch*; (adjective) *Scottish* or *Scots* rather than *Scotch*, exceptions being *Scotch* broth, whisky (note no *e*), terrier, Guards, and a few subject-specific words such as *scotch thistles*. Note that *Scotch tape*, although it has no clear association with Scotland, is capitalized because it is a trade name.

scoundrel   See KNAVE/RASCAL/ROGUE/SCOUNDREL.

scrip/script   *Scrip* most often designates a substitute for regularly authorized paper money. It is ordinarily issued only in emergencies. *Script*, a much more common word, is used as in these examples: "The document was in script, not type." "Script type resembles handwriting." "Each actor was given a copy of the script."

scrupulous   See METICULOUS/PUNCTILIOUS/SCRUPULOUS.

scrutinize   Because *scrutinize* means "to examine carefully," *carefully*, *closely*, and the like are not used with it in SWE. See also SCAN/SKIM.

sculpt/sculpture   Interchangeable as verbs.

seasonable/seasonal   Although these words are often used interchangeably, many careful writers differentiate them. *Seasonable* means "appropriate to this season": "In the North in January, seasonable high temperatures are usually below freezing." *Seasonal* ordinarily means "dependent on or controlled by the season or time of year"; "One seasonal difference in hiring is caused by the annual influx of job-seeking June graduates."

secondly   See FIRSTLY, SECONDLY.

secret tryst   It wouldn't be a tryst if everyone knew about it. SWE omits *secret*.

sectarian/secular   *Sectarian* refers to religious sects: "Sectarian differences have divided many denominations." *Secular* means "worldly rather than spiritual": "Some members asserted that the priest was too much interested in secular matters."

secure   See GET/OBTAIN/SECURE.

see if I can (*can't*)   "See if you can (*can't*) borrow the money." Both are used, although *can* has logic on its side. Either way, it's FF. SWE: "Try to borrow . . ."

see, saw   "Zoos see a bright future, conferees asserted today." "World

War II saw an end to fortifications such as the Maginot Line." How can things without eyes see anything? The usage is SWE, illogical though it seems.

see where FF for "see that." In SWE one does not "see in the newspaper where the telephone workers may strike." Instead one "sees that . . ."

seeing FF for *because* or *as*: "Seeing (*Seeing as, Seeing as how*) we're late already, we . . ."

seem 1. Overused by the timid. Robert Frost wrote, "The woods are lovely, dark, and deep." The timid write, "The woods seem . . ." 2. *Can't seem to* is FF, marginally SWE, for "seem unable to." See also CANNOT (3).

seldom ever/seldom if ever/seldom or never *Seldom if ever* and *seldom or never* are SWE idioms. Each means that something seldom happened if it happened at all. *Seldom ever* is FF. See also RARELY EVER/SELDOM EVER.

select See EXCLUSIVE/SELECT.

-self, -selves In SWE the pronouns ending in *-self* or the plural *-selves* have two legitimate uses: (1) as intensives: "She herself told the story," and (2) as reflexives: "She told herself that Pete would not get drunk again." Generally considered FF in their use as subjects, objects, or the like, the terms appear in FF in these ways: "Betty and myself easily got work." "Xerox hired Betty and myself." "This is for Betty and myself." SWE substitutes *I, me, me*, respectively. (The *-self* pronoun in such sentences is a resort of someone who is uncertain about *I* vs. *me*.)

self-confessed As in "self-confessed killer," *self-* is redundant.

self-deprecation/self-depreciation *Self-deprecation* is a form of modesty, disavowing a real accomplishment as unimportant: "Aw, shucks, fellas, I didn't do much." *Self-depreciation* is unrealistic and excessive claims of lack of self-worth: "Nothing I do ever turns out right. I'm a failure as a wife, as a mother, as a businesswoman, as a . . ."

sell, sold Marginally SWE in expressions such as "You can't sell me such a theory" or "I'm sold on that idea," these verbs are often used by members of Congress, among others.

semi- See BI-.

senior citizens Certainly SWE, the term is disliked by some older people who consider it condescending. But what is a short substitute? *Older people* is an unfinished comparison – older than whom? Because *oldsters* sounds rather slangy or "cute," it has never caught on, nor (so far) has *generians*, which suggests that these people have *generated* and are partly responsible for the world today. *Generians* calls to mind *sexagenarians* and similar decade words. *Old folks* suggests Stephen Foster and the Swanee River. So, unless *generians* or some other word unexpectedly takes hold, SWE settles for *senior citizens*.

sensibility/sensibleness/sensitiveness/sensitivity *Sensibility* is not "sensibleness." *Sensibility, sensitiveness,* and *sensitivity* all mean "being sensitive," but *sensibleness* is "being sensible."

sensual/sensuous   SWE has blurred a useful distinction between these words. The most careful writers use *sensual* for "fleshly, voluptuous," usually referring to sex or, in a somewhat uncomplimentary way, to gratification of the senses. They use *sensuous* in a neutral or favorable way to refer to what is experienced through the senses: "sensuous descriptions," "sensuous impressions." Our sexually liberated age has so intertwined the two words, however, that few people can now tell them apart. A best-selling book of 1969 dealt almost exclusively with female sexuality and was called *The Sensuous Woman.*

sentiment/sentimentality   *Sentiment* refers to honest but not overwrought tenderness. Carried to extremes, sentiment becomes *sentimentality* – shedding tears for every fallen sparrow, imagining that one's relatives and closest friends are perfect, remembering only the good in "the good old days."

separate   SWE checks on whether it is needed, as in "The ambassador had separate conversations with the vice-president and the secretary of state," or unneeded, as in "The ambassador made five separate requests."

seraph   See CHERUB/SERAPH.

series   Everyone knows that *World Series* is as singular as *Super Bowl.* So is *series* in other meanings, unless more than one series is meant: "A series of explosions was (not *were*) heard." "Several series of explosions were heard."

serious   See CRITICAL.

seriously consider   Is *seriously* needed?

serve/service   SWE usually says that maintenance people *service* automobiles, refrigerators, computers, and the like, but ordinarily prefers *serve* in other contexts: "This telephone company serves only a few thousand customers." "Our cab company does not allow us to serve Newark passengers." "We serve the entire city."

set/sit   To *set* means "to place"; to *sit,* "to take a sitting position." People confused by these verbs may compose and say *aloud* repeatedly sentences such as these: "*Set* it on the table." "I *set* it on the floor." "You had *set* it in the wrong place." "Now you are *setting* it in the right place." "*Sit,* Rover." "Rover is *sitting* here." "He *sat* here yesterday." "He has *sat* here every day." "Why does he *sit* in this spot?" "He enjoys *sitting* here." Oddities: Hens *set* or *sit* on their eggs to hatch them (at other times they may *sit*). The sun *sets.* We *sit* or *seat* a person.

several   Although *several* has no precise numerical value, it is about the same as *a few* but fewer than *fairly numerous.* Dubious: "During its history, England has had a role in several wars" (*numerous* or *many* would be more accurate).

sewage/sewerage   *Sewage* is what passes through sewers. *Sewerage* can mean either the system of sewers, as in "the sewerage of Dayton," or "the removal of waste matter through sewers," as in "Increasing problems with sewerage are likely." Although *sewerage* sometimes is used for *sewage*, confusion may result.

sexy Now SWE. Of three dictionaries published between 1971 and 1981, one labels *sexy* slang, one says informal, and one treats it as standard. More recent ones appear unanimous in considering it standard. The word is relatively new, having been traced only to 1928, but the biblical King David and probably Adam and Eve themselves seem to have recognized the qualities it summarizes.

shake down, shakedown The verb, noun, and modifier one by one have become SWE: "The gang shook down ("extorted money from") leading politicians." "The shakedown ("extortion") was revealed only yesterday." "The shakedown ('testing') cruise revealed several weaknesses."

shall Except in questions starting with "Shall I (*we*)," *shall* is, if not dead, moribund. Only a few purists try to obey the old rules, which were not based on actual use and were never consistently followed. For the pure at heart, these are the rules in simplified form:

	Simple Future	Determination or Promise
I, we	shall	will
you, he she, it, they, Jones	will	shall

she Although no scholar has convincingly explained why, for at least two thousand years people have used a feminine gender pronoun for a ship. So: "My yacht is the *Mark Twain*. She . . ." Some owners, more or less affectionately, call their cars "she," probably never "he."

She See HE, SHE.

shell See BULLET/CARTRIDGE/ROUND/SHELL . . .

shenanigans Suppose that you witness some high-spirited behavior, a practical joke or a trick or two, a little drinking, and a great deal of semi-innocent fun. Suppose that you had to invent a word to cover all that. You probably wouldn't come up with *shenanigans*, but you might not find a better one. Nobody is certain where *shenanigans* came from – the Irish, maybe – but in the absence of an equally descriptive term, the word has deservedly reached SWE status.

ship See BOAT/SHIP; SHE.

ships that pass in the night Cliché. Longfellow wrote that many possibly compatible people meet like "Ships that pass in the night, and speak each other in passing,/Only a signal shown and a distant voice in the darkness." The metaphor is excellent and worth repeating – but not over and over (and not misquoted as "two ships passing in the night").

shod The past tense of the verb *shoe*. The past participle is *shod*, *shoed*, or *shodden* (take your choice). The sports commentator who said that a locker-room attendant has "enough football shoes to shod a centipede" offered an amusing comparison but should have said "to *shoe*" if he followed SWE usage.

shop   Generally used as an intransitive verb, as in "He shops on the Miracle Mile" or "She shops for Swiss chocolate," *shop* is now SWE as transitive also: "He shops the stores on the Miracle Mile." Used in this way, the emphasis is on both looking and buying, but *shops on (in, at)* stresses the buying.

shore   See BANK/SHORE.

shortly   In SWE this word is not used when "briefly" is meant. "He spoke shortly" probably means "curtly," and "He may speak shortly" probably means "soon." To avoid ambiguity, SWE chooses *briefly*, *curtly*, or *soon* – whichever is intended.

shot   See BULLET/CARTRIDGE/ROUND/SHELL/SHOT.

should/would   Pupils were once taught to say, "I should like to have one" rather than "I would . . ." But times have changed. Now *should* is used mainly for "ought to": "I should go to Denver tomorrow." Less frequent uses are illustrated in "I should think so," "We should ('are likely to') get there before dark," "If Mr. Clayton should ('does') call, tell him . . ."

show up   Once considered only informal, *show up* is now SWE in these senses: come, arrive – "He showed up at noon"; reveal faults – "The official report showed him up as a liar"; be revealed clearly – "Her courage shows up best in her battle against cancer." *Show up* is probably still FF for "outdo, defeat": "I showed him up in the pole vault."

shuttle back and forth   *Shuttle* means "move back and forth." The other three words are unnecessary.

[*sic*]   Usually enclosed in brackets (not parentheses) and italicized (underlined) because it is a foreign word, *sic* follows or is included in a quotation. It means "That's really the way it is printed. I'm not responsible for this stupid mistake." Example: "Shakespeare's home-town of Avon-on-Stratford [*sic*] was . . ."

sick at (*to*) one's stomach   SWE uses both. However, one is *sick with* a cold, and *sick of* ("tired of") the rainy weather.

sick (for "morbid")   *Sick humor* and *sick joke* are SWE terms in which *sick* means "morbid, unwholesome." See also BLACK HUMOR/SICK HUMOR; MORBID.

sick/sickly   A *sick* person may be temporarily ill, as with a cold. A *sickly* person has one or more enduring illnesses, or is sick much or most of the time. See also *ill/sick*.

sidewalk   See PAVEMENT/SIDEWALK.

sideways, sidewise   See EDGEWAYS, EDGEWISE/ENDWAYS . . . ; -WISE.

sight   See CITE/SIGHT/SITE.

sillily   SWE: short for "in a silly way." But the word looks and sounds odd, and for some people is hard to say. SWE must choose here between verbiage and oddity, or borrow the still FF "He behaved silly," recommended by SANE.

similar See CORRESPONDING/SIMILAR.

similar(ly) to SWE checks to see whether *like* will be equally clear.

(for the) simple reason that *Obvious* may be better than *simple* here. Or the whole phrase may be replaced by *because* or *only because*: "We stopped feeding birds for the simple reason that (or *because*) squirrels and raccoons were eating most of the seed."

simple/simplistic A *simple* solution and a *simplistic* solution are not the same. The simplistic one is actually oversimplified. The word implies that the person offering such a solution is not aware of or chooses to disregard some of the complexities.

simulate See DISSIMULATE/SIMULATE.

since See BECAUSE/SINCE.

singlehanded(ly) Although the adverb *singlehandedly* still exists, many respected authors use the less cumbersome *singlehanded* instead: "Singlehanded, Fred installed the garage door opener." SANE approves.

sink down Because sinking can be only downward, SWE deletes *down*.

sinus A *sinus* is one of several cranial cavities. SWE writes, "His sinuses were bothering him again," not "His sinus were . . . " Sinus is not an ailment. One does not get treatment or take medication for sinus, but for sinusitis or a sinus infection.

Sir See DAME/SIR.

sit See SET/SIT.

sitcom Well on the way to replacing *situation comedy*. It follows the frequently traveled path of *mob*, which Jonathan Swift decried as a replacement of *mobile vulgus*. (The language survived the shortening.)

site See CITE/SIGHT/SITE.

size/sized With *large, small*, and similar words, *sized* appears in SWE more often than *size*: "large-sized brushes." Often, however, as in that example, it can be omitted.

skeptical See CYNICAL/SKEPTICAL.

skim See SCAN/SKIM.

skirt around "Senator Raddles skirted around the issue but never quite discussed it." To *skirt* is to "go around" or "go along the edge of." SWE omits *around*.

slacks (verb with) SWE: "This pair of slacks *is* new." "These slacks *are* new." Verbs with *hose* ("legwear"), *stockings, pants*, and *trousers* are similar. See also *pair*.

slander See DEFAMATION/LIBEL/SLANDER.

SLANG William Lyon Phelps, a nineteenth-century professor of English at Yale, wrote: "Our slang's piquant as catsup. I decry it / Not as a condiment, but as an entire diet." Slang originates in various ways, as these outworn words reveal. *Vamoose* is a variant of Spanish *vamos*, "Let's go." *Square* ("an ultraconservative person") is a poetic or at least metaphorical way to say that the person lacks the smooth-running qualities of a wheel; *wheel* itself ("an important person") emphasizes in another way this century's idol. Some slang expressions are only overused ordinary terms, such as *drop dead*. A few, like *punk* or *moll*, have been borrowed from the argot of crime; thieves' language has been notably inventive for centuries, perhaps as a protective device. The jargon of an occupation or a sport, when used in another context, is often slang but may become SWE; *hit a homer* is good baseball talk, but when used to mean in business "succeed in an undertaking," it becomes slang. Much slang results from teenagers' wish to break away from the supposed conservatism (linguistic and other) of their elders, and from the attempt, also observable in some of their younger siblings, to create a secret language that only the initiated can understand.

Slang has four major weaknesses, writers of SWE believe, and for that reason they, like Phelps, use it mainly as a "condiment." One weakness is that it is a transitory language; a grandfather, using the slang of his youth, has difficulty in conversing with his grandson, who uses today's slang. The second, and related, weakness is that slang may not be understood even by others of the same generation. Third, the endless repetition of any expression, slang or not, becomes tiresome, and the users of slang tend to repeat endlessly. Finally, most slang expressions are not precise. For example, *real cool* (a 1950ish term that earlier was *real George* and still earlier *swell*, and later became *ba-ad* and will be something else when you read this) signified vague approval but suggested no reason for the approval, no identification of the good quality. The constant use of such easy and inexact terms leads to shoddy thinking and contributes to mental debilitation. You know, like, man, that's the name of the game.

In its place, though, if not overused, slang may be valuable. Its place is almost always an informal one (FF) – at a party or picnic, on the beach, at a ball game, in conversation with close friends. But occasionally in SWE a slang term may lend force, on a few occasions a surprising or even poetic effect.

SLANTING Slanting is the rhetorical device of omitting whatever material may harm one's cause and selecting materials and words that favor it or are hurtful to the opposing view. For example, here are headlines from two newspapers with differing political and economic views. Both headlines were used for the same story: "Congressional Leaders Threaten New Taxes." "Congressional Leaders Promise Tax Reforms." Note *threaten* vs. *promise* and the unpleasantness of *new taxes* in contrast to supposedly good *tax reforms*.

slattern/sloven/slut A *slattern* is an extremely unkempt woman. A *sloven* is an extremely untidy man or woman. A *slut* is a woman, often but not necessarily untidy, who is considered sexually immoral or promiscuous.

slaughter See ANNIHILATE, DESTROY, FLAY . . .

slay 1. If it weren't for headline writers, who like its brevity, this word might have become obsolete, but they have kept it as vigorous as the descendants of Cain. The principal parts are *slay, slew, slain*. 2. With the meaning of "greatly amuse," as in "His funny stories slay me," *slay* is FF. See also ANNIHILATE, DESTROY, FLAY . . .

sleek/slick Both words convey the idea of smoothness, but *sleek* is more often figurative for "well-groomed, well-fed, thriving, polished in manner." *Slick* most often means "slippery," but also may mean "shrewd" or "tricky," especially in informal usage: "a slick trader." It may also mean "superficially attractive."

sleeper Flexner says that in the 1930s *sleeper* for "unexpected success" was first applied to a movie. It has since become rather frequent in regard to horses, investments, politicians, athletic teams, and many other things. It occurs at times in SWE.

sleight/slight *Sleight*, meaning "skill, dexterity" or "cunning, craftiness" appears most often in the expression *sleight of hand*. For other meanings, *slight* is the accepted spelling.

slick See SLEEK/SLICK.

slob *Slob* is a contemptuous word for a person who is crude, uninformed, and slovenly. Sitting in his T-shirt the slob guzzles beer while he takes part vicariously in a television wrestling match. When the female slob is in the kitchen, she wears a dirty housecoat, ignores the sinkful of dishes, and sets on the grimy table an open can of beans and a couple of beers. People who pride themselves on their standard English sometimes need a word for such persons, but most dictionaries call *slob* informal or slang. It's a good, understandable word and should be SWE. A word ought not to be called nonstandard because its surroundings or its meaning is unpleasant.

slow drawl Redundant. By definition a drawl is a slow manner of speaking.

slow/slowly Both *slow* and *slowly* may be used as adverbs. In fact, *slow* is the older. So both "Go slow" and "Go slowly" are SWE. Euphony may sometimes determine the choice. "The two deer slowly went behind the trees" sounds better to most people than "went slow." *Slow* is more likely in short sentences, *slowly* in long, especially in writing. Similar comments apply to *loud, loudly; quick, quickly;* and *soft, softly.*

small See LIMITED/LTD./SMALL.

smaller, smallest See LEAST, LESS/LITTLER, LITTLEST/SMALLER, SMALLEST.

smash See ANNIHILATE, DESTROY, FLAY . . .

smell (and its synonyms) Pleasant: *aroma, bouquet, fragrance,* PERFUME, SAVOR; neutral: *odor, smell;* unpleasant: *stench, stink. Odor* and *smell* are general words. Sometimes they need to be qualified with adjectives such as *strong* or *flowerlike,* or be replaced by another of the words listed above. *Aroma* often means a spicy or savory smell, especially one that fills a considerable area: "the aroma of Grandma's kitchen." *Fragrance* refers to a light, perhaps flowery smell, as does *perfume*. *Bouquet* usually applies to wine. *Savor* combines the senses of taste and smell, emphasizing the former. *Stench* is stiffer than *stink*. Both appear in SWE.

smell (verb) See also FEEL (GOOD/WELL; BAD/BADLY).

smog Blends involve combining two words, a practice popularized several decades ago by *Time*. Some blends are meant mainly to amuse, as *infanticipating* ("expecting a baby") perhaps is. Some blends are useful and become standard, as is true of *brunch* (although the imitations *linner* and *lupper* have little value and have never caught on). Like *brunch, smog* ("a combination of smoke and fog, as well as pollutants and sometimes sunlight") has become SWE.

snide Either not listed or else labeled as slang in older dictionaries, *snide* is now an SWE adjective for "derogatory" or "slyly insinuating." More rarely it is a noun meaning "a dishonest person or act" or "a counterfeit."

snooty George Orwell said that a bourgeois belief he had encountered in his youth could be summarized "The lower classes smell." People who figuratively tilt their noses up to reduce such a smell are described as "snooty." It's a picturesque word, occasionally a good SWE substitute for *disdainful* or *haughty*.

snow job FF (slang), rare in SWE, for "flattery intended to persuade": "Dillard tried a snow job on me, but I held my ground."

snuck *Snuck* is FF for *sneaked*.

so (in comparisons) "It was *so* hot yesterday!" Conservatives call such sentences "unfinished comparisons" and recommend completion, possibly "It was so hot yesterday that every newspaper ran pictures of eggs frying on sidewalks." Another interpretation is that *so* in such a sentence is an intensifier, like *very* or *extremely*. In this case, no completion is necessary. However, most writers use *so* as an intensifier mainly in informal contexts. The male chauvinists say that it sounds feminine: "It's *so* lovely!" With some exceptions, SWE avoids unfinished comparisons.

so as Redundant when followed by an infinitive, as in "We crossed the road (so as) to see the cows." FF when followed by a clause: "We crossed the road so as we could see the cows."

so . . . as/as . . . as See AS . . . AS/SO . . . AS.

so . . . so In student writing, *so . . . so* sentences are marked almost as frequently as *and . . . and* sentences. *So* is especially overused in the sense of "for that reason": "My parents could not afford to send me to college, so I had to find other sources of money, so I . . . " Revising the sentence is usually the best remedy: "Because my parents could not afford to send me to college, I . . . The first thing I tried was . . . "

so/so that "They rose early so (or *so that*) they would not miss the plane." Both are used in SWE, with *so* increasing in frequency, although conservative writers and editors still favor *so that*.

soar Journalists tell us often that prices (the inflation rate, humidity, temperature, or what-have-you) soars. Unless the increase is remarkably large and rapid, *soar* may be too strong. One dictionary definition: "climb swiftly or powerfully."

so-called SWE uses *so-called* only when some people actually do use a designation that may be undeserved or unsuitable: "A so-called moral victory is neither moral nor a victory." Note that no quotation marks are needed around *moral victory*. When SWE does use the apologetic marks, it deletes *so-called*. SWE hyphenates *so-called* when it comes before the modified noun, as in "her so-called uncle," but not after: "her uncle, at least so called."

sociable/social For the meaning "friendly, affable, eager to converse," *sociable* is more common in SWE, but *social* is also used. An old-fashioned name for a lawn party or other informal gathering is *social,* which old-timers often called a *sociable*: "an ice-cream social (*sociable*)." Both forms are FF and geographically limited.

social disease This euphemism has been largely replaced in SWE by the more frank *venereal disease* or the specific name.

soft/softly See SLOW/SLOWLY.

software See HARDWARE/LIVEWARE/SOFTWARE.

softwood See HARDWOOD/SOFTWOOD.

soliloquy See MONOLOG(UE)/SOLILOQUY.

some See A/SOME.

some (adverb) "The farmer bought some sixty feeder calves." *Some* in this adverbial use, meaning "about," is SWE.

some/somewhat FF (dialectal or informal): "He's some better today," "The temperature has dropped some." SWE substitutes *somewhat*.

some thing vs. something/some time vs. sometime *Something* and *sometime* are the forms almost always needed. *Some thing* is standard when a contrast is intended: "This time don't bring me some live animal; bring me some *thing*." *Some time* is standard when time is what is being talked about, as in "Some time is what we need" or "I have some time to spare."

somebody/someone Interchangeable. Each is singular. A verb and a pronoun with it are also normally singular in SWE usage: "Somebody is certain to lose his (*her*) wager." *Somebody . . . they (their)*, however, has been endorsed by some groups within the National Council of Teachers of English, to the dismay of many members. In FF, *somebody . . . they (their)*, is almost universal. See also THEIR, THEM, THEY.

sometime See OCCASIONAL/SOMETIME; SOME THING VS. SOMETHING . . .

sooner 1. In the sense of "rather," *sooner* is SWE: "He would sooner vote for a crocodile than for Brown." **2.** After *no sooner, than* rather than *when* is the usual SWE preference: "She had no sooner reached cruising altitude than her radio went dead."

sore FF for "annoyed, angry": "Don't get sore about this."

sort of See KIND OF/SORT OF.

soul As an adjective for "black in origin, rooted in the black experience," this word is SWE but slightly informal: "soul food (*music, sister*)."

sound out In the sense of "learn the opinion or attitude of," *sound out* is SWE: "They sounded out the provost before they asked for the president's approval."

southerly See EASTERLY/EASTERN.

souvenir See REMEMBRANCE/REMINDER/SOUVENIR.

spaded/spayed *Spay* means "remove the ovaries of an animal": "We took Queenie to the veterinarian to be spayed (not *spaded*).

spark SWE in the sense of "serve as the immediate cause of": "The assassination of a relatively unimportant man sparked World War I." (The spark is usually not the real, underlying cause.)

spat (noun) SWE: "A short-lasting quarrel over a small matter." As a rule a few spats between a couple do not lead to divorce, and *spat* is too light a word to apply to disagreements between nations. The same definition and comments apply to *tiff.* See also ROW; RUCKUS. For the verb see SPIT/SPITTED.

spayed See SPADED/SPAYED.

speak to (*with*) Often interchanged, although it is logical to use *to* for one-sided speaking, *with* when two or more persons are conversing: "The captain spoke to his crew to inform them of the new danger." "The captain spoke with the first mate, frankly exchanging opinions." A similar distinction is usually drawn between *talk to* and *talk with.*

spearhead Overused, by journalists especially, for "direct, lead, take charge of."

special Some merchants have given *special* a bad reputation. "Today's Special" at the lunch counter may be last night's dinner warmed over or disguised. The "Special Markdown" on the used-car lot may indeed be a marked-down price – say, by two hundred dollars after being marked up by three hundred. What is special about a "special invitation to subscribe"? Some things in life are indeed special, but it's not always easy to recognize them. In SWE, context shows specifically what is special, unusual, exceptional, or distinctive. See also ESPECIAL/SPECIAL.

specially See ESPECIALLY/SPECIALLY.

specie/species *Specie* is coined money (not paper). In rare instances its plural, *species,* is used: "the species of England and France." Even in such a sentence, however, *specie* is probable. *Species* ordinarily means "a kind" and is most often used in biology for a classification ranking below *genus*: "a rare species of butterfly." In *Homo sapiens,*

Homo represents the genus, *sapiens* the species. Both the singular and plural are *species*. FF: "a specie," "one specie."

SPECIFICITY See **ABSTRACT AND GENERAL WORDS**.

specimen See **EXAMPLE/SAMPLE**.

spectators See **AUDIENCE/CONGREGATION/SPECTATORS**.

spell The verb *spell* meaning "take over a job for a short time" is SWE: "to spell the helmsman." So is the noun *spell* as in "a short spell," "a warm spell," "did a spell in prison," although the noun use is most likely in informal contexts.

spell out Although Bernstein calls *spell out* "a tired old workhorse," it is still frequent in SWE in the sense of "state explicitly": "Even some IRS officials cannot clearly spell out the implications of this new tax regulation." *Spell out in detail* is redundant.

spend time See **KILL TIME/PASS TIME/SPEND TIME**.

sphere See **REALM/SPHERE/WORLD**.

spick-and-span Sometimes people classify words as slang or informal simply because they *sound* informal. This is true of *spick-and-span*. Its first recorded use is in the admired translation of Plutarch's *Lives* by Sir Thomas North in 1579 or 1580, and many other reputable writers have used it since. But Morris in 1975 reported that the term was still "generally regarded as close to slang." Sir Thomas North deserves more respect. The term is SWE.

spiral "Prices are spiraling once more," a news story said. Perhaps it is easy to guess the direction of this spiral, but ordinarily the context should make clear whether downward or upward is meant. A spiral may go either way. We may climb or descend a spiral staircase.

spire/steeple A church or other building may have a spire, a steeple, or a spire on top of a steeple. A steeple is a tower, sometimes containing bells. A spire is normally slimmer and may be either hollow or solid.

spit See **EXPECTORATE/SPIT**.

spit/spitted 1. Yes, *spitted* is one past tense of *spit,* but only in the sense of "thrust a rod through": "He spitted the dressed chicken and suspended it over the fire." 2. In the sense of "expectorate," both *spat* and *spit* are SWE for the past tense, with *spat* perhaps more frequent.

splutter/sputter Interchangeable. *Splutter* is the newer word, perhaps a blend of *sputter* with *splash*. (One person with a good ear says that *splutter* "sounds wetter than sputter.")

spoof As both noun and verb, the word is SWE to refer to a parody or gentle ridicule: "a spoof of modern literary criticism," "a comic opera that spoofs the grand solemnity of Wagner."

sprain/strain A *sprain* is a painful wrenching or tearing of ligaments – for instance, in the ankle or shoulder. *Strain* usually results from overuse or overexertion and is customarily applied to muscles or ligaments that are extended too far but are not torn. Emotional and mental strain also exist, but most of us need not worry often about the latter.

spray/spume Sometimes an ocean wave strikes a rock as it pounds ashore, sending water high in droplets. These are *spray,* as are the droplets blown from a fountain by the wind. If you look out to sea, you may see foam or froth atop some of the waves, or churning around on the surface. This is *spume.*

sprint/spurt (running) A *sprint* lasts longer than a spurt. For example, a one-hundred-meter dash is often called a *sprint.* Near the end of a longer run, a good runner has conserved enough strength to sprint for the final fifty or more meters. A *spurt* is a short burst of speed, perhaps faster – while it lasts – than the same runner's sprint would be.

225

spume See SPRAY/SPUME.

spurious See ARTIFICIAL/ERSATZ/FAKE . . .

spurt See SPRINT/SPURT.

sputter See SPLUTTER/SPUTTER.

square FF (outmoded slang) for a person looked on by the speaker as old-fashioned, "out of it," "not with it," "not hip or even hep."

square miles SWE distinguishes between *square miles* and *miles square.* Nine square miles of land could be, for example, 3×3 miles or $4\frac{1}{2} \times 2$. Nine miles square, however, would be nine miles on each side; $9 \times 9 = 81$ square miles. Obviously the same distinction is made between *square inches* and *inches square,* and so on.

squoze Sometimes used humorously in SWE, *squoze* is FF for *squeezed,* by analogy with *froze.*

stabilize When manufacturers or other businesspeople refer to stabilizing prices, they often have no interest in keeping them steady. They overuse (and misuse) *stabilize* to mean "to prevent from going down." OPEC oil ministers, for instance, apparently used an Arabic equivalent of that word each time they raised the price during the 1970s.

staid/stayed The adjective (meaning "dignified, sedate") is *staid:* "The attorney's staid manner was comforting."

stalactite/stalagmite In a cave a *stalagmite* builds from the base upward, but a *stalactite* hangs down from the roof like an icicle. An old mnemonic device: the stala*c*tite is *tight* against the ceiling.

stalemate Headline: "Wage Stalemate to Be Broken Soon." In chess a *stalemate* or a checkmate ends the game. Each is impossible to break, remove, overcome. It's as final as nuclear winter. The headline writer could, however, have written "Wage Stalemate to Be Averted" or "Wage Agreement Near."

stall In the sense of "delay," the verb *stall* was labeled slang in many dictionaries early in this century, but now is SWE in sentences such as "He stalled to catch his breath." In athletic and other contexts it is also used as a noun or a modifier: "The team has gone into a stall," "a stall offense." *Stall for time,* although widely used, is redundant, because *for time* is implicit in *stall.*

stammer/stutter   To *stammer* is to speak hesitantly and with pauses and occasional repetitions: "I – I find – I find it – it's hard to – to talk about it." High emotion is the usual cause, but embarrassment or failure to remember may also be at fault. To *stutter* is ordinarily to repeat sounds (less often whole words): "B-b-but Bob-Bob d-d-didn't tell me." *Stutter* is the term used in this sense by speech therapists.

stamp/stomp   **1.** Often interchanged, although *stomp* suggests heavier, more violent action. People, especially women, usually stamp their feet, but a large, cruel man may stomp on a fallen opponent. Large animals may stomp around, but a pony delicately stamps a front hoof. **2.** *Stamp out* is usual for "eliminate": "stamping out use of illicit drugs."

stance   Related to *stand, stance* basically means "a standing position" but has been legitimately extended to "an intellectual or emotional position." SWE avoids, however, statements in which the idea of "standing" is absurd, as in "My stance is that we should stage a sitdown strike."

stanch/staunch   Used interchangeably in SWE, although some people prefer *stanch* as the verb: "to stanch the flow of blood," and *staunch* as the adjective: "a staunch friend." That distinction is useful.

stand in line/stand on line   The usual idiom is *stand in line,* but *stand on line* is frequently spoken – less frequently written – in parts of the eastern United States.

stanza/verse   In popular use, a *verse* is the same as a *stanza.* To literary scholars, however, a verse is a single line, and a stanza is a group of lines, often rhyming in a patterned way. *Verse* is also used to distinguish poetic writing from *prose.*

starboard   See LEE/PORT/STARBOARD . . .

state of the art   This term originated in the 1960s and quickly became SWE. It is used both as a noun and (usually hyphenated) as an adjective, especially in referring to the most advanced developments in a technology, a science, or education: "The state of the art in computer technology changes before there is time to describe it in print." "This state-of-the-art metal detector . . . "

state   See also SAY.

stationary/stationery   *Stationary* means "not moving": "a stationary engine." *Stationery* is material for writing, especially paper. Children are sometimes told that they can remember the distinction by thinking of the *er* in *stationery* and in *letter.*

statue/stature/statute   The stone man or woman standing in the park is a *statue.* He or she may have a *stature* of about twelve feet. A local *statute* makes it illegal to deface a statue.

statuesque/statuelike Both mean "similar to a statue," but *statuelike* is more literal, recalling the hardness and immobility of a real statue. *Statuesque* refers more to graceful appearance, stateliness, or superb proportions. Actress Grace Kelly was often described as "a statuesque blonde," but her easy movements and expressive face were certainly not statuelike.

staunch See STANCH/STAUNCH.

stay home SWE in the United States, but some conservatives prefer the British *stay at home,* arguing that *home* cannot be used as an adverb. Words, however, keep jumping over fences.

stay/stop If you *stop* at a hotel or motel, do you only pause there – perhaps for a meal – or do you spend the night? Because of possible ambiguity, SWE writers generally use *stay* for an overnight or longer sojourn. In FF, *stop* is frequent.

stayed See STAID/STAYED.

steal See ROB/STEAL.

steeple See SPIRE/STEEPLE.

sterling (silver) Not synonymous with *pure. Sterling* silver is 92.5 percent silver, 7.5 percent copper or other metal. A person of "sterling character," it may possibly be inferred, is highly praiseworthy, but like the rest of us has a little alloy to prevent excessive softness.

stewardess The modern preference is for (*flight*) *attendant* or *steward,* regardless of sex. See also -ESS.

stick up for FF for "uphold, defend, side with": "Louise always sticks up for her husband."

still and all This phrase is almost meaningless. SWE settles for *still, yet, anyhow,* or *nevertheless.*

still continue, still remain, still stay SWE omits *still.*

stomp See STAMP/STOMP.

stone See ROCK/STONE.

stonewall (verb) Popularized by denizens of the Nixon White House to mean "insist that one knows nothing about a subject," *stonewall* (like *at this point in time*) has become fairly well established in journalistic and other writing.

stop by *Stop by* is now SWE for "come for a brief visit." See also STAY/STOP.

straddle (an issue) SWE in the sense of "appear to favor both sides." Some politicians have straddled issues of corporate greed by speaking publicly about helping "us little fellows" against the "giants," but then quietly voting for bills that help generous campaign contributors.

straightened/straitened *Straightened* means "make straight" or "put-in-order": "She straightened her stockings." *Straitened* means "narrowed, squeezed." A financially straitened person is squeezed financially, "feels the pinch," is "in financial straits."

strain   See SPRAIN/STRAIN.

straitjacket/straitlaced   Preferably not *straight-*. A strait, such as the Strait of Gibraltar, squeezes water between land masses. A *straitjacket* squeezes the person inside it, and a *straitlaced* person is figuratively squeezed by a narrow interpretation of morality, as women used to be squeezed by laced corsets.

strange   See ODD/PECULIAR/QUAINT . . .

strangled to death   If you have been *strangled,* you're dead.

strata/stratums   The usual plural of *stratum,* meaning "layer," as in "a stratum of rock," is *strata,* although *stratums* is occasionally seen.

stutter   See STAMMER/STUTTER.

subconscious/unconscious   To a psychologist, *subconscious* refers to what goes on, in human thought and emotions, that a person is not aware of: "strong soldiers of hate and love fighting it out in his subconscious." *Unconscious* in ordinary use means "temporarily without consciousness" or "involuntary": "knocked unconscious by his opponent," "unconscious sneering tone."

subject   Perhaps for some legal or legalistic reason, police reports frequently refer to a person as a *subject.* The word is vague enough to cover all races, ages, and genders, and may conceivably include such nonpersons as monkeys or dogs. The result is sometimes amusing, as in this quotation from an Indiana police blotter: "A subject was reported to be throwing objects into the street." SWE, unless preparing police reports, uses a more specific word to refer to a person: *boy, woman, young person, man in a checkered jacket,* and so on.

subject matter   "The subject matter of the discussion was . . . " *Subject* alone is usually enough, although the two words may be needed in expressions such as "the subject matter of this course."

subject/topic   Often interchangeable: "the subject (*topic*) of discussion." Some writers, however, consider it useful to regard topics as divisions of a subject. Thus the subject "polar exploration" can yield a large number of topics, such as the Peary expedition, the question of who really reached the Pole first, or some recent exploratory techniques.

SUBJECTIVE COMPLEMENT   See IT'S I/IT'S ME.

subsequent to   *After* is more concise.

subsist   See EXIST/SUBSIST.

substitute   See REPLACE/SUBSTITUTE.

success   See GOOD BENEFIT/GOOD SUCCESS.

such a   **1.** With occasional exceptions, SWE avoids unfinished comparisons, as in "It was such a hard job!" SWE might complete that like this: "It was such a hard job that we had to call for help." **2.** In *no such a thing,* the *a* is unnecessary. See also *so* (*in comparisons*).

suffer from/suffer with   Both are SWE, although "suffer from arthritis" (or other ailment) is more likely.

sufficiency   *A sufficiency of* is wordy for *enough.*

sufficient number Instead of *a sufficient number* (or *amount*) *of*, SWE prefers *enough, ample,* or *sufficient.*

sufficiently Usually followed by an adjective and an infinitive, or an adjective and *for*: "The engine is sufficiently powerful to lift five tons," " . . . sufficiently powerful for the tasks you described." Wordy: " . . . sufficiently powerful that it will perform the tasks you described."

suggest *Suggest* is standard when what is said is tentative, when it is presented as one possible solution. Sometimes a stronger word is suitable, for example, *advocate, assert, declare, predict, recommend.*

summarize See RECAPITULATE/REPEAT/SUMMARIZE.

summary See PARAPHRASE/SUMMARY.

super Overused FF adjective or exclamation for anything favorable – perhaps often for *exceptional, great, marvelous,* or any other word of high or ecstatic praise.

supersede (Note the spelling.) *Supersede* does not indicate superiority. When one person (*regulation,* and so on) supersedes another, he, she, or it replaces the other and may or may not be better. However, in some instances something is superseded when it becomes obsolete.

supersonic/ultrasonic *Supersonic* means "beyond the speed of sound": "This plane flies at supersonic speed." *Ultrasonic* refers not to speed but to acoustic frequencies – those above the range audible to most people: "Dogs can hear ultrasonic whistles." Such sounds are above twenty thousand cycles per second.

supine See PRONE/PROSTRATE/SUPINE . . .

supplement See AUGMENT/SUPPLEMENT.

supplemental inflatable restraints Hoity-toity. A General Motors advertisement says that "supplemental inflatable restraints" are available. Quick, G.M., the air bags!

supporter See PROPONENT/SUPPORTER.

suppose See CALCULATE/RECKON/SUPPOSE.

suppose(d) to *Supposed to* is SWE in "Mr. Bedrosian is supposed to ("is expected to, has promised to") call this afternoon." *Suppose to* in such a sentence is FF.

supreme sacrifice As in "For his country he paid the supreme sacrifice." Criticized as "stock pathos" in some stylebooks, and certainly not to be used often. It is true and forgivable, though, in writing about people who gave their lives for causes they considered worthy. Sometimes it is used ironically, as in referring to a person who abstained from smoking for a day, or to someone who missed a rock concert.

sure/surely "I sure like pistachio ice cream" is FF, with *sure* used as an adverb. SWE requires *surely*, as in "The candidates surely will soon begin to discuss the issues." *Sure enough* is SWE, although informal in tone, in "Sure enough, the gun was loaded" or similar sentences.

suspect (verb)/suspicion 1. Illogical: "Drugs are suspected of being involved in the murders." Better: "Sellers (or *Users*) of drugs are suspected . . . " Despite the lack of logic, sentences like the first sometimes occur in SWE. **2.** *Suspicion* as a verb is FF (dialectal). The SWE verb for "to be suspicious of" is *suspect*.

sustain   Some stylebooks assert that *sustain an injury* is inferior to *suffer an injury,* but the expression is used so frequently in SWE that it may no longer be condemned. *Sustain a loss* is almost never criticized.

swallow down   In SWE, *down* is deleted here. In FF, however, Mama says to her reluctant little patient, "Swallow it down, honey," even though she knows that swallowing up is unlikely. (Granted, a whale and a wolf, respectively, swallowed *up* Jonah and a grandmother. But maybe their anatomy isn't like the little patient's.)

swap   A few years ago, many people would have called *swap* a good word in horse-trading but too informal for international exchanges. However, when the Reagan administration was interested in trading arms for Americans held hostage, *swap* was in constant use by the media, including the most reputable. So horse-traders and *swap* now find themselves in select company. Consider the word SWE.

SWEEPING GENERALIZATION   A sweeping generalization is an inclusive statement that cannot be proved but that often can be at least partly disproved: "Women are not good liars." "Mexicans are short." A statement containing one of these words is often a sweeping generalization: *all, no* or *none, everybody* or *nobody, always, never*: "All Swedes (Poles, or you name them) are brilliant." "No women are great artists." "Always distrust a cross-eyed man." "It never rains but it pours." Seldom, if ever, is a sweeping generalization appropriate. "All generalizations are false, including this one."

swell   Obsolescent slang word intended to praise. See also LOUSY; SUPER.

swoon (verb)   **1.** Still SWE, *swoon* is now usually replaced by *faint* for the meaning "lose consciousness." **2.** It is also SWE for "become ecstatic about": "Teenagers in the 1940s swooned over Frank Sinatra."

sympathy   See EMPATHY/SYMPATHY.

syndrome   Too often used by people who do not know that a syndrome to a doctor is a group of symptoms that, taken together, characterize a disease. So a *syndrome* is not a "disease." One doesn't say, "My husband is in the hospital with a syndrome." Outside medicine a syndrome is a group of signs indicating an undesirable condition. The Super Bowl Weekend syndrome, for example, has been caricatured as massive sandwiches, huge dishes of popcorn, six-packs of beer, and five men staring hypnotized at a television screen. It is inaccurate to refer to something as a syndrome if only one symptom is observable. Dubious: "a Vince Lombardi syndrome."

synthetic   See ARTIFICIAL/ERSATZ/FAKE . . .

T

taciturn See LACONIC/RETICENT/TACITURN.

tacky SWE, *tacky* has in recent years added to its meaning of "physically shabby, dowdy" a more figurative sense: "inconsiderate, un-
worthy, undeserved, cheap": "a tacky remark."

tact see DIPLOMACY/TACT.

tad/tad bit Dictionaries agree that *tad* is informal for "a small boy"
or "a small child." But in recent years the word has been used widely
to mean "little": "Move it just a tad." And *tad bit* has been trying to
compete with *little bit*, as in "a tad bit noisy." These are still FF.

tailor-made See CUSTOM, CUSTOM-BUILT.

take A dozen or more clichés start with *take*. Here is a bit of nonsense
using several of them: "Why don't we take time by the forelock,
take the bit in our teeth, take the bull by the horns, and take the
enemy by storm? That would take the wind out of their sails."
"Maybe so, but I'd rather take cognizance of the situation and take
to my heels."

take for example FF if *take* has no clearly indicated object, as in
"Take, for example, the parents can't agree on the baby's name."
SWE says, "For example, some parents cannot . . ." or "Consider as
an example parents who cannot . . ." or "Take, for example, new
parents who cannot . . ."

take in Has moved from FF to SWE in the sense of "attend, go to,
see, hear": "While in St. Louis they took in a Cardinal-Cub game."

take into consideration *Consider* is often enough.

take off FF or shakily SWE in the sense of "depart, leave": "They took
off for Vancouver by car." It is solidly SWE, though, for the taking
off of an airplane.

take on SWE for "hire" or "combat": "The factory took on new
employees." "The new champion said he would take on any qualified
opponent." FF for "scold" or "show excitement": "Ma really took
on whenever Pa came home drunk." "Laurie took on over Gina's
diamond bracelet and then took off after its donor."

take part See PARTAKE.

take place See OCCUR/TAKE PLACE.

take sick FF (regional) for *become (get) sick (ill)*, *take sick* sometimes
appears in SWE.

talent See GENIUS/TALENT.

talk (noun) *Talk* is SWE for reference to informal remarks such as a
coach's pep talk or to any other rather conversational, not fully
prepared oral presentation. For more formal occasions, *address*, *lecture*, or *speech* is appropriate. See also ADDRESS/LECTURE.

talk to/talk with See SPEAK TO.

tall   See HIGH/LOFTY/TALL.

target   This word often contributes to brevity. *Target date* is obviously shorter and less awkward than *the date by which completion of the task is hoped for*. But *target* is used too often in contexts where it is neither appropriate nor helpful. Often more accurate: *quota, goal, objective. Targeted* can often be omitted, as in "the targeted objective."

task (verb)   This is a vogue word, as in "This office is tasked with the responsibility for . . . " Although nouns are often made into verbs, such transformation is desirable only when no existing verb does the job. In our example, *has* or *has been assigned* or *is responsible for* would be the usual SWE preference.

232 **teacher**   See EDUCATOR.

technic/technique   Interchangeable for "method of doing something," but few people use *technic*. However, *technics* is frequent in SWE for "the theory or study of a process or an act" or "technical methods or details."

technician   See ENGINEER/SCIENTIST/TECHNICIAN.

teeming   *Teeming* means "swarming": "a pond teeming with carp." Dubious: "Savannah and Charleston are teeming with history." Exaggerated: "Nashville, Indiana, is teeming with art dealers." For the first, *rich in* may be more suitable. For the second, perhaps "has almost a dozen art dealers."

teen-age(d)   See MIDDLE-AGE(D)/TEEN-AGE(D).

telecast/televise   The verbs are interchangeable: "PBS will telecast (or *televise*) the debate." *Televise* has become more frequent. The past tense and past participle of *telecast* may be either *telecast* or *telecasted*, usually the former. *Telecast*, but not *televise*, may be a noun: "The telecast can be seen on CBS."

tell it like it is   FF. Not yet old, but already tired, for "be honest about it, face the facts, be realistic."

tell tales out of school   Cliché. SANE recommends *tattle*.

temblor   *Temblor*, based on a Spanish verb for "shake," is standard – not *tremblor*, even though the earth "trembles" during an earthquake.

temerity/timidity/timorousness   *Temerity* is boldness, audacity: "She had the temerity to say that my mascara was too thick." *Timidity* is almost the opposite: "timidity, shyness, fear." *Timorousness* also involves fear or shyness, but hesitation, too.

temperature   See FEVER/TEMPERATURE.

tempo   Refers to relative speed or characteristic rhythm – not to something not moving. Poor: "The tempo of the international situation has changed." This would be improved if *discussions* or another action word replaced *situation*.

temporal/temporary   *Temporal* is sometimes misused for *temporary*. *Temporal* is in contrast to *spiritual* or *eternal*; it means "pertaining to this life": "Ministers tell us that we think too much of temporal life, not enough of the hereafter." *Temporary* means "not expected to last long": "Some 'temporary' buildings were moved to college campuses after World War II and are still in use there."

tend to   Shortened from *attend*, *tend* is SWE in "tend the sick," "tend bar," "tend the store," and similar expressions. Conservatives, however, object to "tend to business," "tend to a child," and the like, preferring *attend to*. SWE usage is divided. Since the choice is not clear and not really important, follow your own preference.

tender (verb)   See OFFER/TENDER.

tenet   See DOGMA/TENET.

term as   SWE usually omits *as* in sentences such as "We termed him (as) recalcitrant." "He was termed (as) a traitor."

terminate   Often high-flown for "end."   233

terrible/terribly   Conservatives say – accurately – that *terrible* and its adverb have degenerated from "filling with terror" to mean "bad" or "painful": "My leg cramp was terrible" or to "very" as in "We are terribly happy." There is little chance to reclaim the meanings. Today, to express the similar meaning of *terrible*, we must rely on a substitute such as *terror-filled*, *terrifying*, *frightening*, or the much weaker *scary*.

tetchy/touchy   Interchangeable, although *tetchy* is unlikely in serious contexts. A variant of *tetchy* is *techy*.

than (in incomplete comparisons)   SWE avoids unfinished comparisons such as "He liked movies more than his mother." An added *do*, *does*, or *did* generally makes the intended meaning clear.

than any/than anyone   Suppose that Walter, seven feet tall, is the tallest member of a basketball team. He is not taller than any member, because he *is* a member. He is taller than any *other* member of the team. He is taller than anyone *else* on the team. The principle: In using *any* or *anyone* in comparing things or people belonging to the same group, logic requires *any other* and *anyone else*. (In FF, *other* and *else* are often left out.) See also OTHER.

than I (*he, she, we, they*)/than me (*him, her, us, them*)   SWE: "He argued more successfully than I." The meaning is "than I did," with *I* the subject of a shortened clause. Similarly, "He worked harder than I (*she, we, they*)." Usually FF, but found now and then in informal SWE: "He argued more successfully than me (*her, us, them*)." SWE: "His remarks hurt my sister more than me." The meaning is that he hurt me, although he hurt my sister more. *Me* is an object of *hurt*. Similarly, "His remarks hurt her more than us (*them*)." FF: "His remarks hurt my sister more than Clara and I." In "He called her more often than I [did]" and "He called her more often than (he called) me," the words shown here in parentheses are often added to prevent misunderstanding, but are not grammatically necessary.

than what   In many sentences, such as "Hamburger costs more than what it did last year," *what* is unneeded.

than whom   SWE usually avoids the expression because of its awkwardness. When used, it is generally in sentences such as "Senator

Clancy, than whom no more loyal follower of the president could be found, was . . ." (Grammatically, *than who* would be required, like *she* in "worked harder than she (did)," but centuries of usage have established *than whom*.)

thank you in advance Somewhat discourteous, for this phrase suggests that the writer does not want to take the trouble to write another letter to express his gratitude.

thanks to SWE in sentences such as "Thanks to an early winter storm, the school bus driver could not make his rounds."

that (adverb) Yes, *that* can be an adverb, although usually it is a pronoun or an adjective. In "You won't need an overcoat, it's not that cold," *that* modifies *cold*. The use is SWE, but more frequent in informal contexts. *This* may similarly be employed adverbially.

that of SWE: "The upholstery of the sofa is better than that of the chair." (*That of* is needed. Else *upholstery* would be compared with *chair*.) Illogical: "One of the more interesting sports in Minnesota is that of curling." (*That of* should be omitted. The sport is curling.) *That of* is not followed by a possessive case, which would create a double possessive; not "the theory was that of Mrs. Dipple's" but ". . . that of Mrs. Dipple." Still better: "The theory was Mrs. Dipple's."

that (omission of) *That* may be omitted before a following clause if no lack of clarity results. SWE: "He said (that) he would need more time." Dubious: "I want to point out my opponent was . . . ," which needs *that* before *my opponent* to prevent momentary misreading.

that (position of) "The coach said on Friday he would start Hanson at center." First note the meaning when you insert *that* after *said*. Then note the difference when you place it after *Friday*. Draw your own conclusion.

that (referring to a clause) See WHICH (REFERRING TO A CLAUSE).

that there/this here Why are *that there book* and *this here book* FF, while *that book there* and *this book here* are SWE? The reason is that *there* and *here* are customarily adverbs, but in *that there book* or *this here book* they seem to be adjectives modifying *book*. In *that book there* or *this book here*, however, those words have the clearly adverbial meanings of "in that place" or "in this place." We can say "that book in that place" but not "that in that place book." In most sentences, of course, *there* and *here* are not needed at all. *That book* and *this book* suffice.

that/which In introducing clauses *that* and *which* can often be interchanged. However, many careful writers use *that* with restrictive clauses (essential to the meaning of the sentence) and *which* with nonrestrictive (helpful but not essential). Restrictive: "All eggs that are cracked must be discarded." (Note that the meaning changes if *that are cracked* is omitted.) Nonrestrictive: "All eggs, which are high in cholesterol, are excluded from this diet." (The clause adds but is not essential to the basic meaning.) *Which* is also sometimes useful in a sentence that would otherwise be overburdened with *that*'s.

that's for sure (*certain, real*)   Widely used in popular speech, apparently in the mistaken belief that *for* adds emphasis. SWE drops *for*: *that's sure (certain, real).*

thaw   See MELT/THAW.

theft   See BURGLARY/HOLDUP/ROBBERY.

their, them, they   SWE generally avoids *their, them,* or *they* to refer to *anybody, anyone, each, everybody, everyone, no one, many a person, a person, somebody,* or other singular pronouns or nouns. Instead it uses *he, him, his, she, her, hers* as appropriate. Informal: "Everybody thinks that such an accident can't happen to them, but they are wrong." SWE most often substitutes *him* and *he,* or recasts: "Most people think that such an accident cannot happen to them, but they are wrong."

their/there/they're   Their: *belonging to them* – "their house"; there: *in that place* – "Look over there! There it is!"; they're: *they are* – "They're late."

theirs   Never use an apostrophe in *theirs.* It is not to be confused with *there's,* meaning "there is."

then too   Overused and sometimes inexact. Dubious: "I hope to make the football team; then too I plan to go out for basketball." More clear: "I am trying out for the football team, and in the winter I plan to go out for basketball."

thence, thenceforth   See HENCE, HENCEFORTH.

theory   See OPINION/THEORY.

therapy   May include both physical and mental treatment, but ordinarily not surgery.

there is (*are, was, were*)   **1.** Sentences beginning with one of these forms are sometimes unnecessarily wordy. For example, "There are three swans in the pool," although not objectionable, is a word longer than "Three swans are in the pool." Besides, *there* is a colorless, almost meaningless word, but *swans* immediately creates a picture. **2.** Grammatically, *there* as in 1 is called an expletive, meaning "a filler word." It is not the subject. The subject in the example is *swans,* which requires the verb *are* rather than *is.* Similarly, "There *were* three swans," "There *is* one swan," "There *are* ten pies left," "There *is* no pie left," "There *were* ten pies left." **3.** In a sentence such as "There were only two swans got into the water," the *there* construction is FF. SWE would phrase it in either of these ways: "There were only two swans that got into the water" or preferably "Only two swans got into the water."

therefor, therefore, thereof, thereto, theretofore   Useful in law and sometimes in business, but except for *therefore* these words are obsolescent or obsolete elsewhere. (*Therefore* is in general use meaning "for that reason." The legalistic *therefor* means "for that thing" or "for those things": "purchased said property and paid therefor the sum of ten thousand dollars.") See also HEREOF/HERETOFORE/HEREUNTO . . .

these kind See KIND OF, SORT OF.

they (indefinite) English lacks a pronoun like the French *on*, which can be used indefinitely to mean "people," "most people," "the inhabitants," "everyone," or "some people." Speakers of English try to overcome the deficiency by using *they*, but then conservatives ask the unanswerable question, "Who are *they* in 'They say that the murderer will never be known' or 'They have cold winters in Montana'?" *They* survives the implied criticism and frequently, even in reputable publications, does serve as our equivalent of French *on*. Often, though, writers of SWE prefer a clear, specific replacement, such as "Townspeople say . . ." or "Montanans have cold winters," but sometimes turn reluctantly to the indefinite *they*.

they're See THEIR/THEM/THEY.

think to 1. FF (regional) for "remember to": "She didn't think to bring her pipe wrenches." 2. SWE for "expect to": "Before he noticed that the rope was frayed, he had thought to use it to climb over the wall."

thing An essential word, but when a more specific one fits the context, SWE gives *thing* a rest.

thinking Overused for *opinion*: "What is your thinking about this?"

Third World This "world" includes undeveloped or developing countries, especially those in Asia and Africa but sometimes also in South or Central America, that are not clearly allied with either Communist or non-Communist powers.

this (for *a*) FF: "There was this man who could stand on his head for two hours." SWE: ". . . a man," unless there has been an earlier reference to him.

this, that (reference) SWE makes sure that readers can immediately understand what *this* or *that* represents. Dubious: "She wanted to buy either the plain or the plaid shirt, but this was difficult." (Does *this* mean the buying or the deciding?) "City officials are making plans for the construction of a new library. That cannot be done quickly." (The planning or the construction, or both?)

this See also the entries for *that*.

thither See HITHER/THITHER/WHITHER.

thoroughbred See PUREBRED/THOROUGHBRED.

thoroughfare Although it survives in "America the Beautiful" in the line "A thoroughfare for freedom beat," the word can be confusing. It can mean either a highway or a street connecting two other streets, and the sign "No Thoroughfare" is equivalent to "Dead End." Because of possible misunderstanding, SWE rarely uses it.

thoroughly (completely) satisfied Usually *satisfied* can stand alone.

those kind See KIND OF, SORT OF.

though See ALTHOUGH.

thousand "Several thousand immigrants" refers to an entire group, "several thousand of the immigrants" to part of a larger group. See also MILLION.

thrash/thresh SWE generally uses *thrash* for "flog, beat," and *thresh* with reference to harvesting grain. See also ANNIHILATE, DESTROY, FLAY . . .

thresh See THRASH/THRESH.

thrice Now rare for "three times."

thrifty In SWE, people can be thrifty but things cannot. The word means "frugal, wisely economical." Inanimate things cannot be wise or unwise. Used dubiously in advertising: "the thrifty flour (*soft drink*, and so on)." See also ECONOMICAL/FRUGAL/THRIFTY . . .

throe/throw *Throe* refers to spasm, struggle, or pain (often emotional). Its Old English ancestor is a verb meaning "to suffer." SWE: "in the throes (not *throws!*) of despair."

through In the sense of "completed, finished," as in "When Congress was through amending, the bill was unrecognizable," *through* is SWE. Conservative editors, however, consider too informal *through* in sentences such as "Our relationship is over. We are through" or "The injury finished his career. He was through." The distinction seems too trivial to worry about, although 25 percent of the AHD usage panel do so.

through thick and thin This cliché was clearer when, as in Chaucer's day, *thick* was understood as short for "thicket" and *thin* meant "open space."

throughout Because of the redundancy, SWE avoids using *throughout* with any word meaning "all" or "whole"; not "She sewed shirts throughout the entire day" but ". . . throughout the day."

throw See THROE/THROW.

thrust As in "the thrust of this proposal" or even "this plan has thrust," the word has only vague meaning but a strong suggestion of the masculine power that many executives and politicians admire. It is SWE.

thus/thusly **1.** *Thus* is one of many adverbs with no -*ly*, so *thusly* is never needed. **2.** *Thus* is a rather stiff word, often better replaced by *so* or *as a result* or *that is why*. *Therefore* also is sometimes possible but is equally stiff.

tied Redundant: "Both (or The two) teams are tied." Obviously if one team is tied with the other, both are included. Similarly redundant: "All three teams are tied." SWE says: "The three teams are tied."

tie-in This term is overused for "connection" but useful in specific meanings. For example, businesspeople talk about tie-in sales of one product with another. Newspaper editors or television news directors may be interested in tie-ins between news events.

tight(ly) **1.** In "Screw the lid on (*tight* or *tightly*)," either may be used. *Tight* is both an adjective and an adverb. **2.** "Sleep tight" is standard, although most likely in informal contexts. Never "Sleep tightly."

till, until Interchangeable. Note that *till* has no apostrophe. A short form of *until*, written *'til*, appears mainly in verse of a bygone day.

tiller See HELM/RUDDER/TILLER.

tilting at windmills The nearsighted Don Quixote rode with his lance to attack windmills, which he thought were huge, fearsome knights. Note that the phrase uses *at*, not *with*, as it is sometimes mistranslated. Note, too, that until a better metaphor for opposing imaginary enemies is found, the phrase suits well, even though it has become a cliché.

timber/timbre In American use *timber* ordinarily refers to large growing trees (which become *lumber* after they are cut down and sawed into boards). *Timbre* refers to the quality (not pitch or loudness) of a speaking or singing voice or of a musical instrument: "Two violins may differ slightly or greatly in timbre."

times less "Scientific tests show that Brand X is three times less strong than Brand Y." Third-grade arithmetic teaches children that *times* refers to multiplying, not dividing. Usual SWE: "Brand X is only one third as strong" or "Brand Y is three times as strong."

timidity See TEMERITY/TIMIDITY/TIMOROUSNESS.

tinker's dam(n) SWE writers take their choice, *dam* or *damn*, according to their choice of conflicting etymologies: (1) In mending metal pots, tinkers used a bit of cloth or clay – a sort of dam – to hold the solder in place until it set. (2) Tinkers swore a great deal.

tiny little, wee small Authors of children's books are justified in using expressions such as "tiny little rosebud" or "wee small children" because many children like repetition and reinforcement. But writers for adults need not put one *little* word after another. Similar comments apply to *big huge* and the like.

-tion "The installation of new evaporation instrumentation seems a confirmation of the corporation's intention of remaining in contention." SWE dislikes many *-tion* words close together. It lets verbs do more of the work: "The installing of new evaporating equipment suggests that the corporation intends to continue fighting for a larger share of the market."

tirade See HARANGUE/TIRADE.

tired cliché So it is.

'tis Once used in not very good verse, and now almost never. Same comment: *'twas, 'twere, 'twill*.

titanic Even bigger than *gigantic* and stronger too. But the sinking of the *Titanic* in 1912, with the loss of 1,517 lives, gave the word a bad connotation.

to SWE omits unless really needed. In "Where is she going to?" it deletes *to*. See also **PREPOSITION AT END**.

to all intents and purposes A shortened version of a legal phrase, but still too long, since *practically, in practice,* or *in effect* says the same thing.

to be (omission of) FF (dialectal): "The rug needs vacuumed," "The engine needs worked on." SWE: ". . . needs to be vacuumed (*worked on,* and so on)." Apparently *need* is the verb most often mistreated in this way.

to me Except after verbs like *seem, to me* is FF for "in my opinion." FF: "Sandy Koufax to me was the smartest pitcher of that decade." SWE: "Sandy Koufax in my opinion was . . ."

to we the people Because the Preamble to the U.S. Constitution begins "We the people," some of the descendants of those people believe that the phrase is inviolable. Even congressmen have been heard to say "to (*with, from,* and so on) we the people." In the Constitution, however, *we* is the subject of a sentence, not an object of a preposition. SWE says, "We the people are . . . ," "to us the people," "may hurt us the people."

to wit Except in law, *to wit* has been replaced by *as follows* or *the following.*

together with See ALONG WITH, AS WELL AS, IN ADDITION TO . . .

tome Not generally applied to an ordinary book but to one volume in a series or, especially, to a sizable scholarly work or an unusually large book of any sort.

tomfoolery SWE, equivalent to *foolish behavior* or *shenanigans.* OED traces *tomfool* to 1356–1357, *tomfoolery* to 1840. Age may deserve respect.

ton SWE: "a two ton (or *two-ton*) truck," "It weighs two tons," "two tons of coal." British and sometimes American: "two ton of coal" (infrequent in SWE). Incidentally, an American ton is 2,000 pounds; a British ton, 2,240.

tony Once a favorable adjective meaning "aristocratic," the word is now used as a pejorative similar to "hightoned, pretentious, showy": "lives on the toniest street in town." It is infrequent in SWE, but possible in lightly critical remarks.

too 1. Although *too* in the sense of "very" is now seldom declaimed against, as it once was, it sometimes seems a bit silly, as in "Prospects for peace do not look too good." *Too* usually means "more than enough," and obviously prospects for peace could not be more than enough. Other examples of questionable usage: "She doesn't sing too well." "Glisson is a good fielder, but he doesn't hit too well." See also NOT . . . TOO. 2. *Too* is weak as a sentence opener, in the sense of *further* or *furthermore:* "Too, girls usually have more verbal facility than boys have." 3. A few conservatives still object to *too* before a past participle, saying that *too much alarmed* is preferable to *too alarmed.* SWE accepts both.

top Headline writers' love of three-letter words has led to overuse of *top.* Possible substitutes: *chief, foremost, highest, leading, main, most important, primary.*

topic See SUBJECT/TOPIC.

tornado See CYCLONE/TORNADO.

tortuous/torturous *Tortuous* means "crooked, unpleasantly winding": "a tortuous road," "tortuous reasoning," "the tortuous path to a presidential nomination." *Torturous* is associated with *torture*, extreme pain: "Visits to a modern dentist are seldom as torturous as they once were."

total (verb) In the sense of "demolish (an *automobile*)," *was totaled* is useful to claim adjusters to indicate that a vehicle would cost more to repair than its worth. Dictionaries still list this meaning of *total* as slang or informal, but the verb is appearing more and more in SWE, especially in newspaper accounts of accidents.

total of Often can be deleted. The words may be used to avoid starting a sentence with a figure: "A total of 1,415 dressed turkeys were (not *was*) shipped."

toted/totted *Toted* is a pleasant SWE informality: "They toted their gear into camp." *Totted*, past tense of the verb *tot* derived from *total*, is usually followed by *up*: "We totted ("totaled") up the day's receipts." *Toted (up)* is sometimes substituted in FF.

touchy See TETCHY/TOUCHY.

tough As a synonym for *difficult* or *unfortunate, tough* is knocking on the doors of SWE but is not always admitted. "It's tough to get a job now." "Yes, it's tough to be out of work these days."

toward, towards Interchangeable, with *toward* extending its lead.

track/tract In referring to land, you could be on the right *tract*, but otherwise you are likely to be on the right *track*. Trains run and autos or horses race on tracks, and animals leave tracks in the snow. Some evangelists may leave religious tracts with us.

trade See OCCUPATION/PROFESSION/TRADE.

tragedy, tragic Junior spills his chocolate milk, messing up the new carpet – unfortunate, but not *tragic*. Joan's date doesn't show up – maybe a good riddance, but not a *tragedy*. Aside from special literary definitions, a *tragedy* is a disastrous event with lasting and often fatal consequences. It may be only personal and familial but possibly may reach international proportions.

trained expert See QUALIFIED EXPERT.

traipse Flesch is rightly puzzled about why this four-hundred-year-old verb for "stroll aimlessly" is still labeled informal, and suggests that it may be because the word suggests "unbusinesslike meandering." A word should not be excluded from any context simply because it doesn't sound businesslike. People who *traipse* are probably not businesslike, anyway, but they're still people. The verb should be SWE, and in the minds of some editors it is.

transient/transitory Although almost synonymous, *transient* is more likely with concrete things, *transitory* with abstract: "transient guests," "the transient sands of a windswept shore"; "transitory grandeur (*beauty, hopes*, and the like)."

translucent/transparent   See DIAPHANOUS/TRANSLUCENT/TRANSPAR-
ENT; OPAQUE/TRANSLUCENT.

transpire   In science, to *transpire* is to give off vapor. In SWE general
use it means "to come to light, to become known": "It transpired
that Clark had been robbing the till." Some people misinterpreted
sentences like that to mean "it happened that . . ." So arose a
controversy that still goes on. May or may not *transpire* mean "to
happen"? Correspondents have written erudite and witty letters to
the (London) *Times* favoring one side or the other. The conservative
AHD usage panel voted against, 62–38 percent; editors might split
50–50. The issue is not earthshaking, does not affect clarity. Most
things that happen do become known to someone. SWE writers
choose the side they prefer.

treachery/treason   Although sometimes used interchangeably for
"betrayal of trust," the words are often differentiated in SWE. The
victim of *treachery* is ordinarily a person, small group, company, or
the like, but the victim of *treason* is one's government, sovereign,
nation, fellow citizens. As a result, treason is certainly a crime, but
treachery is not unless clearly illegal activity is present.

trek   This Afrikaans word for a journey by ox-drawn cart or wagon
suggests that the noun or verb should be used for something slow,
long, arduous. Dubious: "a trek to the neighborhood supermarket."

trendy   A good word for "following a trend." It is SWE, a favorite
of the *New York Times Magazine*.

trigger (verb)   *Trigger* is SWE in the sense of "activate, serve as the
impulse to," but perhaps is overused. See also SPARK.

TRITE EXPRESSIONS   Expressions that become trite are generally
somewhat figurative. If not, they are likely to be a set combination
of modifier and noun. When first used, they may have been startlingly appropriate; imitators of the phrasemaker picked up the expression; their own hearers and readers borrowed it in turn. Because
of overexposure it lost its verve, like ginger ale spread over the
bottom of a saucer.

It is impossible to list all the trite expressions. Some are mentioned
elsewhere in this book. Here is a small, random assortment of others:

abysmal ignorance	days of old (olden days)
beat a retreat	every waking hour
better half	fair sex
blind justice	Father Time
blushing bride	generous to a fault
brutally murdered	grateful earth
busy as bees	the Grim Reaper
charming hostess	hoary with age
clear as crystal	honeyed words
crack of dawn	host of friends
dark secret	icy wastes

immaculately dressed	primrose path
the last one on earth to	quick as a flash
manly chest	rolling prairie
Mother Earth	roar of battle
motherly advice	ruby lips
nestling in the valley	streamlined efficiency
off the beaten track	stubborn pride (. . . as a mule)
pluck up courage	throw caution to the winds
point with pride	walk on air
pretty as a picture	white as a sheet

242

trip FF (slang) for "a prolonged hallucination": "I had a bad LSD trip last week." Informal: *ego trip, guilt trip*.

triumphal/triumphant *Triumphal* ordinarily involves things and celebrations: "triumphal banners, processions," "the triumphal march in *Aïda*." *Triumphant* also is celebratory but usually with reference to people: "triumphant team members hugging one another," "triumphant voices."

trivial See ACADEMIC; PALTRY/PETTY/TRIVIAL.

-trix Along with another feminine ending, *-ess, -trix* is dying out. For example, *aviatrix* has been largely superseded by the generic *aviator*.

troop/troupe *Troupe* is used almost solely for an itinerant group of entertainers.

trooper/trouper The first is a mounted soldier or police officer; his horse has usually been replaced by a motor vehicle. A *trouper* is one of a troupe of entertainers.

troublous Obsolescent for *troublesome*, as in "We live in troublous times."

trousers The word requires a plural verb.

truism/truth A *truism* is a *truth* but is so obvious that perhaps it need not be stated: "It is a truism that formal weddings are expensive." An author, however, may write a sentence like that to introduce a topic, and go on to add some fresh comments.

trustee/trusty The plurals of these nouns are *trustees* and *trusties*. A trustee is (1) a person authorized to administer property or affairs for someone else, or (2) a member of the governing board of a college or other institution. A *trusty* is most often a prisoner given unusual privileges, degree of freedom, or responsibility. Trustees of a university are not flattered when students or alumni write about them as trusties.

try (noun) Although *try* is normally a verb, its noun use is also SWE in expressions such as "make a good try."

try (verb) News story: "Identities given by the Vietnamese as those of dead Americans will try to be confirmed." No. Identities cannot try anything. In using *try*, SWE shows who or what is making the attempt. The example could be written, "American investigators will try to confirm . . ."

try/attempt, endeavor, strive   *Try* is a workhorse, patient and unassuming. *Attempt, endeavor,* and *strive* can be rather pretentious. (To show this, Evans suggested substituting one of the other words in "If at first you don't succeed, try, try again.") *Endeavor* is the most formal of the three synonyms and suggests continued effort. *Strive* is the most vigorous, suggesting strenuous, conscientious work on a difficult task.

try and/try to   SWE treats *try to* as more logical than *try and.* We *try to do* something (one action), but *try and do* seems to imply two actions, trying and doing. *Try and* is FF.

tummy   A word that children like, *tummy* is cutie-pie as a name for an adult abdomen: "Tuck in your tummy with a Tutweiler." It is sometimes used in SWE for a light touch.

tumult/turmoil   The two are often used interchangeably. If the disorder is noisy, or if large numbers of people are involved, *tumult* is the more likely.

turbid/turgid   *Turbid* means "muddy," "dark with soot, smoke, or fog." Figuratively: "muddled, confused, in turmoil": "a prostitute's turbid life." *Turgid* means "swollen, inflated" and by extension "overornate in language or style": "the turgid styles of some Victorian writers."

twice as many . . . than   Not customary in SWE: "Twice as many cases of flu were reported locally in 1988 than in 1987." SWE usually replaces *than* with *as.* The construction is similar to *twice as large as.*

twins   Seldom if ever is *both* needed with *twins.* In "Both twins like ice cream," SWE replaces *Both* with *The,* although *both* may add a little emphasis. In "pair of twins," *pair of* is ordinarily expendable. However, *pairs of* or *sets of* is needed in "Their children are a girl, a boy, and two pairs of twins" (or ". . . twin boys and twin girls," and so on). To indicate a boy and a girl, either *a mixed pair of twins* or *mixed twins* is customary.

two first, two last   See FIRST TWO/TWO FIRST.

tycoon   Now SWE for "powerful businessman."

type of   SWE: "this type of architecture," "one type of quince." FF: "this type architecture," "an old type sewing machine."

U

ugly as sin   This is not only a cliché but an inaccurate one. Most "sin" is on the surface temptingly attractive, like Heinrich Heine's devil: "a handsome, charming man . . . obliging and courtly . . . who speaks well of Church and State."

ultrasonic See SUPERSONIC/ULTRASONIC.

unabridged See ABRIDGED/UNABRIDGED.

unalienable Despite being in the Declaration of Independence, *unalienable* has been largely superseded by *inalienable*.

unanimous A member of a president's cabinet: "The nomination was unanimous by almost everybody." That's like saying that something is perfect except for the imperfections, or that a bin is full except for the third that is empty. *Nearly unanimous*, however, is logical.

unauthorized trespassers A hand-lettered sign on a fence: "Unauthorized Trespassers Will Be Persecuted." Since all trespassers are unauthorized, that modifier should have been deleted. See also PERSECUTE/PROSECUTE.

unaware(s) Because *unaware* can be either adjective or adverb, why bother with the *s*? "They were unaware of . . ." (adjective), ". . . caught us unaware" (adverb).

uncomparable See INCOMPARABLE/UNCOMPARABLE.

unconscious See SUBCONSCIOUS/UNCONSCIOUS.

under water/underwater To modify a noun, SWE uses *underwater*: "the underwater scenery at Silver Springs." Otherwise it uses two words: "They could see fish swimming ten feet under water."

underlay/underlie See OVERLAY/OVERLIE.

understand See COMPREHEND/UNDERSTAND.

underwhelm *Overwhelm* is derived from an Old English word for "to turn over." A person may be overwhelmed if he or she is figuratively turned upside down. *Underwhelm* is a humorous variant meaning "not excited, not turned upside down." It is not yet SWE, but deserving. It is easily understood and provides a light touch.

undue, unduly These words mean "excessive, excessively, or unwarranted" and are omitted in SWE if something else in the sentence suggests excess: "She overpraised him (unduly)." "His (undue) alarm was not warranted."

unexceptionable/unexceptional *Unexceptionable* means "beyond reproach, beyond objection": "Few people live completely unexceptionable lives." *Unexceptional* may mean either "common, ordinary, usual" or "without any exceptions": "Our day was routine, completely unexceptional." "Your adherence to this diet must be unexceptional. Eat nothing not listed here."

unfavorable See OPTIMISTIC/PESSIMISTIC; FAVORABLE/UNFAVORABLE.

UNFINISHED COMPARISONS "Our trucks are sturdier." "This toothpaste makes teeth whiter." "The analgesic that works faster." Sturdier, whiter, or faster than what? An advertising writer likes such unfinished comparisons because they imply what cannot be proved: that Ford trucks are sturdier than Chevrolets, Aim will make your teeth whiter than Crest, and so on. In all writing, not just advertising, SWE users check to be sure that they show what is being compared with what. See also SO (IN COMPARISONS); SUCH A.

unflappable British slang for a World War II air-raid warning was *flap*; from that came *unflappable* ("not capable of being alarmed.") The word crossed the ocean and in recent years has become an SWE synonym for *calm* or *imperturbable*.

uninterested See DISINTERESTED/UNINTERESTED.

unique The language needs a word meaning "pertaining to the only one of its kind": "She made a beautiful but unique dress." Common usage, although not most SWE usage, has weakened the word to mean no more than "unusual." As a result, to express the example unmistakably we must write, "She made a beautiful dress that was the only one of its kind" or ". . . dress unlike any ever seen before." In its strict meaning, nothing can be *more, less, rather, somewhat,* or *very unique.* SANE pleads for restoration of a unique heritage. See also **COMPARISON OF ABSOLUTES.**

United Kingdom See BRITISH ISLES/ENGLAND/GREAT BRITAIN . . .

universal(ly) Earth is not the universe. Phrases such as *universally believed* cannot be used honestly, because who knows what is believed in other galaxies? But despite the illogicality, the phrases are SWE.

universal panacea See PANACEA/REMEDY.

unknown Probably there is no person not known to someone else. Almost always, then, a person should be described as *unidentified* rather than *unknown.* With reference to things, such as sums of money or itineraries, some may accurately be called "unknown": total losses in a forest fire, for example, may be incalculable and therefore never known. SWE checks, though, to see whether *undecided, undisclosed, uncertain, unannounced, undetermined,* or some other such word may be more accurate.

unless and until SWE generally finds that one of the conjunctions will suffice.

unless/without FF (regional and illogical) says, "People cannot sneak up on a Doberman without he knows it." SWE says, ". . . without his knowing it" or "unless they are extraordinarily cautious." Note that SWE does not use *without*, a preposition, as a conjunction. FF: "You can't get to the Frobishers without you ford a stream."

unorganized See DISORGANIZED/UNORGANIZED.

unprecedented If something is truly unprecedented, it has no precedent. It or something much like it has never happened before. SWE seldom uses it for "strange, uncommon, rare." A drouth, for example, is unprecedented only if the region has never before been so dry for so long. See also UNIQUE.

unqualified See DISQUALIFIED/UNQUALIFIED.

unseemly This is a slightly old-fashioned word for "in poor taste, inappropriate."

unthinkable Nothing is unthinkable (or *inconceivable*) if anyone has ever thought it. But despite this illogicality, *unthinkable* and *inconceivable* are SWE.

until See *till, until; unless and until*.

untold wealth The meaning is not "concealed wealth" but "wealth so great that it has not been counted and perhaps cannot be." (One meaning of *tell* is "count," as in "telling her beads.")

unwieldy (Note the spelling.) The word is an adjective: "three unwieldy bags of cabbage." (The opposite, *wieldy*, is also SWE but is seldom seen or heard. People are more likely to talk about things hard to handle rather than easy.)

up **1.** Redundant: *Up* can be omitted after a verb if it does not affect the meaning. For example, in "I picked up the scissors and opened up the package," the first *up* is needed but not the second. Ordinarily *up* can be deleted after *open, close, add, divide, settle, finish, hurry*, and many other verbs. **2.** With *until, till, to*: SWE usually omits *up* in phrases such as "up until 1991." **3.** Informal SWE: Large dictionaries list various phrases using *up* in SWE, especially in informal contexts; for example, *up to you, up to mischief, not up to it*. More likely in FF are *hard up, on the up and up*. **4.** As a verb: The verb *up* is part of the jargon of card-playing: "up the ante, upped the bid," and as a figure of speech has moved into other contexts, including international diplomacy: "Once again Iran upped its demands." Athletics coaches, like military officers in fiction, may say, "Up, men, and go get 'em!" or "Up and at 'em!" in both of which *up* has the force of a verb. Elsewhere: "Restaurants are again upping the price of coffee." (Incidentally, they seem never to *down* the price.) FF: "She upped and hit him."

up to the hilt Cliché. An unpleasant metaphor suggesting the depth to which a dagger may be plunged. Unwisely used in gentler contexts such as "up to the hilt in party preparations."

upcoming As a synonym of *forthcoming* or *approaching, upcoming* is up and coming. Now SWE, despite William Safire's remark that the word reminds him of food being regurgitated.

upon See ON/UPON.

uppity A delightful FF (slang) word for "snooty" or "snobbish." "She gave him an uppity look before she noticed how handsome he was." Sometimes appears in SWE.

upshot See FINAL COMPLETION.

uptight FF. As used by some blacks, hippies, and others in the 1960s and 1970s, *uptight* meant any of several things: "tense," "nervous," "angry," "without money," "having a closed mind," "too conventional," "intimate," or "OK." The chameleonic word has not yet decided on the color(s) it prefers. Even aging hippies cannot always be sure about which definition is intended, although intonation and context give useful hints.

upward revision Used by semantically sensitive politicians and businesspeople to mean "It will cost you more."

upward(s) *Upward* is usual in the United States as both adjective and adverb: "an upward trend," "moved slowly upward."

us men/we men   SWE uses *we men* as a subject and generally as a predicate nominative: "We men sometimes disagreed." "It was we men who disagreed." In the second example, *us men* may sometimes occur in light SWE. *Us men* is the form used as an object: "Their unkind words hurt us men." "Some of us men wanted revenge." Obviously, the same principles apply to *we* (*us*) *women, boys, girls*, or *teddy bears*.

usage/use   Although these words are sometimes used interchangeably as nouns, *usage* is customary with regard to the ways that language is spoken or written: "modern English usage." It may apply also to other customary practices: "according to the usages of the Roman Catholic Church." In other senses *use* is much more frequent: "the use of this tool," "a medicine in wide use." *Usage* in such expressions sounds stilted, comparable to *wastage* when *waste* is meant.

use to/used to   Without *did* or another auxiliary verb, *used to* is SWE: "Australians used to resent references to early convict-settlers." In such sentences it attaches the meaning "formerly" and indicates past time. In statements such as "She became used to his bragging," it means "accustomed to." With *did, didn't*, or less frequently other auxiliaries, *use to* is customary, although some SWE writers prefer to avoid the construction. "Did they use to come here?" "They didn't use to come here." For the latter, "They used not to come here" is also frequent.

user-friendly   SWE. A computer term, long needed in other contexts but now overworked, as in an advertisement that calls milk "the user-friendly food."

utilize   The response to "May I utilize your facility?" is likely to be "What?" "May I use your bathroom?" will probably bring "First door on the right." SWE tries to avoid highfalutin words, especially in everyday contexts.

V

vacillating   See AMBIVALENT.

VAGUENESS   *Vague* means "not specific." "She felt uncomfortable" is vague. Did some part of her body hurt, was she embarrassed, or did she have only undefinable feelings that something was wrong? "The room was long" is vague. Was it fifteen feet long, thirty, as long as half a football field, or what? At times there is no need for precision. In "The flames leaped high above the roofs of the little houses," dimensions for *high* and *little* would detract from the effect: "The flames leaped ten or eleven feet above the roofs of the houses, which averaged twenty by thirty feet in size." Amateur writers, however, are much more often vague than overprecise.

valuable/valued   A *valuable* item has monetary value or is useful. A *valued* possession is prized by its owner. It may have only sentimental value; it is not necessarily costly or even useful. For example, an old snapshot may be valued but not valuable in dollars. *Valuable,* however, may sometimes be appropriately modified: "valuable as a reminder of the family's earlier poverty."

vanity See ARROGANCE/CONCEIT/HAUGHTINESS . . .

variety See BRAND/KIND/VARIETY.

variously "The robber was described variously as dark-haired and thirty, and red-haired and forty." Only two descriptions are given, but *variously* implies several. SWE may say "described as either . . . or . . . ," or "described by some witnesses as . . . and by others as . . . "

vault See SAFE/VAULT.

venal/venial "The venal governor became a multimillionaire in two terms, although his salary was only $75,000 a year." A person is *venal* if corruptible, mercenary to an excessive degree. "Such kissing is only a venial sin if it is a sin at all, the priest told her." An act is *venial* if it is forgivable, not really a very serious transgression. In contrast, a *mortal* sin, such as suicide, causes spiritual death.

verbal See ORAL/VERBAL.

verbiage/verbosity Both signify wordiness. They are sometimes used interchangeably in SWE. However, *verbiage* generally refers to the wordiness of a piece of writing or speaking: "the verbiage of her legal opinions." *Verbosity* is more likely to refer to the wordiness of the speaker or writer: "the notorious verbosity of Senator Glickens." Rarely, *verbiage* means one's choice of words, one's manner of expression: "her clear, impeccable verbiage." Since the unfavorable meaning is much better known, this use may be misinterpreted.

verdict Technically, a jury but not a judge may bring in a *verdict.* The judge can make a decision, ruling, or finding, and can pronounce a sentence.

vermin The word refers to harmful or annoying insects as well as small animals such as rats and mice. Once the word was used as a singular, "A vermin was caught," but now is regarded as plural: "Vermin (not *vermins*) were keeping us awake every night."

verse See POETRY/VERSE; STANZA/VERSE.

verve/vim Both refer to energy and liveliness. *Verve* adds the idea of enthusiasm and is often used to describe style in literature or other artistic endeavors. *Vim* emphasizes physical vigor; in fact, *vim* and *vigor* are often teamed up – needlessly.

very Overused. An apocryphal story is told of a young writer with inherited wealth whose literary agent advised him to use *very* less often. A few days later the writer cabled the agent from a cruise ship, "Thank you very, very, very (84 more *very*'s) much." SWE favors *much, very much,* or another adverb rather than *very* alone before past participles showing physical states: *much worn, badly burned, very much strengthened.* Usage here, however, is not consistent.

via   In Latin, *via* means "by way of." Conservatives like to preserve that meaning: "to Denver via St. Louis." In general, SWE follows the conservative preference, but some good writers use *via* for "by means of": "via private automobile," "via telephone," or even "became rich via oil-drilling." *By* is simpler and unpretentious.

viable   The basic meaning is "capable of surviving," but that has been supplemented by "practicable, workable" and then has moved on to something almost as vague as "good." As a result of so much weakening, *viable* often needs to be replaced by a more precisely defined term, as context demands.

vice/vise   Something considered evil is a *vice*: "the twin vices of drunkenness and gambling." "Vice isn't nice." A *vise* is a tool to hold something tightly, as a carpenter's vise holds a piece of wood or metal. Dictionaries list *vice* as an alternative spelling, but SWE (in this instance tool catalogs and books on carpentry) almost invariably use *vise* for the tool.

vicious   See ABANDONED/DEPRAVED/VICIOUS.

victim   See MARTYR/VICTIM.

vim   See VERVE/VIM.

violin   See FIDDLE/VIOLIN.

virile   In SWE, not applied to women. (The ancestral word is Latin *vir* ("man"). The word does not refer solely to sexuality but also to strength, physical endurance, or the like.

virus   In SWE one is not "hospitalized with a virus" (that sounds much too cozy), although the expression is common in FF. Nor, obviously, is one "hospitalized with a germ." Viruses and germs cause diseases but are not themselves diseases. One can, however, be "hospitalized *by* a virus."

vis-à-vis   Sometimes used in FF but not in SWE for "about, concerning": "What do you think vis-à-vis Poland?" Today's SWE uses it most often in the sense of "compared with, in relation to," as in "What is your opinion of Senator Ream's revised bill, vis-à-vis her original proposal?"

vise   See VICE/VISE.

visionary   *Prophetic* has good connotations, *visionary* usually bad. A visionary scheme is an imaginative one that farsighted people believe has almost no chance of success. Sometimes, however, a visionary person is able to turn visions into reality, as the inventors of airplanes and radios did.

visit with   Informal, now SWE, for "chat with," but may also mean "pay a visit to." You need not be with your friend when you visit with him, however; you may do so by telephone.

viz.   An obsolescent abbreviation for *videlicet,* meaning "namely," *viz.* is still used in some reference books or legal documents but almost never elsewhere.

vocation   See AVOCATION/VOCATION.

VOICE (of verbs)   See **PASSIVE VOICE**.

vow Appropriate in a solemn context, *vow* refers to an earnest promise, an oath, not something trivial. Dubious: "I'm going to eat all the candy," she vowed.

wages (verb with) According to the King James usage in Acts 6:23, "The wages of sin is death," but modern English prefers a plural verb. See also SALARY/WAGES.

wait for/wait on In SWE a clerk or waiter *waits on* customers in a store or restaurant. The customers sometimes need to *wait for* help or *wait for* someone to come to them. *Wait on*, then, means "to serve," and *wait for*, "await." In FF, *wait on* is often used in both senses.

waive/wave *Waive* is used only in the sense of "relinquish voluntarily" or, less often, "postpone": "Cline waived his right to trial by jury." "The legislative committee waived action until next year." An arm gesture is a *wave*. A flag waves, a woman waves her hair, and water has waves.

wander See MEANDER/WANDER.

want *Want* is FF when followed by a noun clause: "Do you want I should go now?" "He wanted that we should wait." SWE uses a noun or noun equivalent: "Do you want me to go now?" "He wanted us to wait."

want for FF in expressions such as "Your mother wants for you to ride to town." SWE deletes *for*.

want in (*off, out*) FF for "want to come in (*get off, go out*)," these expressions have not become SWE perhaps because they seem to use prepositions as objects, although some grammarians explain that here *in, off*, and *out* are simply elliptical for "to come in" and so on.

want to "You want to study hard for Professor Warner's tests." *Want to* for "should" or "must" is FF.

want/wish Often interchangeable, *want* is more likely for physical things and *wish* for abstract or remote things: "He wanted some rye bread." "He wished immortality." Some people regard *wish* as slightly prissy.

ward off See AVERT/AVOID/PREVENT.

wave See WAIVE/WAVE.

wax (verb) For "become" or "grow," as in "He waxed eloquent," *wax* seems old-fashioned.

way (adverb) FF. A shortening of *away*, used by Stephen Foster in the line "Way (or '*Way*) down upon the Swanee River" from his song "My Old Kentucky Home." It is also used in conversation by countless others in expressions such as "way off in the distance," "That's way too hard."

(the) way In sentences such as "He played it the way the old violinist had taught him," many users of SWE prefer *in the way* or *as* instead of *the way*.

way in which Often *in which* can be deleted: "The general explained the way (in which) he wanted his subordinates to respond."

way out This FF expression (persistent hippie slang) is often intended to praise or to describe something extraordinary, almost unbelievable: "Way out, man!" "That chick is way out!" "Allen's poetry is way out." Appears occasionally in SWE but lacks specificity.

way/weigh (nautical) Seamen *weigh* ("raise") anchor, and soon the ship gets under *way*.

way(s) SWE avoids "a ways" as illogical, but in FF "a long ways off" and the like frequently occur.

251

ways and means Maybe a House of Representatives committee really deals with both, but probably few of its members can tell which is which. We ordinary folk can get by with either one.

we (editorial, royal, and presidential) An editorial that presents the opinion(s) of a newspaper rightly uses *we* (as in "we believe") unless it is signed by one person. When *we* is used to mean all the people, a distinction such as "we Americans" is necessary. A king, queen, or pope customarily has used *we* to refer to the singular self, and U.S. presidents have used it ambiguously to refer to self, self and staff, the whole government, all Americans, or everybody in the world – which one often not specified.

we (reference) "In America we follow the precepts of Christianity." Who are *we*? All Americans, some Americans, most Americans? Users of SWE try to make clear the meaning of *we* or any other pronoun. The example should probably begin with "*Many (some* or *most) Americans.*" (In the same example, *the precepts* may also be questioned. All the Christian precepts? Most? Some? Selected ones of?)

wealthy See AFFLUENT/OPULENT/RICH . . .

WEASEL WORDS Theodore Roosevelt popularized this term for words that are slippery and elusive in meaning, that are slightly misleading, and that leave their users a way to escape if cornered. In "Savings up to 50 percent," the weasel words are *up to*, which here can mean anything from below 1 up to 50 percent. On seeing "All prices reduced," the weasel-word watcher asks, "Reduced from what?" "Compare our prices and save" – two good bits of advice, certainly, but compare with what and save how much? "Priced as low as (or *starting at*) $12.95" – and how high do the prices go? "Swish fights bad breath" – but who wins? "Water-resistant" – not to be confused with *waterproof.* "Doctors recommend ____" – which doctors, witch doctors?

wedding See MARRIAGE/NUPTIALS/WEDDING.

wee small See TINY LITTLE/WEE SMALL.

weigh (nautical) See WAY/WEIGH.

weird   Dictionaries define *weird* as "supernatural" or "highly unusual." The word is overused (FF) to describe almost anything at all out of the ordinary: "I had a weird day." "What a weird blouse!"

weirdo   FF (slang, but moving toward SWE for an unusually strange person whom one holds in contempt.

well and good   "Everything seems well and good." SWE generally settles for "All is well" or "Everything seems (or *looks*) good." See also GOOD/WELL.

well-nigh   Has been well-nigh replaced by *nearly*.

westerly   See EASTERLY/EASTERN.

wharf   See DOCK/PIER/WHARF.

what (verb with)   *What* may be singular or plural according to its context: "What sounds like a bird is actually a chipmunk." "What sound like birds are actually chipmunks." "She is wearing what seems to be a split skirt." "She is wearing what seem to be green tights."

what all, who all   Once considered regional but now more widespread, *what all* and *who all* are intensive forms of *what* and *who*, asking in effect, "What are all the things?" and "Who are all the people?": "What all did you talk about?" "Who all were at the dance?" Still found only infrequently in SWE.

what it's all about   FF. Cliché, beloved of sports commentators, for "the most important thing," or something similar: "Defense – that's what this game is all about."

what ever/whatever (in questions)   Although *whatever* is SWE in most instances, as in "Tell me whatever you can" or "Whatever you say will be held against you," in questions such as "What ever became of Kenneth Mahoney?" the two-word form is standard.

What's the matter?   SWE, but somewhat informal, for "What's wrong?" Used frequently by Shakespeare, but usually in a different sense.

whatsoever at all   "I felt no pain whatsoever at all" is redundant. SWE deletes *whatsoever*, *at all*, or both.

when, as, and if   To introduce a clause, SWE ordinarily chooses one, not all three.

when, where (in definitions)   A thing is not a when or a where. "A leopard is when a cat has spots" is not SWE, although comparable sentences occur often in FF. SWE: "A leopard is a large, spotted, wild member of the cat family" or "A leopard is a spotted cat."

whence   See HENCE/THENCE/WHENCE.

where (for *when* or *that*)   "Where full payment is impossible, credit terms may be arranged." In this statement, probably place (as suggested by *where*) is not really involved. SWE prefers *when* or *if* unless the reference is to place.

  FF: "I saw in the paper where oil has been found in Wyoming." SWE: ". . . that oil . . ."

where (in definitions)   See WHEN, WHERE.

where . . . at (or *to*)   See PREPOSITIONS.

where I'm coming from   FF for "what I believe, what I insist on, what I'm trying to do." Sometimes results in odd sentences like this of Senator Robert Dole in 1988: "We need to keep a Republican in the White House, and that's where I'm coming from."

whereabouts (verb with)   1. "Used with a singular or plural v[erb]," RHD says. However, a plural verb is essential when two or more persons may be in different places: "Their whereabouts ('locations') are unknown." 2. (adverb) In sentences such as "Whereabouts is she now?" the word is only a long substitute for *where* and is not likely in SWE.

whereas   Useful in legal documents and formal resolutions as a short way of saying "because it is a fact that." Today used only seldom elsewhere because it seems stilted.

whereby, wherefore, wherein, whereof   Legalese for (respectively) "by which," "for that reason," "in which," "of which."

whether or not   A few conservatives still insist that *or not* must accompany each *whether*, but most now grant that the chief use of *or not* is for emphasis, and only occasionally for clarity. Optional use: "Tell me whether (or not) you will be there." For emphasis: "I must know whether or not you will be there." For clarity: "You will be there whether you like it or not."

which   Not used in SWE to refer to persons; not "the man which" but "the man who (*that, whom*)."

which (referring to a clause)   "Marie asked her brother for some advice, which seldom happened." Such sentences are not uncommon in conversation, and usually not misunderstood, but are questioned in SWE. *Which* is intended to mean that Marie's asking was rare but seems to say that the advice seldom happened. Ambiguous: "She was not noted for her beauty, which was surprising." In using *this* or *that* to refer to a clause, SWE checks for clarity just as it does for *which*.

WHICHMIRE   James Thurber coined this word for long, *which*-filled sentences in which even conscientious readers, which all writers hope for but which not everybody is, may become mired as in a swamp which they cannot get out of, for which they can't be blamed. Remedies: Cut irrelevancies. Shorten a clause to a phrase or a word. Divide the long sentences into two or three shorter ones, maybe like this: James Thurber coined this word for long, unclear *which*-filled sentences. Even conscientious readers may become mired in a verbal swamp created by too much whichcraft.

while   See ALTHOUGH/WHILE.

whilst   Frequent for *while* in Great Britain, but almost unknown in the United States.

whip(ped) cream   The SWE form is *whipped*, simply because the cream has been whipped.

whiskey/whisky   Scotch or Canadian *whisky*, Irish or American *whiskey*.

whither   See HITHER/THITHER/WHITHER.

who else's   See ELSE'S.

who/whom   *Whom*, almost never used in FF, is a leading trouble-maker for those striving to master SWE. Here we will concentrate on formal style. Use *whom* (1) as object of a preposition: "To whom should we address the complaint?" "The complaint came from whom?" (2) as object of a verb: "She called whom?" "Whom did she call?" (object of *did call*). "Tell me whom she called" (object of *called*). *Who* is used as the subject of a sentence or clause: "Who is coming?" "Tell me who is coming." "Who shall I say is coming?" (subject of *is coming*). "I called Gomez, who I felt should be consulted" (subject of *should be consulted*; *I felt* is a clause on its own). Suggestions: (1) Make up several sentences closely resembling these examples. Repeat them *aloud* until all seem natural to you. (2) If in doubt, choose *who*. "Tell me who she called" may be excused as conversational English, but "Whom is calling" sounds idiotic. See also DOG WHO; WHOEVER/WHOMEVER.

whoever/whomever   The same principles apply to these words as to *who*, *whom*: use *whoever* as a subject, *whomever* as an object. Consider the function of the word in the clause of which it is a part, and ignore the rest of the sentence. Examples of formal use: "Whoever comes to our door is a friend" (subject of *comes*). "Tell whoever comes to our door to go away" (subject of *comes*). "Tell whomever you see that we are having a party" (object of *see*). "For whomever you invite there will be a welcome" (object of *invite*). "For whoever is invited there is a welcome" (subject of *is invited*).

whole other   "That's a whole other problem" is FF. SWE: "That's an entirely (or *wholly*) different problem." FF: "That's a whole nother problem" (*whole* splits the word *another*).

whom   See WHO/WHOM.

who's/whose   SWE uses *who's* only when it is replaceable by *who is* or *who has*: "Who's ('Who is') in the penalty box?" "Who's ('Who has') been charged with the penalty?" "Whose fault was it?" (*Who is* or *who has* will not fit there.)

whose else   See ELSE'S.

whose/of which   May *whose* be used to refer to animals and things, not just to people? Yes, according to SWE. "The flowers, whose scent is more noticeable at night . . ." is preferable to the awkward "The flowers, of which the scent . . ." See also DOG WHO.

widow/wife   Newspaper people have sometimes debated whether an obituary writer should say that a deceased man is survived by his *widow* or his *wife*. The decision is not always the same. Obviously, she has now become his widow, but some journalists argue that in the few days of transition, *wife* is the kinder choice. Except possibly for the obituary, the surviving woman is a widow. However, in references to her past married life, SWE calls her the wife of so-and-so. Similar comments apply to *husband/widower*.

widow woman   FF. Of course a widow is a woman! Delete *woman*, says SWE.

wieldy   See UNWIELDY.

wiggle/wriggle   Often used interchangeably, *wriggle* is customary for a writhing, snakelike motion that results in a change of location, but *wiggle* is more often a back-and-forth movement in approximately the same spot: "The snake wriggled away from the dog." "Can you wiggle your ears?"

win (noun)   "The team desperately needs a win" is standard on the sports page. Now the noun use has moved into SWE with reference to musical, political, and other competitions: "To stay in the race, Senator Read needs a win in the New York primary."

win out   SWE asks, "Is *out* necessary?"

windward   See LEE/PORT/STARBOARD . . .

-wise   Long established in such words as *sidewise, lengthwise, crosswise,* and *likewise, -wise* has become an overworked combining form and sometimes an object of ridicule late in the twentieth century. It has shown up in such possibly useful forms as *timewise* ("in regard to elapsed time") but also in such absurd combinations as *jumping-ability-wise, movie-acting-wise, word processor-wise,* and "It's been a difficult season, *competitivewise*" or "We're really in a hole *heightwise.*" *Wise*wise it must be said that SWE considers it unwise to overuse *-wise.*

wish I was (were)   If I am in Louisville but would rather be in Paducah, "I wish I were in Paducah" is standard. We wish for something that is contrary to fact. See also IF I WERE/IF I WAS.

wish   See WANT/WISH.

wishful thinking   A cliché, but how else can you say "thinking that something is true but not realizing that you are only wishing it to be true"? Frequent in SWE.

with   If a sentence containing *with* seems awkward, SWE checks to see whether a substitute may help; for example, "With increasing use of cocaine by young people, a solution to the entire drug problem becomes even more urgent than before." The *with* phrase is not accurately related to the rest of the sentence. Here SWE substitutes *Because of* for *With.*

with bated breath   Cliché, *bated* is archaic for "reduced." SWE reasons, "If few modern people understand the word, why use it?"

with telling effect   A dying cliché for "highly effective."

with the exception (*intention, purpose,* and so on)   Many phrases using *with the . . . of* can be shortened. "Everybody with the exception of two girls decided to stay" becomes "Everybody except two girls . . ." "He accepted the job with the intention of resigning after one year" becomes "He accepted the job, intending to . . ."

within the framework of Pretentious. Often *in* or *in relation to* can substitute.

without See UNLESS/WITHOUT.

witness As a verb this is often pretentious for "see" or "go to." Stuffed shirts witness a basketball game; basketball fans go to or see the game, or even enjoy it.

woman See LADY/WOMAN.

womanize SWE, as is the noun *womanizer.* The verb may mean either "give feminine characteristics to" or "pursue women excessively for sexual purposes." (Why are there no comparable *manize* and *manizer?*)

womanlike See LADYLIKE/WOMANLIKE, WOMANLY.

womanly See EFFEMINATE/FEMALE/FEMININE . . .

wont Old-fashioned for "custom" or "habit": "He rose at six, as was his wont."

workaholic SWE. Clearly modeled on *alcoholic* and meaning "a person addicted to work," *workaholic* is a valuable addition to the language. Wayne Oates, who probably coined it, also coined *workaholism,* for what lazy people consider a disease from which a workaholic suffers.

world of Overused for *much, plenty of,* etc., in phrases such as "a world of time," "a world of difficulty," "worlds of problems."

world See REALM/SPHERE/WORLD.

worn-out See OUTWORN/WORN-OUT.

worry See ANXIETY/APPREHENSION/CARE . . .

worse (*worst*) comes to worst The four-hundred-year-old idiom is "if worst comes to worst." Logic calls for "if worse comes to worst." Who can argue successfully with tradition or logic? SWE uses both forms or ducks the question and says "if worse changes to worst."

worsen Once dialectal but now SWE for "to become worse" or (less often): "to make worse": "The pain worsened." "Scrubbing floors worsened the pain in her back."

worst way **1.** FF and sometimes unclear as an expression of intensity: "She wanted Joe in the worst way." SWE might substitute "She longed for Joe" or "She intensely wanted to hold Joe in her arms again." **2.** Expressions such as "What she needed in the worst way was sympathy" seem illogical. *Most* is more likely in SWE. **3.** A newspaper's advertising consultant understandably advised a garage owner to change the wording of this proposed ad: "We want to repair your car in the worst way possible." SWE finds few, if any, uses for that expression.

worth while/worthwhile A rule of thumb: one word when used before a noun, two words after the verb: "a worthwhile plan," "The plan is worth while." If the expression makes sense when *one's* or *your* is inserted between *worth* and *while,* two words are SWE. Strunk and White caution that both words are rather vague. They recommend something more precise, such as *promising, worth reading,* or *worth trying.*

worthless See INVALUABLE/PRICELESS.

worthy The Nine Worthies discussed in medieval times included persons such as Charlemagne and Alexander the Great. But the term has lost repute, and to talk today of someone as "a worthy" is ironic and disparaging, perhaps humorously so. Charles Dickens contributed to the pejoration in his *Sketches by Boz*: "stirring the taproom fire and . . . taking part in the conversation of the worthies assembled around it." The adjective *worthy*, though, has kept its reputability.

would Although *would* may indicate customary or frequent action, as in "He would prepare the same breakfast," *would* is unnecessary with a specific time phrase such as *each day* or *every month*. SWE often changes "Each day he would prepare the same breakfast" to "Each day he prepared the same breakfast."

would be Announcer: "A player is down on the twenty-yard line. That would be Scott Graham." SWE prefers *is*.

would See SHOULD/WOULD.

wrack See RACK/WRACK.

wriggle See WIGGLE/WRIGGLE.

X

Xmas Infrequent in SWE, except in advertising, *Xmas* for *Christmas* is frowned on and regarded by many people as mostly commercial, and irreverent at that. The accusation of commercialism is well founded, but not the other. *X* was the first letter in the old Greek name for Christ and was often used to represent His name.

Y

Yankee Has four meanings: (1) a New Englander; (2) to some Southerners any Northerner (often with *damn* or *dam* as an inseparable prefix); (3) to foreigners any resident of the United States, to whom the term may be applied affectionately, indifferently, or hostilely; (4) a member of a baseball team. It occurs occasionally in SWE for any of the above definitions.

ye As in "Ye Olde Clocke Shoppe," *ye* is not only overused but also based on misinformation. An Old English symbol for *th*, called a "thorn," looks somewhat like a *y,* and later printers confused the two. So this *ye* is simply *the* and should be so pronounced.

Yiddish See HEBREW/ISRAELI/JEWISH . . .

yon Somewhat old-fashioned. Shakespeare used it in "Yon Cassius has a lean and hungry look." It is still heard occasionally in *hither and yon*. *Yonder* has the same meaning, "over there," but is also infrequently heard and rarely appears in SWE.

you No longer regarded as unsatisfactory in addressing the reader, except in highly impersonal prose. SWE avoids, however, mixing *one* with *you*. Not SWE: "One must be sure that you do not come down too hard on the floor." See also ONE (IMPERSONAL).

you all Generally considered only a Southern expression, as in "Y'all come," *you all,* as well as *all of you,* is actually SWE in all parts of the country, used to emphasize the inclusiveness of *you*: "You all know that most television programs are now recorded." Robert Gorrell has said that in one small town some newcomers were considered uncouth because they used *you all* and *we all* instead of the "correct" *you-uns* and *we-uns.*

You can say that again Tiresome FF substitute for "I agree." Similar is "You took the words right out of my mouth."

you know Especially overused in speaking, *you know* usually has no more meaning than the *uh* that signifies hesitation. Hearing excessive *you know*'s irritates many people and makes them doubt the speaker's intelligence. One such listener is reported to have inserted a quick "No, I don't" after each *you know* used by a friend. (She lost the friend.)

young/youthful Often interchangeable, *young* is more likely to refer to actual age, *youthful* to appearance or actions: "a young man, about twenty-two," "She still has a youthful figure."

your earliest convenience Old-fashioned phrase, once widely used in business letters or duns: "Please remit at your earliest convenience." Today *immediately* or a similar word is probable.

yummy Most dictionaries say that *yummy* is slang, and it must be admitted that the word is unlikely in a letter to a corporation president unless to praise his company's candy bars. But even though not SWE, *yummy* is a wonderful word to use in talking to children or in complimenting Aunt Mabel for her should-be-famous fried chicken.

Z

zap An FF verb or exclamation that became widely used during the computer games craze when trillions of "baddies" were zapped. Vague in meaning – perhaps "obliterate, shoot down, cripple, kill, turn off, turn on," or what you will. It appears occasionally in SWE.

zeal/zest *Zeal* is keen desire, enthusiasm. It implies a cause or goal: "zeal to become a nurse," "zeal to reduce the probability of war." *Zest* emphasizes enjoyment, gusto: "zest for life," "zest for gourmet food."

zero See AUGHT/NAUGHT.

zilch FF (slang). SWE prefers *nothing, none,* or *zero.*

zip (noun)   Marginally SWE, this word sounds as zippy as its name. Much more lively than *alacrity,* and more suggestive of quick movement than *vim* or *vigor. Energy* has little zip, either; it suggests Con Edison.